Four Centuries of Jewish Women's Spirituality

FOUR CENTURIES *of* JEWISH WOMEN'S SPIRITUALITY *- a sourcebook*

EDITED AND WITH INTRODUCTIONS BY
Ellen M. Umansky and Dianne Ashton

BEACON PRESS - BOSTON

Beacon Press
25 Beacon Street
Boston, Massachusetts 02108–2892

Beacon Press books
are published under the auspices of
the Unitarian Universalist Association of Congregations.

99 98 97 96 95 94 93 92   8 7 6 5 4 3 2

This book was published in part with the support of The Lucius N. Littauer
Foundation.

Text design by Gwen Frankfeldt

Library of Congress Cataloging-in-Publication Data

Four centuries of Jewish women's spirituality: a sourcebook / edited by
Ellen M. Umansky and Dianne Ashton.
p. cm.
Includes bibliographical references and index.
ISBN 0-8070-3612-9 (cloth)
ISBN 0-8070-3613-7 (paper)
1. Judaism.   2. Jewish meditations.   3. Women, Jewish—Religious life.   4. Women,
Jewish—Biography.   5. Jewish literature—Women authors.
I. Umansky, Ellen M.   II. Ashton, Dianne.   III. Title: 4 centuries of Jewish women's
spirituality.
BM43.F68   1992
296.7′082—dc20   91-32959
CIP

*To those
Jewish women
whose spiritual lives
remain unrecorded*

We must not speak of
women writers in our
century (as we cannot
speak of women in any
area of recognized
human achievement)
without speaking also
of the invisible, the
as-innately-capable:
the born to the wrong
circumstances—
diminished, excluded,
foundered, silenced.

—Tillie Olsen, *Silences*

Contents

Part III · 1890–1960: URGENT VOICES

CONTENTS

THIS volume of spiritual writings offers the reader reflections on Jewish, religious self-identity as seen through the eyes of almost one hundred Jewish women. Reflecting a wide variety of literary genres, the material that we have included was written between 1560 and 1990, that is, from the very beginnings of modern Jewish history up through the present day. Much of this material has never before been published, and, for the most part, material that has appeared in print has not previously been anthologized and thus has not been easily accessible to the contemporary reader.

In collecting material, we attempted to draw on as wide a variety of sources as possible, including the voices of North American and European Jewish women and of women living in the land of Israel. Well aware of the importance that historical and familial contexts play in shaping one's spiritual life, we further sought material by Jewish women of different ages, sexual orientations, and educational and socioeconomic backgrounds, responding to a variety of historical and personal situations.

The authors whose works follow include women identifying with modern Jewry's four major religious movements—Orthodoxy, Conservatism, Reform, and Reconstructionism—as well as those who identify their spirituality as Jewish but are not part of a particular Jewish "denomination" or define their community as other than, or outside of, the mainstream. Among contemporary women, for example, alternative communities include the North American *havurah* movement begun in the 1960s, which consists of small, usually egalitarian fellowships of Jewish women and men; P'nai Or, an international network of Jewish renewal communities catalyzed by the spiritual teachings of Rabbi Zalman Schachter-Shalomi; and various Jewish feminist communities that, within the last ten years, have been created, and are continually being created, throughout Canada and the United States. Finally, we have included writings by religious leaders and laypeople. In so doing, we have included writings intended to be spiritual works (e.g., sermons, addresses, rituals, blessings, and prayers) as well as those (such as letters, sisterhood minutes, and committee reports) that similarly express, although often less self-consciously, the spiritual concerns of their authors.

Because we recognized from the outset the enormity of this project, we decided not to include fiction. While acknowledging that fiction can be, and indeed for some modern Jewish women has been, a very important means of spiritual self-expression, we also realized that fiction is less easily excerpted than sermons and essays and far longer than the poems and prayers that we include here. It also seemed to us that published fiction by Jewish women is more readily available to the contemporary reader than are the nonfictional material that we decided to include (see, e.g., *America and I: Short Stories by American Jewish Women Writers,* ed. Joyce Antler [Boston: Beacon, 1990]).

We initially intended to organize the book around the themes of God, Torah, and Israel: the three central categories of Jewish religious thought. Yet, as this volume took shape, it became clear to us that the materials we had collected could not easily be subdivided into three thematic sections. Indeed, almost all the writings seemed to reflect on all three themes. On the other hand, there also seemed to be important differences among the writings, differences based on the historical periods in which the pieces were written. It thus seemed to make the most sense to arrange the volume chronologically, from 1560, the earliest dated material we uncovered, through 1990, the year in which this volume was completed. While in some respects the exact dates that we have chosen to define the four sections of this book are arbitrary, there do seem to be important similarities among the material collected in each of the book's four parts.

The first section, 1560–1800, consists of early modern (or late medieval–early modern, depending on when one dates the beginnings of modern Jewish history) writings that reflect traditional understandings of God, religious teachings (Torah), and Jewish peoplehood (Israel). While the communal activities engaged in by some of the writers—and, in particular, by the seventeenth-century Italian poet Sara Coppia Sullam and her contemporary, the German merchant Glückel of Hameln—help identify these women as "modern," the religious ideas expressed in their writings in no way challenge religious concepts developed through almost two thousand years of rabbinic interpretation and teaching.

Spiritual literature produced by Jewish women between 1800 and 1890 takes on greater diversity both in the literary forms it assumes and in the concepts it expresses. Among many of the writers, one further finds a stronger sense of female religious self-identity and a conscious desire to articulate what the authors perceive to be their religious mission as women and as Jews. Perhaps most striking, material dated after 1800 reflects the stronger public voice that Jewish women began to assume within their religious and secular communities. Unlike the material dated prior to 1800, which consists largely of private letters, memoirs, and prayers, one finds in the book's second section published poems, essays, hymns, and excerpts from lengthy theological treatises.

After 1890, spiritual literature produced by Jewish women increases both in volume and in variety of expression. One also finds a new sense of urgency, reflecting such specific historical circumstances as the massive immigration of Eastern European Jews into Western Europe and North America between 1881 and 1914; the events of the First and Second World wars, including the decimation of European Jewry; and increased Jewish settlement in the land of Israel, culminating in 1948 in the establishment of Israel as a modern Jewish state. Out of this sense of urgency emerges a more widespread commitment to personal and communal action. This too is clearly revealed in most of the works included in this section.

While this sense of urgency does not disappear after 1960, the vast amount of published and unpublished spiritual writings that have been produced by Jewish women during the last thirty years made it necessary for us to create a final section simply entitled "Contemporary Voices." Perhaps most striking about the material included here is the vast range of both literary and creative genres on which Jewish women today are drawing in order to give their spirituality self-expression and the diversity not only of religious thought but also of suggested modes of religious action. While many contemporary Jewish women, like generations of Jewish women before them, have developed a sense of spirituality that is essentially private rather than communal in nature, others have sought to express their spirituality through public roles previously open only to men (e.g., rabbi and cantor) and, in some cases, through rituals and observances from which women traditionally have been exempt if not excluded. One finds, too, increasing numbers of women undertaking serious study of Jewish texts, again creating a spiritual path very different from that undertaken by previous generations of Jewish women. If anything, this final section reveals that it may no longer be possible to speak in a unified way about "Jewish women's spirituality." The diversity of contemporary Jewish religious life, in general, is clearly reflected in the writings included here, as are the diverse spiritual paths that have been taken, and continue to be taken, by growing numbers of Jewish women.

The historical essay on Jewish women's spirituality that introduces this book was written by Ellen Umansky. The additional essays introducing each of the volume's four major sections were all collaborative efforts, as was the gathering of primary source material for the book as a whole.

The title of Ellen's introductory essay—"Piety, Persuasion, and Friendship"—was first suggested to her as a title for an essay she wrote several years ago on the spirituality of a number of modern Jewish women who functioned as unordained religious leaders. The book in which this essay appeared was entitled *Embodied Love: Sensuality and Relationship as Feminist Values,* edited by Paula M. Cooey, Sharon A. Farmer, and Mary Ellen Ross (who suggested the title to her), and was published by Harper and Row in 1987. While broader in scope than the essay that appeared in *Embodied Love,* the historical essay that Ellen wrote for this sourcebook similarly focuses on piety, persuasion, and friendship as reflective of the Jewish concepts of God, Torah, and Israel.

The term *piety* suggests a personal, inner search for both God and godliness that has characterized the spiritual journeys of Jewish women for almost two thousand years. *Persuasion* is meant to suggest deeply held religious convictions that Jewish women have attempted to share with others through thoughts and actions. For many Jewish women, these convictions are identical to what Jews have traditionally identified as "Torah," while for some, especially among contemporary Jewish women, these convictions go beyond, and sometimes call into question, the teachings of "Torah" itself. Finally, the term *friendship* reflects a concern not only for "Israel"—that is, for the Jewish people and, for many Jewish women, for the land of Israel itself—but also for other human beings, recognizing the extent to which personal relationships and the communities that they sustain can strengthen one's sense of religious commitment.

Given the huge undertaking that we set ourselves, this volume could not have been completed without the assistance and enthusiastic support of many people. First, we both want to express our deep gratitude to Caroline Birdsall, who first brought this project to Beacon's attention, and to Deborah Johnson, who provided invaluable editorial assistance. We also want to thank Robert Gottlieb, for all his help, and Lauren Bryant, the editor who saw this project through to completion. Her careful reading of the entire manuscript as well as her patience and great moral support have helped us not only sharpen this book's focus but also get through what often seemed to be an insurmountable task. In addition, we want to thank all those who contributed to this volume. We especially want to thank Sara Horowitz, for supervising interviews and providing insights regarding women and the Holocaust; Faith Rogow, for suggestions and material about the founding of the National Council of Jewish Women; and Marcia Falk, Kathryn Hellerstein, Sue Ann Wasserman, and Chava Weissler, for their great interest in this project and for their ideas as well as their translations.

As in any collaboration, there are many people whom we want to thank individually. Dianne Ashton wants to express her deep appreciation to the American Jewish Archives in Cincinnati for awarding her a research fellowship to find source material by Jewish women, many of whom lived in the United States for at least part of their lives. Jacob Marcus, Jonathan Sarna, Michael Meyer, and Abraham Peck, the faculty of Hebrew Union College most closely associated with the archives, listened to ideas and made helpful suggestions about sources and issues. The archives staff, then headed by Fanny Zelcer, was always helpful, encouraging, patient, and energetic, as was the staff of the American Jewish Periodicals Center at Hebrew Union College. Mary Kate McDonald, a student at the University of Delaware, conducted interviews for Dianne and made valuable suggestions for transcription, while Dianne's husband, Richard Drucker, patiently read several versions of material that she prepared for this volume. To him go her thanks for his encouragement, interest, love, and support.

Ellen Umansky's gratitude goes to the library staff at the New York School of Hebrew Union College–Jewish Institute of Religion for all their assistance in helping her gather material for this book and to all those at Emory University responsible for the sabbatical leave that allowed her to devote her time to the book's initial preparation. She is especially grateful to Linda Kuzmack and Jonathan Sarna for their critical readings of the introductory essay to this volume and to Linda especially for suggesting, and providing, additional source material that has substantially strengthened this book. She also wants to thank her colleague David Blumenthal for his constant and genuine encouragement of her work on Jewish women's spirituality; Stephan Loewentheil, David Ellenson, Ali Crown, Stephanie Stern, and Donald Aslan for their encouragement and words of wisdom; Marc Levy, for sharing his computer expertise; and her husband, Alan Kannof, for almost twenty years of sound literary advice, emotional support, and friendship. This book could not have been completed without the help of various friends, relatives, and baby-sitters who gave Ellen time to work. In this regard, she especially wants to thank her husband, Alan; her mother, Dorothy Umansky; and her housekeeper of almost three years, Rosario Tarqui. She also wants to thank her sons, Abraham, Ezra, and Seth, for not turning off her computer while she was in the middle of writing and for filling her life with so much joy. Finally, she wants to thank the members of B'not Esh, the Grail Women at Cornwall-on-Hudson, and everyone at the Jewish Community Center of White Plains for challenging her notions of spirituality and supporting her spiritual growth.

Ellen M. Umansky
Dianne Ashton
January 1991

Piety, Persuasion, and Friendship: A History of Jewish Women's Spirituality

Ellen M. Umansky

JEWISH spirituality, like many other forms of spirituality, can be seen as an expression of individual and/or communal yearnings toward the divine and a life of holiness. As Arthur Green has written recently, Jewish spirituality can be defined as "life in the presence of God" or, more specifically, "the cultivation of a life in the ordinary world bearing the holiness once associated with sacred space and time, with Temple and with holy days." According to Green, this definition of spirituality "should allow talmudist, halakhist, and commentator to take their deserved place within the collective 'spiritual' enterprise alongside the more obvious prophet, philosopher, and mystic." [1] As this present volume of prayers, poems, sermons, essays, rituals, *midrashim,* and blessings written by Jewish women from the late sixteenth century through the present reveals, modern Jewish women have also actively engaged in a search for God and attempted to achieve a life of holiness. Like the male legal experts and scholars to whom Green refers, these women also deserve a place in the collective spiritual enterprise of the Jewish people.

While historians and scholars of religion have only begun to explore the spirituality of Jewish women, past and present, Jewish women have sought God's presence from the very beginnings of Jewish history. [2] Although exempt from the dual obligations of religious study and participation in regularly scheduled public worship—two important, if not central avenues through which Jewish men have traditionally sought God—Jewish women were obligated to pray. [3] Unlike the prayers of their husbands, sons, and fathers, however, those of Jewish women were primarily private, spontaneous, and emotional in nature, reflecting the realities of their everyday existence.

Prior to the seventeenth century and the advent of modernity, Jewish women received a minimal religious education because of their exemption from the obligation to study, set out in Jewish legal material written during the earliest centuries of the common era. Consequently, the Hebrew *siddur* (prayer book) was inaccessible to most of them. This led to the creation of the communal institution of the *zogerke,* a woman able to read the Hebrew text who led women with little knowledge of Hebrew through the synagogue service. One such woman whose name has come down to us was Urania of Worms, who lived in the thirteenth century. According to her epitaph, "With sweet tunefulness, [she] officiated before the female worshippers to whom she sang the hymnal portions [of the worship service]." [4]

Their exemption from regular participation in communal worship and their subsequent exclusion as members of the *minyan* (the quorum of ten necessary for public worship) and as leaders in communal prayer encouraged Jewish women to cultivate their spirituality privately.[5] This sense of spirituality was fostered by women's own perception that the home (as opposed to the synagogue) was indeed their religious domain. It was they, for example, who were responsible for maintaining the dietary laws and preparing their homes for Shabbat (the Sabbath) every week—cleaning, baking *challah* in a ritually prescribed way, and kindling the Sabbath lights. Preparations for other home-centered Jewish holidays were also seen as women's obligations. The most time consuming was Passover, which required, among other things, thoroughly cleaning the home and removing all leavened products, putting away regularly used dishes, pots, and utensils and taking out those used only for Passover, and preparing special foods for the family *seder.*[6] Women were further responsible for following the laws of *niddah,* biblically based rabbinic laws that regulated the times during which sexual relations between married couples were permitted.[7] In so doing, they were said to ensure the "ritual purity" of their homes.

Equally time consuming were the obligations set out for women in the Mishnah, the earliest corpus of Jewish law, completed circa 200 C.E.[8] According to the Mishnah, for example, "These are works which the wife must perform for her husband: grinding flour and baking bread and washing clothes and cooking food and giving suck to her child and making ready his bed and working in wool." As a prescriptive rather than descriptive document, the Mishnah may simply be presenting those tasks that ideally women were to perform rather than those actually assumed by them. Indeed, the Mishnah goes on to maintain that if a woman brings her husband "one bondwoman she need not grind or bake or wash; if two, she need not cook or give her child suck; if three, she need not make ready his bed or work in wool; if four, she may sit [all the day] in a chair." Yet, according to Rabbi Eliezer, a rabbi of the early second century C.E., a man should force his wife to work in wool even if she brings him one hundred bondwomen, for "idleness," he said, "leads to unchastity." [9]

Revealed here is a mind-set that undoubtedly reflected the realities of traditional Jewish women's lives. While the mishnaic authors were concerned that certain tasks within the home be performed, their wives did not necessarily have to perform them. Thus, while they were responsible for upholding the laws regarding *niddah, challah,* and *hadlaqat ha-ner* (kindling the Sabbath lights), women were not specifically obligated to cook, weave, or make beds. Indeed, those wealthy enough to afford household help were welcome to do so. Yet the real concern, as expressed by Rabbi Eliezer, was that, if women hired someone to do those tasks for them, they would be idle. It never occurred to Rabbi Eliezer, it seems, that wealthy women might wish to spend their free time learning Torah or attending the three regularly scheduled synagogue services each day. While it may have occurred to some Jewish women—as it did, for example, to the second-century Beruriah (the wife of Rabbi Meir), whose scholarly opinions were cited in the Mishnah even when they diverged from those of male authorities of the day— most probably shared the view held by Rabbi Eliezer, that the world of scholarship was reserved for men.[10]

There is no evidence to suggest, however, that, prior to the seventeenth century and the entrance of European Jewry into modernity, most Jewish women thought of their world—the world of the home—as either subordinate or peripheral to Jewish religious life.[11] Indeed, since much of Jewish religious life, including the celebration of the holidays and Shabbat, was home centered, women were undoubtedly aware of the extent to which the continuation of Jewish life depended on them. Moreover, women had the responsibility of bearing and nurturing children, equally important for the physical and spiritual preservation of Judaism. Although technically, according to *halakhah* (rabbinic law), only men were obligated to have children, women were fully expected to procreate.[12] They were to do so not only to enable their husbands to fulfill their obligations but also to fulfill what the rabbis assumed was their natural desire to bear children, a desire whose fulfillment, again, was central to the continuation of Jewish life.

If, prior to the seventeenth century, few Jewish women recorded the content of their religious lives, reasons why this is so are many. First, most Jewish women may well have been illiterate and thus *could* not have recorded a written description of their lives had they desired to do so.[13] Second, among those women who were able to read and write, only a few, it seems, were scholars and none rabbis. None, in other words, were among the scholarly elite who produced Jewish spiritual literature, whether we define that literature as liturgy, mystical texts, or rabbinic codes. Third, literate women may have refrained from writing prayers because they perceived the world of scholarship as men's domain—women's contribution to Judaism lay elsewhere. Fourth, even if women wanted to write prayers and homilies, few would have had the opportunity to do so. Excluded from the Bet Hamidrash, the Jewish house of study, they would have had to write at home, surrounded by their children and inundated with household obligations. As a clearly sex-differentiated society that viewed the religious worlds of men and women as separate from one another, traditional Jewish society simply did not create either the motivation or the opportunity for women to write spiritual literature. If anything, such efforts would have been actively discouraged. There remains the possibility that a few exceptional Jewish women *did* produce spiritual literature prior to the late sixteenth and early seventeenth centuries.[14] If they did so, however, their writings either were not preserved or have not yet been uncovered.

1560–1800: TRADITIONAL VOICES

For the most part, then, we have little access to Jewish women's voices prior to the seventeenth century. Nevertheless, as we have already seen, it is possible to speculate about the content of premodern Jewish women's religious lives. By the early seventeenth century, European rabbis began to write prayers, folklore, and homiletic tales in the vernacular specifically for women. Included among these was the *Ts'eno Ur'eno* (Go out and see), a Yiddish version of the Pentateuch, along with legends and moral principles, first published in 1622. Popular among late medieval and early modern Eastern European Jewish women, its division of the Torah into weekly sections enabled its female readers to follow at home the portion of the Torah that was being read in *shul* (synagogue). Some of the religious literature written for women also appealed to uneducated men (i.e., those who did not know Hebrew and did not have a great familiarity with traditional Jewish texts). Yet the primary goal of its authors was to appeal to women as a means of education, edification, and devotion.[15]

During the seventeenth century, Ashkenazic women (Jewish women in Central and Eastern Europe) began to recite *tkhines,* Yiddish supplicatory prayers written mostly by men, although a significant number appear to have been written by women.[16] These prayers, popular among Ashkenazic women at least through the nineteenth century, were voluntary prayers that focused on important religious events in women's lives. Despite their exemption from public worship, many women, especially those who knew Hebrew, apparently chose to recite the Hebrew liturgy and to attend synagogue, if not daily, at least on the Sabbath and on holidays. Yet, as Chava Weissler has noted in her extensive study of the *tkhines* literature, "to the extent that they also recited *tkhines,* they defined for themselves an alternative rhythm as well." Unlike the *siddur,* whose prayers were phrased primarily in the plural, *tkhines* were private prayers, to be recited, for example, when lighting candles, baking *challah* (see, e.g., "The *Tkhine* of Three Gates" in this volume), or, following the laws of *niddah* (women's special commandments), on becoming pregnant, recovering from illness, welcoming the New Moon, visiting a cemetery, or confessing sins—even "on no particular occasion." As Weissler writes: "An inventory of the occasions for which *tkhines* exist shows us a world organized very differently from that of the *siddur,* a world structured by the private events of the woman's domestic life as much as by the communal events of the Jewish calendar."[17]

The matriarchs of the Bible—Sarah, Rebecca, Rachel, and Leah—played a striking role in the *tkhines* (see the two "*Tkhine* of the Matriarchs" included in this volume). In contrast to the Hebrew prayers of the traditional *siddur,* which often described God as the God of the patriarchs—Abraham, Isaac, and Jacob—the *tkhines* more frequently referred to God as the God of the matriarchs, actively invoking their spirits in prayer. The invocation of these spirits reflected a personal rather than communal understanding of faith. What was asked of the matriarchs was not intercession on behalf of the entire Jewish people but rather intercession with God on behalf of the individual worshiper and her children. Through these and other female intercessors, like the biblical Hannah, the mother of Samuel, God as "heavenly Father" became less remote and more actively concerned with the worshiper's daily existence. These supplicatory prayers are the first example of Jewish spiritual literature known to have been written, at least in part, by women.[18] As such, they provided their authors (who Weissler speculates were most likely middle-class or wealthy women of the urban elite) the opportunity to express, in writing, their own personal religious vision.[19]

Additional written expressions of spirituality by Jewish women during this period can be found in memoirs (the most notable of which is the full-length memoir of the seventeenth-century merchant Glückel of Hameln, excerpted in this volume) and letters addressed to children, husbands, and other family members (three of which are included here). Although not focusing exclusively on spirituality, they reveal the importance that many of the authors attached to God, religious observance, and the preservation of Jewish self-identity. Finally, exceptional women like the Italian poet Sara Copia Sullam wrote polemical letters defending Jewish religious claims. Sullam's letter (included in this volume) to Baldassar Bonifaccio, later bishop of Capodistria, testifies to the variety of spiritual literature produced by at least some Jewish women during the early modern era.

By the end of the seventeenth century, the emancipation of European Jewry allowed many Jews to end their physical and intellectual isolation and to participate more fully in the social, economic, and political life of the non-Jewish world. As thousands of Jews, especially those of the middle and upper classes, began to avail themselves of these new opportunities, the religious mind-set that governed medieval European Jewish communities began to disintegrate, as did the communities themselves.[20] Led to view Judaism as part of life rather than all of life, growing numbers sought to redefine their understanding of Jewish self-identity, to achieve an identity that was fully modern as well as fully Jewish.

Women, it seems, at least among the elite, were the first to gain the benefits of emancipation. In Central and Western Europe, for example, middle- and upper-class Jewish girls had begun to study piano, foreign languages, and other secular subjects by the eighteenth century. In marked contrast to their brothers, whose education continued to be composed primarily of traditional religious study, girls began to take advantage of the educational opportunities emancipation provided. Their education, encouraged and financially supported by their families, served as a visible sign of Jewish acculturation, proof, in other words, that their families had indeed adapted to modernity.[21] While some of the Jewish women who gained access to enlightened education and culture eventually converted to Christianity—both to escape what they perceived to be their inferior social status as Jews and to find within Christianity what they believed to be greater opportunities for spiritual self-expression and growth—the vast majority remained within the Jewish community.[22] Like their male counterparts, these women attempted to forge for themselves a modern Jewish self-identity.

Not surprisingly, however, given the new social and educational opportunities available to them, many middle- and upper-class women found traditional justifications for their exclusion from religious study and their unequal participation in communal life and public worship to be inadequate. Their traditional religious roles within the home seemed limited and circumscribed in comparison to those greater opportunities available to them in secular society.[23] The stress on individualism, dating back to the Renaissance and the Protestant Reformation, had a particularly strong effect and led many Jewish women, as it did their Christian counterparts, to reevaluate their own religious identification.

1800–1890: STRONGER VOICES

By the beginning of the nineteenth century, Jewish literary women began to seek written expression for this reevaluation. Some, perhaps spurred on by similar efforts among non-Jewish women, began to write essays, poems, and prayers that voiced their spiritual concerns and aspirations (see, e.g., the poetry of Rahel Luzzato Morpurgo, Rebekah Hyneman, Rosa Emma Salaman, and Adah Isaacs Menken as well as the theological writings of Englishwoman Grace Aguilar included in this volume). While some women continued to espouse the values and expectations of traditional Judaism, others began to question whether a sex-differentiated society afforded them full opportunity for spiritual growth. Without necessarily questioning the belief that men and women were different by nature, growing numbers of women began to look for greater, more public arenas through which to express their spirituality.[24] In so doing, Jewish women began to claim a stronger spiritual voice.

Beginning in the 1830s, numerous urban, middle-class Jewish women in England and the United States sought to counter Protestant missionizing efforts and to preserve Judaism and Jewish culture through the creation of new social, philanthropic, and educational organizations. In the United States, for example, Philadelphian Rebecca Gratz (1781–1869) created the nation's first Hebrew Sunday School as a means of educating Jewish boys and girls (most of whom were the children of immigrants) in what Gratz and her female coworkers took to be a blend of the practicalities of American life and the essence of traditional Judaism.[25] Often starting their classes with an original prayer and continually looking for intelligible and personally meaningful ways in which Judaism could be presented, many women, including Gratz, found teaching religious school to be an important means of publicly affirming and expressing their spirituality. Religious schools, then, both armed their students with the means of combatting Protestant evangelical claims (and at the same time learning more about Judaism) and afforded their female teachers new opportunities for spiritual expression and for participation in communal religious life.

Many Jewish women, whether consciously or not, succeeded in combatting Protestant missionary activity simply by cultivating a greater religious atmosphere within their homes.[26] Indeed, the Hebrew Sunday School trained its female students to do just that. Without any communal or governmental means of enforcing religious standards, the personal piety of traditional Jewish women in nineteenth-century England and America *in general* took on special significance. Through the dual powers of persuasion and friendship, it was these women who effectively guarded and transmitted the importance of Jewish values to their families and their communities and helped preserve and transmit the significance of religious observance as well.

In England and North America, the high level of tolerance, if not outright acceptance, that many Jews experienced accelerated the process of acculturation and fostered new, more intimate communication between Christians and Jews. Most Jewish women, like their male counterparts, saw themselves as sharing with their Christian neighbors not just a common language but a common culture. As English replaced Yiddish as the vernacular of most English and North American Jews, fewer and fewer Jewish women could read the Yiddish Bible stories and supplicatory prayers that had been written for them. Looking for new sources of religious edification and devotion, many turned to non-Jewish literature. This literature was easily accessible since it was written in English and often serialized in the popular press. Moreover, Jewish women may have been more inclined than Jewish men to read explicitly devotional popular literature since contemporary claims that women were more innately spiritual than men led many authors—both male and female—to write such literature specifically for women.

The close cultural and social relationship that Jews and Christians shared in nineteenth-century England and, to a lesser degree, the United States facilitated missionizing efforts among Jews by Protestant evangelicals. In contrast to the experience of earlier evangelicals missionaries, those active during the nineteenth century in compact urban areas like London and New York City found themselves with a greater Jewish population to target, a population that, given the cultural and social contact between Christians and Jews, they could more easily meet.[27] Like those Jewish actively engaged in antimissionizing efforts, many Jewish women sought ways in which to combat missionary activity. Jewish women who took nineteenth-century ideas about women's special moral influence seriously may well have considered resistance to missionary activity to be women's particular responsibility.

Some literary Jewish women responded to missionizing by writing religious novels and essays. Many of these (such as Grace Aguilar's *Women of Israel*) focused on the biblical matriarchs as a means of positively asserting the authors' own Jewish self-identity and as a direct refutation of evangelical claims that Judaism traditionally debased its women. Other women founded or joined already existing associations aimed at either countering Protestant missions or promoting greater understanding between Christians and Jews. Such associations published and distributed scholarly defenses of Judaism, sponsored Jewish-Christian dialogues and debates, and featured prominent speakers addressing both traditional religious themes and major concerns within contemporary Jewish life.

By the mid-nineteenth century, women were said to constitute the majority of the reading public in England and the United States and, at least among Protestants, the bulk of educated churchgoers.[28] Consequently, growing numbers of literary women began to write books for other women like themselves. Highly sentimental and frequently autobiographical or semiautobiographical, these works sought to exert a spiritual influence over their readers. Using what they believed to be women's great power of moral persuasion, many of these writers actually viewed themselves in quasi-clerical terms. As the popular Unitarian minister William Ellery Channing noted in 1849, referring to American women novelists, "Woman, if she may not speak in the church, may speak from the printing room, and her touching expositions of religion, not learned in theological institutions but in the schools of affection, of sorrow, of experience, of domestic charge, sometimes make their way to the heart more surely than the minister's homilies." [29]

While Jewish women were more frequently readers of these works than they were authors, a fair number of Jewish literary women, primarily, although not exclusively, in England and the United States, wrote spiritual autobiographies, religious novels, and theological essays of their own. First appearing in the 1840s, such works were produced well into the twentieth century. Especially noteworthy were essays, poetry, and novels by Englishwoman Grace Aguilar (1816–47), whose writings enjoyed enormous popularity in both England and the United States. Her most heavily theological work, *The Spirit of Judaism*, first published in 1842 and reprinted four times during the next thirty years (excerpts from which appear in this volume), was considered by many nineteenth- and early twentieth-century Jewish women on both sides of the Atlantic to be among the most influential theological works they had ever read.[30]

Women's activities as mothers often provided them justification for expression of their personal spirituality; indeed, mother-child communication provides a core of oral and folkloric tradition in almost every religious culture. Throughout the nineteenth and early twentieth centuries, Jewish mothers wrote farewell letters to their children who formed the increasing number of Jews immigrating from continental Europe to England and North America in search of greater economic and political freedom. Rarely expecting to see their children again, mothers often wrote these letters in the form of the Jewish ethical will, a document traditionally written by an elderly parent, usually a father, summing up his acquired wisdom and advising his children on how to conduct their moral lives after their parents' deaths.[31] As literacy grew among Jewish women, an increasing number began to write ethical wills as a means of imparting to their children both wisdom and hopes for their future. Like the letters written by nineteenth- and early twentieth-century Jewish women in a similar form, these wills became written expressions of their authors' spirituality. The ethical will of American Grace Nathan and the farewell letters of Europeans Yette Beckman and Lena Roth (included in this volume) reflect the piety of their writers, their moral sensibility, and the meanings they attached to personal religious observance. Initial studies of ethical wills suggest that, unlike those written by men, wills written by women draw on "psychological insights to personalize their hopes and counsels."[32] Indeed, the ethical wills that we have included in this volume reflect an intensely personal faith grounded primarily in religious feeling.

By the mid-nineteenth century, a growing number of Jewish women in Western and Central Europe and in North America turned to the nascent Reform movement, seeking greater opportunities for spiritual self-expression through expanded participation within the synagogue itself. Although in some ways more theoretical than real,[33] Reform Judaism's declaration of women's spiritual equality appealed to thousands of emancipated women. Viewing the relegation of women to a separate gallery in the synagogue as an old-fashioned "orientalism" that needed to be abandoned, abolishing the traditional benediction recited by Jewish men thanking God for not having been created a woman, and insisting that women be obligated "from youth up to participate in religious instruction and the public religious service and be counted for a *minyan*," the Reformers believed that the "spirit of the [modern] age" demanded that women be entitled, in both the synagogue and the home, to "the same religious rights and subject to the same religious duties as men."[34] While women were not ordained as Reform rabbis until 1972, by the mid-nineteenth century Reform Judaism offered women religious education and participation in a worship service based on a liturgy that was largely in the vernacular and therefore easily accessible to them.[35] In America, women were further afforded the opportunity to sit alongside men and to assume some leadership roles within the synagogue, an opportunity that grew more widespread as the century progressed.

Equating Judaism with ethical monotheism, the Reformers placed greatest emphasis on personal faith and moral behavior. But Jewish women had traditionally been encouraged to cultivate a sense of private, or personal, religiosity. At the same time, rabbinic

Judaism—and in the nineteenth-century the secular Cult of True Womanhood—held them responsible for establishing a spiritual (i.e., moral) atmosphere within the home. In some ways, then, Reform Judaism's equation of spirituality with inner piety and moral behavior served simply to validate and value what Jewish women—as women—had long since understood to be true religion.[36] (For an example of the equation of spirituality and piety, see the hymns of American Penina Moise included in this volume.)

Liberal (or Reform) Judaism's understanding of spirituality was particularly well suited to women, wrote Lily Montagu: "Just as women were oriented inward, so did Liberal Judaism place ultimate authority for belief and practice within the individual soul." Moreover, in demanding reverence for all of life, Reform, she said, presented a synthetic, unifying conceptualization of existence characteristic of the female intellect, a conceptualization in opposition to a more male, scientific analysis of creation.[37] (Montagu was the founder of the Liberal movement in England. One of her writings is included in this volume.)

Just as Reform acknowledged that one need not be a scholar to find God, it also acknowledged that one need not lay *tefillin* (phylacteries, which Jewish men traditionally wrap around their arms and forehead each morning) or wear a *tallit* (a prayer shawl traditionally worn by Jewish men during morning prayers). By taking the position that these external (male) symbols of religiosity are inessential to true worship (indeed, Kaufmann Kohler, a leader of American Reform, considered *tefillin* a primitive talisman and the wearing of the *tallit* "fetishim"),[38] the Reformers again validated the traditional piety of Jewish women who had long sought to find God without benefit of *tefillin* or *tallit* and without benefit of regular participation in daily worship services, which the Reformers similarly devalued.[39]

Not all nineteenth-century Jewish women, of course, even among the most emancipated, turned to Reform Judaism as an outlet for spiritual self-expression. Many, especially among the working classes, either retained the traditional faith of their foremothers, were attracted to Samson Raphael Hirsch's modern Orthodoxy, which offered women new educational and communal opportunities but at the same time continued to espouse the importance of sex-differentiated roles, or were drawn to such secular movements as socialism (and, by the end of the century, Zionism) that redirected and redefined spiritual activity.

While some male (and female) Reformers found it difficult, if not impossible, to understand why thousands of Jewish women, even among those who saw themselves as modern, refused to abandon traditionalism, those nineteenth-century women who in varying degrees came to identify themselves as Orthodox believed that what Reform offered them was not a means of becoming more fully Jewish but rather a means of becoming less so. Along with what may have been the potential allure of Reform Judaism—for example, the abolishment of a separate women's gallery in the synagogue, mixed choirs, prayers and sermons in the vernacular, and the positive valuation of inner piety and moral action—the movement devalued those personal observances through which they as women sought God. The dietary laws, for example, for which women had long claimed expertise and through which they were able to sanctify their lives and their homes, were denigrated by the Reformers, viewed not simply as inessential but, as the Reformers later declared, as apt to "obstruct [rather] than to further modern spiritual evaluation." [40] The laws of *niddah* (family purity) were, again, not simply abolished but looked on with disdain. Modern concessions made by the Reformers regarding the celebration of the Sabbath and of holidays undoubtedly led many women, as it did men, to conclude that the concern of the Reformers was not, as they claimed, to ensure the sanctification of these celebrations but rather to seek new ways to adapt to non-Jewish society, a path that would ultimately lead to the destruction of Judaism itself.

By the second half of the nineteenth century, an increasing number of Jewish women, particularly in England and the United States, began to seek ways of expressing their spirituality as Jews and their particular moral sensibility and sensitivity as women within both a domestic and a communal setting. Their voices became stronger as they grew more confident of their own capabilities and of the particular contribution that they needed to make to the Jewish community and to the spiritual treasury of the world. Whether they expressed their voices through essays, poems, prayers, or public addresses or simply chose to join their voices with those of others engaged, as they were, in social, philanthropic, and educational efforts, growing numbers of Jewish women demanded to be heard. One sees this newly crystallized sense of religious mission reflected in women's spiritual writings. Before 1890, spiritual writings by Jewish women viewed God primarily as a father in heaven to whom one owed gratitude, obedience, and humility (see, e.g., the published works of Rahel Morpurgo, Penina Moise, and Rosa Emma Salaman as well as the private devotions of Judith Montefiore included in this volume). After 1890, these writings increasingly came to view God as one who demands moral and social action. Like the written works of many non-Jewish women during this same period, those by Jewish women echoed both the belief that one serves God best by serving others (a view also common among increasing numbers of men)[41] and the belief that, given their innate spirituality and powers of moral persuasion, women had a special obligation to transform their homes and their communities, if not the entire world.

1890–1960: URGENT VOICES

During the latter years of the nineteenth century and well into the twentieth, the voices of Jewish women assumed greater urgency in those countries in which Jews had been emancipated[42] and women subsequently were given new opportunities for personal growth and religious self-expression. In Europe and the United States, among both traditional and Reform Jews, women and men continued to espouse the view that women were religious by nature and that it was thus women's obligation to impart spiritual values to their children and their husbands, creating a religious, moral atmosphere within the home.

With religion firmly associated in the popular imagination with so-called feminine influence, women's activities in general increasingly reflected the conviction that it was up to them to share their own understanding of true religion with others.[43] Among Jews and Christians, literary women continued to write essays, prayers, religious novels, and spiritual autobiographies. As in previous generations, these works were written both by women who were professional writers and by women who simply felt the need to express in writing their understanding of religion and their own religious faith.

Within a Jewish context, such works included Josephine Lazarus's *The Spirit of Judaism,* published in 1895 (excerpts from which appear in this volume), and spiritual autobiographies by communal leaders Hannah Greenbaum Solomon and Rebekah Kohut detailing their involvement in the creation of the National Council of Jewish Women (NCJW). In England, Lily Montagu wrote a collection of prayers (*Prayers for Jewish Working Class Girls,* 1895), a theological treatise (*Thoughts on Judaism,* 1904), two religious novels and a book of short stories all focused on religious themes, a spiritual autobiography (*Faith of a Jewish Woman,* 1943), a liturgy compiled and in part written by her and intended for Sabbath celebrations at home (1944), and a devotional work entitled *God Revealed* (1953). (Despite her output, Montagu did not consider herself a professional writer.) American Sarah Kussy, a member of the Conservative movement's National Women's League, published the essay "Judaism and Its Home Ceremonies" in the *America Jewess* (a periodical, published between 1896 and 1899, that frequently devoted space to Jewish women's spiritual writings), while German social worker and feminist Bertha Pappenheim (1859–1936) wrote numerous prayers, several of which are included in this volume.

Sermons and public addresses centering on religious themes delivered by Jewish women often made their way into print. These included numerous sermons and addresses by preachers Ray Frank (1865–1948) and Tehilla Lichtenstein (1893–1973) in the United States and by Lily H. Montagu in England (some of which are excerpted here).[44] They also included speeches by American NCJW leaders Hannah Greenbaum Solomon, Sadie American, and Rebecca Kohut, addresses by Bertha Pappenheim (one of which, delivered at the 1912 Women's Congress in Munich, is included here), and committee reports and addresses by American educators and communal workers Julia Richman (1855–1912) and Minnie D. Louis (1841–1922), published either in conference proceedings (such as the address by Richman included in this volume) or in such periodicals as the New York–based *American Hebrew* (see, e.g., the piece by Louis included here).

Some Jewish women, again like their non-Jewish counterparts, kept diaries that not only served as a written record of daily happenings, family occurrences, and local, national, and international events but also discussed, with great candor and emotion, their authors' sense of Jewish self-identity. Others wrote memoirs, often intended for family distribution only, that sought to convey to their children and grandchildren what the nature of their lives had been.[45] While some Jewish women (e.g., Judith Lady Montefiore) kept diaries and wrote informal memoirs prior to the end of the nineteenth century,[46] the majority of those to which we have access were written after 1870. Perhaps fewer Jewish women wrote diaries and memoirs before this period; perhaps fewer were preserved; or perhaps scholars simply have not yet uncovered many of those that were written. In any case, by the end of the nineteenth century, as secular and religious educational opportunities for Jewish women increased (and, at least in the United States and England, as Jewish women gained access to higher education), as women began to play a wider and more significant role than they had previously in Jewish communal life, and as growing interaction between Jews and non-Jews led a great many Jewish women to reflect on religion in general, Christianity in particular, and the role of faith in modern life, an increasing number of Jewish women began to keep written records of their lives.

Most of these records have never been published. Those that have been preserved—either in archives or privately, by family members—reveal a great deal about modern Jewish women's sense of spirituality. Some, especially those written by Sephardic Jews (Jews of Spanish, Mediterranean, or African descent) and Eastern European immigrants to England and the United States, reveal a traditional understanding of Jewish piety and of women's role in maintaining traditional observances within the home. Others, particularly those written by native-born English and American Jews of the middle and upper classes, reflect a sense of religious identity shaped largely by the teachings of Reform.

A number of writings reveal the extent to which some Jewish women used non-Jewish teachings alongside Jewish teachings in coming to a sense of spiritual self. In the United States, for example, during the decades around 1900, thousands of Jewish women turned to the writings of Mary Baker Eddy, founder and leader of Christian Science. While some who did so actually left Judaism for membership in the Christian Science church, the majority continued to identify themselves as Jews while at the same time turning to Eddy's writings, attending Christian Science meetings, and visiting Christian Science practitioners for spiritual guidance and healing.

Clara Lowenburg Moses, for example, a New Orleans Jewish woman who lived from 1865 to 1951 and identified as a Jew throughout her life, recalled in her memoirs that in 1914, when her brother-in-law was stricken with leukemia, she and her sister engaged several nurses and had him treated by a Christian Science practitioner. "When we left to go to Asheville, North Carolina," she wrote, "we got another healer to treat him there. . . . We had a [Christian] Science teacher in New Orleans who insisted that it was thru [sic] her healing and work with him that he had improved, so both Helen and Marguerite too [her sister and niece] read the *Science and Health* books, as well as the Bible for hours at a time."[47] Moses went on to describe later visits to Christian Science practitioners as well as reading Eddy's *Science and Health* along with portions of both the Old and the New testaments with her sister. Her belief that the teachings of Christian Science served to strengthen her religious faith is echoed in the diaries, memoirs, and published letters of other American Jewish women (both native born and immigrant) during the late nineteenth and early twentieth centuries.

By 1921, the allure of both Christian Science and the Protestant-based alliance called New Thought (similar to Christian Science but believing in the use of modern medicine) led two Jewish women in New York—Bertha Strauss and Lucia Nola Levy—along with three Reform rabbis—Alfred Geiger Moses, Morris Lichtenstein, and Clifton Harby Levy—to search for ways of presenting a vision of happiness and health within an explicitly Jewish context. While the result of their efforts, a movement called Jewish Science, never attracted more than one thousand members, the vast majority of whom were women, many more faithfully subscribed to the *Jewish Science Interpreter,* published by Lichtenstein's Society of Jewish Science as early as 1925 and continuing to appear monthly even today. In 1938, Lichtenstein's wife, Tehilla, assumed leadership of the society. In so doing, she became the first Jewish woman formally to assume a position of religious leadership in America.

Diaries, memoirs, and letters published during the late nineteenth and early twentieth centuries both in Yiddish newspapers in the United States and England and in English-language Jewish newspapers were frequently written by Jewish women who did not identify themselves as religious. Among these were Zionists, Bundists (members of the General Jewish Worker's Union founded in Russia in 1897) and other socialists, Communists, anarchists, and Yiddishists (i.e., those interested in preserving and perpetuating Yiddish culture). While the definition of *spirituality* as "life in the presence of God" might preclude us from seeing most of these women (along with their male counterparts) as spiritual, many of their writings do seem to express a modern, secular form of religious faith.

Cultural Zionists, for example, following the lead of Ahad Ha'am, spoke of working for Jewish national renewal in Palestine as a "spiritual obligation." For them, this obligation was not mandated by God but rather expressive of the spirit of the Jewish people. Ahad Ha'am and his followers thus spoke of a cultural "spiritual inheritance," one that could be developed fully only by Jews working together in Palestine, the Jewish national home.[48] Most of those who worked to preserve the Yiddish language and culture similarly did not identify their activities as religious. Yet again, like cultural Zionists, they too believed that there was a Jewish cultural inheritance that they had received and that, through their efforts, would grow and flourish. These efforts were directed not toward rebuilding Palestine as a cultural center for Jews all over the world but toward preserving in the Diaspora Yiddish language and culture—the "spiritual inheritance" of modern Eastern European Jewry.

In decrying existing social, economic, and political orders and working to create new ones, many Jewish socialists and Communists believed that it was they who would help bring about a "universal brotherhood" (sic) of peace and justice. While Reform Jews spoke of the establishment of such a "brotherhood" as part of their religious mission, Jewish socialists, both male and female, denounced Reform sentiments as hypocritical, maintaining that the Reform movement did little, if anything, to make such sentiments a reality.[49] In contrast, Jewish socialists, Communists, and even anarchists believed that their actions would indeed help create a better world. Speaking in religious terms, one might maintain that such Jews sought to attain a life of holiness for themselves and others by repairing the world (tikkun olam) and making it whole.

Not all Jewish activists, of course, were secularists. Some—women in particular, reflecting commonly held beliefs concerning their superior moral nature—explicitly saw their actions as having religious significance. Many women believed therefore that they could be particularly effective in bringing about a new social order.

Similar sentiments motivated thousands of more conservative Jewish female social reformers. In the United States and Great Britain, for example, many native-born middle- and upper-class Jewish women eagerly participated in nonsectarian charitable, educational, and philanthropic organizations. Notable among these were Lily Montagu's sister, Henrietta Franklin, a president of the National Union of Women's Suffrage Society and one of the founders of an educational system (P.N.E.U.) that dominated English educational theory during the first quarter of the twentieth century, and Maud Nathan (1862–1946), a wealthy Sephardic Jew active in the New York Exchange for Women's Work, the New York Woman Suffrage Party, the Women's Auxiliary of the Civil Service Reform Association, and the Consumers' League of New York, an organization that sought to ameliorate, through consumer pressure, the working conditions of women and children in New York City department stores.

Other elite women worked to create women's organizations specifically for Jews. By the turn of the century, for example, few Jewish communities in the United States lacked a ladies' aid society. Attempting to extend their help beyond the Jewish community, members visited hospitals, established loan funds for the poor, and offered cultural events to which all women were invited. In Chicago, for instance, the Chicago Women's Aid, an association founded in 1862 as the Chicago Young Ladies' Aid, helped introduce penny lunches in schools, hired a dietician, and provided the Associated Jewish Charities with a visiting nurse. It was also actively interested in and provided financial support for the Sheltering Home and Creche for Poor Jewish Children. Like other Jewish communities, Chicago also had a Ladies' Sewing Society (in fact, it had two). These societies hired poor women to sew clothing that would then be distributed to the needy.[50] For their members, these societies functioned as both social and spiritual outlets. They not only afforded Jewish women the opportunity to meet other women of similar backgrounds and socioeconomic class but also enabled them to bring their "feminine influence" into the larger community, providing other, less fortunate women with adequate clothing, food, and shelter so that they too might transform their homes into pious havens.

Similar efforts were made by those women, both Jewish and non-Jewish, who worked to establish and run settlement houses. Lillian Wald (1867–1940), for example, perhaps American Jewry's best-known female social worker, championed such causes as child welfare, public health nursing, vocational guidance, the establishment of scholarships for talented children, and woman suffrage. Born in Cincinnati into a well-to-do middle-class family, the well-educated Wald turned to social service, especially nursing, as a means of helping others. Although she, like many other of her female contemporaries, felt more comfortable at meetings held by the humanistic Ethical Culture Society than she did at synagogue services, Wald continued to identify herself as a Jew.[51] While the extent of her Jewish identity may have been primarily cultural, her efforts to help others were to a great extent conditioned by her own upbringing and, more specifically, by what she had been taught to regard as women's sensitive and moral nature.

Some Jewish social workers, like Goldie Stone, an Americanized Lithuanian immigrant who worked with members of the native-born female Jewish elite in Chicago to create social and philanthropic opportunities for impoverished Russian Jewish immigrants, summed up their religious faith with the phrase "Be kind."[52] Yet many of the Jewish women who engaged in social reform, unlike Stone and Wald, explicitly described their activities as an outgrowth of what they understood to be women's particular religious mission.

By the beginning of the twentieth century, Jewish women's organizations in the United States proliferated among the native-born elite on both the local and the national levels. Most notable were the local sisterhoods, established as social, educational, and philanthropic organizations, that, by the second decade of the century, were in existence in almost every Reform temple in the country. By 1913, these groups were coordinated on a national level as the National Federation of Temple Sisterhoods (NFTS).[53] The National Women's League of the United Synagogue of America, founded in 1918 by Matilda Schechter (and renamed the Women's League for Conservative Judaism in 1972), engaged in similar activities.[54] The work of these organizations was explicitly driven by religious sentiment, attested to in sisterhood minutes, handbooks (see, e.g., the *Women's League Handbook* excerpted in this volume), and published essays by sisterhood members.

The National Council of Jewish Women (NCJW), founded in 1893 following the first Congress of Jewish Women, organized by Hannah Greenbaum Solomon (1858–1942) as part of the Parliament of Religions held at the Chicago World's Fair, was unusual in its independence from any male-dominated religious movement. The national leadership of the council coordinated the educational, religious, and philanthropic work of local chapters (guiding this work through the creation of a national platform) and sought to unite Jewish women of different social and religious backgrounds. The council succeeded to some extent in this endeavor, although the overwhelming majority of its early members were of German origin and religiously identified as Reform. Seeking first to tap the spiritual potential of their members and then help them exert a moral influence over the American Jewish community as a whole through specific philanthropic and educational efforts, such early leaders of the council as Rebekah Kohut (1864–1951), president of the New York Section, firmly believed that every Jewish woman was obligated to become a "missionary of God" (see the NCJW address by Kohut, as well as the address by Solomon echoing similar sentiments, both included in this volume).

Americanized immigrant women were increasingly attracted to women's organizations founded by native-born Jews. By the 1920s and 1930s, for example, thousands had joined the National Council of Jewish Women as well as Hadassah, the enormously successful women's Zionist organization cofounded and led by Henrietta Szold (1860–1945) in 1912. Not all these women who joined Hadassah viewed themselves as religious. Yet even those who identified themselves simply as cultural Jews shared with Szold the belief that the perpetuation of both Jews and Judaism depended on Jewish resettlement of Palestine. While Hadassah's goals were not explicitly spiritual, the organization provided hundreds of thousands of American Jewish women with the opportunity to engage in important Jewish philanthropic, educational, cultural, and even political activities.[55] If one understands Jewish spirituality as extending beyond study and prayer, then raising money to send a contingent of nurses to Palestine, helping the poor, working for Jewish-Arab rapprochement—in short, working for practical change—can be a reflection, as they were for Szold, of religious and moral convictions (see the letters by Szold included in this volume). Thus, participation even in such seemingly nonreligious organizations as Hadassah became—and continues to be—a way for many American Jewish women to give their own understanding of Jewish self-identity greater public expression.

The same was undoubtedly true for the thousands of women active in the Jüdischer Frauenbund (JFB), the Jewish feminist movement founded in 1904 by Bertha Pappenheim and other German

Jewish activists. During the thirty-five years of its existence, the JFB fought for women's equality in Germany and in the Jewish community both as an end in itself and as a means of reinvigorating German Jewish life. It was the conviction of Pappenheim and other JFB leaders that Jews were turning away from Judaism primarily because women, who should be cultural transmitters, either knew nothing of Jewish traditions or were alienated from Jewish customs owing to their subordinate status. If women were granted equality, the JFB believed, they would return to Judaism and in so doing revitalize German Jewry.

Like their counterparts in England and the United States, most JFB members, including Pappenheim (who served as president and driving force of the JFB for most of its existence), believed that men and women were different by nature. Maintaining that women's maternal instincts made them uniquely qualified for social work, the JFB launched a major campaign against international trafficking in white slavery, supported orphanages, assisted foster children and unwed mothers, and provided job training for young women whom they feared might otherwise turn to prostitution. Drawing on what many of its members believed to be women's innate piety, their powers of moral persuasion, and their friendships with other women, the JFB leadership encouraged thousands of German Jewish women to engage in the many ongoing struggles for social reform, including that for women's equality. In so doing, they succeeded in opening up for their members what Pappenheim viewed as an important path to God.[56]

During the first few decades of the twentieth century, Jewish women who actively fought for woman suffrage, particularly in England and the United States, frequently couched their calls for equality in religious terms. Moreover, as Linda Gordon Kuzmack has persuasively shown, many Jewish suffragists fought to achieve the vote not only in the national political arena but also within the religious-communal sphere, demanding a vote in the synagogue and membership on communal and synagogue governing boards. Within the Reform movement, the religious movement in which they gained the greatest headway, women succeeded in being seated on some of its governing boards.[57]

By the late 1930s, the political situation in Germany signaled the demise not simply of the JFB but of German Jewry. Letters, diaries, poems (such as those by Gertrud Kolmar included in this volume), and memoirs written by scores of Jewish women in Germany and, indeed, throughout Europe are important resources to be explored in any attempt to understand how Jewish women have defined both spirituality in general and Jewish spirituality in particular. They further reveal how the Nazis' rise to power and the subsequent destruction of European Jewry led these women to reevaluate and often redefine their concepts of God and of Jewish self-identity.

As Sybil Milton has pointed out, women remain invisible in most contemporary studies of the Holocaust. Thus, for example, the different experiences of female and male prisoners remain unexplored.

Yet the vignettes and diaries by women interned in Gurs, Ravens-bruck, Auschwitz-Birkenau, and Bergen-Belsen that Milton has ex-amined reveal that there were important gender-related differences separating the experiences of women from those of men. Drawing on these memoirs, Milton writes that "religious Jewish women, who, once married, kept their hair covered in public under either a wig or scarf, felt both a physical and a spiritual nakedness, thus unprotected and exposed to the whims of their Nazi tormenters." Orthodox Jewish women from Hungary and Subcarpathian Russia used "hollowed-out potato peels filled with margarine and rag wicks" for Sabbath candles and secretly carved Hanukkah *dreidels* (tops) from small pieces of wood, while "religious Jewish women interned in Gurs during 1940 and 1941 sometimes refused to take advantage of Saturday releases from the internment camps, because of the traditional prohibitions against travel on the Sabbath. By staying, they were sometimes trapped and later deported to Ausch-witz, where they perished."[58]

Not all women prisoners, of course, were Orthodox or remained so. Indeed, many, if not most, female prisoners (like their male counterparts) focused their thoughts less on God than on sheer sur-vival. Yet, as some memoirs written by Holocaust survivors suggest (such as the testimony of Itka Frajman Zygmuntowicz included in this volume), when women's thoughts did focus on the presence or absence of divinity as well as on their fears and hopes in general, the language used and the events recalled were frequently gender based, rooted in their experiences as women.

In *Fragments of Isabella*, for example, Isabella Leitner describes the moral and physical degradation that she and her sisters, who fought to stay together in Auschwitz, suffered. In the death camps, she writes, they no longer looked like girls. Their heads were shaved, and they had ceased to menstruate. A year after the war, when her American aunt insisted that she put on lipstick so as to look more attractive, she demurred, for, as she told her aunt, she no longer knew how people lived, only how they died. Although sur-rounded by death, she once experienced what she called the "real smell of real life" at Auschwitz. A woman whose pregnancy had gone undetected by the Nazis gave birth, and Isabella and a number of other women prisoners were able to hold the baby before she was discovered and sent to the crematorium. "We touched the dear little one before she was wrapped in a piece of paper and quickly handed to the *Blockälteste* so the SS wouldn't discover who the mother was," writes Leitner, "because then she too would have had to ac-company the baby to the ovens. That touch was so delicious. Are we ever to know what life-giving feels like? Not here. Perhaps out there, where they have diapers, and formulas, and baby carriages—and life." Sometime later, after she and her sisters had been moved from Auschwitz to Birnbaumel in eastern Germany, she was forced to carry the body of a young girl murdered by the SS to her grave. She remembered thinking, "Rest in peace, young girl. The flickering stars above must be the weeping children of your womb. The womb, the glorious womb, the house that celebrates life, where life is alive, where the bodies of young girls are not carried out into the night. Rest in peace, young girl." [59]

As her memoir reveals, Leitner may have lost faith in a supernatural God, if indeed she ever believed that such a God existed, yet she retained faith in what she identified as the "god in man" (sic) or that which is good in all of us. This abiding faith in humanity, despite the reality of evil, stands in sharp contrast to the disillusionment described by Nechama Tec in her memoir Dry Tears. Tec describes, for example, the shattering of her mother's faith immediately following the Nazi occupation of Poland, where she and her family lived. Securing a job as housekeeper for a high Nazi official, her mother often brought home baskets of food with which her employers rewarded her. "Of course the meat that was a part of these gifts," writes Tec,

> was not kosher. But my mother, who until then had kept a kosher home and had refused to taste any of the forbidden foods, stopped objecting. Appalled by the destruction around her, she had concluded simply: "There is no God. If there were a God he could not tolerate all the murdering and torturing of innocent people." Just as she previously had no doubts about observing religious rituals, now she did not hesitate to give them up. Those few simple words were all the justification she needed. She was a person of action, not given to brooding.[60]

Surviving the war by passing as Christian, Tec and her family returned to their home in Lublin, only to discover that, of the forty thousand Jews who lived there before the war, fewer than 150 had survived. Polish anti-Semitism had not disappeared, and, indeed, as Tec discovered firsthand, Poland was still not safe for Jews. Her memoir, unlike that of Leitner's, ends without an affirmation of faith either in God or in humanity.

As new Holocaust memoirs are written by male and female survivors, as previously written memoirs and diaries are uncovered (although apparently fewer wartime memoirs have been published by women than by men),[61] and as interviews with survivors are either published or filmed, we may gain an even greater understanding of the ways in which gender helped shape one's experience of the Nazi occupation of Europe and the destruction of European Jewry. Claudia Koonz's recent study of women in Nazi Germany includes two excellent chapters that help illuminate specific ways in which the experiences of Jewish women—as women—differed from those of men.[62] Still, by focusing almost exclusively on women's physical and emotional suffering as well as on their struggle for survival, these chapters tell us almost nothing about how these experiences affected women's religious faith. Perhaps future studies of the Holocaust will explore this further.

Throughout the twentieth century, both before and after 1948, Jewish women living in the land of Israel wrote essays, devotional hymns, and poems (such as those by Anda Amir included in this volume) that reflected their own sense of spiritual self-identity and the spiritual dimensions of the land of Israel and the Jewish people as a whole. After Israel was declared a state by a vote of the United Nations in 1948, thousands of Jews emigrated there, bringing their cultural and spiritual heritage with them. Among them were the Yemenites, eager to leave a country in which their status as Jews was politically, economically, and religiously inferior to that of the Muslim majority. While Yemenite Jewish men wrote Hebrew devotional poems that were often inspired by mystical traditions, Jewish women sang songs in the vernacular that were passed down orally and sung at weddings and other celebrations. As the Yemenite songs that we have included in this volume reveal, some directly appealed to God for aid or comfort; most reflected the daily circumstances of Yemenite women's lives.[63]

1960–1990: CONTEMPORARY VOICES

In the last thirty years, an increasing number of Jewish women, especially in North America, have begun to explore the meaning of Jewish spirituality, both for previous generations of Jewish women and for themselves, as contemporary Jews. To a large extent, these explorations have been stimulated by the development and growth of feminist awareness within American society and within the American Jewish community itself. By the early 1970s, as thousands of Jewish women, along with their non-Jewish counterparts, continued to demand social, political, educational, and economic equality within American society, many Jewish women also began to turn inward, subjecting the American Jewish community to intense scrutiny. They demanded greater opportunities for participation and even leadership not only in American Jewish organizations but also within the synagogue itself.[64]

Women in the Conservative movement have sought to be, and to a large extent have succeeded in being, counted in the *minyan* (the quorum of ten necessary for public worship), gaining the privilege of being called to the Torah to recite blessings before and after the Torah reading (*aliyot*) and, in recent years, gaining entrance to both the cantorial and the rabbinical programs at the movement's Jewish Theological Seminary of America.[65] Reform and Reconstructionist women have become increasingly active in every aspect of their movements' religious and organizational lives. While in many ways early Reform pronouncements concerning women's equality were more theoretical than real, both Reform and Reconstructionism have long afforded women the opportunity to serve as congregational presidents and heads of important synagogue and organizational committees and recognized them as full participants in public worship. Worship services in both movements are egalitarian, with women assuming leadership roles as members of the laity and the rabbinate (having been ordained as Reform rabbis since 1972 and as Reconstructionist rabbis since 1973). In the Reform movement, where there is a cantorate, women are also invested as cantors (and have been since 1975) and today make up more than half the student body of Hebrew Union College–Jewish Institute of Religion's School of Sacred Music.

The bat mitzvah ceremony, introduced into the synagogue by Mordecai Kaplan, founder of Reconstructionism, in 1922 to celebrate his daughter Judith's religious maturity, continues to offer twelve- and thirteen-year-old girls the equivalent of the bar mitzvah, giving them the opportunity to affirm and celebrate their knowledge of and commitment to Judaism publicly (for a recent reflection by Kaplan's daughter on her religious faith, see Judith Kaplan Eisenstein's "The Spiritual Power of Music," written expressly for this volume). Gaining widespread acceptance in Reconstructionist congregations by the 1950s and now universally accepted in the Reform movement (along with confirmation, a ceremony introduced by Reform well over a hundred years ago celebrating the graduation of boys and girls from religious school), bat mitzvah is also celebrated in the majority of Conservative synagogues today. Some Conservative synagogues, however, unlike Reconstructionist and Reform synagogues, hold bat mitzvahs on Friday evenings instead of on Saturday mornings (when bar mitzvahs are held). The intent is to afford women a religious celebration comparable but not directly parallel to the bar mitzvah, the girl reading not from the Torah (as they do in Reconstructionist and Reform congregations—an innovation that some rabbis maintain cannot be justified within the framework of traditional Jewish law) but from the *haftarah,* a selection from the Prophets that accompanies the week's Torah reading.[66] Some congregations in all three movements have recently begun to offer classes in adult bat mitzvah, culminating in either a group or an individual ceremony. In short, all three movements, largely but not exclusively at the initiation of women, have come to offer women increasing opportunities to affirm and express their spiritual self-identity publicly.

Although such public opportunities have been more limited for Orthodox women, a few Orthodox synagogues now have a *bat Torah* ceremony for girls. As part of this ceremony, girls may give a *dvar Torah* (a commentary on the week's Torah portion), read a special selection of prayers, recite a poem, or give a speech that they have written. While such opportunities are still not the norm in Orthodox synagogues, an increasing number of American Orthodox synagogues have apparently begun to ask, "Within the Orthodox restrictions, how do we expand the possibilities for Bat Mitzvah?"[67]

First conceived in the late 1970s, Orthodox women's prayer groups have also slowly begun to proliferate. Offering women the opportunity to participate fully and lead public worship services (albeit women-only services taking place outside the synagogue), they provide traditional women with the means of exploring their spirituality in a communal setting. Without replacing private, home-centered explorations of spirituality (e.g., preparing for Shabbat and holidays, candle lighting, observing the laws of *nid-*

dah, etc.), the prayer groups have enriched the spiritual lives of a growing number of Orthodox women and may represent the first step toward Orthodox women's demanding a greater role in the synagogue itself.[68]

In looking at the religious writings of contemporary American Jewish women, one often finds the identification of spirituality with inner piety and of Jewish spirituality with communion with God and obeying God's teachings (including those that focus on ethics and morality).[69] Yet this understanding of spirituality, found primarily among women who either identify themselves as Reform Jews or grew up in the Reform movement, may have less to do with gender than with the teachings of Reform Judaism itself. As first articulated in nineteenth-century Germany, Reform Judaism viewed ethical monotheism, that is, belief in one God and observance of God's moral teachings, as the "essence" of Judaism. Although in the last one hundred years—particularly in America—Reform has gained a greater appreciation of traditional ceremonies and observances, it still views moral behavior, seen in the light of God's covenant with Israel, as central. Indeed, for many, if not most, Reform Jews, the ethical realm is more central than study and public prayer.

Yet, while a focus on "Jewish values" as opposed to "Jewish skills" may be particularly characteristic of Reform Judaism, what does seem to be a common thread running through the spiritual visions of many contemporary American Jewish women is a willingness to share our own experiences, what Reform Rabbi Laura Geller has called the "Torah of our lives as well as the Torah that was written down" (see her address included in this volume). From deeply personal sermons written by Reform, Reconstructionist, and Conservative women rabbis (several of which are included in this volume), to poems such as Merle Feld's "Meditation on Menstruation," "Healing after a Miscarriage," and "We All Stood Together," to Savina J. Teubal's "Simchat Hochmah" (literally, the celebration of one's acquiring wisdom), a ritual written for the celebration of her sixtieth birthday, to Penina Adelman's fertility ritual for the biblical Hannah, written, at least in part, as an expression of her "frustration, despair and uncertainty" as to whether she herself could bear a child, these varied spiritual expressions reveal a sense of spirituality that to a great extent is gender based.

The desire to forge a link between individual experience and Jewish teachings as a way to find personal meaning in Jewish rituals, observances, and texts may simply reflect the historical reality that the male framers of Jewish liturgy and law were not particularly concerned with women's spirituality. Thus, women have been forced to create new rituals, stories, and blessings that forge a connection between religious faith and the realities of their everyday lives. As the work of the psychologist Carol Gilligan has suggested in another context, these women's writings may indeed echo a "different voice," rooted in women's own inner natures.[70] In either case, however, these newer spiritual expressions, like those articulated by previous generations of women, have been shaped by such cultural and social factors as current beliefs about women's nature, access to Jewish learning, and, specifically, the study of Jewish texts. The increasing feminist awareness, within American society in general and the American Jewish community in particular, has created an atmosphere among both traditional and liberal Jews that has encouraged women to find our own voices and to articulate our own spiritual visions.

In Israel, North American Jewish women (studying or working in Israel or permanently living there) have helped create "the Women of the Wall," a religiously diverse group of Israeli and foreign Jewish women formed in January 1989 who regularly pray together, "raising their voices in prayer and reading from the Torah on days when this is customary in Jewish practice" and praying without a Torah service at the Western Wall (the Kotel) in Jerusalem every Friday morning.[71] The target of great opposition, and on occasion violence, by ultra-Orthodox Jews (at first because the women came to the wall carrying a *sefer Torah*, a Torah scroll; now, presumably, because of their opposition to women's prayer groups in general), the Women of the Wall see as their continued purpose the facilitating of women's spiritual expression and the providing of mutual support "to help each member enhance her experience of prayer at the holy site."[72] While the Women of the Wall is unique in bringing traditional and liberal Jewish women together in prayer, other opportunities exist in Israel for Jewish women to explore their spirituality as Jews. Despite the fact that most Israeli Jews identify themselves as nonreligious, there are notable examples of opportunities that exist for Israeli Jewish women to define and explore Jewish spirituality, among them traditionally run schools for girls, institutes of Jewish study open to both sexes, newly created Reform and Conservative synagogues in which women have been encouraged to participate more fully in worship, and the Jerusalem school of Hebrew Union College–Jewish Institute of Religion, which admits women to its rabbinical program (studying alongside North American rabbinical candidates, male and female).

Listening to the voices of contemporary Jewish women reminds us that Jewish spirituality is not (and, indeed, never has been) monolithic. Although, as we have seen, Jewish women were traditionally encouraged to develop a particular kind of spirituality (i.e., one that was largely private, spontaneous, and emotional in nature), women's greater access to Jewish learning, their assumption of more public religious roles, and the creation of new rituals, blessings, and *midrashim* by women, along with recent articulations of a more systematic, Jewish feminist theology,[73] have led many Jewish women to explore other, less traditionally female ways of discovering the divine. In so doing, the religious paths that they have taken have been, and continue to be, remarkably diverse.

Notes

1. Arthur Green, introduction to *Jewish Spirituality from the Bible through the Middle Ages* (New York: Crossroad, 1988), xiii, xv.
2. The historical study of Jewish women's spirituality is, in fact, a field still in its infancy. While, to date, no book-length work focusing specifically on this area

has been published (with the exception of the present volume), essays by Ross S. Kraemer ("Jewish Women in the Diaspora World of Late Antiquity"), Judith Baskin ("Jewish Women in the Middle Ages"), Chava Weissler ("Prayers in Yiddish and the Religious World of Ashkenazic Women"), Renée Levine Melammed ("Sephardi Women in the Medieval and Early Modern Periods"), and Ellen M. Umansky ("Spiritual Expressions: The Religious Lives of Twentieth Century American Jewish Women") in *Jewish Women in Historical Perspective* (ed. Judith Baskin [Detroit: Wayne State University Press, 1991]) discuss women's spirituality at length. See also essays by Chava Weissler on the *tkhines* literature (esp. "The Traditional Piety of Ashkenazic Women," in Green, ed., *Jewish Spirituality,* 245ff.; and "Woman as High Priest: A Kabbalistic Prayer in Yiddish for Lighting Sabbath Candles," *Jewish History* [in press]) and by Ellen M. Umansky on modern Jewish women's spirituality (e.g., "Piety, Persuasion and Friendship: Jewish Female Leadership in Modern Times," in *Embodied Love: Sensuality and Relationship as Feminist Values,* ed. Paula M. Cooey, Sharon A. Farmer, and Mary Ellen Ross [New York: Harper & Row, 1987], 189ff.). For a discussion of Sephardic women, see Susan Sered, "The Domestication of Religion: The Spiritual Guardianship of Elderly Jewish Women," *Man* 23 (1988): 506–21. Works of related interest include Bernadette J. Brooten, *Women Leaders in the Ancient Synagogue,* Brown University Series, no. 36 (Chico, Calif.: Scholars Press, 1982); Rachel Biale, *Women and Jewish Law: An Exploration of Women's Issues in Halakhic Sources* (New York: Schocken, 1984); Judith Romney Wegner, *Chattel or Person? The Status of Women in the Mishnah* (New York: Oxford University Press, 1988); Ross S. Kraemer, *Maenads, Martyrs, Matrons, Monastics: A Sourcebook on Women's Religions in the Graeco-Roman World* (Philadelphia: Fortress, 1988); and Judith Baskin, "Some Parallels in the Education of Medieval Jewish and Christian Women," *Jewish History* (in press).
3. According to the Mishnah, "Women, slaves and minors are exempt from reciting the Shema and from putting on phylacteries, but they are subject to the obligations of prayer and *mezuzah,* and grace after meals" (Berakhot 3.3).
4. Israel Abrahams, *Jewish Life in the Middle Ages* (1897; reprint, New York: Atheneum, n.d.), 26, quoting A. Löwy in the *Jewish Chronicle,* 30 December 1892, p. 11.
5. For a more detailed discussion of this point, see Biale, *Women and Jewish Law,* 20ff.; and Weissler, "The Traditional Piety of Ashkenazic Women," 245ff. As Linda Gordon Kuzmack points out (correspondence with Ellen M. Umansky, 22 August 1990), "Midrashic literature further provides evidence of the power and importance of women's private spiritual prayers that abound during the Talmudic period." See Judith Hauptman, "Women in the Talmud," in *Religion and Sexism: Images of Woman in the Jewish and Christian Traditions,* ed. Rosemary Radford Ruether (New York: Simon & Schuster, 1974), 184–212; and Linda Gordon Kuzmack, "Aggadic Approaches to Biblical Women," in *The Jewish Woman: New Perspectives,* ed. Elizabeth Koltun (New York: Schocken, 1976), esp. 252–54, and "Rabbinic Interpretations of Biblical Literature" (M.A. thesis, Baltimore Hebrew University, 21 April 1975), 136–41.
6. For a better idea of how time consuming preparations for Passover can be, see Blu Greenberg, *How to Run a Traditional Jewish Household* (New York: Simon & Schuster, 1983), 398ff.
7. According to these laws, a married woman could not have sexual intercourse with her husband during her menstrual period (identified as being at least five days) and for seven blood-free days after that. She also could not have sex with him for seven days following the birth of a son and thirty days following the birth of a daughter. Following this period of time, she needed to immerse herself in a *mikvah* (ritual bath). Only then could sexual relations be resumed.
8. The Mishnah, redacted by Judah ha-Nasi (Judah the Prince) ca. 200 C.E., was "the intellectual crystallization of the orally transmitted teachings of scribes, Pharisees, and sages from the Second Temple period down to Judah ha-Nasi [in the third century]. The authority of the Mishnah was said to derive from Sinai, and to constitute, together with Scripture, 'Torah' in the broad meaning given to it by the rabbis" (Robert M. Seltzer, *Jewish People, Jewish Thought* [New York: Macmillan, 1980], 251). Although a prescriptive rather than descriptive docu-

ment, because its teachings were believed to be part of the "oral law" revealed at Sinai, we can assume that it was regarded as authoritative by most Jews through the seventeenth century, and it remains authoritative for many Jews (including Orthodox Jews, who continue to maintain its divine origin) today.

9. Mishnah Ketuboth 5.5 (in *The Mishnah,* trans. Herbert Danby [London: Oxford University Press, 1933], 252).

10. For a detailed discussion of the legend of Beruriah in Jewish tradition, see Rachel Adler, "The Virgin in the Brothel and Other Anomalies: Character and Context in the Legend of Beruriah," *Tikkun* (November/December 1988), 28–32, 102–5.

11. Jewish modernity begins with a process identified as "emancipation." Whether one dates this process back to the seventeenth century, as historian Salo Baron suggests in his multivolume *A Social and Religious History of the Jews* (2d ed. [New York: Columbia University Press, 1952]), or to the early eighteenth century, as social historian Jacob Katz maintains in *Tradition and Crisis* (New York: Free Press, 1961) and *Out of the Ghetto* (Cambridge, Mass.: Harvard University Press, 1973)—and both agree that emancipation occurred at different times in different countries—*emancipation* can be defined as the participation of Jews in the political, social, economic, and educational life of the non-Jewish world (participation either limited or denied them prior to this period).

12. "The duty to be fruitful and multiply falls on the man but not on the woman" (Mishnah Yevamot 6.6). For a discussion of women's exemption from the mitzvah of procreation, see Biale, *Women and Jewish Law,* 198ff.

13. While, admittedly, this point is speculative, it is clearly a subject for further investigation.

14. Since, for the most part, emancipation was a process rather than an event, it is difficult if not impossible to assign an exact date to the beginnings of modernity. Thus, although we have referred to the seventeenth century as the beginning of modernity, it is possible to date its origins somewhat earlier, as Baron suggests *A Social and Religious History of the Jews.* The earliest piece of spiritual writing by a Jewish woman that we discovered dates back to 1567 (Rachel to her son Moses in Cairo). While this document can be considered either late medieval or early modern because it is so similar to letters written by many Jewish women after 1700, we have included it in this volume.

15. See Weissler, "The Traditional Piety of Ashkenazic Women," 268.

16. Ibid., 246.

17. Ibid., 248.

18. With the possible exception of such biblical prayers as the songs of Miriam and Deborah, which some scholars believe were in fact written by women.

19. See Weissler, "The Traditional Piety of Ashkenazic Women," 269, n. 6.

20. The religious mind-set was one that did not compartmentalize religious life, differentiating between the secular and the sacred; rather, it viewed Judaism as an all-encompassing framework whose teachings governed all of one's life.

21. For a fuller discussion of this, see Katz, *Out of the Ghetto,* 84ff.

22. Most notable among these women were the so-called salon Jewesses of the eighteenth and early nineteenth centuries, e.g., Rahel Varnhagen, Henriette Herz, and Dorothea Mendelssohn (daughter of the famous Jewish thinker Moses Mendelssohn), who participated in leading intellectual non-Jewish circles of their day.

23. For a discussion of ways in which, by the end of the nineteenth century, thousands of Jewish women in England and America "modified or rejected traditional Judaism by moving from the home into the public sphere and by demanding a more equal role in Jewish religious and communal life," see Linda Gordon Kuzmack, introduction to *Woman's Cause: The Jewish Woman's Movement in England and the United States, 1881–1933* (Columbus: Ohio State University Press, 1990), 3.

24. Beth Wenger ("Jewish Women and Voluntarism: Beyond the Myth of Enabler," *American Jewish History* 79, no. 1 [Autumn 1989]: 37–54) argues that American Jewish women actually used the so-called myth of domesticity to expand their roles within the community.

25. For an analysis of Rebecca Gratz's role and the establishment of new roles for women in the American Jewish community, see Dianne Ashton, "Rebecca Gratz and the Domestication of American Judaism" (Ph.D. diss., Temple University, 1986), 174–260.

26. This is not to imply, however, that women attempted to cultivate a greater religious atmosphere in their homes *solely* as a means of combatting missionary activity. While this may have been one of the intentional or unintentional outcomes of their efforts, many if not most nineteenth-century Jewish women considered ensuring the sanctity of one's home and exerting a spiritual and moral influence over one's family to be important responsibilities in and of themselves.

27. I am grateful to Linda Gordon Kuzmack for helping me clarify this distinction.

28. For a discussion of women increasingly filling the pews of churches and synagogues in nineteenth-century America and England, see Kuzmack, *Woman's Cause*, chap. 1.

29. William Ellery Channing quoted in Ann Douglas, *The Feminization of American Culture* (New York: Knopf, 1977), 130.

30. Among her other popular works was *Women of Israel,* in which Aguilar extolled the women of the Bible. As Kuzmack writes, "Over a hundred Anglo-Jewish women responded [to its publication] with a collective letter of appreciation to Aguilar: 'You have taught us to know and appreciate our dignity. . . . You have vindicated our social and spiritual equality'" (*Woman's Cause,* 15).

31. Ethical wills were also written by rabbis, whose testaments "often include, in addition to messages directed to their own kindred, ethical insights addressed to Jews everywhere" (Nathaniel Stampfer, introduction to *Ethical Wills: A Modern Jewish Treasury,* ed. Jack Riemer and Nathaniel Stampfer [New York: Schocken, 1983]).

32. Riemer and Stampfer, eds., *Ethical Wills,* 175.

33. For an elaboration of this point, see Riv-Ellen Prell, "The Vision of Women in Classical Reform Judaism," *Journal of the American Academy of Religion* 50, no. 4 (December 1982): 576.

34. Report of the Commission on the Position of Women, given at the Breslau Conference, 13–14 July 1846, cited in David Philipson, *The Reform Movement in Judaism* (New York: Ktav, 1967), 219.

35. Equally appealing to women was the weekly sermon delivered in the vernacular during Saturday morning worship services (Michael Meyer, *Response to Modernity: A History of the Reform Movement in Judaism* [New York: Oxford University Press, 1988], 55).

36. According to Jonathan Sarna (letter to Ellen M. Umansky, 6 April 1990), at this time the locus for religion actually began to shift from the home to the synagogue. With less and less actually practiced in the home, the religious sphere that women traditionally occupied actually grew narrower, perhaps explaining why they, like their Protestant counterparts, increasingly came into the synagogue. This development may help explain, at least in part, why the Reform movement, which afforded women a greater role in that area of religious life (i.e., the synagogue) that had come to take on new importance, succeeded in appealing to thousands of Jewish women.

37. Meyer, *Response to Modernity,* 218, summarizing Montagu's views expressed in "Liberal Judaism in Its Relation to Women," *Jewish Religious Union Bulletin* (June 1914), 5.

38. Kohler quoted in ibid., 273.

39. This does not mean, however, that they did not create their own ritual garb. Many women did use forms of head covering when they prayed (and in many cases even when they did not pray). As Jonathan Sarna has pointed out "There was a strong tradition of women 'dressing up' for the Sabbath and holidays" (letter to Ellen M. Umansky, 6 April 1990). Although traditionally women did not wear the fringed garments (*tzitzit*) that men were obligated to wear, the Shulchan Arukh, a sixteenth-century compendium of Jewish law, apparently tells what a woman must do if she wears one (Mark Zborowski and Elizabeth Herzog, *Life Is with People: The Culture of the Shtetl* [New York: Schocken, 1951], 139). Few women, however, if any, wore *tzitzit* (similarly devalued by the Re-

formers). What is more, while the special clothes that women wore on the Sabbath and holidays undoubtedly had spiritual significance, as Jonathan Sarna suggests, Reform Judaism not only continued to value women's dressing up for Sabbath and holidays but also recommended that men do so too (as opposed to wearing traditional male ritual garb). While most women (and men for that matter) may not have thought of this recommendation as a "feminization of Judaism" (and in fact there is no indication that the leaders of Reform intended this recommendation to be such), one can argue that, subconsciously at least, women were attracted to houses of worship in which their form of "ritual garb"—i.e., special clothing—was accorded universal recognition.

40. The fourth point of the Pittsburgh Platform of 1885, cited in Philipson, *The Reform Movement in Judaism,* 356.

41. This view was given even greater credence through the twentieth-century "Social Gospel," which emphasized the intrinsic connection between religion and moral action (i.e., social justice). Directly or indirectly, the Social Gospel influenced thousands of liberal British and American Protestants and Jews.

42. Including the United States and Canada, the land of Israel, and most, if not all, of Central and Western Europe.

43. The term *feminine influence* was coined by Ann Douglas in *The Feminization of American Culture.* Although her reference here is to nineteenth-century American women, it also reflects commonly held ideas about women's nature and the role of women in religion in Europe, both in Great Britain and on the Continent, among Christians and among emancipated Jews.

44. Although a few sermons and addresses by Montagu appeared in various conference proceedings, in publications of the World Union for Progressive Judaism and the National Federation of Temple Sisterhoods (in America), and in such periodicals as *Liberal Judaism,* the vast majority of her sermons and addresses did not appear in print until the publication of *Lily Montagu: Sermons, Addresses, Letters and Prayers,* ed. Ellen M. Umansky (Lewiston, N.Y.: Edwin Mellen, 1985).

45. See, e.g., the memoirs of Americans Maud Nathan (*Once upon a Time and Today* [reprint, New York: 1974]) and Rebecca Kohut (*My Portion* [New York: Albert and Charles Boni, 1927]) and of Englishwomen Louisa Lady De Rothschild (see Lucy Cohen, *Lady De Rothschild and Her Daughters, 1821–1931* [London: John Murray, 1935]) and Constance Lady Battersea (*Reminiscences* [London: Macmillan, 1923]).

46. See, e.g., the unpublished diary of Eleanor H. Cohen, an American Jew from South Carolina, written between 1865 and 1866, in the American Jewish Archives in Cincinnati. An excerpt from this diary is published in Jacob Rader Marcus, ed., *The American Jewish Woman: A Documentary History* (New York: Ktav, 1981), 260–67. An outstanding example of a memoir written by a Jewish woman prior to the twentieth century is Eastern European Pauline Wengeroff's *Memoir of a Jewish Grandmother,* published in German between 1908 and 1910. While brief excerpts from her diary are published in English in Lucy Dawidowicz's *The Golden Tradition: Jewish Life and Thought in Eastern Europe* ([New York: Schocken, 1968], 160–68), no English translation of this memoir as a whole has yet been undertaken. English communal worker Rachel Simon apparently kept a diary prior to 1890 yet did not publish extracts from it until 1894 (some of which are included in this volume). For a rare example of a memoir written by a Jewish woman prior to the nineteenth century, see the memoirs of the seventeenth-century merchant Glückel of Hameln (also excerpted in this volume).

47. Clara Lowenburg Moses, "My Memories," typescript, American Jewish Archives, Cincinnati.

48. This point is made by Arnold Eisen in "Secularization, 'Spirit,' and the Strategies of Modern Jewish Faith," in Green, ed., *Jewish Spirituality,* 299.

49. As Meyer notes in *Response to Modernity,* it was not until the second decade of the twentieth century, largely through the influence of the American Progressive Movement and the Christian Social Gospel, that the Reform rabbinate began to agitate "for the transition to social activism" (pp. 286ff).

50. Marcus, ed., *The American Jewish Woman*, 465–67. According to historian Jonathan Sarna, Jewish women's sewing societies date back to the early nineteenth century. One congregation (Shearith Israel) called its sewing society a "Dorcas Society," a (perhaps unconscious) reference to the New Testament figure of Dorcas that indicates that the founding of the society was due largely to Christian influence (correspondence with Ellen M. Umansky, 6 April 1990).

51. As Jonathan Sarna points out, Ethical Culture "was a movement that held a special attraction for women, precisely because it allowed them to express their 'personal faith and moral behavior' in a public arena, without being fettered by ritual and sectarianism" (correspondence with Ellen M. Umansky, 6 April 1990).

52. Marcus, ed., *The American Jewish Woman*, 604.

53. By 1928, over three hundred temples were represented, and membership had grown to fifty-five thousand (June Sochen, *Consecrate Every Day: The Public Lives of Jewish American Women, 1880–1908* [Albany: State University of New York Press, 1981], 129).

54. The smaller size of the Women's League (in comparison to Reform's NFTS) may simply have reflected the smaller size of the Conservative movement itself. Twenty-six local sisterhoods affiliated with the league on its founding in 1918. By 1925, 230 sisterhoods had joined, totaling twenty thousand members (Pamela Nadell, *Conservative Judaism in America: A Biographical Dictionary and Sourcebook* [Westport, Conn.: Greenwood, 1988]), 330–31).

55. For a fuller description of Hadassah's activities, see Joan Dash, *Summoned to Jerusalem: The Life of Henrietta Szold, Founder of Hadassah* (New York: Harper & Row, 1979); and Sochen, *Consecrate Every Day.*

56. For a fuller description of both the Jüdischer Frauenbund and Bertha Pappenheim's role in its creation and development, see Marion Kaplan, *The Jewish Feminist Movement in Germany: The Campaigns of the Jüdischer Frauenbund, 1904–1938* (Westport, Conn.: Greenwood, 1979). See also Marion Kaplan, "Bertha Pappenheim: Founder of German-Jewish Feminism," in *The Jewish Woman: New Perspectives,* ed. Elizabeth Koltun (New York: Schocken, 1976), 149–63, and "Sisterhood under Siege: Feminism and Anti-Semitism in Germany, 1904–1938," in *When Biology Became Destiny: Women in Weimar and Nazi Germany,* ed. Renate Bridenthal, Atina Grossman, and Marion Kaplan (New York: Monthly Review Press, 1984), 174–96.

57. Kuzmack, *Woman's Cause*, 187.

58. Sybil Milton, "Women and the Holocaust: The Case of German and German-Jewish Women," in Bridenthal, Grossman, and Kaplan, eds., *When Biology Became Destiny,* 312, 314–15.

59. Isabella Leitner, *Fragments of Isabella: A Memoir of Auschwitz* (New York: Dell, 1978), 58, 68.

60. Nechama Tec, *Dry Tears: The Story of a Lost Childhood* (New York: Oxford University Press, 1982), 7.

61. Claudia Koonz, *Mothers in the Fatherland: Women, the Family and Nazi Politics* (New York: St. Martin's, 1987), 348, n. 3. According to Linda Gordon Kuzmack, however, the National Holocaust Memorial Museum in Washington, D.C., has many unpublished memoirs by women (correspondence with Ellen M. Umansky, 22 August 1990).

62. See Koonz, *Mothers in the Fatherland,* chaps. 10 ("Jewish Women between Survival and Death") and 11 ("Consequences: Women, Nazis, and Moral Choice").

63. Mishael Maswari Caspi and Deborah Lipstadt, introduction to *Daughters of Yemen,* ed. and trans. Mishael Caspi (Berkeley and Los Angeles: University of California Press, 1985), 1–9. For a guide to work on Yemenite culture in Israel, see Nitza Druyan, "Yemenite Jews in Israel: Studies of a Community in Transition," *Jewish Folklore and Ethnology Review* 2, nos. 1–2 (1989): 32–38.

64. For a detailed discussion of the impact of feminism on American Jewish life, see Ellen M. Umansky, "Feminism and the Reevaluation of Women's Roles within American Jewish Life," in *Women, Religion and Social Change,* ed. Yvonne Yazbeck Haddad and Ellison Banks Findly (New York: State University of New York Press, 1985), 477–94.

65. The faculty of the Jewish Theological Seminary voted to accept women into the rabbinical program in 1983, and women entered the program soon after. Although in the past few years women have also gained formal entrance into the cantorial program and as such can be invested as cantors, members of the Conservative movement's professional cantorial organization continued to bar women from becoming members of their organization for some time. In August 1990, through a motion adopted by its Executive Committee, women finally succeeded in gaining membership in the Cantors' Assembly.

66. On the other hand, many Conservative synagogues do hold bat mitzvahs on Saturday morning, with the girl reading from the Torah.

67. Arlene Agus quoted in Susan Weidman Schneider, *Jewish and Female: Choices and Changes in Our Lives Today* (New York: Simon & Schuster, 1984), 137. Schneider also provides a discussion of the bat mitzvah in general.

68. For a fuller discussion of these groups, see ibid.

69. This is not to imply that women outside the Reform movement do not see inner piety as an important aspect of spirituality. However, these women also seem to emphasize the intrinsic religious value of rituals and ceremonies (see, e.g., the works of Susan Grossman, Amy Eilberg, and Dvora Weisberg included in this volume).

70. See Carol Gilligan, *In a Different Voice: Psychological Theory and Women's Development* (Cambridge, Mass.: Harvard University Press, 1982), esp. chap. 6.

71. The quotations from a pamphlet issued by the International and Philadelphia Committee for the Women of the Wall, January–February 1990.

72. In an attempt to stop the acts of violence leveled against them by ultra-Orthodox Jews and apparently tolerated by the Ministry of Religion and the police, members of the group have initiated a lawsuit before the Supreme Court of Israel to assure the right of Jewish women to group prayer. The International Committee for the Women of the Kotel, Inc., formed to support the actions of the Women of the Wall group in Israel, has recently initiated a parallel, supporting suit.

73. See Judith Plaskow, *Standing Again at Sinai: Judaism from a Feminist Perspective* (San Francisco: Harper & Row, 1990).

Part I

1560-1800: TRADITIONAL VOICES

A S this section reveals, there were some Jewish women during the earliest periods of modern Jewish history who did produce written expressions of their spirituality. Their works included letters, memoirs, and *tkhines*, supplicatory prayers written in Yiddish (i.e., "spiritual literature") that in part at least reflected their authors' understanding of God, religious teachings, and the Jewish religious community of which they considered themselves to be part.

Although, after 1800, the number of Jewish women who wrote about their spirituality increased significantly (an increase reflected in the greater amount of material that we have included in the remaining three sections of this volume), those, perhaps exceptional, early modern Jewish women who wrote prior to 1800 revealed an understanding of spirituality that shared a great deal with that of Jewish women of earlier generations. For the most part, these women attempted to cultivate a sense of inner piety, not through the study of religious texts, or through participation in regularly scheduled public worship services, but simply by opening themselves up to God, attempting to discover a connection between spirituality and the realities of their everyday existence.

The first selection, "A Yiddish Letter to Her Son Moses in Cairo," was written in October 1567 by Rachel, the wife of Rabbi Eliezer Susman Ashkenazi of Jerusalem. Although not focusing on spirituality, the letter reveals its author to be a traditionally pious woman who looked to God as the omnipotent source of justice and mercy. Frequently using such phrases as "Thanks be to God, thanks be to God," and "God be praised," and constantly referring to the divine as her "Rock and Redeemer," she views her family's poverty as God's just punishment for the many sins that they have committed. Although the many references to her financial misfortunes may well have been intended to make her son feel guilty both about leaving her and about the pain she suffered in childbirth, hoping, perhaps, that these feelings would lead him to offer her financial assistance, the religious faith expressed in this letter, both implicitly and explicitly, seems genuine, revealing a life rooted in traditional religious belief and observance.

The next two selections, dated November 1619, were also originally written in Yiddish: two of the fifty-four letters written by Jewish men and women in Prague at the beginning of the Thirty Year's War and given to a messenger on 22 November to deliver to Jews in Vienna. These letters were in all likelihood intercepted. Eventually falling into the hands of the Austrian authorities, they were stored in the archives of the Viennese imperial court, where they were discovered early in the twentieth century.[1] The first selection is a letter written by a woman named Sarel to her husband, Loeb Sarel Gutmans, a merchant in Prague, the second a letter by Henele, daughter of Abraham Ha-Levi Heller, to her sister and brother-in-law in Vienna. Like the letter by Rachel, Rabbi Eliezer Susman Ashkenazi's wife, these reveal the authors' traditional religious faith. Viewing God as omnipotent, merciful, and benevolent, the authors allude to their frequent, spontaneous, and private devotions. God, for them, is both Lord and protector. They turn to the divine to deliver them from their misfortunes and to secure not just their own health but that of others.

The next selection, an abridged version of a pamphlet by the Italian poet Sara Copia Sullam (1590–1641), is an exceptional document. Unlike most Jewish women of her day, Sullam developed her concepts of spirituality largely through her own study of religious and philosophical texts, both Jewish and non-Jewish. Possessing an excellent knowledge of Hebrew, Greek, and Latin, she was well known among Christian intellectuals and Jewish poets and scholars, who met frequently in her home. This pamphlet, published in 1621, is noteworthy not only because it is one of the first polemical letters to have been composed by a Jewish woman but also because it is the only extant work by Sullam, hailed in her day as one of the outstanding women poets of Italy. The pamphlet was addressed to Baldassar Bonifaccio, later bishop of Capodistria. Based on rumors he had heard claiming that Sullam did not believe in divine revelation, Bonifaccio charged her with not believing in the immortality of the soul. In the light of the fact that the Inquisition, established since 1454, was still powerful in Venice, Bonifaccio's public denunciation placed her in serious danger.[2] Her pamphlet, which appeared two days later, affirms that the soul is "incorruptible, immortal, and divine," that the Ten Commandments are indeed the work of God, and that she herself, far from being a religious heretic, is in fact an observant Jew. While Sullam's pamphlet tells us little, if anything, about the faith of more "ordinary" Jewish women, her work reminds us that, although generalizations can be made about the nature of traditional Jewish women's religious faith, there were always exceptional women like Sullam who were able, and who chose, to cultivate their spirituality in very different ways.

The excerpts from the memoirs of the German Jewish merchant Glückel of Hameln (1646–1724), written in Yiddish to her children, are also exceptional, not so much in the author's understanding of spirituality, as in the fact that hers is the only full-length memoir written by a Jewish woman prior to the nineteenth century to which we have access. If other Jewish women wrote memoirs—and there is no reason to think that they did not—these memoirs have not yet been discovered.

Begun shortly after the death of her first husband in 1689 and completed in 1719, Glückel's memoir vividly chronicles her childhood in Hamburg, her marriage at fourteen, the birth of her thirteen children, her activities as a businesswoman working alongside her husband, and, following his death, her assuming sole responsibility for the family's financial matters. She sold pearls, set up a store, attended merchant fairs throughout Germany, and promoted desirable matches for her children. Later, after the death of her second husband, a wealthy banker in Metz who went bankrupt soon after they had married, leaving her in dire financial circumstances, Glückel went to live with her daughter and son-in-law, by whom she was apparently well treated and respected. Although, in many ways, the world that Glückel inhabited was a medieval one (e.g., she and her children lived in self-contained Jewish communities with traditional Jewish law providing the framework in which all of life was to be lived), one sees in her memoirs the beginnings of modernity. Her business activities, for example, reflect the rise of capitalism and the subsequent, growing participation of Jews in the economic life of the non-Jewish world, while the religious and secular education that she and her siblings received reflects the new educational opportunities available to Jews of both sexes.

Glückel tells her children that the purpose of her memoir is not to instruct them in moral behavior but simply to reflect on and thus share with them the story of her life. In so doing, Glückel frequently reveals her understanding of religion and, more specifically, the various ways in which she attempted to live as a religious Jew.

The first excerpt, the opening of book 1, is one of many places in which Glückel—despite her disclaimer—offers her children moral advice. Emphasizing those religious values and teachings that she hoped they would follow, she attempts to impart to her children the importance of religious study, ritual observance, and the doing of good deeds. The second excerpt is one of Glückel's brief digressions. In the midst of telling her children about her life, she frequently halts the narrative and addresses herself directly to God. These addresses, which form part of her memoirs but sound like spontaneously composed prayers, reveal Glückel's unswerving faith in the divine as the omnipotent Lord of heaven. To her, God is both creator and preserver, the source of mercy, justice, and eternal truth.

It should be noted that, while much of Glückel's spiritual life appears to have been composed of private, spontaneous devotions (as the second excerpt reveals), she also went to synagogue. Sitting in the women's gallery, she describes being "absorbed in the [written] prayers." Although she mentions attending synagogue only in passing, the few references that she gives indicate that she discovered there a sense of religious community with other Jewish women (including her daughters) and a means of publicly affirming her identity as a Jew.

Finally, this section concludes with four *tkhines*,[3] translated and selected for this volume by Chava Weissler, who, as noted in the introduction, has written extensively on this genre.[4] According to Weissler,

> The remarkable woman who is the author of the first text was noted in contemporary sources for her talmudic learning, an accomplishment that was extremely rare for a woman. Sarah Rebecca Rachel Leah Horowitz was probably born in the first or second decade of the eighteenth century.[5] She is by far the most learned female author of *tkhines* I have yet encountered. In her Hebrew introduction to this *tkhine*, she stresses the great power of women's prayer to bring about the messianic redemption. She argues forcefully that women should attend the synagogue more regularly and pray with copious and redemptive tears. This prayer, entitled *"Tkhine of the Matriarchs,"* is intended to be recited in synagogue on the Sabbath preceding Rosh Hodesh, during the ritual of blessing the coming month.
>
> The second text, also entitled *"Thkine of the Matriarchs,"* is intended for the penitential season, when God judges each person and weighs his or her sins in the balance, deciding, in the words of the Rosh Hashanah liturgy, "who shall live and who shall die, who at the end of his days, and who untimely."
>
> The portion of the text quoted is taken from a prayer to be recited when the *shofar* is blown on Rosh Hashanah. This act reminds God of the binding of Isaac, for whom a ram was substituted as a sacrifice, and thus awakens God's mercy for Isaac's descendants. According to more popular tradition, the blasts of the *shofar* serve to confuse and silence Satan, who, on Rosh Hashanah, the annual day of judgment, accuses Israel before the heavenly court, reminding God of its people's sins.
>
> There is no direct evidence about Serel, the author of this *tkhine*. However, her husband, Mordecai Katz Rappoport, was head of the rabbinical court of Oleksiniec, a small town in Volhynia; he also seems to have been an apothecary. A book he wrote was published in Oleksiniec in 1767, presumably during his term of office.[6] Although Serel, like Leah, was a rabbi's wife and seems to have known a certain amount of Hebrew, the tone of her *tkhine* is more popular and less scholarly than the previous text.
>
> The third text comes from a work entitled *Sheloshah she'arim* (The three gates) and is attributed to the legendary Sarah daughter of Mordecai, known as Sarah bas Tovim.[7] This sophisticated, powerful, and erudite work was reprinted numerous times and was perhaps the most beloved of all *tkhines*. It includes three sections, the "gates" of the title: the first contains *tkhines* for women's special *mitzvot*,[8] the second contains a prayer for making memorial candles for the dead, and the third is a series of prayers for the New Moon, which includes a description of the women's paradise, the text included in this volume.
>
> This remarkable passage derives from the Zohar,[9] the great classic of medieval Jewish mysticism, via an intermediate source in Yiddish, the *Sefer Ma'asei Adonai*.[10] Both Yiddish versions of this motif—that found in the *tkhine* and that found in the *Sefer Ma'asei Adonai*—

differ from the original in ways that expand, somewhat, the spiritual aspirations deemed appropriate for women.[11]

The final text, a prayer for baking the weekly Sabbath loaf, returns us from the heights of paradise to the family hearth. This prayer was published in an anonymous collection entitled, simply, *Tkhines* that appeared in Amsterdam in 1648. The compiler of this collection was probably a man, and many of the *tkhines* it contains are reworkings of Hebrew models. This prayer, however, in its humble simplicity, sounds as if it originates in women's oral tradition. Only two of the matriarchs appear in the text; they are pictured, like the woman reciting the prayer, as baking bread for the Sabbath. This lovely text shows how a woman could make of her kitchen a holy place and sanctify the homely act of baking bread.

Notes

1. Franz Kobler, "Introduction to Document 66: Private Letters from the Ghetto of Prague Written on the Threshold of the Thirty Years' War," in *A Treasury of Jewish Letters: Letters from the Famous and the Humble,* ed. Franz Kobler (Philadelphia: Jewish Publication Society of America, 1953), 2:449.
2. According to Kobler (ibid., 442).
3. The Yiddish word *tkhines* is derived from the Hebrew *tehinnot,* "supplications."
4. For a fuller treatment of the *tkhine* genre, see Chava Weissler, "The Traditional Piety of Ashkenazic Women," in *Jewish Spirituality from the Sixteenth Century Revival to the Present,* ed. Arthur Green (New York: Crossroad, 1988), 2:245–75.
5. According to the autobiography of Dov Ber Birkenthal (1723–1805), she was living as a young married woman in the home of her brother, who was the rabbi of Bolechow, a city in Polish Galicia, in the year 1735. Birkenthal remarks on her great Talmudic learning (*Zikhronot R. Dov mi-Bolehov* [Berlin: Klal, 1922], 44).
6. *Encyclopedia Judaica* (Jerusalem: Keter, 1972), s.v. "Novy Oleksiniec"; Hayyim Liberman, "Tehinnah imahot u-tehinnat sheloshah she'arim," in *Ohel Rahel* (New York, 1979–80), 432–54, esp. 434, n. 9.
7. Her epithet means "Sarah daughter of notable people." (*Tovim* is a term for a certain type of Jewish communal official.) There appears to be no firm historical evidence about her apart from the unusually detailed autobiographical material that appears within the texts of the two *tkhines* attributed to her, which can be reliably dated to the eighteenth century. S. Niger ("Di yidishe literatur un di lezerin," in *Bleter Geshikhte fun der yidisher literatur* [New York: Sh. Niger Bukh-komitet baym alveltlekhn yidishn kultur-kongres, 1959], 83–85) and Israel Zinberg (*A History of Jewish Literature,* trans. Bernard Martin, vol. 7, *Old Yiddish Literature from Its Origins to the Haskalah Period* [New York: Ktav; Cincinnati: Hebrew Union College Press, 1975], 252–56) are, however, convinced that she actually existed. The issue is complicated by the fact that she seems to have become a sort of folk heroine; Y. L. Peretz depicts her as a kind of fairy godmother in his short story "Der ziveg, oder Sore bas Tovim" (*Ale verk,* vol. 5, *Folkstimlekhe geshikhten* [New York: Cyco, 1947], 373–79).
8. *Hallah:* the separation of a small portion of dough in memory of the system of priestly tithes; *niddah:* the observance of the rituals of purity surrounding menstruation; and *hadlaqah:* kindling the Sabbath lights.
9. Zohar III 167a–b (Shelah Lekha).
10. This work contains translations and paraphrases of material from a variety of mystical works. The author of the *tkhine* used the Amsterdam edition (1708) or an edition descended from it.
11. For further discussion of this passage, see Chava Weissler, "Women in Paradise," *Tikkun* 2, no. 2 (April–May 1987): 43–46, 117–120.

A mother does not forget the pain she suffered with her child.

RACHEL, WIDOW
OF RABBI
ELIEZER SUSMAN
ASHKENAZI

A Yiddish letter to
her son Moses in
Cairo

Jerusalem, 3 October 1567

May life, health and peace be bestowed upon thee by the Creator of
the world, and blessing and prosperity in all undertakings of thy
hands, my beloved son, the dear and excellent Rabbi Moses, may
his Rock and Redeemer keep him, and thy wife, may she live, and
thy son, may he grow to learning and good works, and all thy relatives, may their Rock and Redeemer keep them. I inform you of my
health, and may nothing but good be your share.

My dear son, may thy Rock and Redeemer keep thee, I am very
worried because I have not received any letter from thee for such a
long time. I have also been worried by the removal of thy daughter,
may she live. Her husband considered it right that she did not want
to stay with her mother-in-law; she herself is in need. And I was not
able, because of our many sins, to maintain her. If I could have done
so, I certainly would have taken her to me.

My dear son, do the best you can for them, but avoid doing harm
to thyself. Thy son-in-law is, because of our many sins, heavily indebted to the non-Jews. His house has gone, they have sold all the
belongs of Beile [the daughter of Moses, the addressee] so that she,
because of our many sins, does not possess any clothes. She has
made him two suits from thy silken coat, one for the engagement,
another for the wedding. He has almost torn them already. I cannot
describe to thee what foolish things he has done. He offered guarantees for his brother and to get Moses and thy mother-in-law out
of their difficulties. He was, however, unable to pay, and therefore
he was obliged time and again to pay interest after interest. Beile's
goods were to be used for the payment of the interest, and so were
the movables which have been in his mother's house. Therefore, my
dear son, be careful that he may not drag thee into his affairs, and
by no means agree to be a guarantor for him or for anybody else.
And be watchful that he may not go away and leave thy daughter
destitute, God forbid! I would have preferred her to have stayed

here, and would have obtained from him the letter of divorce. But she did not want to do so. So great is her love for him. When everybody told her, "Let not thy goods be taken away! Weep and cry!", she answered: "I wish to let him take everything. If the Lord, may He be praised, helps him, He will change him." This is why nobody was able to help her. Therefore, my dear son, do not worry about this matter; thou canst not change it. What the Lord does in His mercy is the best. He does what is best in His eyes.

Thy Beile, may she live, has clever hands; she embroiders very nice things from silver and gold. If thy wife is willing to work she could help her. She is quite reliable, God be praised, and she likes to work, but she was not very fond of learning. But I do not want to enlarge upon this. Only may life and peace be thine in abundance, thanks be to God, thanks be to God. Thy mother Rachel, who writes in great haste.

Written on the 29th of Tishri. May thy days be prolonged in gladness.

As to Zevi, I let thee know that Rabbi David gives him his daughter. She is a fine girl. He gives him his house and all his books, furniture and fine clothing. He wishes to have an Ashkenazi [as his son-in-law] at any cost. . . .

R[abbi] Benjamin, may his Rock and Redeemer keep him, has married his daughter to a young man, an orphan, the grandson of Isaac Cohen, a Hungarian of fifteen years. He will study with him and keeps him in his house. The young man has about three thousand of his own, and R[abbi] Benjamin, may his Rock and Redeemer keep him, will after go to Hungary to the city of Ofen. The Lord, may He be praised, help him to go there and come back in peace. And may this be His will. Mayest thou too experience happiness through thy children, may their Rock and Redeemer keep them, and through all that you likest. And may this be His will. Thanks be to God, thanks be to God. Thy mother Rachel who, may it not be said of thee, is troubled. And thus peace and many years.

I should like to see thee come hither to take care of thy books. When I, God forbid, close my eyes, they will take away everything. This must not happen. And the honored and learned R[abbi] David is, may it not be said of thee, not always too well. He is an old man of eighty. Mayest thou also grow as old as he, thou and thy children, and may they live for learning and good works. I should like to see thee take with thee the pledges of the children, may their Rock and Redeemer keep them. I wished to send thee the candlesticks and the hanging lamp, but nobody was prepared to carry them. God forbid that any changes should occur, may it be not said of thee. This must not happen. Therefore come hither with thy children, may their Rock and Redeemer keep them. Everything here is cheap. I have prepared half a measure of wine for thee. And let me know fully always about thy health. The saying "Out of sight, out of mind" is not always correct. For a mother who has experienced pain does not do so. She does not forget the pain she suffered with her child. It was my wish to send something for thy child, but, because of our many sins, I do not possess anything. . . . My dear, write me what thou hast heard about the children, may their Rock and Redeemer keep them, how they are.

Breindl Korkes sends thee greetings and begs thee to take care of the letter.

Thee is nothing for which I care so much as your long life to a hundred years, this is my prayer in the morning and late. . . .

Prague, November 1619

Many good, blessed and pleasant years, may they surely come to you and to your head and hairs! To the hands of my lovely, dear, beloved husband, the pious and prudent, worthy Rabbi Loeb, may his Rock and Redeemer keep him.

First know of our good health; you, too, shall be so always and in every hour. Further, my lovely, dear, beloved husband, you shall know that I was very eager to write you much but I was afraid that I should have to pay too great a fee to the messenger, so much I have to write to you. I have been ever grieved because I have not heard a word from you for seven weeks, where you are in the world, especially in such a situation as that which we have now. May the Lord, be He praised, turn everything to good soon. I was, indeed, at my wits' end, and did not know what I should think about all that. Honestly, I do not know how I live in my great distress, the Lord, be He praised, knows how I feel. I do not eat, I do not drink, I do not sleep, my life is no life for me. For in good days, if I did not have two letters a week, I thought that I should not be able to live longer. . . . And now I do not at all know for such a long time where you are in the world. But what shall I do now? I have worried about so many things, I must rely upon God, may He be praised. But there is nothing for which I care so much as your long life to a hundred years, this is my prayer in the morning and late, may He grant it. What shall I do? Will the Lord, be He praised, let me witness happily your homecoming now in good trim? Believe me, therefore, I shall do my best and shall certainly never let you go away, for if somebody had ever told me about such a sorrow, I would surely have lost my temper. What shall I do? I must say to everything: even this will be for good.[1]

Now my heart has been calmed a little, because a messenger came from Linz today, who met Jokel at the fair; he had asked Jokel about you, and he said that you are in Linz. You can believe me, I have heard an angel, if I may say so. First I was troubled again that you have not written. I wonder that you let a bird fly [namely, the messenger] in such a time without writing, as this is not your manner. But at any time if I had been given 100 ducats it would not have pleased me so much, although for me every penny is now like a thousand, you can believe me indeed. Nevertheless cursed be all

---

SAREL, DAUGHTER OF MOSES

to her husband, Loeb Sarel Gutmans

money, and the only good is if I hear of your dear health to long years. I thank God, may He be praised, for this [so much], as I cannot write you.

I had much to write you about horrible things, but I cannot write, about the affliction we had to endure here when riots almost occurred in our streets. It was like at the destruction of the Temple. What shall I tell you about this? I think you are clever enough to imagine what could happen in such a time. Now we have been saved from this peril, we have certainly profited by the merits of our ancestors. And I particularly have suffered terribly. I have not saved a penny for my own needs, if, God forbid, my life were to be endangered. Nowadays nobody is ready to lend anything to other people, from one hand into the other. When I needed something for living, I was obliged to offer double pledges and to pay high interest. What shall I do? I wriggled about like a worm before I was prepared to borrow money on pawn in such a time. The saying goes: Need breaks iron, if you will or not. You must eat, domestics must eat, you may be as careful as you like, you must have money anyhow. I had waited for ages, as I supposed that you would conclude a loan with the son-in-law of the righteous priest or with R[abbi] Moses, son of Joel Hazan, but by now I had seen it was coming to nothing, so I had to give as pawn what I had in my possession. May God, be He praised, help me further with honor. What shall one do? The rich and the poor are nowadays all equal, one gains just as much as the other. Believe me, therefore; my head tells me not to wish you now here, I think you are yourself prudent enough for this, it is not necessary to teach you much. If I only hear where you are in the world, if I only hear about you and I have a letter from you every week and know that you have a good job. For here one cannot do anything nowadays, until the Lord, be He praised, will change it soon for the better.

Besides, you should know that they have crowned the King here with great honors, and her too: him on Monday, the 28th of Heshvan,[2] and her on Thursday, the New Moon of Kislev.[3] Write, too, what is going on, so that one may know what is happening. . . . Besides, you may know that Kalman is here and walks about and asks whether he should come to you, whether he could assist you so that you would not be so lonely. I myself would give much for this if you would have him with you so that somebody would take care of you; this is my greatest sorrow; for myself I do not care. Therefore, my dear beloved husband, do not otherwise for sure than to write me a letter whenever you can, and delight me once again with news about your health, long may it last, Amen.

Further you may know that just as we were writing,[4] people arrived from Vienna and did not bring me a letter either. This has frightened me even more, and they told me that you have sent a letter through a messenger and are looking forward to my answer. But I have not seen any letter at all. Therefore do not upset me any longer and write me certainly about all things and thoroughly. I have no rest in my heart. They told me that you were having quite a nice time there. I, too, should like to enjoy it. But I do not blame you. You have never become entirely settled, and thus you think: out of sight, out of mind. . . .

And thus, good night from your loving wife, who remembers you always, and who has no rest in her heart until she hears of your good health, to long years.

Sarel, daughter of Moses, may his memory be blessed

Notes

1. Taanit 21a.
2. The coronation of Frederick took place on 4 November 1619 (27 Heshvan).
3. Elizabeth was crowned three days after her husband.
4. This passage may be taken as an indication that this letter was not written but dictated by Sarel, the writer (apparently) having been Meir Epstein, her son-in-law. The handwriting of this letter is identical to that of one known to have been written by Epstein.

HENELE, DAUGHTER OF ABRAHAM HALEVI HELLER

Letter to her sister Bona and to Simon Wolf Auerbach, the husband of the latter

The Lord, may His name be praised, is my witness that what I suffer for you means much more to me than my own sorrows.

Prague, 22 November 1619

Much peace and health, ever and always: as much as you desire and can speak with your mouth, to my most beloved sister, the virtuous and pious, the king's daughter all glorious within,[1] the wife of the Rabbi, lady Bona, may she live, and to your lovely and beloved husband, the dear, sensible and God-fearing man, his learned excellency, Rabbi Wolf, may his Rock and Redeemer keep him, and to your dear little children, each of them, according to their names.

First of all you shall know that I am well; I wish to hear the same of you as well, my most beloved sister and most beloved brother-in-law [whom I love] like my own brother. You shall know that I was very pleased when I heard that you, [may you live] for long years, are well and that the Lord, may His name be praised, let you reap the reward of your righteousness and piety and has saved and helped you that no harm, God forbid, has been done to you.[2] May the Lord, praised be His name, further protect all of you from affliction, and let you come, with God's help, to great joys. I knew nothing until Matel came and I read the letter of your dear father, the honorable man, may His Rock and Redeemer keep him. You can imagine how pleased I was, may it be for long, and I pray to God, praised be His name, that He may further save you and all Israel from that and from all evil. The Lord, may His name be praised, is my witness that what I suffer for you means much more to me than all my great sorrows, and you can imagine that I have now many sorrows. May God the Omnipotent turn the misfortune of everybody to good. I don't want you to read anything that will disgust you, and will, therefore, not complain, because the Lord, may His name be praised, has done us such miracles and restored you, thanks to God. Everybody says how you and your lovely dear husband have done so many kind and good works. I have also been told how your dear husband stayed with you and did not move from you; he has behaved not like a husband but like a father.

Otherwise, my lovely dear sister and brother, you shall know that I have written you about three letters since you last wrote one. . . . Matel told me that you wanted to send me linen-cloth, but you have none now. . . . God knows it would have come to me now at the right time. Let us make this our sacrifice and expiation. But I wonder that R[abbi] Moshe does not send me the money for the Mahzor[3] I have sent him. Ask him to give the money to R[abbi] Simon,[4] the righteous priest, may his Rock and Redeemer protect him, son of the very learned excellency Isaac, the righteous priest, may his Rock and Redeemer keep him.

My lovely dear sister and brother, I have been told that the Duke of Bavaria[5] has captured Nördlingen,[6] I should like to know whether this is true. I had no letters from our sister Gutle, may she live, I should like to hear and see much good for good, therefore write me often, please, so that each may at least know of the other's health, particularly in these days when sinful man has so much trouble again. One trouble always comes after the other. May the Lord, praised be His name, have mercy upon all Israel and, with God's help, give health and peace. I don't waste words; nobody knows in whose hands the letters may fall. You shall know that Samuel son of R[abbi] Abraham Wallerstein arrived here naked and stripped of everything except a shirt and an old suit. He told us that they took everything from him in Nikolsburg. His father gave him a nice suit. He will go away again whatever the danger. . . . I don't want to waste words until I shall receive, with God's help, good letters from you.

And thus may the Lord protect you from all trouble, this is the desire and prayer of her who loves and honors you, your sister Henele, daughter of my father and teacher, the excellent and learned Abraham Levi Heller, his memory be blessed in the world to come, who day and night thinks of you for good, and would like to see you. . . .

In great haste Friday, on the eve of the holy Sabbath, 15th Kislev 380 of the small number.

Notes

1. Ps. 45:13.
2. Allusion to the plague that was then raging in Vienna.
3. High holy day prayer book.
4. Rabbi Simeon, son of Rabbi Isaac ben Simson, son-in-law of Rabbi Loew ben Bezalel, the "Hohe Rabbi Loew."
5. Maximilian of Bavaria, head of the Catholic League. He opposed the Protestant Union and immediately after Frederick's coronation set his army in motion against Bohemia.
6. A town in Bavaria situated on the Eger, a free city of the empire since 1215. In the course of the Thirty Years' War, two great battles (in 1634 and 1645) were fought near this city.

I do not know that there is to be found in Holy Scripture another autograph written by the hand of God than the Decalogue, to which I cling with my faith and also with works as much as is in my power.

SARA COPIA
SULLAM,
Italy

Letter to Baldassar
Bonifaccio

Venice, 1621

The human soul, Signor Baldassare, is incorruptible, immortal, and divine, and infused by God into our body at that time when the organism is formed and able to receive it within the maternal womb: and this truth is so certainly, infallibly, and indubitably impressed on me, as I believe it is impressed on every Jew and Christian, that the title of your book, in which you have dared to deal in a farcical way with this matter, reminded me of the saying of that brave Roman who, having been invited to deliver an oration in praise of Hercules, exclaimed, "Eh, who has said anything against Hercules?" And in a similar spirit I, too, said: "Is there any need for a tract like this, particularly in Venice, and what is the purpose of printing such treatises among Christians?" When, however, I read the treatise properly later on, I discovered that it was addressed to me on the entirely false assumption that I cherish an opinion opposed to this clear truth. I was astonished and indignant at the shameless calumny which you have thus cast directly upon me, just as if you were the true investigator of the human heart. You must know that my soul is known to God only. . . .

Since, therefore, your calumny is without any foundation I should have been entitled to use against you quite a different means of defence than that of the pen, by an indictment for open libel. But pity, which is embodied in our law, makes me merciful also toward your simplicity, which made you believe that you could gain immortal fame by saying something about the immortality of the soul. And as you had no better opportunity, you have yourself invented one. But instead of dealing with more important matters I felt that I had to spend two nights in countering your intrigue, on the plotting of which you have wasted night work for two years. I shall prove by this writing how false, unjust and senseless is your imputation that I deny the immortality of the soul. I do this in order to clear myself before those who do not know me, and who perhaps might believe your charge. . . .

Tell me then for God's sake, Signor Baldassare, what has induced you to write and print this tract and to involve my name in it. You say in Virgilian verses that God has chosen you for this purpose. This is ignorance indeed! So the Lord had at his disposal for such a sublime and important purpose no other more illuminated spirit and no more learned servant than just you! Of the host of all scholars He has chosen nobody but you to deal with such a worthy matter! If the belief in the immortality of the soul were not implanted in the human spirit by other means than rational grounds, it would be served badly if there were not other than yours which, although they emanate from learned authors, have been misunderstood and reproduced so badly by you. Such a worthless treatment of so important a matter serves rather to strengthen the arguments of the opposition. You will say, perhaps, that God often chooses vile and abject instruments to do great works, that His omnipotence reveals itself particularly in this way, and that, after all, Balaam's ass spoke once—yes, in those cases the effects were obviously divine, and the baseness of their instruments did no harm to them. You, who have pretended to prophesy without any inspiration but that of an extreme arrogance, have in the upshot shown more of ignorance than of any wonderful divine virtue! You would, therefore, have done better if you had applied to yourself instead of the verses of Virgil those of Dante:

> Midway upon the journey of our life
> I found myself within a forest dark
> For the straightforward pathway had been lost.

You want to deal with the soul? with immortality? with the most difficult and arduous question in all philosophy, which would perhaps have been obscure to you in various aspects if theology had not come to your aid? You are certainly well aware of the fact that you are neither a philosopher nor a theologian, and, if I am not mistaken, I have heard from your own mouth that these sciences do not belong to your profession. And in spite of this you have dared to touch with your fingers such a sublime matter. . . .

It is not enough, my dear Sir, to possess the title "Juris utriusque Doctor" to deal with the immortality of the soul. And in order to convince you how little skill you possess in theological writing as well as in philosophical reasoning, it may be sufficient to remind you of that nice little calumny you threw at my head in the beginning of your book, in which, after having falsely supposed that I deny the immortality of the soul, you declare that I am the only one who, after so many centuries, has fallen into such an error. That you have not read Scripture nor the historian Josephus Flavius, who reports the various opinions of the Jewish people, I can forgive you; but I cannot forgive you that you have not present in your mind the Gospel of your own creed; otherwise you would have remembered that in St. Matthew, chapter 22, the Sadducees, a Jewish sect that denied the immortality of the soul, came to Christ to submit their objections, and he answered them wisely and reduced them to silence.

You add that I do not believe in the infallible autograph written by God: I do not know that there is to be found in Holy Scripture another autograph written by the hand of God than the Decalogue, to which I cling with my faith and also with works as much as is in my power. If you have another writing made by the hand of God I would be delighted to see it. But let us see how well and with what linguistic skill and knowledge of Hebrew you have used the word *ruach* in order to produce an argument for your purpose. You declare that the proper meaning of this expression is the human, or rather the angelic and Divine spirit. I would be entitled to ask you for the strictest evidence of this interpretation, if you had spoken out of your understanding of this language. As I, however, know that you are without the slightest knowledge of Hebrew, and that this was only whispered to you by other people, I clearly see that you are an ignoramus concerning other matters about which you have spoken as well. You would have acted wisely if in this case, especially when you are engaged in a controversy with a Jewess, you had consulted an expert, because *ruach* means originally nothing else than atmospheric wind or the air which we breathe; thus it can clearly be seen how incorrect are the conclusions drawn by you from that word. Where you pretend that you can prove by that expression that the soul is bodiless and immaterial, it would be necessary for one inclined to follow your conclusions to resort to another logic than that of Aristotle. But if you are so eager to defend the immortality of the soul, why do you attack a woman who, although somewhat versed in studies, has not made this science her profession? If you wish to show yourself fearless and brave, it would have been necessary to attack the Empedocleses, the Anaxagorases, the Epicuruses, the Aristotles, the Alessandri Afrodisei, the Averrhoi. . . . But as far as I can see you wanted to play the gallant man by withdrawing behind a barricade where nobody is present who would raise your glove. . . . Oh, you valiant fighter against women, the battlefield is entirely yours. Pass from one end to the other, batter the air with your magnificent strokes, and listen, since no other noise is heard, to nothing but the sound of your own hoarse trumpet! . . .

I repeat what I have said already: this is not an answer to your challenge, but a simple manifesto to excuse my not making my appearance. There is no reason for a combat where no resistance exists, neither in words nor deeds. As far as I am concerned, you may remove your armor, but even if you provoke me again with insults, I have no more intention of answering you, first because I do not want to waste my time, and then because I have no desire whatever to attract the attention of the public by my writings as you have shown yourself so ambitious to do. Live happy! You will attain the immortality which you preach so eloquently, if you observe your Christian teaching as well as I observe the law of Judaism. . . .

· I ·

In my great grief and for my heart's ease I begin this book the year of Creation 5451 [1690–91]—God soon rejoice us and send us His redeemer!

I began writing it, dear children, upon the death of your good father, in the hope of distracting my soul from the burdens laid upon it, and the bitter thought that we have lost our faithful shepherd. In this way I have managed to live through many wakeful nights, and springing from my bed shortened the sleepless hours.

GLÜCKEL OF HAMELN, Germany

From her memoirs

This, dear children, will be no book of morals. Such I could not write, and our sages have already written many. Moreover, we have our holy Torah in which we may find and learn all that we need for our journey through this world to the world to come. It is like a rope which the great and gracious God has thrown to us as we drown in the stormy sea of life, that we may seize hold of it and be saved.

The kernel of the Torah is, Thou shalt love thy neighbor as thy-self.[1] But in our days we seldom find it so, and few are they who love their fellowmen with all their heart—on the contrary, if a man can contrive to ruin his neighbor, nothing pleases him more.

The best thing for you, my children, is to serve God from your heart, without falsehood or sham, not giving out to people that you are one thing while, God forbid, in your heart you are another. Say your prayers with awe and devotion. During the time for prayers, do not stand about and talk of other things.[2] While prayers are being offered to the Creator of the world, hold it a great sin to engage another man in talk about an entirely different matter—shall God Almighty be kept waiting until you have finished your business?

Moreover, put aside a fixed time for the study of the Torah, as best you know how.[3] Then diligently go about your business, for providing your wife and children a decent livelihood is likewise a *mitzvah*—the command of God and the duty of man. We should, I say, put ourselves to great pains for our children, for on this the world is built, yet we must understand that if children did as much for their parents, the children would quickly tire of it.

A bird once set out to cross a windy sea with its three fledglings. The sea was so wide and the wind so strong, the father bird was forced to carry his young, one by one, in his strong claws. When he was half-way across with the first fledgling the wind turned to a gale, and he said, "My child, look how I am struggling and risking my life in your behalf. When you are grown up, will you do as much for me and provide for my old age?" The fledgling replied, "Only bring me to safety, and when you are old I shall do everything you ask of me." Whereat the father bird dropped his child into the sea, and it drowned, and he said, "So shall it be done to such a liar as you." Then the father bird returned to shore, set forth with his second fledgling, asked the same question, and receiving the same answer, drowned the second child with the cry, "You, too, are a liar!" Finally he set out with the third fledgling, and when he asked the same question, the third and last fledgling replied, "My dear father, it is true you are struggling mightily and risking your life in my behalf, and I shall be wrong not to repay you when you are old, but I cannot bind myself. This though I can promise: when I am grown up and have children of my own, I shall do as much for them as you have done for me." Whereupon the father bird said, "Well spoken, my child, and wisely; your life I will spare and I will carry you to shore in safety."

Above all, my children, be honest in money matters, with both Jews and Gentiles, lest the name of Heaven be profaned. If you have in hand money or goods belonging to other people, give more care to them than if they were your own, so that, please God, you do no one a wrong. The first question put to a man in the next world is, whether he was faithful in his business dealings.[4] Let a man work ever so hard amassing great wealth dishonestly, let him during his lifetime provide his children fat dowries and upon his death a rich heritage—yet woe, I say, and woe again to the wicked who for the sake of enriching his children has lost his share in the world to come! For the fleeting moment he has sold Eternity.

When God sends evil days upon us, we shall do well to remember the remedy contrived by the physician in the story told by Rabbi Abraham ben Sabbatai Levi. A great king, he tells us, once imprisoned his physician, and had him bound hand and foot with chains, and fed on a small dole of barley-bread and water. After months of this treatment, the king dispatched relatives of the physician to visit the prison and learn what the unhappy man had to say. To their astonishment he looked as hale and hearty as the day he entered his cell. He told his relatives he owed his strength and well-being to a brew of seven herbs he had taken the precaution to prepare before he went to prison, and of which he drank a few drops every day. "What magic herbs are these?" they asked; and he answered: "The first is trust in God, the second is hope, and the others are patience, recognition of my sins, joy that in suffering now I shall not suffer in the world to come, contentment that my punishment is not worse, as well it could be, and lastly, knowledge that God who thrust me into prison can, if He will, at any moment set me free."

However, I am not writing this book in order to preach to you, but, as I have already said, to drive away the melancholy that comes with the long nights. So far as my memory and the subject permit, I shall try to tell everything that has happened to me from my youth upward. Not that I wish to put on airs or pose as a good and pious women. No, dear children, I am a sinner. Every day, every hour, and every moment of my life I have sinned, nearly all manner of sins. God grant I may find the means and occasion for repentance. But, alas, the care of providing for my orphaned children, and the ways of the world, have kept me far from that state.

If God wills that I may live to finish them, I shall leave you my Memoirs in seven little books. And so, as it seems best, I shall begin now with my birth. . . .

· II ·

Thou knowest well, Almighty God, how I pass my days in trouble and affliction of heart. I was long a woman who stood high in the esteem of her pious husband, who was like the apple of his eye. But with his passing, passed away my treasure and my honor, which all my days and years I now lament and bemoan.

I know that this complaining and mourning is a weakness of mine and a grievous fault. Far better it would be if every day I fell upon my knees and thanked the Lord for the tender mercies He has bestowed on my unworthy self. I sit to this day and date at my own table, eat what I relish, stretch myself at night in my own bed, and have even a shilling to waste, so long as the good God pleases. I have my beloved children, and while things do not always go as well, now with one or the other, as they should, still we are all alive and acknowledge our Creator. How many people there are in this world, finer, better, juster and truer than I, such as I know myself for patterns of piety, who have not bread to put into their mouths! How, then, can I thank and praise my Creator enough for all the goodness He has lavished on us without requital!

If only we poor sinners would acknowledge the everlasting mercy of our God who from the dust of the ground formed us into men, and that we may serve our Creator with all our heart, gave us to know His great and terrible and holy Name!

Behold, my children, all a man will do to gain the favor of a king, flesh and blood that he is, here today and tomorrow in his grave, no one knowing how long may live he who asks or he who gives. And behold the gifts he receives from the transient hand of a king. Honors the king can grant him and put him too in the way of wealth; yet honors and money are but for a space and not for eternity. A man may hoard his honors and his gold until the very last, and then comes bitter Death to make all forgotten; and his honors and his gold are of no avail. Every man, he knows this well and yet he strives loyally to serve a mortal king to gain the passing reward.

How much more, then, should we strive day and night, when we come to serve in duty bound the King of kings who lives and rules forever! For He it is whence come the favors we receive from human kings, and He it is who gives these kings their all and who puts it in their heart to honor whomsoever His holy will decrees, for "the king's heart is in the hand of the Lord." [5] And the gifts of a human monarch stand as naught against the gift of the God of Glory upon those whom He delights to honor: eternity without stain, measure or term.

So, dear children of my heart, be comforted and patient in your sorrows and serve the Almighty God with all your hearts, in your evil days as in your good; for although we often feel we must sink beneath our heavy burdens, our great Lord and Master, we must know, never lays upon His servants more than they can bear. Happy the man who accepts in patience all that God ordains for him or for his children.

Wherefore I, too, beg my Creator give me strength to bear without fret the contrarieties of the world, all of them, be it said, of our own making. "Man is bound to give thanks for the evil as for the good." [6] Let us commend all into the hands of God, and I will now resume my tale. . . .

Notes

1. Rabbi Akiba said, "Thou shalt love thy neighbor as thyself—that is the greatest commandment" (Sifra, Kadoshim, 4.12).
2. Talmudic gloss on Eccles. 5:1.

3. Shammai said, "Set up a fixed time for thy study of the Torah" (Sayings of the Fathers, 1.15).
4. Rabbah said, "When one stands at the judgment-seat of God, these questions are asked: Hast thou been honest in all thy dealings? Hast thou set aside a portion of thy time for the study of Torah? Hast thou observed the First Commandment? Hast thou, in trouble, still hoped and believed in God? Hast thou spoken wisely?" (Talmud, Shabbat, 31-a).
5. Prov. 21:1.
6. A great rabbi and hero in Talmudic days, Jochanan ben Zakkai belonged to the school of Hillel, lived through the fall of Jerusalem, and died in Jabneh ca. 108 C.E.

This *tkhine* was written by the woman, the rabbi's wife, Mistress Sarah Rebecca Rachel Leah, daughter of the brilliant and famous rabbi Yokel Segal Horowitz, head of the rabbinical court of Glogau; wife of the brilliant and acute luminary, our teacher Rabbi Shabbetai, head of the rabbinical court of Krasny.

Lord of the world, almighty God! In your great mercy, you have created heaven and earth and all their creatures in the first six days, with only ten words. And on the seventh day, which is the Holy Sabbath, you rested from your words, and [thus] also have you done with your dear people Israel, with whom you celebrate yourself, as it says in the biblical verse "Israel, in whom I will be glorified" [Is. 49:3; quoted in Hebrew].[2] This means in Yiddish, You dear folk Israel, with you I celebrate myself, that they, too, should also rest on the Sabbath, from all work and from words that you ought not to speak. [On the Sabbath, one] should speak only words of Torah, and one should study Torah, each according to his ability. And he who cannot study Torah, and also women, should read in Yiddish, and should also understand how to serve God; they should know how to observe their commandments, which God has commanded [them].

You have also given us New Moons, which the Sanhedrin used to consecrate. Today, when we consecrate the New Moon, when we say the blessing on the Sabbath [that is before] Rosh Hodesh, then it is a time to petition God. Therefore, we spread out our hands before God, and pray that you bring us back to Jerusalem, and renew our days as of old.

For we have no strength, we can no longer endure the hard, bitter exile, for we are like the feeble lambs. Our Sabbaths and festivals and our New Moons have been ruined. We are like orphans, like sheep who have gone astray without a shepherd. For the nations have too much power over us. You are a God of vengeance, and you reckon up accounts with the wicked. Therefore, we pray you, Lord of the world, take revenge on those who cause us suffering, for the sake of the merit of the patriarchs and matriarchs. O God, just as you answered our forebears, so may you answer us this month, by the merit of our mother

SARAH, for whose sake you have commanded and said, "Touch not my anointed ones" [Ps. 105:15; quoted in Hebrew], which means in

FOUR TKHINES
Translated by Chava Weissler

Tkhine of the Matriarchs[1]

Yiddish, You nations! Do not dare to touch my righteous ones! Thus too, may no nation have any power over any of her children to touch them for evil.

By the merit of our mother

REBECCA, who caused our father Jacob to receive the blessings from Father Isaac [Gen. 27]. May these blessings soon be fulfilled for Israel her children!

By the merit of our faithful mother

RACHEL, to whom you promised that by her merit, we, the children of Israel, would come out of exile. For when the children of Israel were led into exile, they were led not far from the grave in which our mother Rachel lay. They pleaded with their captors to permit them to go to Rachel's tomb. And when the Israelites came to our mother Rachel, and began to weep and cry, "Mother, mother, how can you look on while right in front of you we are being led into exile?" Rachel went up before God with a bitter cry, and spoke: Lord of the world, your mercy is certainly greater than the mercy of any human being. Moreover, I had compassion on my sister Leah when my father switched us and gave her to my husband Jacob in my place, and I told her the signs that my husband and I had decided on, so that my husband would think that I was the one. No matter that it caused me great pain; because of my great compassion for my sister, I told her the signs. Thus, even more so, it is undoubtedly fitting for you, God, who are compassionate and gracious, to have mercy. God answered her, I acknowledge that you are right, and I will bring your children out of exile. So may it soon come to pass, for the sake of her merit.[3]

And for the sake of the merit of our mother

LEAH, who wept day and night that she not fall to the lot of the wicked Esau, until her eyes became dim.[4] For the sake of her merit, may you enlighten our eyes out of this dark exile.

We will certainly be called the Daughter of Abraham, the children of Abraham our father, but today we must be in unmerciful hands. Thoroughly cleanse us of our sins [Ps. 51:9], for we have been thoroughly smitten because of our sins; therefore, renew us, and bring us this month to joy, and may all be turned around for us for good. Pride of our power [Ps. 89:18; quoted in Hebrew], you are our great power. May you elevate us; may you turn everything around for good, for the sake of the merit of the holy patriarchs, Abraham, Isaac, and Jacob.

Lord of the world, you call us "my peculiar treasure," which means in Yiddish, you are my dear people, and we call you our dear father. And we pray to you to grant to us, and to all who exert themselves in the study of your holy Torah, and who compose holy books, and who arrange prayers and *tkhines* for us, that we may be privileged to have worthy, living, and healthy offspring. May they be scholars, and may they serve God with perfect hearts and with love, [together] with [all] the pious ones, Amen, so may it be his will.

This new *tkhine* was written by the woman, the rabbi's wife, Serel, daughter of the famous rabbi Jacob Segal of Dubno; wife of the rabbi, the luminary, expert in wisdom, Mordecai Katz of blessed memory, Rappoport, head of the rabbinical court of Oleksiniec. . . .

TKHINE OF THE MATRIARCHS
FOR THE *SHOFAR*

Lord of the world, merciful father, have mercy on us and accept our prayers. For you have commanded your people Israel to blow the *shofar* in order to confuse Satan so that he may not accuse us. . . .

Today I stand at my judgment, today you reveal your tribunal. Lord of the universe, if I must stand trial, may your attribute of mercy overcome the attribute of justice, and forgive us our sins. . . . And especially now, when we have heard the sound of the *shofar*. . . . Blow away all our sins with the sound of the *shofar*. For with our ninefold blowing of the *shofar*, may the merit of the four matriarchs and the three patriarchs and Moses and Aaron stand by us in this judgment, for they have arisen [to plead for us].

First we ask our mother Sarah to plead for us in the hour of judgment, that we may go out free from before this tribunal. . . . Have mercy, our mother, on your children. And especially, pray for our little children that they may not be separated from us. For you know well that it is very bitter when a child is taken away from the mother, as it happened to you. When your son Isaac was taken away from you, it caused you great anguish. And now you have the chance to plead for us. For he is now blowing the *shofar*, the horn of a ram, so that God will remember for us the merit of Isaac, who let himself be bound like a sheep on the altar [Gen. 22]. Therefore, Satan will be confused, and cannot at this moment accuse us. So you have a chance to plead for us, that the attribute of mercy may awaken toward us.

And I also ask our mother Rebecca to plead for our fathers and mothers, that they may not, heaven forbid, be separated from us. For you know well how one can long for father and mother. When Eliezer, the servant [of Abraham] took you away from your father and mother to your husband, Isaac [Gen. 24], you also wept copiously. Therefore, you know how bad it is without a father and without a mother. May they have a year of life, a good year, and a year of livelihood, a year in which I and my husband and children will have sustenance and livelihood.

And we also ask our mother Rachel to plead for us, that we may be inscribed and sealed for good, and that we may have a year of life, and a year of livelihood. And may we never suffer any sorrow. We know well that you cannot bear to hear of any sorrow. For when your beloved son Joseph was led to Egypt, the Ishmaelites caused him great sorrow, and he fell on your grave and began to weep, "Mother, mother! Have mercy on your child! How can you look on my sorrow, when you had such love for me? And today, I am so embittered, and you have no compassion for me!" And you could not bear to listen to the sorrow of your child, and you answered him, "My dear child, I hear your cry, and I will always have compassion when I hear your sorrow." [6] Therefore, have compassion on our sorrow and our anguish and our trembling before the judgment, and plead for us that we may be inscribed for a good year in which there will be no sorrow, Amen.

Also we ask our mother Leah to plead for me and for my children. For now you can all plead for us, for today is the first day of the Ten Days of Penitence. This is the last moment; for I know how much time I have let slip away without turning in repentance for all [my evil deeds]. . . . Therefore, we ask all our mothers to plead for us that we may be inscribed for life and for peace and for livelihood. May we not, heaven forbid, need to depend on human charity, which is a greater disgrace than God's gift, but rather may we be nourished by your holy hand, Amen, Selah.

The T*khine* of Three Gates[7]

This *tkhine* was made by the virtuous woman, Mistress Sarah, may she live long, daughter of our teacher the Rabbi Mordecai, of blessed memory, grandson of the rabbi, our teacher Mordecai, of blessed memory, who was head of the rabbinical court in the holy community of Brisk, may God defend it. . . .

Lord of the world, I pray to you, God, as Queen Esther prayed. Lord of the whole world, with your right hand and your left hand, you have created the whole world with both your hands. May you spread your mercies over me.[8]

There are also there in Paradise six chambers in which there are several thousand righteous women who have never suffered the pains of Hell. Bithia the Queen, daughter of Pharaoh,[9] is there. There is a place in Paradise where a curtain is prepared to be opened, which allows her to see the image of Moses our Teacher. Then she bows and says, How worthy is my strength and how knowing is my power! I drew such a light out of the water, I brought up this dear light! This happens three times a day.

In the next chamber, there are also thousands upon thousands upon myriads of women, and Seraḥ daughter of Asher[10] is a queen. And every day it is announced three times, Here comes the image of Joseph the Righteous! Then she bows to him and says, Praised is my strength, and how worthy is my power, that I was privileged to tell my lord Jacob that my uncle was alive. And in the upper chamber, he studies Torah, and in the other chamber, they sing hymns and praises, and study Torah.

In the third chamber is our mother Jochebed, the mother of Moses our Teacher, with many women, and they praise God, blessed be he, three times every day, and say the Song of the Sea [Exod. 15:1–18] with great joy. "Miriam the prophet . . . with the timbrel in her hand" [Exod. 15:20; quoted in Hebrew] is there, and says this verse by herself, and many holy angels who are with her praise God's blessed Name.

In the fourth chamber sits Deborah the Prophet with many thousand women, and they praise God's blessed Name, and they sing the Song [Judg. 5].

And the chambers of the matriarchs cannot be described; no one can come into their chambers. Now, dear women, when the souls are together in paradise, how much joy there is! Therefore, I pray you to praise God with great devotion, and to say your prayers, that you may be worthy to be there with our Mothers. . . .

On Putting the Sabbath Loaf into the Oven

This the woman says when she puts the Sabbath loaf into the oven: Lord of all the world, in your hand is all blessing. I come now to revere your holiness, and I pray you to bestow your blessing on the baked goods. Send an angel to guard the baking, so that all will be well baked, will rise nicely, and will not burn, to honor the holy Sabbath (which you have chosen so that Israel your children may rest thereon) and over which one recites the holy blessing—as you blessed the dough of Sarah and Rebecca our mothers. My Lord God, listen to my voice; you are the God who hears the voices of those who call to you with the whole heart. May you be praised to eternity.

Notes

1. My translation is based on the 1796 edition, published in Horodno. While this is not the first edition of this work, the Yiddish portion of the text in this edition seems slightly better than that found in the first edition (Lvov? n.d.).
2. *Tkhines* often include phrases, quotations, or biblical verses in Hebrew, which are usually translated or paraphrased in Yiddish.
3. The source of this is the *midrash* on Lamentations, *petiḥta* 24:23–25, which builds on Jer. 31:15–17.
4. This is the rabbinic explanation of Leah's "weak eyes" (Gen. 28:17).
5. This translation is based on an undated edition published in Lvov, probably between 1780 and 1820.
6. Compare Louis Ginzberg, *The Legends of the Jews* (Philadelphia: Jewish Publication Society, 1969), 2:20–21.
7. In my quotations from the *Sheloshah she'arim*, I have relied primarily on an undated, probably late eighteenth- or early nineteenth-century, probably Eastern European edition found in the collection of the Jewish Theological Seminary; I have compared the text to other similarly undated editions and to a late version of the text published in Vilna by Romm in 1864.
8. Compare Targum Sheni of Esther's prayer.
9. Although a Bithia, daughter of Pharaoh, is mentioned in 2 Chron. 4:18, it is not clear that she is the same person as the daughter of Pharaoh who rescued Moses (Exod. 2:5–10). The rabbis, however, made this identification and explained her name as meaning "daughter of God" (Lev. Rabba 1:3).
10. Seraḥ, daughter of Asher, is mentioned in the Bible only in genealogical lists (Gen. 46:17; Num. 26:46; 1 Chron. 7:3). However, the *midrash* portrays her as gently breaking the news that Joseph was alive by playing the harp and singing about it so that Jacob could hear (*Sefer ha-yashar, Va-yiggash*). For a fuller discussion of the rabbinic legends about Seraḥ, see Joseph Heinemann, *Aggadot ve-toldoteihen* (Jerusalem: Keter, 1974), 56–63.

Part II

1800-1890: STRONGER VOICES

Introduction

T HE diversity of literary genres contained in this section reflects the extent to which nineteenth-century Jewish women
began to gain a stronger public voice within their religious
and secular communities. The vast majority of spiritual literature written by Jewish women prior to 1800 was private in nature—for example, personal memoirs written to their children, letters addressed to family members, and prayers that were to be
individually recited at home. In marked contrast, spiritual literature
produced by Jewish women between 1800 and 1890 included not
only private documents such as letters, diaries, and ethical wills but
also published poetry focusing on religious themes, hymns to be
sung during synagogue worship, and lengthy theological treatises
such as those written by Englishwoman Grace Aguilar during the
1840s.

This section begins with three short poems written by Rahel Luzzato Morpurgo (1790–1871), perhaps the first woman to write and
publish modern Hebrew poetry. Born and raised in Trieste, Italy,
Morpurgo grew up in a family renowned for its Jewish learning.
While Morpurgo herself never attended school, she studied at home
with tutors (who were also responsible for teaching her brother,
Isaac, and their cousin, Samuel David Luzzato). She apparently
studied, in Hebrew, the Pentateuch, Bahya Ibn Pakuda's eleventh-
century classic *The Duties of the Heart,* and the biblical commentaries of Rashi (1040–1105). As an adult, she studied Jewish mysticism, presumably on her own, and, although she later claimed that
as a wife and mother of four children she had little time either for
study or for writing, continued to write poetry throughout her lifetime, publishing some of her poems in a Hebrew journal entitled
Kochvei Yitzhak (Stars of Isaac). One hundred years after her birth,
fifty of her Hebrew poems were published in a book entitled *Ugav
Rahel* (lit., Rachel's organ or Rachel's flute). Referring to this collection in 1923, Nina Davis Salaman, who translated many of Morpurgo's poems into English, identified it as *The Harp of Rachel.*[1]

The three poems included here, translated by Salaman, were written by Morpurgo near the end of her life. Placing her trust in God

as the source of goodness and the creator of life, she expresses hope in immortality and in a future, worldly redemption. The first poem, which asks "how long till our redemption's Star shall come?" seems to reflect a longing for the end of Jewish exile and the inauguration of the Messianic age. These hopes do not in any way echo early proto-Zionist aspirations but rather reflect the more traditional belief that the Jewish return to Zion would be initiated by the Messiah, as the messenger of God.

Following the poems by Morpurgo are excerpts from the diary and private travel journal of Englishwoman Judith Lady Montefiore (1784–1862). A member by birth of one of the most prominent Jewish families in England, the Cohens, she received an excellent education as a child. She learned to speak French, German, and Italian well, learned enough Hebrew to translate both prayers and portions of the Pentateuch into English, and formally studied music, drawing, and singing as well as English literature.[2] In addition, as one scholar has written, "that which characterized and enhanced the value of her education most was 'the fear of God' which, she had been taught, constituted 'the beginning of knowledge.'"[3] Married in 1812 to the celebrated Moses Montefiore, whom she affectionately called "Monte," she traveled all over the world with him, keeping journals that reflected both their itinerary and, as the excerpts included here reveal, her deep religious faith.

Unlike most Jewish women of her day, Judith Montefiore regularly attended synagogue, either at Bevis Marks, the Spanish and Portuguese congregation of which her husband was a member, or at the synagogue that they had built on their country estate in Ramsgate. While her regular, and when possible weekly, attendance at synagogue mirrored the churchgoing practices of her non-Jewish peers (as opposed to the more frequent attendance of Orthodox men, including her husband), male friends and family members, with the exception of her husband, attempted to dissuade her, maintaining that, according to Judaism, it was not essential for women to attend synagogue. She emphatically disagreed. Consequently, as Linda Kuzmack notes, "given her social distinction, [her] visibility during synagogue worship established a powerful incentive for other Jewish women to follow her example."[4]

Like her husband, Judith kept diaries, in which she frequently wrote. As the excerpts included in this section reveal, she remained committed to God, family, and duty as well as to the Orthodox community of which she and her husband were members. They reveal her understanding of God as an almighty protector and sustainer, the source of happiness and health, in whom she continually placed her trust. In addition, the excerpt from her travel journal dated 18 October 1836, written in Jerusalem, offers a rare glimpse of the great spiritual power and sense of "inspiring veneration" that at least one nineteenth-century Jewish woman discovered there.

The excerpts following those from Judith Lady Montefiore's diary are taken from chapters 1 and 6 of *The Spirit of Judaism,* by Englishwoman Grace Aguilar (1816–47). Edited by Isaac Leeser, perhaps "the most important Jewish cultural figure in antebellum America,"[5] and first published in America in 1842, *The Spirit of Judaism* enjoyed a wide audience among English-speaking Jews and Christians on both sides of the Atlantic. It was one of several works in which Aguilar attempted to present her understanding of Jewish teachings and values and, at least among middle-class American Jewish women, who were perhaps her most enthusiastic readers, was her most theologically influential.[6] Educated at home, Aguilar apparently studied Hebrew, French literature, music, ancient Greek history, Josephus's histories of the Jews of the Roman Empire, and philosophy. She also read articles on rabbinic literature and ethics in the *Hebrew Review,* a scholarly journal published in England in which many of the poems that she wrote first appeared. To help support their family, she and her mother briefly ran a school for children, but family illness forced them to limit their work to private tutorials. Aguilar herself suffered from ill health, and like her father and younger brother, died at an early age.

The kindness shown to her family by their Protestant neighbors apparently impressed Aguilar deeply. While she had a keen sense of marginality as a Jewish woman in a Christian, male-dominated society, she believed that Protestants and Jews shared both a relationship with God and similar standards of piety. Indeed, although religiously and culturally she identified herself as a Jew, she attended services at both Trinity Chapel in London and Bevis Marks Synagogue, of which her father was president. She wanted her work to be read by both Protestant and Jewish women and, by defending Jewish beliefs against Christian counterclaims, to promote good relations among them. Aguilar succeeded, it seems, in doing so by presenting a vision of spirituality comprehensible, if not accessible, to both Christians and Jews. Central to this vision were the Bible as that which best articulated both the nature of the human-divine relationship and such religious truths as the immortality of the soul, home-centered Sabbath worship as that which encouraged family devotion, and private prayers as that which enabled the individual to open his or her heart to God spontaneously.

The Spirit of Judaism, her most heavily theological work, was directed toward a Jewish audience, although, like all her works, it was intended by Aguilar to have a wider readership. It is a lengthy meditation on Judaism's central prayer, taken from Deuteronomy, which begins, "Hear O Israel, The Lord is our God, the Lord is One." In chapter 1, most of which is reprinted here, Aguilar describes prayer as "the language of the heart," "the hour of communion" between the individual and God. Impressing on her readers the importance of Judaism as a living faith, and staunchly defending Judaism against Christian counterclaims, she describes God as a God of love, justice, and mercy. Accepting the traditional Jewish view that the destruction of the Second Temple in Jerusalem and the dispersion of the Jewish people throughout the world was punishment for sins that they had committed, she further accepts the traditional belief that God's promise of a future messianic redemption will eventually be fulfilled. Until then, she writes, we are to follow the "duty of devotion," a way of life revolving around both good deeds and prayer.

In chapter 6, Aguilar offers her female readers advice regarding the religious instruction of their children. Maintaining that faith is best inculcated not through the formal study of religious texts but through sharing one's own sense of piety, by words and by example, Aguilar impresses on her readers the power of persuasion. In particular, she appeals to mothers to impart biblical teachings to their children through short prayers selected from the traditional prayer book or, drawing on biblical teachings, simply by creating prayers of their own. It is incumbent on every Jewish mother, she believed, to teach her children "the religion of the heart," that is, "the blessing and love of his [or her] Father in heaven," and not merely to inculcate "peculiar forms" and rites. Aguilar believed that this religion of the heart, which she identified as the spirit of Judaism, was even more important to women than to men. A man, she believed, might happily go through life without religion, yet a woman, she insisted, needs to know God, for the peculiar trials that she suffers in fulfilling the "sacred duties of a wife and mother" are so great that only God can offer sufficient comfort.

One of the women most responsible for spreading Aguilar's name and work among American Jews was Philadelphian Rebecca Gratz (1781–1869). As director of America's first Hebrew Sunday School, which educated boys and girls in mixed classes taught by female teachers, Gratz introduced Aguilar's writings into the curriculum (a practice followed by the many branches of the school that were later established and that, by the end of the century, had enrolled thousands of students). While unlike Aguilar Gratz was an Ashkenazic Jew, like Aguilar she and her family belonged to a traditional synagogue that followed the customs of Spanish Jews, conducting the worship service entirely in Hebrew. Also, Gratz's father, like Aguilar's, was a prominent member of the synagogue to which the family belonged, and, like Aguilar, Gratz occasionally attended Protestant services despite her religious identification as a Jew, never married, and enjoyed a social circle of both Jews and Protestant Christians. Gratz's influence can be attributed not to her writings but to her actions. She was among the founders of the Female Association for the Relief of Women and Children (1801), the first women's charity organization in Philadelphia; the Philadelphia Orphan Asylum, founded in 1815; the Female Hebrew Benevolent Society (1819), which was the first Jewish women's charity organization in America; the Hebrew Sunday School (1838); and the first Jewish Foster Home in Philadelphia, founded in 1855.

A middle child in a well-to-do and highly respected family of ten children, Gratz lived with three brothers and a sister who all remained single and whose communal activities provided them with active social and religious lives. Included here are two letters by Gratz as well as a report on the Hebrew Sunday School published in Isaac Leeser's the *Occident* in 1858. The first letter, written to her friend Maria Fenno Hoffmann, reveals both Gratz's belief in the immortality of the soul and her vision of God as creator and almighty being who tests individuals through trials of affliction. Revealed here too, as in all the many letters that Gratz wrote throughout her lifetime, is the importance that she attached to friendship. In the second letter included here, written in 1853 to her niece, Miriam Moses Cohen, she makes what she believed to be a connection between friendship and faith quite clear. Observing that death brings those who mourn closer together, she maintained that, in lending support to each other, mourners gain the strength to bow submissively to God, confident that God knows best and trusting that they and the deceased will partake of eternal life and thus eventually be reunited.

Her report to patrons and parents of the Hebrew Sunday School illuminates what Gratz believed to be the school's major purpose. As she maintains, the school's goal was to teach Jewish doctrines and duties to young children so that they might learn what was required of them as Jews and, armed with this knowledge and "unobtrusive" in their observance, succeed in gaining the respect of Christian neighbors, who otherwise might try to convert them.

Rebecca Gratz's successor as superintendent of the Hebrew Sunday School was Louisa Barnett Hart (1803–74). Active in many Philadelphia Jewish charities, including the Ladies Hebrew Sewing Society, founded in 1838, for which she served as director, and the United Hebrew Charities (1869), on whose visiting committee she served, Hart taught at the Hebrew Sunday School prior to becoming superintendent in 1864, the year that Gratz retired. Hart, who never married, lived her life in the company of communal workers, as did Gratz before her. For many years, she kept a journal of her thoughts and experiences. Excerpts from this journal, along with letters that she wrote, were published in the *Jewish Record* after her death. The excerpt included here is a letter by Hart written to a former pupil about to become a teacher. Echoing the motto of the Hebrew Sunday School—"To learn and to teach"—Hart advises her pupil to remember the importance of the Bible as a guide to right thinking and right living as well as the works of Grace Aguilar, who, she wrote, correctly perceived that the spirit of Judaism is love and obedience toward God and "well doing towards our fellow-creatures."

American Jewish poet, essayist, and short-story writer Rebekah Gumpert Hyneman (1812–75) gave written expression to her understanding of spirituality through poems published during the middle of the nineteenth century.[7] With the disappearance of her husband, Benjamin, a few years after their marriage, her two sons' early deaths (one died of starvation in Andersonville Prison in Georgia), and the death of her sister, Sarah, to whom she was extremely close, soon after, Hyneman often turned to two themes— the tragic heroism of the ancient Israelites and the fall of Jerusalem in 70 C.E.—as a means of reflecting the sense of personal tragedy that pervaded much of her life and of revealing her strong conviction that, despite all that had befallen them, the Jewish people maintained a special relationship to God.

In "The Destruction of Jerusalem," published in 1853, Hyneman suggests that the fall of the Roman Empire was God's punishment for the agony its leaders had inflicted on the Jewish people. Here, as in other poems, Hyneman maintains that, despite their suffering, the Jews continue to be God's chosen people. "Ruth's Song" was one of several poems initially written by Hyneman as part of a poetry series on "Female Scriptural Characters," a series that in theme and content echoed Grace Aguilar's *Women of Israel*. As did Aguilar, Hyneman attempted to develop female biblical role models for her contemporaries. In "Ruth's Song," Hyneman optimistically contends that, despite the weariness and sorrow of everyday life, God continually provides hope that joy may come tomorrow.

Following the selections by Hyneman are two brief entries from the unpublished diary of Virginian Emma Mordecai (1812–1906). In her diary, written during the last year of the Civil War, Mordecai poignantly expresses belief in God's power to protect the defenseless. God, for her, is "the Unchanging One" who gave the Jewish people laws by which they are to live forever. While Mordecai obliquely refers to the "peculiar duties" given to her as an inheritor of God's laws, it is unclear from her diary which duties she actually followed. The diary, for example, makes no reference to specific rabbinic regulations (such as, e.g., the dietary laws). Indeed, it contains only two explicit references to religious observance. The first is a reference to Yom Kippur, the Jewish Day of Atonement, on which, apparently, Mordecai fasted and attended synagogue. The second, included here, dated 10 June 1864, comes when Mordecai writes that, because it was a Jewish holiday (Pentecost or Shavuot), she refrained from her usual work of visiting hospitals. Instead, she remained at home and read from the prayer book, revealing a kind of personal piety largely home centered and rooted primarily, it seems, in belief in the absolute power and goodness of God.

Little is known about Emma Mordecai.[8] Never married, she lived with her family for most of her life. During the Civil War, however, she lived with a female friend who owned a small farm outside Richmond. Although the nature of their relationship is unclear (indeed, during the Civil War, it was not unusual for a woman whose home life had been disrupted to live with another woman), it was apparently a close one: Mordecai writes of "our household" and in other parts of her diary indicates that she and Rose (who presumably was not Jewish) occasionally went to church together and were visited regularly by the local pastor. While religiously Mordecai continued to identify herself as a Jew, we do not know whether she attended synagogue, either before or after the war, nor do we know, more generally, in what kinds of secular and religious activities she engaged.[9]

Somewhat more is known about the American Jewish poet Penina Moise (1797–1881). Born and bred in Charleston, South Carolina, Moise was largely self-educated. Following her father's death when she was only twelve, she began working at embroidery and lace making in order to help support her family. Later, she achieved local renown as a poet. At first, she published her poetry in local newspapers and magazines. Later, in 1833, a volume of poems entitled *Fancy's Sketch Book* appeared (apparently leading the literati of Charleston to label her their poet laureate). To support herself, she ran a small private school for girls in Charleston, working together with her niece, Jacqueline, and her sister (Jacqueline's mother), Rachel Levy.

Moise is best remembered as the author of the first American Jewish hymnal (*Hymns Written for the Use of Hebrew Congregations*), published by Congregation Beth Elohim, to which she belonged, in 1856. This congregation, established in the eighteenth century as an Orthodox synagogue, became, in 1824, the first Jewish congregation in America to ally itself with the nascent Reform movement. Moise's English hymns, some of which are included here (and many of which were originally written as poems), reflect the kinds of liturgical innovations that the Reformers proposed.[10] During the course of her lifetime, Penina Moise composed over 190 hymns. Apparently, the *Union Hymnal,* published by the Reform movement in 1897 and still widely used, "contains more of her hymns than of any other Jewish author."[11]

In the first hymn, taken from the 1856 hymnal, Moise identifies faith as that which shields us from life's harsher realities. Here, as elsewhere, she views religion as a refuge and God as an almighty father who offers an eternal, saving grace to those who submit to him completely. The thrust of this, like most of her hymns, is universal. While toward the end she asks God to defend the "first elected nation" (i.e., the Jews), the religious language that she employs throughout is not particularly Jewish. Indeed, her references to God's grace and the gift of salvation sound more Protestant than Jewish. To Moise, however, who saw herself very much as a Jew, such words as *grace* and *salvation* simply reflect her own immersion in American Protestant culture.

Her understanding of faith is developed further in the other hymns that we have included. In "Piety," for example, Moise, who never married and lived her adult years with her married sister, the aforementioned Rachel Levy, rejects the satisfactions of worldly power and sensual pleasure. Describing piety as the commending of one's soul to God, she views the religious life as one of "high concerns," including, for example, concern for those who suffer alone and thus are in need of comfort. Finally, despite the overarching universalism present in all Moise's hymns, one finds in such works as "Man's Dignity" great importance attached to particularistic allegiance. The synagogue, as she envisions it, is a refuge from the outside world, freeing the Jewish people from all its temptations and calling them to a life of divine service rewarded by immortality.

For Rosa Emma Salaman, a British Jew who published a number of poems both in England and in America during the 1840s and 1850s, comfort and calm could be found in contemplating eternity.

Her poem "The Angel and the Child," published in 1855, echoes a theme found in innumerable poems written by Christians during the nineteenth century. Perhaps in response to a growing infant mortality rate (due at least in part to increasing urbanization, which led to crowded, often unsanitary living conditions, epidemics, and so on), male and female writers began to reflect on ways in which women could best cope with the death of their children. Drawing on religious themes, most writers focused on the promise of eternal life and the assurance that in heaven the child would be lovingly cared for. While unlike similar poems by Christian authors Salaman's "The Angel and the Child" makes no mention of Jesus, she too envisions the angel of death not as a forbidding figure but as a loving, whispering, gentle, divine messenger who envelops the small child in his wings, ready to fly with him to paradise. Moreover, Salaman equates purity and goodness with inexperience, as did many other nineteenth-century English and American writers. The child, then, is seen as "sinless" because of his youth and inexperience and thus tells his mother to rejoice, knowing that he will reach paradise before having been touched by sorrow.

Among the writings of nineteenth-century American Jewish women, most of those that were preserved were written by women respected by their local communities as paragons of womanly virtue. Penina Moise in Charleston and Rebecca Gratz, Louisa B. Hart, and Rebekah Hyneman in Philadelphia were all viewed in this way. Their religious activities as well as their perceived asexuality (Moise, Gratz, and Hart having never married; Hyneman living most of her adult life as a single woman) led them to be viewed as "true women," who by definition were spiritual beings. Nineteenth-century American ideology posited a foil for the true woman, namely, the fallen woman—sensuous, worldly, and impure. Jewish actress Adah Isaacs Menken (ca. 1835–68) seemed to fit this description. Taking over the theatrical role of Mazeppa, wearing nothing but a short white tunic and flesh colored tights, entering the theater riding bareback on a white horse, Menken gained both international acclaim and notoriety. Although her origins are obscure, she seems to have been a Sephardic Jew, born in New Orleans. She married at least four times (her first husband, Alexander Isaacs Menken, who was from Cincinnati, was Jewish; her others were not) and seemed to live the kind of worldly existence that helped earn her the label of fallen woman.[12]

Yet Menken wrote religious poetry, making her an enigmatic figure of great interest, at least to those who knew of the marked contrast between her life and her written work. Well aware of her appeal, Jewish Reform leader Isaac Mayer Wise often included her poems on the front page of his English-language journal the *Israelite*. The poems by Menken that Wise chose to publish were all highly sentimental and conventionally written, focusing on Israel's strength in remaining faithful to God. They also spoke of Menken's personal love of God and her dreams of heaven. Less sentimental and conventional were the poems she collected into a thin volume called *Infelicia* (The unhappy one). Perhaps reflecting the influence of Walt Whitman, whom she knew, these poems were passionate and powerful, written in free verse instead of iambic pentameter, and contained a strong authorial voice.

The selection by Menken that is included here, entitled "Drifts That Bar My Door," is taken from *Infelicia*. While expressing the hope that its author will be granted eternal life, its tone is bleak and at times desperate. Here, Menken addresses the angels, acknowledging that her faith has grown weak and her hope nearly dissolved, pleading with them to release her from despair and the agony of living and to lead her to a place of eternal peace. Unable to pray to a God who speaks yet does nothing to save her, she tells the angels that death has already conquered her. Thus, she asks the angels to be quick and release her soul so that she might finally see some light.

Taken as a whole, Menken's poems do not present a unified spiritual vision. Rather, they suggest the fragmented vision of a woman who alternated between hope and despair, sometimes believing in and even addressing God as protector and redeemer, at other times convinced that God either could not or would not save her.

In marked contrast to Menken's fiery poems are three short documents from Germany and America. Written in sentimental, pious tones, the first is an ethical will, the second two departure letters written in the form of ethical wills. All reflect their authors' absolute faith in God as a source of goodness, strength, and comfort. In an ethical will that she began to write in 1827, American Grace Nathan (1752–1831) tells her son that she dies "in the full faith of my religion," grateful to God for the many blessings given her. She reminds her son of the centrality of religious and moral principles in achieving good and tells him that she hopes his children are as loving and kind to him as he always was to her. A second document, a departure letter written by a German Jewish mother, Lena Roth, to her son, reflects a similar sense of spiritual optimism. The author here equates being religious with trusting in God as the source of goodness, turning to God in prayer, and, armed with faith, doing good and not evil, immune to the "trap of vice" into which the irreligious inevitably fall.

Finally, the letter of counsel to N. Henry Beckman, written before he sailed for America by Beckman's mother, a German Jewish woman, dated 30 September 1880, again speaks of the importance of trusting in God to lead us "in the right way." Unlike the previous departure letter, the author here specifically asks that her son not forget his particular religious identity as a Jew. As in the previous letter, however, there is no mention of either specific Jewish precepts or observances. In both these letters, being religious simply seems to be equated with opening one's heart to God.

The diary entries and brief religious reflections written by Englishwoman Rachel Simon (b. 1824?) span a period of over forty years (1840–83). A communal worker and the wife of Oswald Simon (an early, outspoken advocate of Liberal Judaism and among the promoters of its growth in Great Britain), Rachel Simon's writings reveal a deep sense of inner piety and an earnest desire to "spiritual[ly] progress," that is, to achieve great closeness with God, honesty with one's self, and a sense of responsibility and care toward others. Identifying herself as religiously liberal, she maintains that one can achieve the highest spiritual growth within any religious denomination. Given these sentiments, her reminiscence of a sermon delivered "in the Priory church at Malvern" (included here), and the fact that her religious writings appear more universal than specifically Jewish, Simon may well have been a strong supporter, if not co-initiator, of the short-lived "Sunday movement" founded by her husband in 1899. Its intent was to establish a universalistic "Church of Israel" as a religious fellowship of Christian theists and liberal Jews.[13]

More traditionally religious than Simon was Fanny Neuda, author of the German *Studen der Andacht* (Hours of Devotion), a devotional work first published during the middle of the nineteenth century. A collection of more than fifty prayers and private meditations composed by Neuda for Jewish women during public services, at home, and "for all conditions of woman's life," *Studen der Andacht* enjoyed great popularity among German Jewish women at least through the 1940s.[14] An English translation of the book first appeared in 1866. Unfortunately, the translator, M. Mayer, while citing the book's title, omitted any mention of Neuda, thus rendering her unknown to those hundreds, if not thousands, of nineteenth- and early twentieth-century American Jewish women who found her book to be a rich spiritual resource.

By 1890, the thirteenth revised and expanded edition of Neuda's work appeared in German. While telling us next to nothing about the author, it cites her maiden name as Schmiedl. Further, the dedication page—on which Neuda and her publisher dedicate the book to the "noble, magnanimous Baroness Louise von Rothschild"—indicates that Neuda lived in Frankfort-am-Main, the birthplace of the Rothschild family and the home of Louise and Mayer Carl von Rothschild, who continued to live there.

In the "Morning Prayer" that we have included here, Neuda envisions God as an all-gracious and merciful heavenly father and creator. Thankful for his goodness and especially for his preserving her health, she views her willingness to "faithfully discharge" her religious and domestic duties and to show loving-kindness toward others as expressions of her gratitude to him. "Prayer after Safe Delivery," one of many prayers in her book associated with childbirth and motherhood, again reveals her sense of deep gratitude to God. Here, she asks God to protect her and her child, maintaining that it is in God that she places her trust and hope for the future.

This section ends with several poems by the American poet Emma Lazarus (1849–87), a Sephardic Jew raised in a wealthy and assimilated family whose American roots dated back to the eighteenth century. Acclaimed in Jewish and non-Jewish literary circles, she was perhaps "the most prominent American Jewish writer of her generation."[15] The poems included here have been selected by

Diane Lichtenstein, an American scholar who has done considerable work on Lazarus. According to Lichtenstein,

> Lazarus always defined her Jewishness through her identity as author. In 1866, when Lazarus was only seventeen, her first volume of poetry was published. For the next twenty years, until her untimely death from cancer in 1887 at the age of thirty-eight, Lazarus had a prolific and successful career, publishing poetry, fiction, and essays and catching the attention of such prominent literary figures as Ralph Waldo Emerson. At the same time that she was writing many of the poems included here, she was also publishing essays on American literature and on such American authors as Emerson and Henry Wadsworth Longfellow. Both a self-identified American author and an increasingly outspoken Jew, Lazarus could not ignore either component of her identity. She would not have been as effective on behalf of Jews if she had not believed deeply in her right to be an American author, and she could not have been as moving a writer if she had not discovered the significance of her Jewish identity. Particularly in works produced during the 1880s, Lazarus sought a strong, integrative voice that would establish her as a serious American, as well as a Jewish, writer.
>
> Lazarus's proclamation of a Jewish identity through a literary identity distinguished her from most other nineteenth-century American Jewish women, who used the more conventional gender roles of wife, mother, and teacher to demonstrate religious loyalty. Although this sourcebook makes it clear that Lazarus was not the only Jewish woman who wrote, she was, nevertheless, one of the few who could devote all her time to writing because she had no responsibilities to husband, children, parents, or students. Like the biblical Deborah, Lazarus fought against those who sought to annihilate the Jews, but she fought with words instead of with a sword, aiming her attack at Christians who did not understand or accept Jews and at Jews who themselves had become complacent and therefore vulnerable to anti-Semitism.
>
> Despite a quiet public demeanor, Lazarus asserted herself in the world of words. In that world, she articulated loyalty to what she identified as her Jewish "race" as well as to America. Although she did not write in conventional spiritual forms, such as psalms, as did many other women of her day, she did develop and communicate a powerful commitment to Jewish history and values.

While Lazarus's self-consciousness as a Jew clearly intensified after 1881, when Russian Jewish immigrants fleeing from pogroms began to arrive in America in great numbers, her literary interest in Jewish themes dates back to her girlhood. In 1867, for example, at the age of eighteen, she published a poem entitled "In the Jewish Synagogue at Newport," honoring the so-called Touro Synagogue, the oldest existent Jewish house of worship in the United States. Later, Lazarus's poems looked back at the Jewish past both as a means of remembering what was and as a call to future action.

The sense of Jewish spirituality that emerges from all Lazarus's poems is one rooted in her deep sense of connection to the Jewish people—past, present, and future—rather than in any kind of personal relationship with God (indeed, her personal concept of God owed more to Emerson than it did to specific Jewish teachings). Lazarus, it seems, had little use for either public worship or private devotion. Identifying herself as a socialist and later becoming deeply interested in efforts to reestablish a Jewish state in Palestine as a homeland for persecuted Russian Jews (applying a label that did not come into usage until almost ten years after her death, we might call her an early Zionist), she found her connection to Judaism, not in membership in the synagogue (although as an adult she began to study Hebrew and Jewish history), but rather in a love for the Jewish people, best expressed in such poems as "The Banner of the Jew" and "New Year, Rosh-Hashanah, 5643 (1882)."

Her empathy for the plight of Russian Jewry was reiterated in numerous poems, as was her rejoicing in the freedom that America offered them ("The New Colossus," perhaps her best-known poem, was inscribed on the pedestal of the Statue of Liberty). In many poems, Lazarus articulated her fervent hope that one day Palestine would be fully restored as the Jewish homeland. She also expressed this hope in a prose work written between 1882 and 1883 entitled "An Epistle to the Hebrews." Addressed to acculturated American Jews, it is a plea that they acknowledge their Jewish heritage and do all that is in their power to help those Russian Jews fleeing to America's shores. In the excerpt included here, Lazarus points with pride to Jewish literature and to Judaism's concept of God, in whom "two-thirds of the inhabited globe" believe. She tries to convince her readers that, "until we are free, we are none of us free," that is, that the fate of the Jews as a people is bound together. Finally, she makes a plea for her audience to set as a first priority the reconstruction of Jewish national existence. We as Jews, she writes, cannot be healthy if we feed our souls but ignore our bodies, that is, the national component of Jewish self-identity. Thus, she concludes, it is in the best interest of all Jews to have a physically strong homeland that can serve as a place of refuge to the persecuted and a source of worldwide respect to those who are free.

Notes

1. Nina Salaman, *Rahel Morpurgo and Contemporary Hebrew Poets in Italy* (London: George Allen & Unwin, 1923), 34.
2. Sonia L. Lipman, "Judith Montefiore—First Lady of Anglo-Jewry," *Jewish Historical Society of England Transactions* 21 (1968): 287.
3. Dr. L. Loewe, introduction to *Diaries of Sir Moses and Lady Montefiore* (Chicago: Belford-Clarke, 1890), 1:3.
4. Linda Gordon Kumzack, *Woman's Cause: The Jewish Women's Movement in England and the United States, 1881–1933* (Columbus: Ohio State University Press, 1990), 9.
5. Jacob Rader Marcus, ed., *The American Jewish Woman, 1654–1980* (New York: Ktav, 1981), 4.
6. Other works that focused, at least in part, on theological teachings were *Women of Israel* (a study of the biblical matriarchs), *The Jewish Faith, Home Influence: A Tale of Mothers and Daughters,* and *A Mother's Recompense: A Sequel to Home Influence.* Most of her poems also focused on religious themes.
7. The child of a mixed marriage, Hyneman formally converted to Judaism before marrying Philadelphian Benjamin Hyneman. (While religiously Hyneman may have always considered herself Jewish, according to the rabbinic law of matri-

lineal descent, applicable in cases of mixed marriage, she was not considered a Jew since her mother was Christian and therefore needed to convert in order for her—and her offspring—to be considered Jewish by the Jewish community.)

8. We do, however, know something of her family history. Her father, Jacob Mordecai, wrote a tract defending Judaism, and her sister, Rachel, began an extensive correspondence with Maria Edgeworth, asking that Edgeworth rethink her negative attitude toward Jews. Another of Emma's sisters, Ellen Mordecai, is reputed to have lived her adult life as a member of the Episcopal church.

9. The biographical information on Emma Mordecai included here was gleaned primarily from the Mordecai Family Collection, American Jewish Archives, Cincinnati, Biographies File, 6–7; and Sheldon Hanft, "Mordecai's Female Academy," *American Jewish History* 70, no. 1 (1989): 72–93.

10. According to Harold Moise, author of *The Moise Family of South Carolina and Their Descendants* (Columbia, S.C.: R. L. Bryan, 1961), Penina Moise also wrote hymns, recitations, and poems for use by the second Jewish Sunday School in America, founded in Charleston by a Miss Sally Lopez in 1838.

11. Ibid., 68.

12. After her death in 1868, Menken was buried in the Jewish section of the Montparnasse cemetery outside Paris. Her tombstone says only, "Thou knowest."

13. For a fuller description of this movement, see Ellen M. Umansky, *Lily Montagu and the Advancement of Liberal Judaism: From Vision to Vocation* (Lewiston, N.Y.: Edwin Mellen, 1983), 54–55 (see also references to Oswald Simon in the index).

14. Ellen Umansky is grateful to Liese Kaufman of Atlanta for first bringing *Studen der Andacht* to her attention and for providing her with a copy of the 1890 German edition. She is also grateful to Rabbi Richard (Rim) Meirowitz for providing her with a copy of the fifth edition of the book's English translation and to Deanna Douglas for showing her a copy of the 1888 German edition. Having now spoken of this book in various synagogues across the United States, she has had numerous Jewish women tell her that when they were younger (in Germany) they received the book as a gift from their mothers (many on their wedding day). Several have said that "every Jewish woman in [early twentieth-century] Germany owned the book" and frequently used it in prayer. Of the copies of the book that she has seen, Liese Kaufman's was her mother's, given to her during the Second World War. Her mother's first copy, apparently, was either lost or confiscated by the Nazis, and the copy that eventually passed into Liese's hands was given to her mother by another women when they were in hiding. Deanna Douglas's originally belonged to Babette Mayer of Buchau, Germany, the grandmother of Elsa Alexander Rubin of East Liverpool, Ohio, while Rim Meirowitz's English translation was owned by his mother.

15. Charlotte Baum, Paula Hyman, and Sonya Michel, *The Jewish Woman in America* (New York: New American Library, 1975), 38. This sentiment was first voiced at the turn of the century. In an article on Lazarus published in the *Jewish Encyclopedia* (New York: Ktav, n.d., 7:652), Henrietta Szold said that Lazarus was "the most distinguished literary figure produced by American Jewry."

Lament no more, with sleep no more be dumb!
Let men of understanding now arise
And teach us by their calculations wise
How long till our redemption's Star shall come.
To look at one another can, forsooth,
Avail us nothing, howsoe'er one gaze—
Of old, while Israel walked the desert ways,
When Balaam spake his parable of truth,
"A star shall tread," he said, or spake of calm:
Messiah rests—but only till he ride
Upon an ass straight up the Mountain-side!
So say and sing ye every song and psalm
Of Korah's sons; for on that path afar
There looms, about to rise, the destined Star!

RAHEL LUZZATO
MORPURGO,
Italy
Translated by Nina Davis
Salaman

Untitled poem (1859)

And here also have I done nothing that they should put me into
the dungeon.
GEN. 40:15

Untitled poem (1867)

Ah! Vale of woe, of gloom and darkness molded,
    How long wilt hold me bound in double chain?
Better to die—to rest in shadows folded,
    Than thus to grope amid the depths in vain!

I watch the eternal hills, the far, far lying,
    With glorious flowers ever over-run;
I take me eagles' wings, with vision flying
    And brow upraised to look upon the sun.

Ye skies, how fair the paths about your spaces!
    There freedom shines for ever like a star;
The winds are blowing through your lofty places,
    And who, ah! who can say how sweet they are?

**Last poem
(unfinished)**

Woe! my knowledge is weak,
My wound is desperate.
Behold my days draw nigh—
I confess my sins,
I return to my God.

I serve my Creator—with a willing soul.
I thank Him for all the good—He hath done with me;
And for the children of my house—I lift my hands to Him—
Will He not hear my voice—since all mine iniquity is pardoned?

He will open for me the gates of righteousness,
I shall enter into them, I shall praise the Lord,
For He hath done wondrously.
O save Thy people—bless Thine inheritance—My God—

**JUDITH LADY
MONTEFIORE,
Great Britain**

From her diary

10 June 1812

I was this day united in the holy bonds of matrimony to Moses Montefiore, whose fraternal and filial affection [toward his brother, Abraham] gained in me an interest and solicitude in his welfare at a very early period of my acquaintance with him, which, joined to many other good qualities and attention toward me, ripened into a more ardent sentiment. Human beings have not the power to dive into futurity, therefore cannot say what will be, but trusting in God Almighty and ever keeping reason in view, I have as good a prospect for future happiness as I at present enjoy. Oh! may I continually be thankful to God for his great goodness toward me and my family; suffer me not, Good Heavens, to be ungrateful for Thy bounty, but if misfortune or disappointments are to befall me may I bear them with resignation!

I ought to be particularly thankful for one great blessing we possess, namely, the good health of my dear and honored mother. Pray the Almighty to spare her to us many years in health and happiness! My dear father alas! we have lost, which on this eventful day causes a pang that cannot be described. However, reflecting on his virtues, I checked the sorrow his absence would otherwise have occasioned, in the hope of his being blessed in Heaven in company with my beloved brother, Barent. Grant, good God, that we may have the supreme felicity of meeting them in Heaven at our death!

There was a large party at our marriage, and to dinner, consisting of the major part of my beloved Montefiore's friends, and my own, in the whole between eighty and ninety persons, and the day passed with much joy and conviviality. May God Almighty prosper our union! and may we endeavor to deserve his love.—Amen.

Angel Court, 12 June 1812

We passed the whole of to-day without company, except my sister Hannah [wife of Nathan Rothschild] who called in the morning and took luncheon with us. Nothing particular occurred throughout the day. But on lighting the [Sabbath] candles in the evening with my mother, according to her wish and what is taught us, I experienced a new sensation of devotion and solicitude to act right. I trust that God Almighty will direct us how to perform that which is most pleasing to him. I do not know any circumstances more pleasing to me than to perceive that my dear Monte is religiously inclined. It is that sort of religion which he possesses that in my opinion is most essential—a fellow-feeling and benevolence.

Saturday, 13 June 1812

My dear mother, brothers, Mr. Sebag [later married to Moses Montefiore's sister, Sarah] and Miss [Sarah] Montefiore accompanied my dear Monte and self to synagogue at eight o'clock in the morning, where we said our prayers most fervently, after which returned home to breakfast at ten o'clock. Many of our friends called in the course of the morning to offer their congratulations. A great part of the family drank tea with us, and supped. I passed a very happy day. Thank God!

Monday, 21 September 1812

Notwithstanding our last night's apartment was not the most agreeable, still we found ourselves perfectly refreshed this morning, and went out at nine o'clock. Walked through the town to Portsmouth, where we were fortunate in obtaining an extremely pleasant apartment in the York Hotel, with a delightful view of the sea and shipping. There we took breakfast, after which we went out with an intention to see the Docks. . . . At one o'clock we went back to the inn and passed our time with reading till dinner-time, for which we had a roast duck, boiled salmon and vegetables.[1] We then finished our book, took a pleasant walk, returned back to tea. Read our prayers and retired at eleven o'clock, grateful for having passed a very happy day.

Park Lane, Saturday evening, 17 December 1825

After an interval of more than fourteen [?] years I resume noting in this book the principal, though trivial, circumstances of the day,[2] which I found among the other books in arranging them in the library. On perusing the few preceding pages, written during the first month of my marriage, I could not restrain my tears produced from a variety of feelings of joy and sorrow, joy for possessing in health and prosperity the good and worthy husband of my choice, and that most of our family are equally happy, sorrow at having lost that beloved parent of whom I made mention therein, and whose whole life was devoted to the good of others, and acts of devotion. I trust she is happy in heaven! Thankful to the Almighty for permitting me to enjoy so many years of health and felicity, I pray to deserve His continued protection, and that my future life may be guided by His will. . . .

Friday, 23 December 1825

Called at Justina's to ask her to take a ride and pass the evening with us, which she could not accept. Went to the City to fetch Mon.; did not meet him. We went to the synagogue and walked home; dined at home without company. Mon., after looking over several books read a little from Juvenal, that little however was most instructive and improving, teaching the valuable lesson to be satisfied with the decrees of Providence, the best judge of what can tend to our happiness and not to form vain and unreasonable wishes of our own, which often lead to disappointment and regret. I also read a few pages of "Thinks I to myself." [3]

Yarmouth, Saturday, 31 December 1825

Passed a better night than any since we had been here. After prayers, had a delightful walk on the sands for about two hours, though on first going out it snowed and did not promise to prove pleasant. Saw Miss Paterson at a window; she seemed to wonder how we could venture out. The Market Place appears in perfection to-day, the last day of this year, large turkeys, geese and the best quality of other provisions fill the stalls to contribute to the satisfaction of the ensuing year. May it pass as happily as the last, and may we exert ourselves to merit the protection of the Almighty! I read aloud Clark's Travels [i.e., *Travels in Europe, Asia and Africa*] while Montefiore wrote.

From her private journal of a visit to Egypt and Palestine

Alexandria, Sunday, 30 September 1836

This being the eve of our Day of Atonement, we left the ship early, having engaged the apartment at the Locande. We had confidently hoped to have passed this epoch of the year at the Holy City; and our departure from our friends, together with the inconvenience of our apartment, added to our regret on this solemn day. . . . At half-past five, I went with Montefiore to synagogue; prayers commenced at six. It was lighted as on the preceding holidays. Mrs. Fuor, her sister, and two other ladies, were in the gallery with me, but I cannot say much of their devotion, conversation having been more attended to than prayers. The gentlemen here tell me, it is not considered essential for ladies to observe that strict piety which is required of themselves; but surely at a place of devotion the mind ought to testify due respect and gratitude toward the Omnipotent.

Albergo delle Tre Coronne, Monday, 1 October 1836

It was a beautiful morning, and a dark blue firmament recompensed us for a night of torment; truly might it be termed a night of penance. The mosquitos had never been so relentless to us before; but we were told this is always the case at the fall of the Nile. Montefiore arose at six, and went to the great synagogue at seven. At half-past ten Mr. Mazzara accompanied me to Mrs. Fuor's synagogue, it being only two doors from the inn. The gallery was well attended; among the ladies were many from various parts of Europe, more especially from Leghorn, who are now residents of this city. Italian seemed more generally spoken than Arabic; all the children, as well as the Franks, conversing in that language. It was most satisfactory to see so numerous a class of our brethren so highly respectable and well educated as those were whose acquaintance I had so recently formed in this remote and neglected country. . . .

Jerusalem, Thursday, 18 October 1836

There is no city in the world which can bear comparison in point of interest with Jerusalem,—fallen, desolate, and abject even as it appears—changed as it has been since the days of its glory. The capitals of the ancient world inspire us, at the sight of their decaying monuments, with thoughts that lead us far back into the history of our race, with feelings that enlarge the sphere of our sympathies, by uniting our recollections of the past with the substantial forms of things present: but there is a power in the human mind by which it is capable of renewing scenes as vividly without external aids, as when they are most abundant. There are no marble records of the plain of Marathon, to aid the enthusiasm of the traveler, but he feels no want of them: and thus it is, whenever any strong and definite feeling of our moral nature is concerned; we need but be present on the spot where great events occurred, and if they were intimately connected with the fate of multitudes, or with the history of our religion, we shall experience a sentiment of veneration and interest amounting to awe, and one above all comparison nobler than that which is excited chiefly by the pomp or wonders of antiquity. It is hence that Jerusalem, notwithstanding the ploughshare of the heathen, infinitely exceeds in interest Rome, Athens, and even the cities of Egypt, still abounding, as they do, in monuments of their former grandeur, and wonderful and venerable as they are, above all other places on which the mere temporal history of mankind can bestow a sanctity. No place has even suffered like Jerusalem:—it is more than probable that not a single relic exists of the city that was the joy of the whole earth; but the most careful and enthusiastic of travelers confess, that when they have endeavored to find particular marks for their footsteps, there was little to encourage them in the investigation. But it depends not for its power of inspiring veneration on the remains of temples and palaces; and were there even a less chance of speculating with success respecting the sites of its ancient edifices, it would still be the city toward which every religious and meditative mind would turn with the deepest longing. It is with Jerusalem as it would be with the home of our youth, were it leveled with the earth, and we returned after many years and found the spot on which it stood a ploughed field, or a deserted waste: the same thoughts would arise in our hearts as if the building was still before us, and would probably be rendered still more impressive from the very circumstance that the ruin which had taken place was complete. . . .

I can never be sufficiently thankful to Almighty God for suffering us to reach this city in safety. The obstacles that presented themselves, the dangers with which we were threatened, the detentions and vexations which had actually to be endured, all rose in my mind as I gave way to the feeling of delight with which I at length saw the fulfilment of my dear husband's long-cherished wish. Nor was my satisfaction a little increased at the recollection that I had strenuously urged him to pursue the journey, even when his own ardor had somewhat abated, and when I had to oppose my counsel to the advice and wishes of our companions. . . .

Notes

1. As Sonia Lipman maintains in her excellent essay on Judith Montefiore, this entry, among others in the diary, reveals that the Montefiores did not strictly adhere to the Jewish dietary laws at the time that they married. Later, however, Moses Montefiore became extremely observant, as apparently did his wife, strictly following the dietary laws, the Sabbath laws, etc. This change may have occurred on Moses Montefiore's forty-third birthday, 24 October 1827. On that day, he wrote in his diary, "This day I began a new era. I fully intend to dedicate much more time to the welfare of the poor and to attend Synagogue as regularly as possible on Monday, Thursday and Saturday" (quoted in Sonia Lipman, "Judith Montefiore—First Lady of Anglo-Jewry," *Jewish Historical Society of England Transactions* 21 [1968]: 293).
2. "This refers only to the domestic diary. Lady Montefiore had kept special diaries in the interval, notably, one of a tour in Scotland in 1821, which has never been published, and was probably among those destroyed some years ago" (Lucien Wolf, "Lady Montefiore's Honeymoon," in *Essays in Jewish History,* ed. Cecil Roth [London: Jewish Historical Society of England, 1934], 252).
3. A fashionable novel of the day, written by the Reverend Edward Nares.

GRACE AGUILAR,
Great Britain

From *The Spirit of Judaism* (1842)

The Avowal of Unity
Considered as It Regards the Jewish Nation

There is one portion of the Jewish form of prayer, which every member of that nation is desired to repeat twice, sometimes three times, in every day. It is first taught to our children; either in Hebrew or in English, the words of the *Shemang* are the first ideas of prayer which the infant mind receives, long before any meaning can be attached to them; and it is right that it should be so; for so much of vital importance is contained in this brief portion of our ritual, that we cannot impress it too early on the heart of an Israelite. . . . It contains no actual prayer, but prayer is a word which may be taken in a wider sense than its literal meaning. For prayer is the language of the heart,—needing no measured voice, no spoken tone; thus Hannah's wish was heard and answered, though not a sound had passed her lips. It is the hour of communion between man and his Maker—the hour granted to the fallen man to lift him above this world, to bring his great Creator, his merciful Father, a while from His lofty throne above the heavens, even to his side, listening in mercy to his anguished cry, healing the open wound, bidding the floods of woe subside, and leaving His blessed Spirit on the soul to encourage and to soothe.

And this hour of solemn communing, comprised in the word *prayer*, may be passed either in supplication for that which we most need; in confession and repentance for mortal sin; in praise and thanksgiving for untiring, unchanging mercies; in the study of God's Holy Word; searching for and applying the sacred truths contained therein, till we may know in some degree that which we believe, and the moral, social, and domestic duties stand forth clear and spotless even as they came from Him.

It is this which is comprised in the *Shemang*. It is not the creature supplicating the Creator—it is a brief emphatic summary of all those laws which God Himself inspired to Moses to impart; and if we once consider it thus, our thoughts will have no need to wander in the repetition of this prayer; for the affections and the intellect will alike be fully stored.

Taken as a whole, as the contents of about one-quarter of a page in our daily prayer books, we cannot perhaps be so struck with the impressive solemnity of these six verses as when we regard them, as in reality they are, six verses in the sixth chapter of Deuteronomy. To feel their full force, we shall do well to turn to the sacred writings and examine each verse alone.

"Hear, O Israel! The Lord our God, the Lord is One!" Such is the literal translation of the Hebrew, *sh'ma yisrael adonai elohaynu adonai ekad*, but it is impossible to give the full force of the Hebrew by any English words. Yet even the common translation is such, that we cannot peruse it with any degree of attention, without finding its solemnity appeal to our hearts. It is the avowal of belief, belief in the unparalleled, unchanging, incomprehensible unity of God, the repetition and acknowledgment of which marks us as His chosen people,—His redeemed, His beloved, His first-born,—separates us from every other nation, every other religion of the world. How then, can we utter these sacred words in the light and careless way we are but too apt to do? Can the mere avowal of a belief in Unity be acceptable to our God, when we neither know, nor care, what that belief includes? sometimes perhaps mechanically repeated, even at the very time we are hovering between Judaism and Christianity, knowing little of the one, and tempted by interest to embrace the other? Oh, surely this should not be; surely a few words attempting to explain the full sense, by the analysis of each word, will not be wholly unacceptable to the Jewish nation; and be the means, perhaps, by giving their thoughts full scope, to prevent that evil which in the repetition of this prayer is only too general.

The Hebrew word rendered *Lord* in the English of this sentence is in the original that awful and ineffable NAME, which no true Israelite will utter. It is the name peculiar to the Divine Essence, signifying He who WAS, IS and ever WILL BE—*yih(o)vah*. . . . We are told, first, that this Divine Essence—this ever-existing Being is our God, and then, that this Divine Essence is one.

. . . This word, signifying the Ever-Existent, has very often been turned against us, by those who, from a kindly but mistaken zeal, would convince us that our belief is wrong, and that we are blindly following the path of error. They assure us, the ineffable Name is typical of the Godhead in which they believe, that its three syllables denote the Trinity, its plurality in unity, that even as Elohim, it should convince us that their faith, that which the founder of their system taught, was contained as fully in the Old as in the New Testament. It is this argument which not too often shakes the unenlightened Israelite. . . . And yet that very prayer, which slips from his lips every night and morning . . . tells us that God—however plural the word by which He is called in Hebrew may be in its termination, is One—that the Divine Essence, He who was, is, and ever will be, in One—solely, simply, One, without any division of parts; for that One is formed from the uniting, the compressing of the Essence, if I may so speak without profanation; and therefore we cannot embrace the creed of the Nazarene, which not only inculcates division in the immaterial essence, but that the Father was in heaven and the Son upon earth at one and the same time.

. . . It is enough for us to know that not alone did our Father so reveal Himself in the impressive words with which He answered Moses—*ehyeh asher ehyeh*, I AM THAT I AM—or literally, I will be that I will be; but also in the repetition of His laws He inspired that faithful servant with wisdom to proclaim His unity, in terms so powerful and clear, that it would almost seem, as if His all-penetrating eye, marking the war of argument which would assail His people, provided them in these simple words with an armour of proof, no weapon can assail. . . . Our purpose . . . is simply to impress on the heart of the Israelite the awful responsibility he takes upon himself every time he repeats this first verse of the *Shemang*. If he know not, if he care not, to mark the distinction between his faith and that of the nations around him—let him pause ere he repeat the solemn prayer; but oh, let him not hurl down the anger of his Maker by renewing every day his covenant with God, when he neither knows what that covenant is nor cares what it includes.

. . . We must not remain Hebrews only because our fathers were. The faith we receive merely as an inheritance, will not enable us to defend it from insidious attack or open warfare, will not satisfy the cravings of our nature, will not give us a rock whereon to cling in hope and such deep love, that we could be strengthened even to die for it, if it were needed; nor can it be pleasing unto Him who, declaring himself a God of Truth and Love, will so be worshiped. Our hearts must breathe from our lips in this avowal of our faith—we need not utter it aloud, God alone may hear us;—yet should we so dwell on this important subject, that if called upon we might proclaim aloud our faith in the presence of angry thousands, fearlessly acknowledge our belief in the unity of God—Ay, dare even scorn, and proudly and steadily tread the sainted paths which our fathers trod.

. . . None will say I have exaggerated the glowing of the heart, the holy comfort, which will pervade the believer in the repetition of this solemn prayer. Nor will it be in our closets only, we shall feel all that we have gained; we shall go forth, no longer striving to conceal our religion through SHAME (for it can only be such a base emotion prompting us to conceal it in free and happy England);—but strengthened and sanctified by its blessed spirit, we shall feel the soul elevated within us, and cling to our Father and our God in the deep devotedness of true believers, and filled with the warmest love and charity to our fellow creatures. This would be the visible and palpable fruit of an earnest search after truth. . . .

No efforts of our own, however great and magnanimous they may be, can work out our redemption. His mercy, omnific even as His creating word, it all sufficient; but the TRUST in THAT mercy is not of itself enough to obtain salvation. Our Father rejects those who do good, trusting in their own righteousness to save them, looking to their own works to purchase redemption; but He equally rejects those who supinely sit, contented to trust in His word, and think nothing depends on themselves. As works without faith are unacceptable, so equally is faith without works. . . .

The duties devolving on us by the acknowledgment of unity, though solemnly important, are comparatively few; and it is to know them, which renders the retrospect of our history of so much consequence.

That history tells us we are a chosen and severed people—to be holy unto the Lord—. . . a living witness of the Lord and His word. Do not the enlightened and earnest members of the Protestant church all acknowledge their final redemption will be in some way connected with the restoration of Israel? Do not the truly religious of all sects look upon us with feelings near akin to admiration . . . and love? . . . Can we be lukewarm in His cause, careless in prayer, silent in praise? On us, more than other nations, devolves the duty of devotion—of prayer for grace to walk in His paths—thanksgiving for the privilege of belonging to a people so supremely blessed; of proving by our whole conduct, whether social or domestic, moral or religious, that we receive His holy word as true, and believe in His gracious promises—and that we deem the promise of a Messiah to come and redemption so clear and certain, that we do all in our power, by the circumcision of our hearts and removal of our evil propensities, to draw it nearer. Our scattered and humiliated condition can oppose no barrier to the performance of these sacred duties.

. . . Our duty to our fellow-men, which the retrospect of our history inculcates, is simply charity; charity in its widest sense, perhaps in its most difficult performance; charity to the peculiar tenets of others. . . . We should do all in our power to prove indeed the comfort, the spirituality, the holiness, which our blessed faith includes, by kindly acts of social charity and faithful friendship toward those believing differently from us. . . . And it is this, this universal charity, this self-humiliation, which is the duty, the retrospect of our history commands.

Hints on the Religious Instruction
of the Hebrew Youth

The seventh verse of the sixth chapter of Deuteronomy, and the fourth of the *Shemang*, contains so much important matter in a few words, that each member of the sentence demands to be considered separately. In the preceding verses, we have been desired to reflect on and lay up the words of the Lord in our own hearts; in this, to teach them to our children. "And thou shalt teach them diligently to thy children," i.e., the love of God and all that is therein comprised.

To instruct young children in the dull routine of daily lessons, to force the wandering mind to attention, the unwilling spirit to subjection, to bear with natural disinclination to irksome tasks, all this, as a modern writer very justly observes, is far more attractive in theory than in practice. It is a drudgery for which even some mothers themselves have not sufficient patience; but very different is the instruction commanded in the verse we are regarding. To speak of God, to teach the child His will, to instil His love into the infant heart, should never be looked on as a daily task, nor associated with all the dreaded paraphernalia of books and lessons. The Bible should be the guide to, and assistance in, this precious employment. There are moments when children are peculiarly alive to emotions of devotion. The Hebrew mother who desires her offspring to say their prayers morning and evening, to abstain from writing, working, or cutting on the Sabbath, to adhere to particular forms and observe particular days as she does, has yet not wholly fulfilled her solemn duty. This will not be enough to make the Hebrew child love his God or His religion; not enough to restrain him in manhood from becoming a Christian, if it favor his interest or ambition so to do.

. . . Were love and gratitude to [God] banished from every other human heart, surely they would swell in a young mother's breast, as she gazes upon the little creature undeniably His gift, and feels the full gushing tide of rapture ever attendant on maternal love. Surely in such a moment there must be whisperings of devotion, leading the soul in gratitude to the beneficent Giver of her babe, or swelling it with prayer to guide that precious charge aright. It may be, that doubts of her own capability of executing a task, as solemnly important as inexpressibly sweet, may naturally arise; but these doubts, instead of leading her to give up the task in despair, should lead her to the footstool of her God in prayer; and her petition, even as that of Hannah was, will be granted.

That truly pious Jewess not only devoted her child to God, but so devoted him, that but once in the year she could behold him; and at first he was her only child—the little being for whom morning and evening she had implored the Lord, implored Him in tears, in fasting, in bitterness of soul. Her prayer was heard; and how fervent must have been her gratitude, how great the love SHE bore her God, how implicit her reliance on His love for her, that she stilled the yearnings of a mother's tenderness, and as soon as the boy was weaned, brought him up to the high priest and left him there. And was not her pious faithfulness rewarded? Three other sons and two daughters did she bear; and her eldest, the joy, the hope of her heart, became the favored prophet of the Lord.

To part thus from her child is not now demanded of the Hebrew mother; nor can there now be such a blessed consummation of such a self-conquering struggle. Yet the example of Hannah should be treasured up by all the daughters of her race, whom the same beneficent God has blessed with children. It must be remembered that in the present state of Israel the word of God cannot and must not be taken literally as regards the immediate answers to prayers, or punishment of sin. The lapse of years, the difference of position, must not be forgotten. All the pious actions there described, cannot now be performed, nor dare we expect the same direct manifestation of our Father in reward: yet this is no cause of, nor excuse for, the neglect of the Bible. Vouchsafed in love and mercy as an unfailing guide, it at least teaches what is pleasing in the sight of our God, by the blessings that directly follow or are promised. We learn too "The Lord is merciful and gracious, slow to anger and plenteous in mercy;" that "As the heaven is high above the earth, so great is His mercy toward them that fear Him;" and therefore if the examples set before us in His book are followed according to our ability, aided and strengthened by constant prayer, it is certain we too shall be blessed, if not in this world, in that "where they shall teach no more every man his neighbour, and every man his brother, saying KNOW the Lord, for they shall all know me, from the least of them to the greatest of them, saith the Lord; for I will forgive their iniquities, and I will remember their sins no more."

Philadelphia to New York

10 July 1809

**REBECCA GRATZ,
United States**

**Letter to Maria
Fenno Hoffman**

Yes my Dear Maria your sorrows have indeed a home in my bosom witness the pangs which at this moment rend it. I weep over your affecting little letter, till I can no longer discern a sentence in it— and while I almost adore your virtuous exactions and pious resignation, My soul is wised in devotion to that Almighty Being who has made you so perfect and has tried you with so many afflictions. How rich My love must your reward be in a better world, for all your submissions here, but I trust there is much reward for you yet, in this state to make many future years a blessing to you that your example in happiness as well as in affliction may benefit the world.

I wrote you on Saturday night, when my mind was in a tortured state of anxiety and suspense. It was my wish to have started immediately and endeavored to soothe your sorrows by my presence. All your friends here advised your removal from N[ew] York as a much better plan, and the situation of my sisters rendered my leaving home extremely difficult. My Brother proposed writing to Mr. H[offman] and I sat down to make the same request to you. If it is possible dear Maria, do comply with our wishes—bring all your family. . . . You shall have all the consolations friendship can bestow—your feelings shall not be violated by the intrusion of strangers—your children shall be attended with the greatest care—we will pass every hot day in the country—everything affection can do to heal your wounds shall be administered, and we shall be a thousand times your debtor for the trust. . . .

May God Bless and comfort you, My dearest Girl
prays most fervently your ever faithful

RG

Letter to Miriam Moses Cohen

Philadelphia to Charleston, South Carolina

12 September 1853

My Dearest Miriam,

I feel the deepest sympathy for your sorrow stricken family. The bereaved parents & sisters of poor Maria Minis are a mournful group! yet each so strives to support the other than one cannot withhold a sentiment of respect and affection added to their sympathy—and a hope that they "may yet see peace together." No event in this troubled life brings us nearer to our God than the taking away from us of those so loved & cherished—whose innocent life gives us an assurance that they are happier far than we could make them. Our human nature is stricken down—& we bow submissive to the Almighty Being who created our immortal thirst for other worlds than this—the scriptures tell us that "God chasteneth whom he loveth." It is because that mourning teaches us our dependence on his will?—and opens our hearts to the daily & hourly blessings his providence bestows even in this probationary state— we thank Him Dear Miriam, as you say, rejoice in trembling—yet while we tremble rejoice that God knows best what is ultimately for our happiness—and will the happiness of all he has created—pain & sorrow are agents of mercy when they prepare us by a "lowly entrance" for the great change which awaits us. . . .

I am glad you have so much satisfaction in the Ministry of Mr. Rosenfeld and that you are learning from the Hebrew. It has been always a regret to me that I only know the sound and very little of the soul of the language. . . .

A heart full of love from Aunt Becky and for your husband & self My Beloved Miriam. The best wishes, affection [?] from your ever loving aunt,

RG

The Superintendent of the Jewish Sunday School has great pleasure in again presenting the pupils of this Institution to its early patrons; and in meeting their parents and guardians, she feels grateful for the confidence reposed in her, and is fully sensible of her responsibility as directress of a school, intended to embrace the most holy and important portion of education. As Israelites in a Christian community, where our youth associate and compete with their fellow-citizens in all the branches of the arts and sciences, it is essential they should go provided with a knowledge of their own doctrines—that they should feel the requirements of their peculiar faith, and by a steadfast, unobtrusive observance of them, claim the respect of others, and the approbation of their own consciences. As descendants of the great nation to whom God entrusted his Holy Law, which was to enlighten all the people of the earth, and the living witnesses of His sacred Legacy, the Jews ought to be among the purest and wisest of the sons of men, and the most faithful adherents to their religious duties; therefore it is incumbent on them to "teach their children diligently."

The tender age of many little pupils, shows that this duty is recognised; though too young to join in the exercises here, they are familiar with school instruction, and can repeat a prayer, the importance of which was appreciated by the Psalmist, who says: "Out of the mouths of babes and sucklings hast Thou ordained strength." On this text may we not urge the benefits of the Sunday School, and plead with parents to encourage regular and punctual attendance; and on teachers to be ready for this weekly, loving task, enjoined by scripture, and amply rewarded by the generous impulses of their own hearts?

Note
1. Presented to parents and patrons (including Isaac Leeser) on 25 April 1858 at the Sunday School and published by Leeser in the *Occident* that May.

LOUISA B. HART,
United States

Address to a graduating student of the Hebrew Sunday School

While awarding a premium for improvement, I like a teacher's privilege in offering some comments, indeed feel that I should scarcely acquit myself of the duty of one, could I permit you to assume the like responsibility without offering such counsel as experience enables me to.

The simplicity of our holy religion, based as it is upon the unity of the Creator of all, in itself implying perfection and without which there is necessarily imperfection, would seem to require little explanation: the purity of its precepts, the propriety of its prohibitions would seem neither to require explanation nor vindication yet, as the first has been alloyed by other nations, the latter violated by our own, it is proper to guard against the like sinfulness. So much ingenuity has been exercised to combine and reconcile mysticism, as to render it essential to meet the arguments of falsehood with the knowledge and intelligence of truth. Your lessons have taught you

A report on the Hebrew Sunday School of Philadelphia

that it is not enough to believe; we must seek to know why we believe, and action must be proof of conviction; therefore dear——— though no longer a pupil, you must teach yourself to instruct others.

Judaism based on the proclamation of God's unity is the very life of life; let not the acknowledgment "blessed be the name of the glory of His kingdom for ever and ever" be uttered by profane lips, voluntary ignorance is profanity; so too is intellectual enlightenment with presumptuous judgment. "But a lowly heart, oh God, Thou wilt not despise." Your Bible,———, is your best, most certain guide; the works breathing its spirit most important as commentaries; ranking high among them are those of Grace Aguilar, whom living we venerated, and dead we mourn, and to whose loving memory the best incense we can offer is the love and obedience to God, the well doing towards our fellow-creatures, that constitute the spirit of Judaism.

May you be enabled to fulfill all the duties that you now have and may be called to, is the affectionate wish of your teacher,

L. B. Hart

REBEKAH HYNEMAN,
United States

The Destruction of Jerusalem (1853)

Jerusalem! the agonizing cry
That broke from thy crushed heart, rose up to heaven,
And called a curse upon thy conqueror's head.
Rome! the destroyer, mistress of the seas,
And vanquisher of nations, where is she?
Where her fierce legions, sending o'er the earth
Havoc and terror, misery and death?
Where her proud Caesars, at whose lightest word
Nations were subjugated, and the earth
Drenched with the blood of myriads?

Alas!
They who upraised the sword against God's own
Have perished by the sword; there lives not one
Who can redeem her from her abjectness,
Or bring her former splendor back again.
She hath fallen! and her utter nothingness
Proves that an all-avenging Hand hath sent
A righteous retribution on her head.

While thou, oh sadly crushed and humbled one!
Poor widowed dove, scared from thy resting-place,
Israel! grief-stricken and forsaken, thou
Livest, and Rome dies! Go forth, ye vain
And impotent of earth, and boast your power
That lives but for a day; behold in this
God's wisdom and man's error. HE hath made
A mighty nation as a thing of naught,
And raised an atom from the lowest depths
Of misery and bondage unto life.

Let slumber fall lightly
  On eye-lids opprest,
And evening beam brightly
  With visions of rest.

The weary day cometh
  With toil and with sorrow,
But hope nightly beameth,
  With job for the morrow.

Then, slumber, fall lightly
  On eye-lids opprest,
And evening beams brightly
  With visions of rest.

Fair angels are keeping
  Their vigils above,
E'en while we are sleeping
  We share in their love.

Then let slumber fall lightly
  On eye-lids opprest,
And evening beam brightly
  With visions of rest.

Virginia, 10 May 1864

**EMMA MORDECAI,
United States**

From her diary

. . . Loud firing of both cannon and musketry commenced briskly between 4 and 5 o'clock—don't know where the fight was, but not very far off. A heavy thunderstorm with abundant rain stopped the firing for a short time. Continued after the storm abated until dark, when Rose went to bed and I sat knitting in the dark till 9, when I went to bed too, after committing our household to the care of the All Powerful and felt no fear. I had taken a cup of tea which kept me awake till near 12, but my thoughts were tranquill [*sic*] and full of trust. R[ose] was asleep all the time.

10 June 1864

I had intended visiting the Hospitals today, but on consulting my Hebrew Calendar, I found it was the first day of Pentecost, so I remained at home to observe the day as well as I could by reading the services and reminding myself of my peculiar duties as an Inheritor of law given to us by Him who said "I, the Lord, change not." Blind and foolish are those children of Israel, who persuade themselves that the laws given to them by the Unchanging One, for them and their descendants to observe forever, are not binding on them.

PENINA MOISE,
United States

Hymn (1856)

I weep not now as once I wept
    At Fortune's stroke severe;
Since faith hath to my bosom crept,
    And placed her buckler there.

Lightly upon this holy shield
    Falls sorrow's thorny rod;
And he who wears it, learns to yield
    Submissively to God.

It breaks the force of ev'ry dart,
    By disappointment hurled
Against the shrinking human heart,
    In this cold, callous world.

Wrestling with this, I have defied
    All that my peace assailed;
Passion subdued hath turned aside,
    And sin before it quailed.

How many wounds would now be mine;
    How many pangs intense!
But for the shield of faith divine,
    My spirit's strong defense.

Oh! when in prayer my hands I lift
    To Thee Almighty God!
The excellence of this Thy gift,
    With fervor will I laud.

O God! to Thy paternal grace,
    That ne'er its bounty measures.
All gifts Thy grateful children trace,
    That constitute Life's treasures.

Light, being, liberty, and joy,
    All, all to Thee are owing;
Nor can another hand destroy
    Blessings of Thy bestowing.

None, save our own! for in man's heart
    Such passions are secreted,
That peace affrighted weeps apart,
    To see They aim defeated.

LIGHT is made dim by human guile;
    EXISTENCE doth but languish;
and FREEDOM loses her bright smile
    'Mid scenes of strife and anguish.

Father! though forfeited by sin
   Are all Thy tender mercies;
There is a TRUSTING FAITH within,
   That ev'ry fear disperses.

Honor and praise to Thee belong,
   O God of our salvation!
Who will defend from shame and wrong,
   Thy first elected nation.

Protector of the quick and dead!
   Thy love THIS WORLD o'erfloweth;
And when the "vital spark" hath fled,
   Eternal life bestoweth.

Piety (hymn)

Oh, turn at meek devotion's call,
   From idle dreams of worldly power;
Which flourishes awhile, to fall
   And perish like an earth-born flower.

Countless are pleasure's bright decoys,
   Unwary mortals to ensnare;
Faith beckons thee from barren joys,
   And points to her immortal sphere.

Wouldst thou thy soul to God commend?
   Forsake the scene of heartless mirth;
Seek those who weep without a friend,
   Bring wine and oil to suff'ring worth.

Let piety direct thy choice,
   In all thy spirit's high concerns:
Then shall the pilgrim's heart rejoice,
   Who in the "vale of tears" sojourns.

Man's Dignity (hymn)

O God! within Thy temple-walls,
   Light my spirit seems, and free;
Regardless of those worldly calls
   That withdraw it oft from Thee.
Faith to the proudest whispers: Here,
   Riches are but righteous deeds,
And he who dries a human tear
   Ne'er to mercy vainly pleads.

Can sorrow at Thy altar raise
   The voice of lamentation?

Oh no! its plaint is changed to praise,
  Regret; to resignation.
To nought all human evil shrinks,
  Where revelation showeth,
That God each soul to heaven links,
  Which ne'er its trust forgoeth.

Oh! brightest, most benignant boon,
  Above all others rated;
With thee, Creator! to commune,
  In temples consecrated;
That when life's boundary is past,
  More glorious still appears;
Since sanctuary, we at last
  Find in celestial spheres. . . .

ROSA EMMA SALAMAN, Great Britain

The Angel and the Child (1855)

"Thou are too beautiful and good,
  Too full of sacred mirth,
Too pensive in thy gayest mood,
  Dear child, for this cold earth."

Thus spoke an angel to a child,
  And fanned with softest breath
His tender cheek and eyelids mild:
  That angel's name was *Death*.

The angel with his folded wings,
  And torch inverted, stands
And whispers to the child and sings,
  And holds its little hands.

The children by the cottage door
  See not the wondrous sight,
But think their brother's eyes before
  Have never looked so bright.

"Oh! Herbert, darling! Herbert, love!
  What is it thou dost see?
Why dost thou smile and look above,
  And move from off my knee?"

"My mother dearest, let me go;
  My brothers, sisters dear,
Detain me not, nor weep with woe;
  There is no cause for fear.

"Oh! didst thou not, my mother, see
  The messenger divine,

That took me gently from thy knee,
    And said I was not thine.

"He spoke of all the flowers that bloom
    Like glittering stars above;
Of wondrous things beyond the tomb;
    But most he spoke of love;

"He said it was the brightest thing
    That shone in that bright sphere;
That from the seraphs' harps one string,
    Still vibrates even here."

"Thou dearest child, what heavenly light
    Is beaming round thy face!
What anguish will be mine this night,
    To see thy empty place!"

"Oh, mother, if thou couldst but see
    The angel by my side,
How lovingly he's clasping me,
    Thy tears would soon be dried.

"Oh! if thou couldst but hear his voice,
    So gentle and so mild,
Just when he whispered me, 'Rejoice,
    Rejoice, thou blessed child;

" 'For thou to Paradise dost go;
    Yes, thou hast reached that goal,
Before one pang of earthly woe
    Has touched thy sinless soul.' "

· I ·

O Angels! will ye never sweep the drifts from my door?
Will ye never wipe the gathering rust from the hinges?
How long must I plead and cry in vain?
Lift back the iron bars, and lead me hence.
Is there not a land of peace beyond my door?
Oh, lead me to it—give me rest—release me from this unequal strife.
Heaven can attest that I fought bravely when the heavy blows fell fast.
Was it my sin that strength failed?
Was it my sin that the battle was in vain?
Was it my sin that I lost the prize? I do not sorrow for all the bitter pain and blood it cost me.
Why do ye stand sobbing in the sunshine?

ADAH ISAACS
MENKEN,
United States

Drifts That Bar My
Door

I cannot weep.

There is no sunlight in this dark cell. I am starving for light.

O angels! sweep the drifts away—unbar my door!

· II ·

Oh, is this all?

Is there nothing more of life?

See how dark and cold my cell.

The pictures on the walls are covered with mould.

The earth-floor is slimy with my wasting blood.

The embers are smoldering in the ashes.

The lamp is dimly flickering, and will soon starve for oil in this horrid gloom.

My wild eyes paint shadows on the walls.

And I hear the poor ghost of my lost love moaning and sobbing without.

Shrieks of my unhappiness are borne to me on the wings of the wind.

I sit cowering in fear, with my tattered garments close around my choking throat.

I move my pale lips to pray; but my soul has lost her wonted power.

Faith is weak.

Hope has laid her whitened corse upon my bosom.

The lamp sinks lower and lower. O angels! sweep the drifts away—unbar my door!

· III ·

Angels, is this my reward? Is this the crown ye promised to set down on the foreheads of the loving—the suffering—the deserted?

Where are the sheaves I toiled for?

Where the golden grain ye promised?

These are but withered leaves.

Oh, is this all?

Meekly I have toiled and spun the fleece.

All the work ye assigned, my willing hands have accomplished.

See how thin they are, and how they bleed.

Ah me! what meagre pay, e'en when the task is over!

My fainting child, whose golden head graces e'en this dungeon, looks up to me and pleads for life.

O God! my heart is breaking!

Despair and Death have forced their skeleton forms through the grated window of my cell, and stand clamoring for their prey.

The lamp is almost burnt out.

Angels, sweep the drifts away—unbar my door!

· IV ·

Life is a lie, and Love a cheat.

There is a graveyard in my poor heart—dark, heaped-up graves, from which no flowers spring.

The walls are so high, that the trembling wings of birds do break ere they reach the summit, and they fall, wounded, and die in my bosom.

I wander 'mid the gray old tombs, and talk with the ghosts of my buried hopes.

They tell me of my Eros, and how they fluttered around him, bearing sweet messages of my love, until one day, with his strong arm, he struck them dead at his feet.

Since then, these poor lonely ghosts have haunted me night and day, for it was I who decked them in my crimson heart-tides, and sent them forth in chariots of fire.

Every breath of wind bears me their shrieks and groans.

I hasten to their graves, and tear back folds and folds of their shrouds, and try to pour into their cold, nerveless veins the quickening tide of life once more.

Too late—too late!

Despair hath driven back Death, and clasps me in his black arms.

And the lamp! See, the lamp is dying out!

O angels! sweep the drifts from my door!—lift up the bars!

· V ·

Oh, let me sleep.

I close my weary eyes to think—to dream.

Is this what dreams are woven of?

I stand on the brink of a precipice, with my shivering child strained to my bare bosom.

A yawning chasm lies below. My trembling feet are on the brink.

I hear again his voice; but he reacheth not out his hand to save me.

Why can I not move my lips to pray?

They are cold.

My soul is dumb, too.

Death hath conquered!

I feel his icy fingers moving slowly along my heartstrings.

How cold and stiff!

The ghosts of my dead hopes are closing around me.

They stifle me.

They whisper that Eros has come back to me.

But I only see a skeleton wrapped in blood-stained cerements.

There are no lips to kiss me back to life.

O ghosts of Love, move back—give me air!

Ye smell of the dusty grave.

Ye have pressed your cold hands upon my eyes until they are eclipsed.

The lamp has burnt out.
O angels! be quick! Sweep the drifts away!—unbar my door!
Oh, light! light!

GRACE NATHAN,
United States

An ethical will written
to her son (begun in
1827)

TO MY SON

This effort will speak to you from the tomb. Years of infirmities lead to the reflection that we must soon part. I am perfectly resigned to meet the last earthly event, grateful to God for the blessings he has given me.

I die in the full faith of my religion. I leave you in the bosom of a virtuous wife, surrounded by numerous offspring, who give promise of comfort.

Long may they live to show you the same filial duties that I have uninterruptedly received from you. Now in this solemn moment when I am taking an eternal earthly farewell let me express my full approbation of your deportment toward me. It has been exemplary, as you have devoted your kindnesses so may be your great reward; more I could not say. Need I exhort you to the cultivation of your endearing children and give them a just idea of their religious and moral principles, these being the cornerstones of all good, and on which the basis of life here and hereafter may be supported. You my son will live in peace and bear a kind manner to those who have shown it to me; by this they will cherish my memory; and I shall live.

Now thou my son who wast the joy of my younger days and the balm of my declining age, let me thrice bless you and say may peace rest with you forever and ever. Amen.

Your mother Grace Nathan

Keep the seven days of mourning and no more; for that time *only* you will keep your beard.

YETTE BECKMAN,
Germany

A letter of counsel to
her son before
sailing for America

11 P.M., 30 September 1880

My dear Son:

The long-expected has come to pass—your trip to America. You realize, my dear son, the heart pangs I suffer at the thought of your going. It is your wish, and so shall it be. May the Almighty guide and protect you from all evil and always be with you.

Put your trust in Him and He will lead you in the right way. Be brave and good and continue your filial affection. Do not forget our sacred religion. It will bring you comfort and consolation; it will teach you patience and endurance, no matter how trying the circumstances or difficult the trial.

Whether your life be one of success or of struggle, whether rich or poor, keep God before your eyes and in your heart.

You are going out into the wide world, far from parents, brothers, or sisters. It will be trying for you, but you are blessed with many good qualities, and my heart is confident that no harm will befall you. Commit your way unto the Lord and He will bring it to pass.

Be careful in your business associations, and particularly in forming friendships. Above all, guard your health, for that is the greatest gift on earth.

I would like to and I could say much more to you, my dear son— but it is very distressing for me. I only say:

"Travel with God, be ever cheerful and courageous, and put to good use all that you have been taught."

Though a great distance separates us, and you are far from parental care, my thought of you will never cease so long as my heart beats.

The hope that our separation will be of short duration is my only consolation.

And so, my dear son, I bid you adieu. Write frequently and let me know your confidante regarding what happens to you. Do not imbue yourself with the idea of settling down so far away from us, and let me live in the expectation of not being without you too long. Tears come to my eyes; you will therefore have to excuse my poor handwriting.

Your ever faithful

MOTHER.

P.S.—Tomorrow marks the advent of your twentieth birthday and the start of your big journey. May everything be for the best and you be rich in happiness.

My dear Moses:

Although your dear father has already told you everything that can be recommended to a young lad of your age, and although I do hope that you will adhere as much as possible to his writing you, I cannot abstain to admonish you, that you be content and patient whenever you may not achieve what you had aimed at. Since it happens to everybody in life once in a while, which you cannot yet anticipate. In such a case you have to be very patient, even if it costs much effort to endure it. Do believe me, dear Moses, I speak from experience, since I was many times among strange people and went through many sufferings that I never before would have believed I could ever be able to bear. Not to succumb to the grief and sorrow, it was my only confidence to which I each time took recourse, my trust to the dear God. I prayed to Him for His help and assistance, and He surely does not forsake anybody who trusts in Him. Believe me, anybody who is religious will not fall in the trap of vice, as will somebody who forgets his faith and has no religion at all. Certainly, nobody thinks highly of somebody who does not keep up his faith, and there may be many a one who forgot his religion and despises it, however returns to it later on. I assure you that you cannot give me greater joy, because besides this I have no joy any more on this earth, but only when hearing good things from my children and when they keep up their faith as much as possible. Now, enough of

LENA ROTH, Germany

Letter to her son (1854)

this matter. Now I will just recommend to you one more point that you should keep in mind especially: I just want to tell you, don't miscalculate ever your own character, especially against other persons who are less worthy than you are yourself. Never act against your own character, be it against men or women. But do not misunderstand me and think I may be proud (which I never was in all my life). I do not even mean those people who are poorer than you are, because poor people are many times just as honest as the richest are. When a person is honest and righteous, he is just as esteemed as people of rank, but I mean this in quite a different sense. You will understand me—even if not at present—but later, when you have matured. The main thing is, you must try to keep up your good reputation, since, once you are despised and in bad memory, you stay there for ever. Otherwise I won't tell you much more. I think when you are once on your own feet you will get enough experience and comprehend how well your parents mean. Your dear father sacrificed so much for all of you, and this is the reason that I expect you to follow our admonitions. Finally I want to ask you just one thing: to take one more hour's time and read through this letter again (since I know you have a bad memory) so that you don't forget it. This is the wish of your faithful mother.

Lena Roth.

RACHEL SIMON,
Great Britain

From Records and
Reflections

Aspiration

3 April 1840, Aged 16

My most earnest desire is to fulfill the will of God in all things. My greatest wish is to become perfectly religious; by this I do not refer to matters of form and ceremony, although the outward garb of religion must not be neglected.

When I speak of religion I mean a constant inward sense of communion with God, and such reliance upon Him at all times that I may be proof against flattery and the vanities of the world.

My object in committing my ideas and feelings to writing is, that in time to come, should I be less earnest in my religious views, I may have recourse to my notes, and gain from them renewed spiritual strength.

In our days of prosperity it is more difficult to sustain a religious spirit than in times of adversity, because we are apt to forget that God who has bountifully given may also take away.

A Reflection

8 December 1854

Life on earth is short and uncertain. We pass away "like a shadow," and are forgotten, while our spiritual life is eternal.

God is the "father of the spirits of all flesh." In His "Image" we are "created." He is infinite in love and goodness. I believe that it is possible for all of us to attain a far greater expansion of soul than we imagine, but we do not give ourselves the time necessary for the cultivation of this higher growth.

In the achievements of science and art we see wonderful results from intellectual development. Why may we not make spiritual progress in like proportion?

History affords many an example of men and women of intellectual distinction who have yet sought companionship among the unworthy, but those whose spiritual development has kept pace with their intellectual culture wield an influence for good that cannot be measured. If we drink from the "Fountain of living waters" we shall be true to God and ourselves, and faithful to our fellow man.

Small Trials
(A few words of Comfort)

1859

Trials of every description are intended for man's good. This is a doctrine generally accepted, and it is preached in every pulpit; but it requires no uncommon experience to prove how rarely the attempt is made to give effect to it in practical life.

We cannot enumerate the sources of those smaller trials allotted to man.

Trials do not necessarily imply a condition of overwhelming sorrow and anguish,—the tearing you asunder from those most dear to you—destitution, privation, or sickness:—none of these may fall to your lot; yet trials will assail you in some form or other. You may suffer from a variety of adverse circumstances. Perhaps you may be so placed in life as to be living in a state of discord with those around you; you may be married [?] to one who can never properly understand your disposition; your best intentions may be frustrated; or you may receive ingratitude from those whom you have served. In the position of parent, guardian, and teacher, the trials cannot be told—even youth is not exempt. Whether in the schoolroom, or at home, how many disappointments, how various the little troubles, to be endured!

To young and old, then, the same advice must be given:—Turn every trial to account; however trifling in its character, make use of it as the polishing instrument that will change the roughest stone into the jeweler's prize.

It is not an easy work; but it must be the effort of our life if we do really believe that trials are intended for our good.

"Despite not the chastening of the Lord; neither be weary of His correction, for whom the Lord loveth He correcteth; even as a father the son in whom he delighteth" [Prov. 3:11–12]. "For He doth not afflict willingly, nor grieve the children of men" [Lam. 3:33].

Then turn your vexed and troubled spirit Heavenward,—even in the trifling details of daily life. You will be surprised to find how much the purification of your inner life will be advanced. Fail to do this and you will find at best only excuses for ill-humor and impatience.

If a dangerous illness attack your household, or death deprive you of some beloved one, or should some unforeseen accident occur, you will receive such visitations with a calm and becoming resignation. The reason of this is, because you call into practical life right and true principles. You have seen and felt the hand of God. You have been led to the consciousness of a Father's love in your heavy trouble; and why not trace the same acting principle in your lesser trials? Depend upon it, the same remedy holds good in both cases.

Sometimes our spirit is clouded by a depression for which we cannot wholly account. Could we, on such occasions, take a microscopic view of our inner self, we might trace back the hidden cause to some of those small trials, for which we must apply no less a remedy. It is only by this consciousness of a Divine Father's love that we can strengthen ourselves against the evil results of little troubles upon our temper and our character. To this end prayer is the efficient aid. Upon every occasion of annoyance call to your help a few simple words, such as the following: "O God! let not little things vex me and disturb my spirit, nor let me be disheartened by my own shortcomings, but help me to overcome my deficiencies. Strengthen me with a fervent faith in you [?] so that I may know and feel the good that is as [?] all Thy dispensations."

Let us then, henceforth, regard the small trials of daily life as a means, under God's good providence, of attaining a more exalted state; and, with this view of our small vexations, we shall daily grow in likeness unto Him in whose image we are created, and on whose divine favor our peace of mind depends.

However dark and difficult our path in life, we cannot be wholly cast down if our spirit be steadfast with God. Let us but fix a steady gaze upon His infinite perfection, let our hearts be true to Him, trust in His parental love, and a holy calm will take the place of a disturbed mind,—a cheerful hope will light up our depressed spirits. This is the strength that God will give us—a strength ever growing, ever enlarging, the nearer we approach the All-powerful and Perfect One: for to trust in God is at once to receive His blessing.

Reminiscence of a Sermon by Lord Alwyne Compton, now Bishop of Ely

5 August 1883, Malvern

This afternoon I have been greatly pleased with a sermon I heard from the Dean of Worcester (Lord Alwyne Compton), in the Priory church at Malvern. It was in behalf of the "Society for the Prevention of Cruelty to Animals." He took his text from Psalm cxlv.:

"The Lord is good to all, and His tender mercies are over all His works." He went on to show how numerous are God's mercies over all His works, including the animal kingdom. He said, that in the possession of mere physical life there was a happiness which the animal shares in common with man. With this text as a basis, he enlarged somewhat upon the sympathy which should exist between us and the animal creation. He said we have only to watch the [?] of cattle in the field, or listen to the singing of birds in the air, to observe that it is given to them to enjoy their lives. Although we as the highest creation possess dominion over the earth for our service and use, we must not abuse this trust. . . .

All-gracious, All-merciful God! Thy paternal goodness has permitted me to awaken after a refreshing sleep, and has sent the gladdening rays of morning to revive me anew.

O Heavenly Father! how great is the mercy which Thou hast shown unto me. My first emotion is, therefore, to thank Thee, from the innermost depth of my heart, for Thy providential watchfulness over my life, and for having protected me whilst the darkness of night surrounded me.

How many of my fellow-creatures but yesternight ascended the couch in good health and hopes, and yet cannot leave it this day, from being bound to it by pains and suffering! how many may have yesternight sunk to sleep amidst riches and affluence, but who are brought to poverty this morning by sudden disaster. Alas! how many others are languishing, perhaps, in the dark gloom of a prison, into which no friendly ray of joy penetrates. And how large may be the number of those who fell asleep last night, never to awaken any more in this world.

How thankful ought I therefore to be, Heavenly Creator! for Thy goodness, wherewith Thou hast warded off every danger from me, hast preserved my health, and restored me to the arms of my relations and friends. Oh! let me ever cherish this feeling of gratitude within my heart, so that I may faithfully discharge my religious and domestic duties; that I may meet my fellow-creatures with loving-kindness, such as Thou hast shown unto me; and that I may ever extol Thee, who causest the sleeper to awake, and who wilt cause those that sleep the sleep of death to awake to eternal life. Amen.

FANNY NEUDA, Germany

Morning Prayer

Translated from the German by M. Mayer

. . . How dark was everything around me but a few hours ago; anxiety filled my heart, and I was afraid of the results of my fears and pain. But when I called in my woe, the Lord heard me, and saved me from my troubles. The hours of anxiety have passed, and now joy and light surrounded me. Thou, O God! hast safely led me through the dangers of the hour of delivery, Thou has done more unto me than I ventured to hope; Thou hast fulfilled my prayer, Thou hast given me a dear, healthful, well-formed child. Therefore,

Prayer after Safe Delivery

Translated from the German by M. Mayer

I praise Thy mercy, and shall never forget Thy benefits; my heart and mouth shall ever overflow with thanks and praises of Thy supreme power and loving-kindness.

And will filial confidence in Thy mercy I commit all my cares unto Thee, trusting that Thou wilt accomplish the work of grace which Thou has commenced. Thou wilt renew my strength, that I may be able to fulfil the duties of a good and faithful mother.

My God and Lord! Bestow Thy protection also upon my new-born infant, that it may thrive and grow, and be healthful in body and soul, to be a pleasure unto Thee, a delight unto me and my beloved husband, an honor unto all men. Yea, Eternal One! in *Thee* I place my trust, I wait upon *Thy* help; he who trusteth in *Thee* shall never be put to shame. Amen.

**EMMA LAZARUS,
United States**

**In the Jewish
Synagogue at
Newport**

Here, where the noises of the busy town,
    The ocean's plunge and roar can enter not,
We stand and gaze around with tearful awe,
    And muse upon the consecrated spot.

No signs of life are here: the very prayers
    Inscribed around are in a language dead;
The light of the "perpetual lamp" is spent
    That an undying radiance was to shed.

What prayers were in this temple offered up,
    Wrung from sad hearts that knew no joy on earth,
By these lone exiles of a thousand years,
    From the fair sunrise land that gave them birth!

Now as we gaze, in this new world of light,
    Upon this relic of the days of old,
The present vanishes, and tropic bloom
    And Eastern towns and temples we behold.

Again we see the patriarch with his flocks,
    The purple seas, the hot blue sky o'erhead,
The slaves of Egypt,—omens, mysteries,—
    Dark fleeing hosts by flaming angels led.

A wondrous light upon a sky-kissed mount,
    A man who reads Jehovah's written law,
'Midst blinding glory and effulgence rare,
    Unto a people prone with reverent awe.

The pride of luxury's barbaric pomp,
    In the rich court of royal Solomon—
Alas! we wake: one scene alone remains,—
    The exiles by the streams of Babylon.

Our softened voices send us back again
   But mournful echoes through the empty hall;
Our footsteps have a strange, unnatural sound,
   And with unwonted gentleness they fall.

The weary ones, the sad, the suffering,
   All found their comfort in the holy place,
And children's gladness and men's gratitude
   Took voice and mingled in the chant of praise.

The funeral and the marriage, now, alas!
   We know not which is sadder to recall;
For youth and happiness have followed age,
   And green grass lieth gently over all.

And still the sacred shrine is holy yet,
   With its lone floors where reverent feet once trod.
Take off your shoes as by the burning bush,
   Before the mystery of death and God.

                       27 July 1867

The New Year
Rosh-Hashanah, 5643
(1882)

Not while the snow-shroud round dead earth is rolled,
   And naked branches point to frozen skies,—
When orchards burn their lamps of fiery gold,
   The grape glows like a jewel, and the corn
A sea of beauty and abundance lies,
          Then the new year is born.

Look where the mother of the months uplifts
   In the green clearness of the unsunned West,
Her ivory horn of plenty, dropping gifts,
   Cool, harvest-feeding dews, fine-winnowed light;
Tired labor with fruition, joy and rest
          Profusely to requite.

Blow, Israel, the sacred cornet! Call
   Back to thy courts whatever faint heart throb
With thine ancestral blood, thy need craves all.
   The red, dark year is dead, the year just born
Leads on from anguish wrought by priest and mob,
          To what undreamed-of morn?

For never yet, since on the holy height,
   The Temple's marble walls of white and green
Carved like the sea-waves, fell, and the world's light
   Went out in darkness,—never was the year
Greater with portent and with promise seen,
          Than this eve now and here.

Even as the Prophet promised, so your tent
   Hath been enlarged unto earth's farthest rim.
To snow-capped Sierras from vast steppes ye went,
   Through fire and blood and tempest-tossing wave,
For freedom to proclaim and worship Him,
         Mighty to slay and save.

High above flood and fire ye held the scroll,
   Out of the depths ye published still the Word,
No bodily pang had power to swerve your soul:
   Ye, in a cynic age of crumbling faiths,
Lived to bear witness to the living Lord,
         Or died a thousand deaths.

In two divided streams the exiles part,
   One rolling homeward to its ancient source,
One rushing sunward with fresh will, new heart.
   By each the truth is spread, the law unfurled,
Each separate soul contains the nation's force,
         And both embrace the world.

Kindle the silver candle's seven rays,
   Offer the first fruits of the clustered bowers,
The garnered spoil of bees. With prayer and praise
   Rejoice that once more tried, once more we prove
How strength of supreme suffering still is ours
         For Truth and Law and Love.

From "An Epistle to the Hebrews" (1883)

. . . Our own people in default of a sufficient acquaintance with the well-springs of our national life and literature are apt to be misled by the random assertions of our Gentile critics, and are often only too apt to acquiesce in their fallacious statements. "Tell a man he is brave, and you help him to become so," says Carlyle, and the converse proposition is equally true. Our adversaries are perpetually throwing dust in our eyes with the accusations of materialism and tribalism, and we, in our pitiable endeavors to conform to the required standard, plead guilty and fall into the trap they set. That our national temper and character have suffered grievous injury during our thousand year long struggle for existence is undeniable, but the injury has been precisely of an opposite nature to that which the world would have us believe. It has been a physical and material loss, as well as a loss of that homogeneity and united national sentiment which it is our first duty to revive in order to concentrate our efforts toward their regeneration and rehabilitation. "Tribal!" This perpetual taunt rings so persistently in our ears that most Jews themselves are willing to admit its justice, in face of the fact that our "tribal God" has become the God of two-thirds of the inhabited globe, the God of Islam and of Christendom, and that as a people we have adapted ourselves to the varying customs and climates of every nation in the world. In defiance of the hostile construction that may be put upon my words, I do not hesitate to say that our national defect is that we are not "tribal" enough; we have not sufficient solidarity to perceive that when the life and property of a Jew in the uttermost provinces of the Caucasus are attacked, the dignity of a Jew in free America is humiliated. We who are prosperous and independent have not sufficient homogeneity to champion, on the ground of a common creed, a common stock, a common history, a common heritage of misfortune, the rights of the lowest and poorest Jew peddler who feels for life and liberty of thought from Slavonic mobs. Until we are all free, we are none of us free. But lest we should justify the taunts of our opponents, lest we should become "tribal" and narrow and Judaic rather than humane and cosmopolitan like the anti-Semites of Germany and the Jew-baiters of Russia, we ignore and repudiate our unhappy brethren as having no part or share in their misfortunes—until the cup of anguish is held also to our own lips.

What we need to-day, second only to the necessity of closer union and warmer patriotism, is the building up of our national, physical force. If the new Ezra rose to lead our people to a secure house of refuge, whence would he recruit the farmers, masons, carpenters, artisans, competent to perform the arduous, practical pioneer work of founding a new nation? We read of the Jews who attempted to rebuild the Temple using the trowel with one hand, while with the other they warded off the blows of the molesting enemy. Where are the warrior-mechanics to-day equal to either feat? Although our stock is naturally so vigorous that in Europe the Jews remain after incalculable suffering and privation the healthiest of races, yet close confinement and sedentary occupations have undeniably stunted and debilitated us in comparison with our normal physical status. For nearly nineteen hundred years we have been living on an idea; our spirit has been abundantly fed, but our body has been starved, and has become emaciated past recognition, bearing no likeness to its former self.

Let our first care to-day be the re-establishment of our physical strength, the reconstruction of our national organism, so that in future, where the respect due to us cannot be won by entreaty, it may be commanded, and where it cannot be commanded, it may be enforced.

Part III

1890-1960: URGENT VOICES

FROM 1890 through 1960, spiritual literature written by Jewish women increased both in volume and in variety of expression. Much of the literature produced carried with it a greater sense of urgency than that produced by Jewish women in the preceding one hundred years. In part, at least, this sense of urgency reflected new historical circumstances. Prior to the First World War, for example, as great numbers of impoverished Russian Jews continued to arrive in the United States and England in search of freedom, native-born Jewish women and men actively sought ways of helping their coreligionists. Their efforts included incorporating the immigrants into the religious life of the Jewish community, by either creating houses of worship at which the immigrants might feel welcome, creating social organizations whose overt or covert purpose was to tap the spiritual potential of those who were religiously apathetic, or reaching out to the immigrants, largely through philanthropic and educational work, as a first step toward acculturation and eventually adaptation of those religious forms already practiced by many if not most native-born Jews.

Many middle-class American and Anglo-Jewish women, accepting the nineteenth-century equation of true womanhood with spirituality, came to believe that stemming the tide of religious apathy, not just among Jewish immigrants but among native-born Jews as well, was their particular responsibility as women. New opportunities afforded them in Jewish communal life, to a large extent reflecting the great degree of acculturation already evident among native-born late nineteenth-century American and British Jews, gave women new platforms from which they could express and attempt to disseminate their ideas. As the documents in this section reveal, these platforms included synagogue pulpits from which some exceptional women began to preach; American Jewish periodicals such as Rosa Sonneschein's the *American Jewess,* published in the 1890s, and the *American Hebrew,* published weekly in New York City, which regularly included articles by women and published proceedings of women's organizational meetings; and public addresses given to members of such organizations as the National

Council of Jewish Women (NCJW), established in 1893 in the United States.

The proliferation of local Jewish women's organizations in the United States during the end of the nineteenth century and early in the twentieth, including local philanthropic societies and temple sisterhoods, gave American Jewish women even greater opportunities than their English counterparts had to articulate through words and actions their understanding of what it meant to be a Jewish woman. The first two documents included in this section—an excerpt from the Minute Book of the Temple Israel Sisterhood in New York City, dated 1891, and minutes from a June 1891 meeting of the Society Esrath Nashim of Philadelphia, a charitable women's organization initially founded in 1873 but reconstituted in 1891 as the Jewish Maternity Association—reveal the kinds of religious activities in which many native-born American Jewish women were engaged.

The next set of documents includes sermons, prayers, and public addresses by Ray Frank (1865–1948), in all likelihood the first American woman to preach from a Jewish pulpit. As a journalist based in Oakland, California, she frequently traveled throughout the American Northwest as a correspondent for several San Francisco and Oakland newspapers. In 1890, Frank happened to be in Spokane, Washington (then known as Spokane Falls), on the eve of Rosh Hashanah (the Jewish New Year) and was interested in attending religious services. After learning that no service was planned, as the Jewish community was quite small and as yet unorganized, she offered to preach at such a service if a prayer quorum could be gathered. At Frank's initiative, and with the encouragement of one of the community's leaders, to whom she had letters of introduction, a special edition of the *Spokane Falls Gazette* was printed announcing that a young woman would be preaching to the Jews of the community at the Opera House that evening.

According to local newspaper reports, the worship service was extremely well attended and Frank's sermon, an appeal to her coreligionists to resolve their differences and form a permanent congregation, well received. She preached again the next morning and again, less than ten days later, on the evening of Yom Kippur (the Day of Atonement), the holiest day of the Jewish year. In her sermon, excerpted here, Frank reiterated her plea to "drop all dissension . . . and join hands in a glorious cause." Her understanding of Judaism, revealed here and in numerous published sermons and addresses, was both practical and simple. She believed that true piety was simple, direct, and earnest. It involved opening one's heart to God and singing God's praises and recognizing that, while the moral laws are from God, external forms of worship (i.e., religious ceremonies and observances) are human creations that must be altered "to suit the times" if they are to retain their meaning.

The speed with which Frank's reputation as a preacher spread is evident from the following two documents, both from 1893. On the morning of 4 September, she offered the opening prayer at the first Jewish Women's Congress, held in Chicago in conjunction with the

Parliament of Religions that met during the World's Fair. The following morning, she delivered an address entitled "Woman in the Synagogue." In her address, Frank spoke of women's spiritual superiority and their consequent responsibility as mothers, wives, sweethearts, and sisters to serve as religious teachers, leading others to God. Although she believed that women had the right and many the natural ability to serve as either rabbis or congregational presidents, she reiterated the more conventional view that a woman's "noblest work will be at home."

While supporting herself as a journalist during the 1890s, Frank continued to preach and lecture widely throughout the western and northwestern parts of the United States. Although at times she was erroneously labeled a "lady rabbi" by members of the local press, she did in fact attend classes for one semester at Hebrew Union College (the Reform movement's rabbinical seminary in Cincinnati) at the invitation of its founder and president, Isaac Mayer Wise, and was asked by at least one Reform congregation in Chicago to serve as its full-time spiritual leader, an invitation that she declined so as to remain free to preach her own spiritual message rather than the message that a particular congregation felt that they were paying her to hear. Her two "careers"—journalist and preacher—ended with her marriage to Simon Litman in 1901. Following the advice she had given to those attending the 1893 Women's Congress, she attempted to do her "noblest work" at home.[1]

The essay by Philadelphian Mary M. Cohen (1854–1911), "The Influence of the Jewish Religion in the Home," that follows the documents by Ray Frank was also delivered at the 1893 Jewish Women's Congress. An essayist and poet, Cohen frequently wrote on Jewish themes and, as a single woman, devoted a great deal of time and energy to various local Jewish organizations and to Mikveh Israel, the traditional synagogue to which she and her family belonged. She served as a teacher in and later superintendent of the Hebrew Sunday School (succeeding Louisa B. Hart), taught English, reading, and arithmetic to working-class women and girls who attended classes run by the (Jewish) Young Women's Union, organized educational activities for the local Young Men's Hebrew Association, and chaired Mikveh Israel's Religious School Committee. Passionately interested in literature, Cohen was also a member of several literary societies, including the Browning Society of Philadelphia, of which she was president, and served as corresponding secretary and a member of the first Executive Committee of the Jewish Publication Society of America.

In "The Influence of the Jewish Religion in the Home," Cohen gives examples of the ways in which Judaism and home life are inseparable. So important, she asserts, are everyday observances that "the synagogue is the home, and the home the synagogue." Claiming the religious significance of women's traditional roles as wives and mothers and defending what for many women was a private, home-centered understanding of prayer, Cohen maintains that, while entering the house of God is always right and appropriate, it is not "indispensable for the performance of religious service." Nor, she implies, are the traditional religious pursuits of men, that is, the study of religious texts and participation in public worship, superior to such traditionally female pursuits as preparing special foods for the holidays and maintaining a kosher home. The spirit and the body, she says, are equally in need of nourishment, and "to closely associate the material and the religious is to dignify the one without injuring the other."

The vision of Judaism offered by American writer Josephine Lazarus (1846–1910) radically differed from that presented by her coreligionists at the Jewish Women's Congress (as well as from that described in the poems and essays of her sister, Emma).[2] Believing that neither Reform Judaism nor Orthodoxy was capable of awakening the modern Jew's inner spiritual power, Lazarus maintained that a new religious vision was needed that went beyond the narrowness and formalism of existing denominations. At the risk of obliterating Jewish distinctiveness, Lazarus called for a more universal understanding of faith. Forsaking all creeds, Jews and liberal Christians should strive to follow that understanding of faith first given to the world by Judaism, namely, faith as a trust in God and the religious life as a striving to live in conscious relation with "a Being that comprehends and transcends our own," offering hope and immortal promise.

Lazarus most clearly expressed these ideas in a series of essays collected into one volume in 1895 under the title *The Spirit of Judaism,* a title inviting the reader to compare her ideas with those of the still popular *Spirit of Judaism,* published by Grace Aguilar in 1842. Included here is a lengthy excerpt from Lazarus's essay "Judaism, Old and New," first written in 1894, which presents her understanding of what a "universal Judaism" might be.

Public Jewish reaction to Lazarus's ideas was swift and condemnatory. Rabbi Kaufmann Kohler, a leader of American Reform Judaism, published an outraged and scathing review in the Jewish journal *Menorah,* claiming that her equation of Judaism with law and Christianity with love proved that Lazarus simply did not understand the Jewish tradition. Similar reviews, as well as debates by Jewish laity and clergy of Lazarus's ideas, appeared in Jewish journals and newspapers such as the *American Hebrew* and the *Jewish Messenger* (in which three of the five essays in *The Spirit of Judaism* initially appeared).

While no serious study of Josephine Lazarus's life has yet been undertaken, it appears that she never married, continued to write on religious themes throughout her lifetime, and, despite her desire to create what she identified as a universal Judaism, retained an interest in such Jewish organizations as the National Council of Jewish Women, of which she was an early and vocal supporter.

The concept of establishing an independent, national organization for American Jewish women was first proposed by Chicagoan Hannah Greenbaum Solomon (1858–1942) at the Jewish Women's Congress. At its final session, ninety-three women representing

twenty-nine cities voted "to unite in closer relation women interested in the work of Religion, Philanthropy and Education" under
the umbrella of the National Council of Jewish Women.[3] Within
three years, the NCJW held its first national convention, and local
chapters had already been established in nearly every American
town with a sizable Jewish population (as well as in two Canadian
towns).[4]

In her welcoming address, Rebekah Bettleheim Kohut (1864–
1951), president of the NCJW's New York Section, expressed the
conviction shared by other council leaders that Jewish women had
a particular responsibility to serve as religious missionaries. Born in
Hungary but raised in San Francisco, Kohut married Alexander Kohut, a widower with eight children and one of the leaders of the
nascent Conservative movement, in 1887. Widowed seven years
later, she turned to lecturing, writing, and teaching as a means of
supporting her family. She also spent a great deal of time engaged
in educational, philanthropic, and religious communal activities in
New York City, where she lived for most of her adult life.[5]

Largely through the influence of her husband, Rebekah Kohut
came to appreciate the importance of retaining traditional ceremonies both as a means of finding God and as a way of sanctifying
one's home. Consequently, her address, which focuses on the importance of observing the Sabbath, is very different in content and
tone from addresses given by the majority of council leaders. As she
makes clear, to be a truly "religious Israelite" there are certain personal sacrifices that one must make, including reinstating the "pristine glory" of the Sabbath. It is unclear from her address how metic-
ulous in the observance of the Sabbath Kohut believed Jewish
women ought to be. Indeed, her allusion to keeping the Sabbath "in
our hearts" and her own lifelong affiliation with the Reform movement seem to indicate that she was not necessarily advocating a return to traditional, rabbinically prescribed observance. Yet, by reminding her listeners, here and in other addresses, not to abandon
completely ways in which Jewish women traditionally sanctified the
name of God, Kohut was able to reach a greater cross section of
council members than could the majority of NCJW leaders.

Among the more articulate of the council's early leaders was educator Julia Richman (1855–1912), who chaired its National Committee on Religious School Work. A graduate of the Female Normal
School (later Hunter College), the first Jewish woman principal and
the first Jew to become a district superintendent in the city of New
York, Richman was a founder of the Young Women's Hebrew Association and director of the Educational Alliance and the Hebrew
Free School in New York City, a lecturer for the Jewish Chatauqua
Society, and an author who wrote on teaching methods and their
relation to good citizenship.[6]

As a single woman, Richman devoted her life to writing, teaching, and other communal activities. Within the New York City
school system, she promoted such innovations as graded classes,
special classes for gifted students, and the use of stories that illus-

trated points to be discussed rather than "preachy" lectures. At the Educational Alliance and the Hebrew Free School Association, she blended social work with education by distributing free shoes, hot lunches, and clothing to poor students. Anxious to improve what she maintained was the moral, religious, and educational backwardness of the Russian Jewish immigrants living in New York, Richman set out as superintendent of schools for the Lower East Side (where most of the immigrants lived) to eradicate what she considered to be an abominable religious school system. Targeting in particular the traditional *cheder*, the religious primary school imported from Eastern Europe in which boys were taught to read Hebrew by memorizing portions of the Bible and the daily prayer book (although in general she had little sympathy for any school in which classes were too large, teachers poorly trained, and textbooks scarce and uninteresting), she sought to create a system of modern-style religious schools featuring women teachers, mixed classes of students, and what she considered to be a rationally structured curriculum.[7] With Rebekah Kohut, Richman edited *Helpful Thoughts,* a monthly magazine for Jewish religious school teachers.

As an educator, Richman had both her supporters and her detractors. In 1908, for example, the Board of Education of the city of New York received several petitions asking that she be transferred to another district because she was "entirely out of sympathy with the needs of this part of the community" (a request that the board decided not to honor). Yet, as a woman deeply interested in tapping the spiritual potential not only of religiously indifferent Russian immigrants and their children but also of native-born American Jews who had turned away from religion, Richman was widely respected and admired. An effective advocate for the teachings of Reform Judaism, she assumed a major role in helping direct the early religious goals of the National Council of Jewish Women.

In her 1896 report on the work of the NCJW's Committee on Religious School Work, included here, Richman asserted the centrality of the Religious School Committee to the "permanent usefulness of the [National] Council of Jewish Women" and to "the permanence of all true, earnest, spiritual American Judaism." Claiming the spiritual superiority of women, Richman insisted that "only with the aid of our Rabbis can the women hope to improve our [religious] schools; only with the aid of our women can the Rabbis hope to gain real influence over their flocks." In her report, she shared with council members ways in which those who were mothers could evoke within their children an awareness of God's presence, a pride in being Jewish, and an interest in continuing their Jewish education and exhorted all council members to make their friends and families aware of their religious mission.

At the close of the 1896 convention, Hannah Greenbaum Solomon delivered an impromptu presidential address, included here. In her address, she assured council members that she believed, as undoubtedly most of them did, that a woman's first duty was in the home. Nevertheless, she said, as "new women," we also dare to enter the world and to follow our convictions. Blessed with a "wide perspective" and "clear vision," we recognize that there is much in the world that deserves—indeed, demands—our sympathy and help. She hoped, she maintained, "that when the call comes to any of us if we can go, it will find us ready."

Minnie D. Louis (1841–1922), a writer, communal worker, and educator who worked closely with Julia Richman in New York City and was a founding member of the NCJW,[8] frequently articulated her understanding of Jewish spirituality in public addresses and published essays, such as the one included here. Published in 1895 in the *American Hebrew* (and initially delivered as a speech to members of the NCJW), her paper, "The Influence of Women in Bringing Religious Conviction to Bear upon Daily Life," emphasizes the importance of religion as a "primary truth" and intuition about the world and its creation. It further emphasizes women's particular mission to influence others spiritually so that each heart becomes a "Temple for God" and every home a temple. While not explicitly Jewish in content, Louis's essay—written for a Jewish audience and utilizing the religious language of Reform Judaism (e.g., "The Fatherhood of God implies the brotherhood of man," the equation of religious mission with bearing witness to God and spreading God's moral teachings)—was intended to show Jewish women all that they had to offer, *as women,* to Judaism and to the world.

Following the essay by Louis are two poems written by Englishwoman Nina Davis Salaman (1877–1925). Wealthy by birth, Salaman was a poet and translator of Hebrew literature as well as a committed Zionist whose circle of friends in England included members of the Jewish literary elite. The works included here, taken from her collection of poetry *Voices of the River,* published in 1910, reveal Salaman's deeply rooted, personal yearning for the divine. In "The Power of the Spirit," she entreats God to let her feel some intimations of immortality, while, in "Of Prayer," she rejoices at the power of privately offered prayers to give solace in times of sorrow.

"The Jewish Woman in Religious Life" by Bertha Pappenheim (1859–1936) was delivered at the Women's Congress at Munich in 1912. Pappenheim had already gained public prominence both as a social worker and founder of Care for Women, a Jewish women's aid society that sought to help the thousands of Eastern European immigrants seeking refuge in Germany, and as cofounder and leader of the Jewish feminist movement in Germany, the Jüdischer Frauenbund, established in 1904 to seek greater political, economic, and social rights for Jewish women in Germany and in the Jewish community. She was also known as a writer and translator, a tireless champion of the fight against white slavery (i.e., women and girls sold into prostitution), and a vocal supporter of women's right to vote.[9]

Pappenheim begins her address with a scathing critique of the role of women in Orthodoxy. Despite the "high standing [that Jewish women have] within the home," she maintains, married Orthodox women are forced to become "domestic recluse[s]," unmarried mothers and their offspring are treated with contempt and scorn, and Jewish women in general receive "deficient mental training," and are so disregarded within the worship service that from childhood Jewish boys naturally come to feel themselves "superior to the female sex." Yet, while Pappenheim sympathizes with those women who have left Judaism precisely because of the low status accorded them as women, she concludes by defending Orthodoxy, insisting that "the majority of Jewish women can find their high vocation anew within their own race and religion." They can do so, she seems to suggest, not by pressing for change within the synagogue, but by assuming a greater role in communal charitable organizations "in which, according to Jewish law, both sexes should participate equally." Following this address are three brief prayers written in German by Pappenheim and later translated into English and published by one of her "grateful pupils." Revealing none of the anger of her 1912 address, they testify to Pappenheim's deep religious faith and to her great sense of connection to Judaism and the Jewish people.

In the poetry of both Miriam Ulinover (1890–1944) and Kadya Molodowsky (1894–1975), one senses the urgently felt need to reclaim the Jewish past in the light of the poets' experiences as modern Jewish women, far removed from the traditional European Jewish communities to which their foremothers had belonged. Writing in Yiddish, Ulinover and Molodowsky both wrote and published their poetry for the frequently antireligious secular Yiddish press. According to Kathryn Hellerstein, who has selected and translated the poetry by Ulinover and Molodowsky included here,

> Miriam Ulinover spent her entire life in or near Lodz, Poland. She published only one volume of poems, *Der bobes oytser* (The grandmother's treasure), in 1922. Her preparations of a second book manuscript were interrupted by World War II, and the manuscript does not seem to have survived. In the Lodz Ghetto, Ulinover was known for the literary evenings she hosted, under dire circumstances. Unlike Molodowsky, who reinterpreted aspects of Jewish tradition in a radical way, Ulinover consciously sought to preserve a particular side of Jewish folk life—the folk religious life of her great-grandmother. Thus, her poems, such as "Der Alter Siddur" (The old prayer book) and "With the *Taytsh Khumesh*" (a book containing homilies in Yiddish on the weekly biblical portion), included here, are written in apparently simple, rhymed stanzas and in folk Yiddish. The simplicity of language and form is deceptive, though, and immeasurably valuable, for it preserves the specific manifestations of belief and language of an earlier generation of women that Ulinover, even in the 1920s, saw vanishing.

> Kadya Molodowsky, born in White Russia, published her first three books of poems in Warsaw and Vilna from 1927 to 1935. She emigrated to New York in 1935 and published her later works—including three volumes of poems, a novel, short stories, children's poems, and essays—in America and Israel. Her poems included here—"Prayers" and "Songs of Women"—are from her first book of poems. The three poems in "Prayers" show her early linking of nature and devo-

tion; the poem from the sequence "Songs of Women" is an example of her bold reinterpretations of traditional Judaism, here in the form of the *tkhines* (supplicatory prayers) that address the matriarchs, the biblical mothers of Israel.

By the beginning of the twentieth century, the influx of Russian immigrants created in England, as it did in the United States and Germany, a sense of urgency among native-born Jews to create ways of providing financial assistance and facilitating the immigrants' social, educational, and religious acculturation. One Jewish woman who was involved in all these efforts was Lillian Helen Montagu (1873–1963), a social worker, magistrate in the London juvenile courts, suffragist, writer, religious organizer, and spiritual leader. Raised in a wealthy Orthodox home, Lily Montagu came to believe that the religious revitalization of Judaism was essential. Only with this revitalization, she felt, could Judaism become a living faith for her and many other native-born British Jews and for the children of the Russian immigrants who for the most part were religiously apathetic. Equating true religion with personal religion and firmly believing that it was the attaching of oneself to God that truly made one religious, Montagu insisted that one need not study particular texts or observe particular precepts to find God. One need only open oneself up to God's abiding presence.

Convinced that the revitalization of Judaism necessitated the creation of a new Judaism, what she called a "Judaism of the future," Lily Montague began to articulate her own religious vision, a vision that owed much both to the ethical teachings of the Hebrew Bible and, given the paucity of her own Jewish education, to the primarily non-Jewish, British authors whose works she had read. From Thomas Carlyle Montagu came to define religious duty as a call to God's service, from George Eliot she learned that "one serves God best from serving others," from Matthew Arnold she came to understand God as a "Power not ourselves that makes for righteousness," and in Robert Browning she found a kindred spirit who shared her belief that "the best is yet to be." In the early 1890s, when Lily Montagu first met Claude Montefiore, Jewish scholar and proponent of what he identified as "liberal Judaism," she discovered that other Jews shared her religious vision. Moreover, she discovered that these Jews, like Montefiore in England and Rabbis Abraham Geiger and Samuel Holdheim in Germany, were calling this vision Liberal or Reform Judaism. Further convinced by their writings, not only that it was possible to view traditional Jewish observances as inessential and to maintain a primarily universal, Jewish religious vision, but also that this vision was indeed the Judaism of the future, Montagu set out to spread her ideas throughout Great Britain and eventually the world.[10]

In 1902, after enlisting the help of Claude Montefiore, who agreed to serve as president, she formed the Jewish Religious Union (JRU), an organization out of which the Liberal Jewish movement in England was created; and, in 1926, she formed an "international

JRU"—the World Union for Progressive Judaism. While her major work within the World Union was organizational (in fact, from 1926 to 1959, its offices were located in her home), she occasionally assumed a religious leadership role, for example, offering opening prayers at meetings and delivering addresses on religious themes. The document included here is a sermon preached by Lily Montagu at the Reform Temple in Berlin in August 1928. Delivered, in German, during the worship service held in conjunction with the World Union's first international conference, it may well have been the first sermon ever given by a woman (certainly the first ever given by a Jewish woman) from a pulpit in Germany. Focusing on the nature of personal religion and its connection to organized religious life, she reveals her understanding of God as imminent and transcendent, the "spirit of goodness," and the creator of all human beings who has given the Jewish people a particular mission, namely, to bear witness to the divine reality and to spread his moral teachings throughout the world.

For those Jewish women who believed, as Lily Montagu did, that women had a special contribution to make to the spiritual treasury of the world, the increase of religious apathy among all segments of the Jewish population, at least in the Western world, was looked on with particular alarm. As secularization increasingly followed the process of acculturation and the acceptance of Jews into modern society, a significant number of Jewish women attempted, with a new sense of urgency, to help stem the growing tide of religious indifference. Sarah Kussy, an American Jewish woman who lived in Newark, New Jersey, undertook such an attempt both through her writings and through her work as a member of the National Women's League, the women's auxiliary of the Conservative movement.

Included here is an article by Kussy that appeared in the *American Jewess* (the first Jewish journal published specifically for and written primarily by women, it appeared between 1895 and 1899 under the editorship of Rosa Sonneschein). Unlike Lily Montagu, Kussy did not think the creation of a new Judaism necessary to revitalize and sustain religious commitment. Rather, as her essay "Judaism and Its Ceremonies" makes clear, she believed that Judaism's traditional, home-based ceremonies and rituals not only had inspired "reverential and devotional feelings" among Jews in the past but were also capable of doing so in the present and future. As editor of the revised edition of *The Women's League Handbook and Guide,* published in 1947 (a portion of which is excerpted here), Kussy again emphasized the importance of stimulating and revitalizing "religious faith and the [traditional] Jewish way of life." Turning her attention to women, she wrote of achieving this aim by organizing synagogue sisterhoods that promoted educational programs for women and children that stressed "the observance of Sabbath and Festivals, of Dietary Laws and other traditional religious home ceremonies." [11]

Like Sarah Kussy, Grace Shohet (1904?–1954) viewed the work of synagogue sisterhoods as of vital significance to the future of

Jewish religious life in the United States. Included here is a brief prayer by Shohet composed for the dedication of the art museum that she helped establish at the Reform congregation to which she belonged in Brookline, Massachusetts. It reveals her love of God, belief in the centrality of moral values, and conviction that it was up to Jewish women to bring God's teachings to others.

Henrietta Szold (1860–1945) devoted most of her life to scholarly and communal pursuits that revealed not only great intellectual and organizational abilities but also her love of Judaism, concern for Jews, and dedication to the Jewish community. The eldest daughter of Sophia and Benjamin Szold, Henrietta was educated both by her father, a rabbi, and in local schools, graduating as valedictorian of her high school class. Subsequently, she taught (including a course in "Hebrew" theology at the then newly established Johns Hopkins University), wrote articles for Jewish periodicals, and organized night classes in English and American history for Eastern European Jewish immigrants in Baltimore, where she and her family lived. In 1893, she moved to Philadelphia and began working for the Jewish Publication Society, editing and translating several important works, including the multivolume *Jewish Encyclopedia*. Moving with her then-widowed mother to New York City in 1903, Szold attended classes at the Jewish Theological Seminary (becoming the first woman to do so) and served as editor for Professor Louis Ginzberg's *The Legends of the Jews*.

Apparently, it was Ginzberg's marriage to another woman that led Szold to take her first trip to Palestine in 1909.[12] Although she had long identified herself as a Zionist, her trip convinced her that, "if not Zionism, then nothing—then extinction for the Jew."[13] Becoming secretary of the Federation of American Zionists in 1910, she subsequently helped found and became president of Hadassah, an American Jewish women's Zionist organization that today is the largest Zionist organization in the world. Established in 1912, Hadassah engaged in a number of educational and medical endeavors (its first major purpose was to provide medical services for Jewish communities in Palestine, a goal that eventually led to the founding of Hadassah Hospital in Jerusalem).

From 1916, Szold devoted her life to Hadassah's many activities and, more broadly, to Zionist affairs. Moving to Palestine (where she lived, off and on, for the remainder of her life), she founded Histadrut Nashim Ibriot, the Society of Hebrew Women, in 1920 to gather statistics on the number of Jewish births in Palestine, the medical condition of mothers, and the Jewish infant mortality rate. Eleven years later, she was elected to the seven-member Vaad Leumi, the National Assembly (and governing body) of the Jews of Palestine, supervising all its health and educational services. Finally, in 1934, she helped establish and directed the Youth Aliyah movement to bring Jewish children out of Nazi-occupied Europe and to resettle them in Palestine. When Szold died in Jerusalem in 1945, she was still actively engaged in the work of Hadassah and adviser to both the Youth Aliyah and the Vaad Leumi.[14]

As the documents included here reveal, Henrietta Szold espoused a Jewish way of life that "was at once deeply religious, strongly ethical, and broadly tolerant." Her understanding of Judaism was shaped by the Conservative movement, yet she rejected much of traditional Jewish practice, choosing to follow "an independent course." [15] Thus, for example, in 1916, she insisted on reciting the *kaddish* (the mourner's prayer) for her mother as she previously had done for her father, even though the *kaddish* is traditionally recited only by men. Writing to her friend Haym Peretz in response to his offer to recite the *kaddish* for her (her letter is included in this volume), Szold maintained that it was important for her to say the prayer as a public manifestation of her wish "to assume the relation to the Jewish community" that her mother had "so that the chain of tradition remains unbroken." Just as he could do that for the generations of his family, she too needed to do that for her own, contrary to the "generally accepted" Jewish tradition.

The subsequent documents by Szold that are included here are letters revealing the extent to which the revitalization of Jewish life in Palestine became for her a moral and spiritual pursuit rooted in her understanding of what human beings, in general, needed for fulfillment and what Jews needed in order to re-create their national existence. In a letter written to her good friend Alice Seligsberg in December 1909, she describes standing in Jerusalem, looking around, seeing misery, poverty, and disease coupled with idealism, enthusiasm, and hope, and feeling that all her "powers had been called forth" to find a way of making the Zionist dream a reality. Writing to Mrs. Julius Rosenwald six years later, Szold made it clear that American Jews needed Zionism "as much as those Jews do who need a physical home." For her, then, Zionism held out to Jews the promise, not only of physical safety, but also of dignity and pride, with Palestine eventually serving as what Zionist thinker Ahad Ha'am identified as Jewry's spiritual center. Finally, in a letter written from Jerusalem in August 1938, she tells her sisters, Adele and Bertha, that it is no use telling her not to overwork and to be careful. All the Jews in Palestine, she writes, have to take chances, yet they do so willingly, believing that the physical and spiritual survival of the Jewish people depend on their efforts.

Anda Amir (1902–1980?) settled in the land of Israel prior to 1948 and the establishment of the Jewish state. Through several volumes of published poetry, she gave expression to a deep sense of spiritual identity, rooted in her identity as a Jew and as a woman. Sometimes using female biblical figures as a means of conveying a sense of connection to the Jewish past, Amir's poetry was for her a way of writing *midrash* (i.e., an explication of a biblical text forming part of a larger Jewish tradition of the interpretive retelling of Scripture).

According to Rabbi Sue Ann Wasserman, who wrote her rabbinic thesis on twentieth-century female Hebrew poets and to whom we are grateful both for the translated works we have included by Amir and for biographical information about her, Anda Amir was born in Galicia, into an assimilated family. Her father worked as an architect for the Austro-Hungarian government. Amir completed secondary school in Lvóv and at the age of eighteen published a book of verse in Polish, with her first poem the prayer of a Polish child for the liberation of his country. After studying at the universities of Leipzig and Lvóv and, in 1921, publishing another volume of verse in Polish, she emigrated to the land of Israel in 1923. Soon after, she began writing in Hebrew.

Amir's poem "Eve" is a *midrash* on the second story of creation (Gen. 2:4–3:24). Recognizing that the biblical text tells us nothing about Adam and Eve's sex life, yet envisioning Eve as an adolescent who, through the eating of the apple, begins to gain awareness of herself as a sexual being, Amir uses Scripture to reveal the intimate connection between sexuality and spirituality. She views sexuality as what James Nelson has called "both a symbol and a means of communication and communion." "It is who we are as bodyselves," Nelson writes, "who experience the emotional, cognitive, physical and spiritual need for intimate communion, both creaturely and divine." [16] The Eve of Amir's poem views pregnancy and childbirth as restrictive yet redemptive. The recognition that in her ability to give birth she is like the "swelling does" and "heavy she-wolves," as well as like the fruit-bearing tree from which she has eaten, provides Eve with a vision of transcendence, enabling her to connect with a power larger than herself. [17]

"Lot's Wife" can be seen as a *midrash* on Genesis 19. Here, Amir tries to answer Scripture's unanswered question, Why did Lot's wife look back at the city of Sodom despite her husband's warning not to do so? Amir tells us that her looking back was an act of self-assertion and defiance. Unlike her husband, she is both unable and unwilling to cut herself off from the past. Feeling both a personal and a communal/historical connection to the land and the people of Sodom (for, according to Amir, "women more than men, weave their lives out of the people, places, and everyday events that they experience"), [18] she consciously meets her destruction.

The selections included here from the diary that Hannah Senesh wrote between 1934 and 1944 reveal her firm resolve to help her coreligionists endangered by the growing Nazi occupation of Europe. Raised in a distinguished, highly acculturated Jewish family in Hungary, Senesh (1921–44) spent her early years attending a Protestant girls' school that had recently opened its doors to Jews and Catholics. [19] Although on graduation her teachers "positively assured" her mother that Hannah would be admitted to the university (presumably the University of Budapest) even though she was Jewish, Hannah had already decided to emigrate to Palestine and to study at the agricultural school in Nahalal. As she told her mother, "Perhaps I ought to be impressed that in view of graduating *summa cum laude,* and with a plethora of recommendations from teachers and friends, I can get into the university, while a Gentile who just barely squeezed through the exams can sail in! Besides, are they really incapable of understanding that I don't want to be just a student, that I have plans, dreams, ambitions, and that the road to their fulfilment would only be barred to me here?"[20]

As her diary entries make clear, her dreams included helping provide a haven and a revitalized homeland for the Jewish people. When her mother questioned her decision to attend an agricultural school instead of a university, Senesh replied, "There are already far too many intellectuals in Palestine; the great need is for workers who can help build the country. Who can do the work if not we, the youth?"[21] Setting out for Palestine in 1939, Senesh returned to Hungary in 1944 as part of a mission of thirty-two Jews from the land of Israel who had volunteered to parachute into Europe to try to save the remaining Jewish population. She was last seen on 9 June 1944, at the Hungarian border. She was captured, tortured, and shot as a prisoner of war in Budapest. After burial in the Martyr's Corner of a Budapest cemetery, her remains were moved to Israel, where, with full military honors, they were reinterred in a cemetery in the Judean Hills. Her tombstone, with its engraving of a parachute, is in a special section of the cemetery where six others who died on that mission are also buried.[22] Senesh's spirituality, as the documents included here show, was rooted in a love for the land of Israel and for the Jewish people and in a continual struggle to "believe and trust in God."

Poet Gertrud (Chodziesner) Kolmar (1894–1943) grew up in Berlin in an affluent, acculturated Jewish family and obtained a conventional education for girls of her social standing, attending a grammar school, a private high school for girls, and a women's home economics school situated on a farm near Leipzig. Early on, she developed an interest in ancient history, the Far East, and France, hanging pictures of Napóleon on the walls of her bedroom, and eventually trained to teach both English and French. During World War I, Kolmar was employed as an interpreter and censor in a prisoner of war compound in Berlin.

Having written poetry since childhood, she assumed the pen name Kolmar in 1917, when her father privately published a volume of her poems.[23] She continued to write after the war, publishing her poems both in magazines and separate volumes. Included among these was a series of seventy-five poems collectively titled "Image of Woman" or "Female Portrait," published between 1928 and 1937. Never marrying, Kolmar served as housekeeper and companion to her aging father. While she had the opportunity to leave Berlin in 1938 and, with her sister, seek asylum in Switzerland, she chose to stay in Berlin with their father, who either could not or would not leave.

As life for Jews in Germany became increasingly precarious, Kolmar began to develop a greater sense of Jewish self-identity. Soon forced by the Nazis to move into a poorer, overcrowded area assigned to Jews, she began to study and write poetry in Hebrew (unfortunately, none of her Hebrew verse was saved). In July 1941, she was consigned to a forced-labor factory in which all her fellow workers were Jews. Coming to know Jews of the working classes for the first time in her life, her affinity for them led her to recognize that "race is stronger than class," that is, that her Jewishness was a far deeper part of her being than she had previously imagined.[24] In September 1942, her father was sent to Theresienstadt. Five months later, Kolmar herself was deported to Auschwitz. She died soon after.[25]

In the following poems, Kolmar's images of womanhood, whether of a woman poet or a Jewish woman, are those of an innocent victim whose cries remain unheard. The victim of the Shoah (the Holocaust) is present in each of her bleak and powerful poems, either directly or implicitly. For her, a woman is a frightened victim asking for mercy, a vast, unexplored continent soon to sink, or an ancient, ruined, and abandoned castle. In the poem "We Jews," she declares her fierce love for her people and her anguish over their sufferings, which she has witnessed, as well as her militant devotion to the idea of Jewish restoration.

The works of Tehilla Lichtenstein (1893–1973) carry with them a different kind of urgency. Written in direct response to the drifting away of twentieth-century American Jews from Jewish religious life, her hundreds of sermons and addresses sought to instill within her listeners belief both in God as a source of happiness, goodness, and healing and in Judaism as a religious tradition capable of awakening within all Jews an awareness of this ever-abiding presence. Born in Jerusalem to Chava (Cohen) and Rabbi Chaim Hirschensohn, she came to the United States with her family in 1904 and grew up in Hoboken, New Jersey, where her father served as spiritual leader for a small Orthodox congregation. Along with her sisters, Tehilla received an exceptionally good secular education. She received a B.A. in classics from Hunter College and an M.A. in literature from Columbia University and had begun to study for her doctorate in English literature when she left school in 1920 to marry (Reform) Rabbi Morris Lichtenstein. Again, like her sisters, and indeed like most Orthodox women of her generation, the religious education that she received was minimal. Yet Lichtenstein saw herself as religious by nature and actively tried to cultivate a personal relationship with God. Largely influenced by the literary works that she read, she came to view true religion as what stimulated inner piety. To find God, she believed, one need not observe specific, externally imposed rituals, as Orthodoxy maintained. One simply needed to be optimistic, hopeful, "in love with humanity," and open to God's reality.

In 1938, following her husband's death, Tehilla Lichtenstein became spiritual leader of the Society of Jewish Science, the movement that Morris Lichtenstein, with Tehilla's assistance, had founded in 1922.[26] Serving in this capacity until shortly before her death in 1973, she attracted hundreds of Jews to the society as members and spread her religious message to thousands of other American Jews through regular radio broadcasts during the 1940s and the monthly publication of the *Jewish Interpreter,* in which many of her sermons were printed.

In "Believing Is *Seeing*," (included in this volume), Lichtenstein directly explores what she understood to be God's nature. While for her God is not an anthropomorphic being, neither is God an abstract force or power. Rather, God is that "fount of infinite goodness and creativeness *within* the universe and *within* [each individual]" whom we see in the form of those attributes we believe God to possess. Thus, if we see God as love, we may see God as father, if we see God as the source of gentle care, we may see God as shepherd, and so on. Her point is not that God in and of himself is really a father or a shepherd (for, ultimately, God is invisible and incomprehensible) but that the God *in whom we believe* is a being (i.e., a father, a shepherd) who is not just capable of entering into a personal relationship with human beings but who, in fact, does enter into a relationship with us as we affirmatively pray to and visualize what we are seeking.

Her focus on daily experience led Tehilla Lichtenstein to emphasize in her sermons relationships between human beings. To her, dwelling on these relationships both underscored her belief that as God's children we have a responsibility toward each other and reminded her listeners that human relationships awaken feelings of love that can serve as a model for the divine-human encounter. Thus, for example, while she continues to identify God as father in such sermons as "God in the Silence" (excerpted here), she also makes the analogy (based on the experiences of her own life as both daughter and mother) between running to one's mother and entering into the presence of the divine.[27]

Thirteen years after Tehilla Lichtenstein became spiritual leader of the Society of Jewish Science, Paula Ackerman (1893–1989) of Meridian, Mississippi, became the first woman to assume religious leadership of a mainstream American Jewish congregation. In early December 1950, following the death of her husband, William Ackerman, Sr., rabbi of the Reform congregation of Temple Beth Israel, the president and board members of the congregation entreated Paula to succeed her husband as their spiritual leader. Reluctant to do so since she was not a rabbi, she prayed to Gòd for guidance.[28] Two months later, having received what she took to be a number of religious signs indicating that she should say yes to their offer, she assumed leadership of the congregation.[29] For almost three years, she served as Beth Israel's religious leader. In this capacity, she led services, preached, taught, and conducted weddings, funerals, and even conversions.[30]

The sermon included here, "Reserve Resources," dated 2 February 1951, was the first that Paula Ackerman preached in her role as spiritual leader. While she apparently borrowed the title from a talk she had heard over the radio, the content of the sermon was her own.[31] Drawing on her experience, she sought to convey to her listeners ways in which each of them could find important resources of wisdom, strength, comfort, and courage in Judaism. Here, and in the brief address to her congregation that we have also included,

Ackerman's equation of Jewish religiosity with personal piety is quite clear. So too is her emphasis on ethics (or on what Reform Judaism identified as "ethical monotheism") and on her nonhierarchical understanding of religious leadership as that which gives one the privilege and responsibility of sharing his or her faith with others, demanding on the part of the leader honesty, sincerity, and a willingness to draw on the examples of his or her everyday life.

This section concludes with songs sung by Yemenite women in the land of Israel since 1948. Written in Arabic and passed down orally, the songs' precise authorship and date of composition are unknown. Like other Yemenite women's songs, the two included here focus on personal relationships. Alluding to the Yemenite custom of arranging marriages for young girls, the songs speak of familial relationships and relationships between women and men. These relationships serve as the organizing principle of a "personally-oriented religious world" interacting with rabbinic Judaism, creating what Susan Sered has labeled "domestic religion."[32] God plays a central role in each of the songs included here. Primarily envisioned as a source of help, God is the one to whom the frightened young girl turns for joy, protection, and comfort.

Notes

1. She was, however, actively interested in the work of the Hillel Foundation at the University of Illinois, where her husband served as a professor. For a fuller biographical treatment of Ray Frank, along with excerpts from many letters, sermons, and addresses, see Simon Litman, *Ray Frank Litman: A Memoir* (New York: American Jewish Historical Society, 1957).
2. Josephine Lazarus was, in fact, present at the 1893 Jewish Women's Congress and delivered a paper as part of the Parliament of Religions (although not before the Women's Congress).
3. Quoted in June Sochen, *Consecrate Every Day: The Public Lives of Jewish American Women, 1880–1980* (Albany: State University of New York Press, 1981), 53. For a more extensive treatment of the NCJW, see Ellen Sue Levi Elwell, "The Founding and Early Programs of the National Council of Jewish Women: Study and Practice as Jewish Women's Spiritual Expression" (Ph.D. diss., Indiana University, 1982); and Faith Rogow, "Gone to Another Meeting: A History of the National Council of Jewish Women" (Ph.D. diss., State University of New York at Binghamton, 1988).
4. Charlotte Baum, Paula Hyman, and Sonya Michel, *The Jewish Woman in America* (New York: New American Library, 1975), 48.
5. For a fuller, although uncritical, account of Kohut's life, see her autobiography, *My Portion* (New York: Thomas Seltzer, 1925).
6. Books by Richman include *Good Citizenship* (1908), *The Pupil's Arithmetic* (1911, 1917), and *Methods of Teaching Jewish Ethics* (1914).
7. Selma Berrol, "When Uptown Met Downtown: Julia Richman's Work in the Jewish Community of New York, 1880–1912," *American Jewish Historical Quarterly* 70 (September 1980–June 1981): 35–51.
8. In fact, she gave an address at the 1893 Jewish Women's Congress ("Mission Work among the Unenlightened Jews") and delivered subsequent papers (such as the one included in this volume) to local NCJW sections.
9. Among other works, she translated the diary of Glückl of Hameln, a distant relative of Pappenheim's, and the *Tzenah Urena*, the sixteenth-century "women's Bible," into German. For a fuller discussion of Pappenheim's life, see Marion Kaplan, "Bertha Pappenheim—Founder of German-Jewish Feminism," in *The*

Jewish Woman: New Perspectives, ed. Elizabeth Koltun (New York: Schocken, 1976), 149–163, and *The Jewish Feminist Movement in Germany: The Campaigns of the Jüdischer Frauenbund, 1904–1938* (Westport, Conn.: Greenwood, 1979).

10. For a fuller discussion of Lily Montagu's understanding of spirituality and her work as a religious organizer and leader, see Ellen M. Umansky, *From Vision to Vocation: Lily H. Montagu and the Advancement of Liberal Judaism* (Lewiston, N.Y.: Edwin Mellen, 1983); and Ellen M. Umansky, ed., *Lily Montagu: Sermons, Letters, Addresses and Prayers* (Lewiston, N.Y.: Edwin Mellen, 1985).

11. As Kussy explains in her preface, the original handbook was "prepared as a labor of love by Deborah M. Melamed in 1924." Kussy then revised and enlarged the handbook and prepared a new edition in 1939. In the preface to the 1947 edition, she expressed the hope that "the material contained in this volume and the suggestions for its use will be of service to all women's groups actively interested in the future of Judaism in America."

12. See Jonathan Sarna, "Henrietta Szold," in *The Encyclopedia of Religion* (New York: Macmillan, 1987), 14:230.

13. Henrietta Szold to Elvira N. Solis, Milan, 12 December 1909 (in Marvin Lowenthal, *Henrietta Szold: Her Life and Letters* [New York: Viking, 1942], 67).

14. A number of full-length studies of Szold's life have been undertaken. These include Alexandra Lee Levin's *The Szolds of Lombard Street: A Baltimore Family, 1859–1909* (Philadelphia: Jewish Publication Society, 1960), which focuses on her early life; Irving Fineman's *Woman of Valor: The Life of Henrietta Szold, 1860–1945* (New York: Simon & Schuster, 1961); and Joan Dash's *Summoned to Jerusalem: The Life of Henrietta Szold* (New York: Harper & Row, 1979).

15. Sarna, "Henrietta Szold," 230.

16. James Nelson, *Between Two Gardens: Reflections on Sexuality and Religious Experience* (New York: Pilgrim, 1983), 6.

17. See Judith Plaskow, *Standing Again at Sinai: Judaism from a Feminist Perspective* (San Francisco: Harper & Row, 1990), 197, who makes this connection between sexuality and spirituality clear.

18. Sue Ann Wasserman, "Women's Voices through the Past and Present" (rabbinic thesis, Hebrew Union College–Jewish Institute of Religion, New York, 1987), 85.

19. Her father was a successful newspaper columnist and playwright who, according to Catherine Senesh, Hannah's mother, "attempted to provide [his] children with as many rich and happy memories as possible. There were all sorts of excursions, visits to the amusement park and the delightful Budapest Zoo, and innumerable 'story-telling' afternoons arranged in our home for the entertainment of the children and their friends" (Catherine Senesh, "Memories of Hannah's Childhood," in *Hannah Senesh: Her Life and Diary,* translated by Marta Cohn, with an introduction by Abba Eban [New York: Schocken, 1973], 5–6).

20. Ibid., 10.

21. Ibid., 11.

22. See Reuven Dâfne, "The Last Border," in *Hannah Senesh,* 170ff.

23. According to Henry Smith (introduction to *Dark Soliloquy: The Selected Poems of Gertrud Kolmar* [New York: Seabury, 1975], 3), "The Chodziesners were [originally] a family of petty tradesmen from the Prussian provinces east of the Oder, and must once have lived in the Polish town of Chodziez, or Kolmar, as it was called under German rule."

24. Ibid., 49.

25. Although, according to Henry Smith, her time of death (and presumably how she died) is unknown (ibid, 51).

26. For a fuller description of Jewish Science, see Ellen Umansky's introductory essay, "Piety, Persuasion, and Friendship: A History of Jewish Women's Spirituality," in this volume. For a more detailed analysis of the origins and development of Jewish Science, including Tehilla Lichtenstein's role as religious leader, see Ellen M. Umansky, *From Christian Science to Jewish Science: Spiritual Healing and American Jews* (New York: Oxford University Press, forthcoming).

27. In other sermons, such as "Corsage for Mother" (American Jewish Archives, MS Coll. no. 22 box 1, folder 6), she maintained that "God has given each one of us, whether blessed by the stimulus of poverty or blessed by the ease of affluence, the same equalizing gift—our mother's love, which is, on this earth, the nearest thing, the closest thing, to the love that God bears for mankind. Mother's love is of the same substance, it is of the same divine fabric, and expresses itself in the same boundless way."

28. Raised in a Reform congregation in Pensacola, Florida, Ackerman received a fairly good religious education. She attended religious school through confirmation at the congregation to which her family belonged (later becoming a teacher there) and, through arrangements made by her father, studied Hebrew privately.

29. For her, the most powerful sign had to do with the cessation of her menstrual period. She was apparently having menstrual pains, and her doctor advised her to have a hysterectomy, but she was reluctant to do so. It was during this time that she was praying to God daily for guidance as to whether she should accept the congregation's offer. Suddenly, her period stopped, showing no indication of reappearing; consequently, she did not need the hysterectomy. "Now don't you think the Lord was telling me something?" she said (conversation with Ellen M. Umansky—she repeated this story to me several times). From 1983 to 1988, I spent time with Paula Ackerman regularly, occasionally conducting formal interviews, first in Atlanta, then in Thomaston, Georgia, where she spent the last years of her life.

30. While the congregation wanted her to stay longer, she told me that she simply found it "too depressing" to bury her friends. From the end of 1953 through 1961, she lived in "hectic retirement" (although she continued to lecture widely). In 1962, she agreed to serve briefly as spiritual leader of Temple Beth-El in Pensacola, Florida, the congregation to which she had belonged as a girl. She then went back into retirement, living in Meridian, Pensacola, and, finally, in Atlanta and Thomaston, Georgia, so as to be near her son, Dr. William Ackerman, Jr. For further information on Paula Ackerman, see Ellen M. Umansky, "Reform's Lost Woman Rabbi: An Interview with Paula Ackerman," *Genesis* 2 17, no. 3 (June/July 1986):18–20.

31. The radio talk "Reserve Resources" was by (Mormon) Richard L. Evans on the nationally broadcast program "The Spoken Word," Sunday, 17 December 1950. A copy of Evans's talk is included among Paula Ackerman's papers (private collection, Dr. William Ackerman, Jr.).

32. S[usan] Sered, "The Domestication of Religion: The Spiritual Guardianship of Elderly Jewish Women," *Man* 23 (1988): 509. Ellen M. Umansky is grateful to Penina Adelman for bringing this excellent article to her attention.

FROM THE MINUTE BOOK OF TEMPLE ISRAEL SISTERHOOD

Organized 1891, New York City

ARTICLE II

The object of the Society shall be

First to assist the deserving poor among the Israelites of Harlem and to do such other philanthropic work as may be practicable

Second to create and foster greater sociability among members of the congregation

Third to assist and encourage such congregational work as shall tend to the development and advancement of the congregation.

ARTICLE VII

It was decided that the present work of the Sisterhood should be mainly to attend to the immediate wants of those poor families with whom we may come in contact. . . . The names and addresses of (the committee in charge of this) will be placed on a bulletin in the Temple, and all cases of need will be reported to one of the . . . heads of committee who will investigate and report at the next meeting.

(In emergency cases the committee is empowered to dispense the amount of $5. Their district will be above 125th street. They will get further instructions from the United Hebrew Charities.)

FROM THE MINUTES OF THE SOCIETY ESRATH NASHIM, PHILADELPHIA

June 1891

Whereas, Almighty God has called from our midst a dear friend and a generous donor to the deserving poor of Philadelphia, the Society Esrath Nashim (Helping Women) having ever experienced the kindly assistance and good wishes of

Miss Ellen Phillips

during her life time, hereby wish to contribute their mite toward perpetuating her memory and honoring those virtues, which in her were the embodiment of love and righteousness.

Resolved—That the Society deplore the death of Miss Ellen Phillips and extend their sympathy to her Sister and relatives in their sorrow.

Resolved—That the Society Esrath Nashim (Helping Women) being about to enlarge its sphere of usefulness as the

Jewish Maternity Association,

honor the memory of this noble Jewess by naming the first bed to be established in the Jewish Maternity Home, founded under the auspices of the Association at 534 Spruce St. Philadelphia,

The Ellen Phillips Bed:

Resolved—That inasmuch as her character was outwardly modest and retiring, so shall the exterior of the Home be unostentatious; as her life was full of beauty and imbued with charity toward all humanity, so shall the Home be fitted with every appliance for the relief and sustanance [sic] of its beneficiaries; and, as she was truly a pious and observing Jewess, so may we conduct our house, in the observance of those laws laid down for the benefit and blessing of all Israel.

Resolved—That a copy of these resolutions be sent to Miss Emily Phillips, and published in the Jewish Exponent.

There being no further business,

The meeting adjourned.

Belle Cohn
Sec'y.

RAY FRANK,
United States

Yom Kippur sermon,
Spokane Falls,
Washington (1890)

My position this evening is a novel one. From time immemorial the Jewish woman has remained in the background, quite content to let the fathers and brothers be the principals in a picture wherein she shone only by a reflected light. And it is well that it has been so; for while she has let the strong ones do battle for her throughout centuries of darkness and opposition, she has gathered strength and courage to come forward in an age of progressive enlightenment to battle for herself if necessary, or prove by being a noble helpmeet how truly she appreciates the love which has shielded her in the past.

I can scarcely tell you how much I feel the honor you have this evening conferred upon me by asking me to address you. For a woman to be asked at any time to give council to my people would be a mark of esteem; but on this night of nights, on Yom Kippur eve, to be requested to talk to you, to advise you, to think that I am tonight the one Jewish woman in the world, may be the first since the time of the prophets to be called to speak to such an audience as I now see before me, is indeed a great honor, an event in my life which I can never forget. . . . I have been requested to speak to you concerning the formation of a permanent congregation. I was informed that the number of Hebrews and their financial standing was sufficient to warrant an established congregation. . . . Then, I said, how is it you're content to go on with having neither schule [*synagogue*] nor a Sabbath school? . . . I was answered that such a difference of opinion existed among you, so many were prejudiced against reform, the remainder stubborn for orthodoxy . . . think of it, ye Israelites, the chosen of the earth, so divided as to how you will worship Jehovah that you forget to worship at all! You who have received divine protection through centuries of danger and oppression, you whom the prophets say are to survive for the grandest destiny of man, you to whom has been vouchsafed every blessing—because you do not agree as to how you will do this or that, how you will say "thank you Almighty," therefore you do not say it at all.

O, you intend saying it all in good time! There may be repentance at the eleventh hour, but who can say which hour may not be the eleventh one? This is the time for action—right now, and our solemn Yom Kippur is right now of our existence. . . . Drop all dissention about whether you should take off your hats during the service and other unimportant ceremonials and join hands in one glorious cause. . . . It is not necessary to build a magnificent synagogue at once; that can be done in time. The grandest temples we have ever had or the world has even known were those which had the blue sky for a roof, and the grandest psalms ever sung were those rendered under the blue vaults of heaven. . . .

In the name of all we Hebrews hold dear . . . be patient with one another. Drop all personal feelings in the matter, and meet each other half way over your differences; give each other a hearty handshake for the sake of the cause, and I prophesy that Heaven will crown your efforts with peace and prosperity. From tonight resolve to do something.

Prayer at the Jewish Women's Congress (1893)

Almighty God, Creator and Ruler of the universe, through Whose justice and mercy this first convention of Jewish women has been permitted to assemble, accept our thanks, and hearken, O Lord, to our prayer.

In times past, when storms of cruel persecution drove us toward the reefs of adversity, seemingly overwhelmed by misfortune, we had faith in Thee and Thy works, ever trusting and believing that Thou ordainest all things well. Because of this faith, we feel that Thou hast, in the course of events, caused this glorious congress to convene, that it may give expression to that which shall spread broadcast a knowledge of Thee and Thy deeds.

Grant, then, Thy blessing upon those assembled, and upon the object of their meeting. May the peculiar circumstances, which have brought together, under one roof, both Catholic and Jew, who, for centuries, have been seeking to serve Thee, though in different ways, be a promise of future peace. Grant, we beseech Thee, that this convention may be productive of that which is in accordance with Thy will.

Bless, O Lord, this our country and the President thereof, and all the people of the land. May love and peace be the heritage of men, to remain with them forever. *Amen.*

Woman in the Synagogue (1893)

Duality manifests itself in all things, but in nothing is this two-foldness more plainly seen than in woman's nature.

The weaker sex physically, it is the stronger spiritually, it having been said that religion were impossible without woman. And yet the freedom of the human soul has been apparently effected by man. I say apparently effected, for experience has demonstrated, and history records, that one element possessed by woman has made her the great moral, the great motif force of the world, though she be, as all great forces are, a silent force.

It may be true that sin came into the world because of the disobedience of the first woman, but woman has long since atoned for it by her loving faith, her blind trust in the Unknown. Down through the ages, traditional and historical, she has come to us the symbol of faith and freedom, of loyalty and love.

From the beginning, she sought knowledge; perceive, it does not say wisdom, but knowledge; and this was at the expense of an Eden. She lost Eden, but she gained that wisdom which has made sure of man's immortality.

She walked upon thorns, she bled; but so sincerely repentant was she, so firmly rooted had become her faith in the Almighty, that no amount of suffering, no change of time and circumstance, could destroy it. With repentance something had sprung up, and blossomed in her being, an imperishable flower, beautiful, fragrant, making the world bright and sweet.

This flower twined itself round man, its odors refreshed and strengthened him; its essence healed him when wounded, and nerved him on to gallant and noble deeds. It is the breath of life in him, and he must needs be careful of its clinging stems, its tender leaves, for they are rooted in a woman's heart.

In mother, wife, sister, sweetheart, lies the most precious part of man. In them he sees perpetual reminders of the death-sin, guarantees of immortality. Think, woman, what your existence means to man; dwell well on your responsibility; and now let us turn to that part of time called the past, more particularly biblical days. The religious life of the early Israelites is so closely interwoven with their domestic and political life, that it cannot be separated and treated alone. Amidst all kind of tribal and national strife, the search for knowledge of Javeh went on in so even a way, so indifferent to men and things, as no other investigation has done. The soul of mankind could not be quieted concerning this matter, and religion from its very nature evolved itself.

That this was, in its entirety, due to no one people is just as true as that it was due to no one sex.

To the Israelite, because of his sensitive, superior nature, was revealed that first great truth of "I am the Lord thy God," and to them, throughout the generations, was given the command to spread his Truth. But when the Lord said to Moses, "And ye shall be unto Me a nation of priests and a holy nation," the message was not to one sex; and that the Israelites did not so consider it, is proved by the number of women who were acknowledged prophets, and who exercised great influence on their time and on posterity.

The Talmud speaks of seven prophetesses: Sarah, Miriam, Deborah, Hannah, Abigail, Huldah and Esther. Ruth not being mentioned in this list, we infer that she was regarded simply as a religious teacher. Except in the Talmud, Sarah is not mentioned as possessing the inspirational power, which made the prophets of old; yet, there is that chronicled of her which gives rise to the assumption that, for a time at least, she was the greatest of them all. For in Genesis xxi. 12 is recorded the only instance of the Lord's especially commanding one of His favorites to listen carefully to a woman: "In all that Sarah may say unto thee, hearken unto her voice."

Evidently, the Almighty deemed a woman capable both of understanding and advising. . . .

. . . However, the ancient Jewish woman was, above all, wife and mother, and as such she was a religious teacher, and closely associated with what might be called the temple-worship of those days. The life of the woman of patriarchal times was clean and elevating, there was nothing slavish about it; and when one considers that the Jewish Law permitted polygamy, and that even with the debasing influences of harem life instituted by Solomon, the Jews became a monogamous people, one can understand the extraordinary influence of the Jewish woman to whom this important fact is due.

"One woman, a good one, is the light of a man's existence," sang an inspired sage.

Women of other nations soon learned to contrast the life of the Jewish woman with their own, and the first converts to Judaism were women from the neighboring idolatrous tribes. The emotional nature of Jewish women made them fit instruments to celebrate the joys of heaven and earth, and the finest things in our sacred literature are believed by many critics to have come spontaneously from our women's hearts and tongues.

If the woman of apocryphal times does not always appear sharply outlined in her work, it is, as we have said, owing to the deep workings of the wife and mother principle, which was striving to manifest itself as the axis of woman's world. Slowly, unevenly, events moved round, and in the Græco-Roman period we find the capricious jolts and jars lessening, until in medieval times the Jewish wife represents all that is pure and noble in womanhood. . . .

The position of the medieval woman differed from that of her ancient sister. Forced by circumstances at times to become a leader, her personality no longer merged itself in that of her husband, but ran parallel with his. Tribal wars for political supremacy did not now agitate the people, for existence had, in most cases, become an individual struggle. The princes of Judah were dethroned, their lands, the possession of strangers; yet the law lived, better understood and more sacredly guarded than ever. That this was owing, in the greatest degree, to the women is shown by the numbers mentioned in the Talmud as learned mothers and teachers. The Jews were stripped of many precious things by their oppressors, ofttimes their relentless persecutors, yet the Torah held such consolations that the family-home became to the Jew the most beautiful, the most sacred thing in the world. Of the love of a pure wife and reverent, obedient children, nothing could rob him, and he was, indeed, blessed beyond all that sought to harm him. The prophecy of Lemuel's mother had been faithfully realized; and as we look through the mist of centuries, the sunlight clears grayness, and we read: "Many daughters have done virtuously; but thou excellest them all."

True help-mate was the mediæval woman, combining with greatest intelligence, stern purpose and the softest maternal qualities.

During the period of happiness permitted them by Moorish and Spanish rule, our women rose to eminence intellectually and socially. But note how the learning always leaned toward the elevation of the home. That part of the Bible which concerned the home life became their especial study, and as practical preachers of religion, they have never been excelled, for they practiced what they preached.

Among the women of early mediæval times, Ima Shalom, Rachel and Beruria are representative. The father of Ima was president of the Sanhedrin, and a descendant of Hillel. Her husband, the most noted rabbi of his day, found in her an intellectual equal, and many were the knotty questions submitted to her judgment. Had it not been for the self-sacrificing and deeply religious nature of Rachel Sabua, history would scarcely have had an Akiba, while Beruria, wife of Rabbi Meïr, who lived about 100 A.D., was of such powerful intellect that she became noted throughout the land. All that she said concerning disputed points of the Halacha received the attention of her contemporaries. Poetry and prose testify to her worth.

Graetz mentions Bellet, the daughter of Menachem, who lived in Orleans in the year 1050 A.D., as one who was talmudically learned, and who taught the women of her town their religious duties. Hannah, sister of Rabbi Jacob Tam, of Orleans, and a whole circle of learned women in the family of Rashi, of whom may be mentioned Rachel, his daughter, and Anna and Miriam, his granddaughters, were highly educated, and acted as teachers of religion. They paid particular attention to instructing women regarding culinary matters, on which Mosaism laid the greatest stress.

Zunz calls the mother of the chief rabbi of France, Mattathias Ben Joseph Provenci, and wife of Rabbi Joseph Ben Jochanan, "well nigh a lady rabbi," and accords her great praise for her original and sensible interpretation of the dietary laws.

Rabbi Samuel ben Hallevi, who flourished in Bagdad in the year 1200, had a daughter, Bath Hallevi, who delivered in public biblical lectures to men. She was screened from her audience by sitting in a kind of box whose windows had in them panes of opaque glass.

A rabbinical college had for its principal Miriam Shapira, and her lectures to the students are said to have compared favorably with those of her contemporaries. Dolce, wife of Rabbi Eleazer ben Jehudah Rokeach, of Worms, a remarkably learned woman, lived a saintly life, preaching to the women their duties. She with her two children died the death of a martyr, being slain by the Knights of Malta, at Erfurt, in 1214.

In the Hebrew encyclopædia compiled by Dr. Goldman and his associates, and edited in Warsaw in 1818, is found an account of a remarkable woman, Donna Benvenida Abarbanel. Her husband was treasurer of the king of Naples, and into her charge the prime minister of Naples gave the education of his daughter, the princess Leonora. The intelligence and righteousness of Donna Benvenida were known throughout the land, and her association with the princess continued long after the latter's marriage. It is said that her royal charge esteemed her as a mother, and that in all her work this good Jewess never forgot her creed and her people.

Inasmuch as all appertaining to Judaism belongs to the temple, so the connection of this great woman with the synagogue is not to be doubted.

In about 1532, the priests who presided over the Inquisition petitioned the king to drive out the remnant of Jews from southern Italy. The petition was granted. But Donna Benvenida, with great diplomacy, succeeded through the princess in having the edict revoked. From various writings by the clever men of that day, one learns that the highest praise was given this woman. . . .

. . . In the early part of the eighteenth century, Krendel Steinhardt, a member of a gifted family of rabbis, obtained distinction for her knowledge of the festival prayers, the Machsor, and for cleverly interpreting the Midrash. She was known as the "Rebbezin." Sarah Oppenheimer, daughter of the chief rabbi of Prague, wrote a Meghilla, a scroll of the book of Esther, while Sprenza Kempler, blessed with beauty, knowledge and piety, could quote the Mishna from memory. Bienvineda, wife of Rabbi Mordecai, of Padua, was of such rare intelligence that she held disputations on the Talmud and the Mishna with some of the greatest scholars of her day.

The list is a long one, and each name reflects intelligence and piety. But enough has been given to disprove all doubts as to the Jewish woman's capability in religious matters, both as pupil and instructor. If to the men of these times be accorded credit for having performed their duties well, if as scholars, as expounders of the Law, they live in fame, what shall we say of the women who, under the most adverse circumstances, rose to eminence in this same field of labor? With one or two exceptions, they were all wives and mothers, most of them wives of rabbis, and in the discharge of their duties no one thing was done at the expense of another.

Intellectually they were the compeers of their husbands; practically, they excelled them. They built synagogues, controlled colleges, and stipended students. All in all, they have in the past earned the right to the pulpit, even as nature created their sensitive beings to act as its finest interpreter.

Jewish woman had earned the right to the pulpit, though she never formally asked it of the people, but that they would not have wholly opposed it, may be inferred from a romance of Bernstein's, "Voegele, der Maggid," probably founded on facts.

Voegele was an itinerant preacher, and that she combined the lovable qualities of the woman with her chosen work is shown by the fervent words of the hero who says to her, "Your hand makes the *Bethhamedrash* light." To our times and to our country in particular, the Jewish woman is indebted for many changes in her relation to the synagogue, and this progress is mainly due to one man, whose decided stand as a liberalist, in all matters concerning woman and her work, earns our hearty thanks. I refer to our revered rabbi, Dr. Isaac Mayer Wise, of Cincinnati.

With added privileges and numberless innovations, let us see what is the religious status of the Jewish woman of to-day. Compare her with the woman of the Apocrypha we will not, for it would be unjust to both. The one was the result of a great spiritual revelation and chaotic material circumstances pressing against and whirling round each other, leaving as a resultant the keen-visioned, practical woman of the Middle Ages, one whose knowledge was of men, and whose wisdom was of God. Calamitous as were the days, our mothers rose to meet them, each time victorious. Their children received, as a heritage, patience, courage, fidelity, reverence, honest, God-fearing souls, the richest treasures of men. What matter how the winds of fortune blew, the Jew was secure from total shipwreck. He carried as a talisman the instructions of his mother. When persecution drove him from shore to shore, he journeyed across unknown seas, and finding a new Canaan cried, "Hear, O Israel, the Lord our God, the Lord is one!" and so dedicated a new home.

Centuries have passed; the wilderness is the pride of the world, for it is all a land of freedom, of homes; and the Jew, we find him so grateful that he has well-nigh forgotten to what he owes his salvation. He has forgotten, else how explain the empty temples, the lack of religious enthusiasm, lack of reverence of children for parents, lack of that sacred home life which has made us an honored place in history? That our women have not made of themselves Dinah Morrises and "Voegele der Maggids" we can forgive, but that we have removed so many of the ancient landmarks which our fathers established, can we forgive ourselves for that?

That we have not possessed ourselves of the wisdom of her who built her own house can hardly be pardoned us, for what can replace the priceless love which has bound the members of the Jewish family to each other and to their God? Learning is not wisdom. Innovation is not progress, and to be identical with man is not the ideal of womanhood. Some things and privileges belong to him by nature; to these, true woman does not aspire; but every woman should aspire to make of her home a temple, of herself a high priestess, of her children disciples, then will she best occupy the pulpit, and her work run parallel with man's. She may be ordained rabbi or be the president of a congregation—she is entirely able to fill both offices—but her noblest work will be at home, her highest ideal, a home. Our women, living in a century and in a country which gives them every opportunity to improve, are not making the most of themselves, and to the stranger, the non-Jew, who views us critically, we are not entirely an improvement upon our mothers of old. We may dress with better taste, we may know more *ologies,* we may discuss high art, but we no longer offer up such reverent homage to the Almighty, as that which was given in times of direst distress and persecution, and which yielded so rich a harvest as an America, in which to enjoy life and liberty to the utmost. How is this liberty enjoyed? Go to the synagogue on Friday night; where are the people? Our men cannot attend, keen business competition will not permit them. Where are our women? Keener indulgence in pleasures will not permit them. Where are the children? Keenest parental examples of grasping gain and material desires will not permit them, and so the synagogue is deserted. Go there on a Saturday, the day of rest, of holy convocation. Where are the people? Our men are at their shops, our women doing the shopping, calling, or at the theatre; *every one and everything can be attended to but God. For Him they have no time.* With whom lies the blame? Where are the wise mothers of Israel to-day? As we sow, so we must reap. Costly temples with excuses for congregations will not do, friends. Better the old tent for a dwelling, the trees and skies for synagogues, and reverent, God-fearing men and women, than our present poor apology for religious worship.

The world calls the nineteenth century Jew materialistic, the Jew denies it, but denial is not refutation.

It is time we stopped calling ourselves chosen, it is time we stopped living upon our past, time we prove we have been chosen a nation of priests by fulfilling His law. Many an one has been chosen for some noble mission who never attempted its completion, and it would be illogical to credit such an one with any great merit. That we are now in the position of backsliders is owing to us women.

Where are the Hannahs who cry as she of old, "For this lad did I pray; and the Lord hath granted me my petition which I asked of Him. Therefore also have I lent Him for my part to the Lord; all the days that have been assigned to him shall he be lent to the Lord."

Sisters, our work in and for the synagogue lies in bringing to the Temple the Samuels to fulfil the Law. As mothers in Israel I appeal to you to first make of our homes temples, to rear each child a priest by teaching him to be true to himself.

If the synagogues are then deserted, let it be because the homes are filled, then we will be a nation of priests; edifices of worship will be everywhere. What matter whether we women are ordained rabbis or not? We are capable of fulfilling the office, and the best way to prove it is to convert ourselves and our families into reverent beings. To simply be ordained priest is not enough, and the awful punishment which befell Eli is the best illustration of this. Nothing can replace the duty of the mother in the home. *Nothing can replace the reverence of children, and the children are yours to do as ye will with them.*

Mothers, ye can restore Israel's glory, can fulfil the prophecy by bringing the man-child, strong love of the Eternal, to his Maker.

MARY M. COHEN,
United States

The Influence of the Jewish Religion in the Home (1893)

. . . I believe sincerely that the influence of the Jewish religion upon the home is a truth so deeply established that all liberal thinkers have but one opinion about it. But there are, in this world, many thinkers not yet able to think liberally, that is, they have been trained in a certain groove of thought, and their minds remain, according to their education, their environments, their beliefs. It sometimes happens, even among Christians of the kindliest nature and the warmest sympathies, that they have never come in direct contact with families of so different a creed as that upheld by the Hebrews. It has been the experience of the writer, over and over again, that members of the popular religion have observed, "We have never known any Hebrews. What are their views? What are their observances? How does their religion affect the home life? Tell us all that you can."

It is largely with reference to this absence of knowledge of the way in which the Jewish religion enters into the home life that I am urged to deal with the theme before this religious congress of the Columbian exposition.

There is very little doubt that the idea with which the Jewish religion was planned was to so engraft it upon the home life that the two should be inseparably joined. The observances of the faith are so entwined with the every-day atmosphere of the home as to make the Jewish religion and the family life one, a bond in sanctity. In this sense the synagogue is the home, and the home the synagogue. I mean that the intelligent and devout Hebrew parent is the priest or priestess of the family alter. There is no need, if there is a desire to worship the God of Israel, to visit the sanctuary; it is always right and appropriate to enter the House of God, but it is never indispensable for the performance of religious service. . . .

The greatest benefit derived from this close connection between the religion and life is the fact that the religion thus became an intensely practical one, and yet lost nothing of its inspired ideality. It was not possible for the Jew to forget his allegiance to Judaism. In the morning when he arose, the binding of the phylacteries turned his thoughts heavenward; before partaking of food, the immersion of the hands in cold water truly reminded him that "cleanliness is next to godliness." At the close of the meal, the Hebrew grace expressed his gratitude to the eternal Father for his bounties. In the daily events, in the transaction of business, either within or without the home, the influence of the religion was very seldom absent. . . .

The influence of the religion in regard to dietary laws is perhaps one of the most marked in close connection with the home routine. In addition to the various observances commanded in the Bible, tradition and the Rabbis have made it customary for Hebrews to partake of special kinds of food on certain festivals; we see this in the use of white stewed fish for the Passover, in the additional decoration of the table during Pentecost, in the serving of apples and new honey on the New Year. The praises of fried fish as prepared by Hebrews have been eloquently set forth, but where is the writer who has done justice to the glories of the white stewed fish as it appears on the Passover table? Golden balls, of delicate flavor, surmounting slices of the whitest halibut; cayenne peppers, with circles of lemon, adding brilliant color and spicy taste to the compound; over all the yellow sauce, almost jelly-like in consistence. Those who have spoken of Judaism as a "kitchen religion" lose sight of the fact that spirit and body are equally in need of nourishment, and that to closely associate the material and the religious is to dignify the one without injuring the other.

There are many other special dishes transmitted to us by tradition for minor festivals. These little customs serve to bind the religious and the domestic life very closely together, and who can doubt it that sees the blessing given by parents to children on the Sabbath eve, or witnesses the solemnity of the Kiddish, the wine which celebrates the approach of the bride, the Jewish Sabbath. I can never see, in the sometimes punctilious care with which some Hebrew women prepare their homes for the religious festivals, the ground for annoyance or ridicule which it seems to furnish to many critics; to me it presents a beautiful union between the religion and the home. The Jewish faith is not to be worn as a cloak on the Sabbath or the festival in the synagogue, and then to be cast aside before entering the portals of every-day existence; it may be carried as a veil, but through it should be seen, still showing brightly, the purity of the domestic altar.

The Jewish wife and mother, as a rule, is faithful to her husband and children. Her religion teaches her to fulfil every duty to these near and dear ones, and in addition, to exercise as generous a hospitality as her means will permit. From the time when Sarah entertained the angels until to-day, the chain of kindly feeling toward the traveler or the visitor has never been broken; in fact, the well-to-do Hebrew woman holds it a privilege to share the fruits of the earth with any one less favored, and knows that in so doing she is only obeying a divine behest: "And thou shalt rejoice with every good thing which the Lord thy God hath given unto thee, and unto thy house, thou, with the Levite, and the stranger that is in the midst of thee."

The influence of the Jewish religion upon the home is of great importance in determining exactly the niche which the inmates are to occupy in the history of moral forces affecting other peoples. For instance, inasmuch as the Hebrew woman *is* a Hebrew woman, just so powerful are her character and example. There are plenty of merely cosmopolitan women, open to the guidance of every creed or no creed, as shifting fancy may dictate; such women may be lovely and excellent in many ways, but they will scarcely command the admitting respect, the deep sympathy, the earnest fellowship which a loyal Hebrew woman receives in overflowing measure from the world at large. Her chief value to the people of other beliefs is that she is a worthy daughter of Israel, in the home first, and then everywhere. Husband and children in the Jewish home show to the wife and mother a profound affection, and hold her in the greatest honor. Jewish men are almost invariably domestic, valuing their homes as the union of material and spiritual good.

The influence of the Jewish religion in the home may well be treasured as the keystone to the lasting happiness and usefulness of all the nations of the earth.

JOSEPHINE LAZARUS,
United States

Judaism, Old and New (1894)

. . . We stand upon the threshold of we know not what,—unable to go backward, not daring to go forward. The future beckons us on with promise of wider, freer life, unchecked growth and scope, broad, unhampered human and spiritual fellowship. The past holds us with invincible weight. "Deny me, and you deny yourself," it says; "your very life, all that makes you what you are." The blood of martyrs seems to cry to us: "Would you be faithless, then, to us, and have we died in vain?"

And whence come these questionings, this doubt and division of soul? Surely from lack of faith and vision, rather than from true loyalty and conviction. Not in vain will be that martyrdom when it has taught us to be faithful as those martyrs were and when we have, as they had, a faith of our own to be true to; when we are ready to trust and follow it wherever it may lead, to deny self and offer up life for its sake. But we have lost the faith, not merely in the narrow historic sense, not alone in allegiance to the past, in outward conformity to external rites and inherited usage, but as an inward, quickening power, a source of our spiritual life and action, a vision of something that makes life holy, beautiful, and blessed, whatever martyrdom we may be called upon to endure, whatever sacrifice we may be called upon to make.

And when we read it aright, the story of our people means, above all else this faith, a perfect trust and confidence in the leading and purpose of the Most High, whatever that leading and purpose may be, and whether or not we understand it. . . .

Whether or not we have the prophetic vision, whether or not we see and understand the promise beyond, we can be faithful still, now that we find ourselves on the verge of a larger deliverance than ever before. They are the faithless who would lag behind.

. . . It is the task of Judaism to be up and doing, alert and ready to receive, not passively accepting what has been handed down, nor yet watching the smouldering fires of a lingering sacrifice. Let us take our Judaism fearlessly out into the world, to be put to any test, but, above all, freely to be used, not in its own service, but in the service of the God in whom it believes, the universal Father of all, and, therefore, in the world's highest service. And in order to do this, first and foremost we must be rid of self, of this intense preoccupation to survive in any form, as race or creed or nation, this desperate struggle to exist in name, if nothing else. . . .

. . . You are not called upon to sacrifice your deepest principles and convictions; on the contrary, you are summoned to be true to them by casting down the barriers that prevent their fullest exercise and freedom in the widest relation with your fellowmen. Search well your own heart, and perhaps you will find that, once placing yourself in this attitude, throwing off the heavy weight of the past, this dead self that clings to you, you will be born again, into your larger heritage; you will no longer be conscious of difference and separation; you will be one with your brother, the liberal Christian who has likewise come out of the narrowness of his creeds and doctrine into the same freedom as you have,—the glorious freedom of the sons of God, the God of Abraham, Isaac, and Jacob: yes, but the God of the living, not of the dead. Creeds are everywhere falling and being disintegrated, losing their hard-and-fast consistency in order that the truth that has been encased in them shall be set free, the light of the spirit shall shine out like a star. Christianity as a sect or creed has no compelling force for Judaism. The Inquisition could not make Christians of us, nor can all the mild but zealous efforts of the Presbyterians ever make a single honest convert.

That which alone has power supremely to attract is the divine-human life, of which the type has been given to the world by a Jew. And by the divine-human life I mean the life which through every human experience keeps sight and touch of the divine,—a life lived always in conscious relation with infinite and eternal things, in personal union and communion with a Being that comprehends and transcends our own, and therefore a life of sublime trust and assurance, of loving obedience, and of immortal promise and hope. And the secret of that life, the truth which it reads into the world, through every contradiction and obstruction of human circumstance, every manifestation of human weakness, human sorrow and sin, is the truth of love,—of an infinite and eternal Love transcending human imperfections, a divine Heart that reveals itself in answering love to our human heart and human needs.

And is not such a life of the very essence of Judaism, you ask? and I answer: it may be, but not while you limit and circumscribe your Judaism as you do, making of it a fetish, a history and tradition instead of an active, living principle, a visible embodiment of the truth; not while you draw about yourselves the lines of a peculiar and chosen people that isolate you and forbid you from entering into the closest human ties with the people around you. . . . Come down from your watch-towers, come out of your Ghettos, and bear witness to that unity in the world to-day, not as an abstract, metaphysical truth, but in spirit and in deed. . . .

Let us not be deceived. We cannot save our Judaism in any narrow, in any broad sense even, unless we lose it, by merging and adding to it that which will make it no longer Judaism, because it is something that the whole world claims, and therefore cannot be the exclusive prerogative of Judaism,—in other words, by entering into the larger, spiritual life which makes no conditions, no restrictions necessary; draws no boundary lines, no arbitrary and external distinctions of race and creed; sets up no barriers between man and man, between man and God; but reaches out in perfect freedom, perfect oneness with man, to perfect oneness with God. . . .

We can still repeat our creed: "Hear O Israel,—and hear all the world besides,—the Lord our God, the Lord is one,"—one with us, with all of us, Jews and Christians alike. For we have taken into it an element that shall so deepen and enlarge it as forever to redeem it from self and every form of selfishness, all possibility of narrowness and sectarianism. No longer shutting itself in, nor shutting any out, on the contrary, it will welcome all with, "Come unto me, whatever sect, whatever race, whatever creed, for in my larger love, my larger faith, all sects, all creeds are one."

Each of us has our special part, our special work to do, which we cannot shirk, even if we would, for it is forced upon us. To the most indifferent of us it must mean something for our good or ill, our weal or woe, that we are born Jews, into just these conditions in which we find ourselves, to work through them, if we can, into still higher conditions. We all stand at different points along the line, with some above us, some below, to help and to be helped. Judaism is to each of us a personal factor, an individual problem, as well as a large race-question, to be solved individually as well as collectively,—a problem as old as the world, which will be older yet before it is solved. But if we see any light, we need not despair. We can believe, we can hope and trust, and above all, we can serve. "For now abideth faith, hope, and love, these three; but the greatest of these is love."

REBEKAH KOHUT,
United States

Welcoming Address,
First Convention,
National Council of
Jewish Women (1896)

Without a doubt a movement towards unity is in the air. Everywhere we see traces of its influence. The lesson that in union is strength has been learned again, and the women of our times have caught it up. The idea existed that women had inherent incapacity for convictions and co-operation. Women could never work together, so it was said. It cannot be said now. The work of this Council since the Parliament of Religions convened and to-night's gathering are refutations of the statement. Jewish women can work together, and working, can achieve definite results. . . .

Upon every Jewess, and more particularly upon the women of this Council, is laid the duty of being God's missionary in the fullest sense of the word. We are not necssarily to win souls by an aggressive propaganda, which too often repels rather than attracts, but simply by the quiet force of a beautiful example. Every true Jewess is a priestess, and by the very strength of her unobtrusive belief is a witness for religion; and when faith in God is the source of her virtues, truth and integrity, gentleness and purity the foundation stones of her life, then truly is she a blessing in Israel. The mother in Israel was never chosen for active warfare in the cause of religious truth, but she was expected to be a witness of religion in her home. And therefore I say that which my heart impels me to speak. May our deliberations be not only harmonious, pervaded by sweet sisterly affection and love, but above all, may the outcome of the deliberations be tangible and perceptible to the physical eye, as well as to the eyes of faith and reason. Let us not attempt too much. Let us be specific. May this convention end its deliberations and find those who have assembled, each of them, a blessing for Israel. May we feel sufficiently inspired that the future may evidence the earnestness of the present. Let us begin with the most important, the Sabbath, Israel's bulwark from time immemorial. May it be brought nearer to our hearts in such fashion that every one, every daughter of Judah, may hallow it in truth. God be thanked, there are noble hearts which throb for the poor, and intelligent minds to distribute wisely the means intended for those whose lot has not fallen in pleasant places. But if not from our ranks, then from where, shall come those who shall teach our children by religious example, and kindle within them the sparks of faith, that which will keep ever burning the lamp of hope, ever glowing the coals of confidence in the God of Israel? Let the impulse of Sabbath keeping among Jewish women be here fairly started and carried into practice. Let it be sounded forth in clear, unmistakable tones, the resolution that the Deborahs in Israel have taken, to lead their children out into the broad highways of religion and not by devious by-paths.

There is no hopelessness so sad as that of early youth, when the soul is made up of wants, and we who are blessed with the sweet memories of a home wherein God dwelt know too well that even to a child there is no purer, sweeter joy than that associated with the poetic sentiment which is the halo of Sabbath or festival. Sabbath! That is the word which we, as Mothers in Israel, must brave again. Ours it is to be the saviors of our people. Ours it is to arouse courage and hope in the leaders of the nation's destiny. They need our sympathies, our active aid.

. . . Members of this Council, yours it is to send the thrill of hope to the hopeless, and by your touch arouse a new enthusiasm, a greater love for our dear Judaism.

This working for our religion can be the only reason for our existence. In every corner of the earth you will find the Jew a patriot in the best sense of the word. The Jew knows no sectarianism in communal work. In matters philanthropic and educational we shall always join our Christian sisters, for this we need no organization; it is for a better knowledge of our history, our religion, and ourselves as Jews that this Council was called into life. Let us have a long and useful existence, let us labor for the preservation of our sacred heritage, until the whole family of Judah shall have become a blessing unto the Lord. . . .

**JULIA RICHMAN,
United States**

**Report of National
Committee on
Religious School
Work (1896)**

. . . The Committee on Religion claims that the future of Judaism depends upon our closer acquaintance with the history and literature of our people, and that through its efforts the permanent usefulness of the Council will be assured. . . .

If noble men and women will come to our aid, if the Rabbis will give us their valuable support and co-operation, if you will, my sisters—especially you who are Mothers in Israel—make up your minds earnestly, faithfully, prayerfully to assume your share of the obligation, I claim for the work of the National Committee on Religious Schools, not only the key to the permanent usefulness of the Council of Jewish Women, but the key to the permanence of all true, earnest, spiritual American Judaism.

. . . In most cities the Rabbis are willing, and often more than willing to co-operate with our Committee to better the work in our schools; in a few—only a very few instances—it has been reported to me that this co-operation has been withheld.

May I say, right here, that only two causes could have produced such a result? Either our women, with more zeal than tact, have offended the Rabbi or made unreasonable demands, or the Rabbi is blind to the best interest of our Church, and is foolishly belittling his own influence and endangering his own success. Only with the aid of our Rabbis can the women hope to improve our schools; only with the aid of our women can the Rabbis hope to gain real influence over their flocks. Then, since each needs the other, let there be an end to misunderstanding, and let there be mutual trust and mutual help. . . .

We begin our religious work too late, and we end it too soon. We begin our religious work badly; and a bad beginning never makes a good ending.

This is no place for a pedagogic sermon, but I must beg your indulgence long enough to outline the plan by which we teach true patriotism to our little ones in the public schools.

First, our noble flag. Baby minds cannot, of course, grasp its significance, but the children see the beautiful colors; they are made to feel that the flag represents something beyond the baby's comprehension, to be sure, but vaguely. They also feel that it means protection; that to the flag they owe love and respect and loyalty. With the symbol in their hearts and before their eyes, we teach them to take the solemn oath of allegiance to the flag. I cannot describe the ceremony: you must visit a school and see and hear, in order to feel what that means. I hear it daily, and yet with each hearing I am stirred to my innermost soul.

But the flag came first, then the oath, and the beautiful soul-stirring national songs. Then the Fourth of July, our birthday, with its accompaniment of bunting and fireworks; then on to our great men, Washington, Lincoln and the others.

Only later, after the love and loyalty for America and its banner and its traditions are deep-rooted, do we burden the child with the historical data, with chronological details, and with other minor issues. And in this wise, American love and patriotism, and interest in American history are implanted unshakably in every child's heart.

So would I have you teach our little ones true Judaism.

First, God.

Baby minds cannot, of course, grasp its significance; but make them feel the Presence. Take your children to the Religious School at a very early age. Select for them a teacher who loves little ones and who loves God. What do these babies care about Adam and Eve, or the order of creation? Introduce them to the wonders of plant and animal life. *Show them God* in the bursting seed, in the budding flower, in the bird-producing egg, the glorious sunshine. Let them see God and learn to love Him for His blessings in which they share. Let them be made to feel that God means protection, that to Him they owe love and respect and gratitude and loyalty. Make God the starting point and the goal. Love of God, confidence in God, fear, not of God, but of His disapproval, these are the steps by which to develop the feeling of moral obligation, first to the world, then to Judaism. . . .

With God as the foundation, with love of God and confidence in God and gratitude for His mercies in their hearts, then teach them our beautiful, soul-stirring Jewish hymns; tell them of our great days, our great men, our great events, our miraculous preservation. . . .

A word for older boys and girls. *Advance* the age of confirmation. Keep our boys and girls, more especially our boys, in the Religious Schools until they are full-grown in soul as well as stature. Twenty-five years ago most of us were taken from our secular studies before we were seventeen. Look at the girls and boys of today. Nineteen—twenty, it is no uncommon thing to find them, girls as well as boys, at twenty-two or three still at their schooling. Have the Religious Schools kept pace with this progress? I find girls everywhere who beg to remain at school or college "just another year." Do you find them coaxing for permission to remain in the Sunday School? Why not? Trace the cause, correct it, and you will have conquered half the evil. I want our girls and boys taught in advanced or Bible classes until they are grown, old enough in turn to teach others. Is it because we are less intelligent and less capable, or because we are less spiritual, than our friends of alien faiths, that we find so many of their and so few of our own young people fitted to assume the noble work of aiding the holy cause of religion by teaching in our Religious Schools?

The Council has much to do, but let us not attempt everything at once. The crying shame of American Judaism today is, that where once stood high, spiritual ideals, we have substituted merely race pride and material ambition, both developed on intellectual lines, not on lines of faith. Even in our Council study circles, is it not the head more than the heart that there receives nourishment? But it is the heart, my sisters, the good old Jewish heart, with its humble faith, its loyalty to God, its noble aspirations, that we want to bring back. God needs hearts more than heads in His service. Judaism needs hearts more than heads to uphold its glory; and it is in our Religious Schools that these hearts must be awakened. . . .

HANNAH
GREENBAUM
SOLOMON,
United States

Presidential Address
at Reception Given
by the New York
Section, National
Council of Jewish
Women (1896)

The greatest trouble that I have had this whole week has been to recognize myself under the various guises in which I have been introduced. That same perplexity I am suffering from at present. It was only when the word "President" was spoken that I realized of whom Mrs. Beer was talking, and I thank her for her kind thoughts and expressions.

When I was asked to speak to you this afternoon I was still in my own home. Mrs. Wallach wrote me that they wished the "President" to make a few parting remarks. When I received the letter I wrote to Mrs. Wallach that the President ought to make a few parting remarks, but I had my serious doubts whether that President would be the one to whom she had written; so I did not prepare a speech at home for that reason. When I came to the Convention and saw the magnificent women whom we had succeeded in bringing together, I was more than ever satisfied that I would not need to make a speech, and even this morning I had my serious doubts. Yet I concluded, if it should fall to my lot, I might have time between hours to prepare an address. This a kind New York hostess, who honored me by giving a luncheon, prevented. So now I come to you without a parting address, but with a few words direct from the heart. I should not have liked to make a genuine parting address, because partings are sad, and we do not wish to be sad after our happy week here together. . . .

The remarks which Mr. Jacobs made to us this afternoon have impressed me deeply. . . . He mentioned an object which I should not dare to thrust upon this meeting—the new woman. Who is the new woman, who has become such an old subject? She is the woman who has the courage of her convictions; who expresses them when she sees fit to do so, and who follows them when the occasion arises. She is the woman who dares go into the world and do what her convictions demand. She is the woman who stays at home in the smallest, narrowest circle, foregoing all the world may offer to her, if there her duty lies; and I am convinced that, as President of the Council, I need not say to a single woman within reach of my voice that never should any secondary duty take away from us the sacredness of the first, the near duty, for I am satisfied that there is not a woman here who needs that advice. When such a conflict of duties presents itself, home and love are ever the magnets that draw us on, promising peace and rest.

But some of us are taken out upon the hillsides and into the open fields, where we have a wide perspective, and where, if we have clear vision, we see many things that call for our sympathy and help; and I hope that when the call comes to any of us, if we can go, it will find us ready.

I feel that one important subject has been missed in Mr. Jacobs' talk. He speaks of the power of the Jewish woman. He said that without Jewish women, Judaism could not exist; but if Judaism must exist for the women alone, we do not want it. I, for one, want my husband to have Judaism, if I have it, and I want my children to have it. . . . I have always been fond both of men and children, I freely acknowledge it. No social life—no church life—no club life, is complete—no civic life is right, where men and women do not work together. The highest and best that we desire we can only accomplish when men and women work hand-in-hand together. Even Paradise was not complete without a woman, and no paradise on earth can be perfectly complete unless we have men and women.

Another point upon which Mr. Jacobs touched is near and dear to us all. It is the question of barriers between women. Now, although the Jewish Council stands upon its platform of Judaism, because we realize that in this country, at least, all Jews need not separate from Christians for any purpose except for the practice of their religion; not, indeed, to study art, music, or anything else, but that only in our religion we have a legitimate purpose for separation, yet I say that within our Council, working along Jewish lines and Jewish thought, we must still foster the thought of the greater humanity that is outside, and hand-in-hand must work with our sisters of other faiths, striving to achieve the greatest and the best for all. And I am glad to see that in every State where they can, our women are joining the State Federations, working along the lines that tend to the bettering of individuals of all classes, for this is one of the purposes of our Council. We do not care particularly if we are excluded socially, especially if we are excluded on account of our religion. At the same time, whenever the occasion presents itself, whenever the opportunity offers, let us work hand-in-hand.

I would just say one word at parting, and that is that when we go home to our respective duties as Council members, there in our own cities, we make use of the truths we have heard here, and that there we should fulfill our duty to the utmost,—helping ourselves, helping others, influencing those near to us and all the rest. For in our own cities we may hope for perfect harmony, for oneness of purpose, which may for the present be lacking in the great whole, but toward which we must work.

A further thought let us take with us, and that is this: The only things we can share, the only things which we can give to the world without making ourselves poorer, are high thoughts and high aims. We make the age richer by them, and yet do not impoverish ourselves. Let us teach ourselves and each other to love the best there is—to love the best in books, in music, in art; to cherish the highest ideals of character that we can find anywhere.

And I feel that I cannot close without saying one word more to you, our New York friends, who have been so kind—the hostesses who have opened their homes and hearts and taken us in. There is a story, an old Talmudic story (I confess I do not know very many of them, but this one expresses just what I would say). Two friends were about to part, and one said to the other: "Give me thy blessing." And the friend replied, "I will tell thee a story: A traveler, weary, tired, and hungry, came to a beautiful tree. It had sweet fruit, beautiful shade, and at its roots ran a stream. He ate of the fruit, rested in the shade, and drank of the water. And when he was about to depart, he said: 'Wherewith shall I bless thee, O Tree? Shall I wish that thou shalt have beautiful shade? That thou has already. Shall I wish that a silver stream of water may flow at thy feet? That thou hast already. I will bless thee, and wish that the trees planted from thy offshoots may be like unto thee." And so I say to you, my friends: what can I wish you? I can only bless you, and wish there may be many like you. And so I say to you all in parting, that I wish, I hope, I pray, there may be many like you, and may we meet again.

MINNIE D. LOUIS,
United States

The Influence of
Women in Bringing
Religious Conviction
to Bear upon Daily
Life (1895)

. . . Woman is the ozone of the metaphysical atmosphere. In the intellectual view of Religion, which sees it at the *alter* height, the very essence of the woman nature predominates. That all-pervading love working within the human soul shows itself in the benevolent instincts, termed by Comte *Altruism*, and, in the still higher, the maternity, the nourishing instinct, termed by Drummond, also *Altruism*. It is through this highest interpretation of Religion that woman instinctively finds her greatest activity and influence. . . .

A compulsory universal University education, which means the thorough education of the head, hand and heart of *every individual* human being, can be the only developer of the real divinity in man, of the altruism which can make earth beautiful with its glow.

I am no pessimist; I rejoice in the God-light that floods the world, and ever more and more beautifies it to my spiritual vision, and which brings to me contentment and joyous peace, my priceless wealth; and I would have this light focused on every soul, glorifying it like the Rembrandt light on a picture. But it seems to me that this light can only be converged through the spirituality of the intellect and the intelligence of the spirituality, both of which are evolved from nothing but the highest education. . . .

Do we not try to cage our God today? Do not our priests devote their lives to guarding Him in walls of porphyry and onyx and every costly adjunct? And will He remain there? Already from cathedral, minster, temple, abbey, there and there, the life has long since fled; many of them are mere mausoleums for both the living and the dead. . . . But, oh! women, it is we with our "sanative conscience" that must turn in the full, strong light, and make chancel, aisle and transept, lectern and pew, glow in the sunbeams of a new spirituality. Let us turn all into lecture halls, study halls and libraries for young and old, for men and women, for aristocrat and plebeian, for employer and employee; turn them into hospitals for the sick, into homes for the homeless and helpless, and have our priests guard *them* until the complete education has come to all, and built in *each* heart a Temple for God, made *every* home a Temple for Him, and *every* voice to sing with one accord—"The Fatherhood of God, the Brotherhood of Man!" Then will the daily life become a unity of purpose directed by an unconditional, unexacting love, a semblance to that universal love that asks no requital, only free ingress into the soul of every human being. When this is done, then, oh! women, we will not glory in our influence, but with humble heart will say, "Blessed art thou, O Lord, who hast made us as we are." . . .

Lord, let me know the power of the spirit; O Lord, let me know
If in its darkest hour on the prisoning earth below,
The spirit be captive and bound with the body, to beat at its walls
Till, deaf with the clamor of sound, it shall hear not the heaven
    that calls.
Shall it sink in the darkness and fail, and be joined to the ruin of
    life?
Is the striving of none avail, and the hope that lives in the strife?
What of the spirit, O Lord? Shall it wait and be never aware?
Wilt Thou not send it a word from the highest where Truth is laid
    bare?
For Hope that hath no defender lives on for a word from Thee;
O God! it will never surrender, 'tis mighty and sure and free.

**NINA DAVIS SALAMAN,
Great Britain**

The Power of the Spirit (1910)

"Out of the depths I call Thee."—What were life
    Lacking such solace to its lonely pain?
    How could the dumb heart suffer, and sustain
The sorrow and the bitterness and strife;

And know the gloom and dream not of the light?
    They watching for the morning wait not so,
    Not as the soul waits, yearning from its woe
Upward to some unknown unending height.

And though no sign nor help come, and no voice,
    Nor any knowledge from the silent peak,
    Trustfully from its pain the soul shall speak,
"Out of the depths I call Thee," and rejoice.

Of Prayer (1910)

BERTHA PAPPENHEIM, Germany

The Jewish Woman in Religious Life

Translated by Margery Bentwich

A Paper read at the Women's Congress at Munich, 1912

In order that my remarks may appeal to a wide circle I would indicate, in a few words, the fundamental differences which underlie the development of communal life in Christian and Jewish religious communities.

The Jewish religion is purest Monotheism. It knows no dogmas, no church, no sects, no proselytes, no mission, no worldly or political ambitions. It is in the best sense a matter of private conscience; it has and needs no outward forms and authorities to bind its members together.

The construction of the community is, as one would expect from its simple premises, of the simplest: the members unite for prayer and for the study of the holy writings; they are bound together by the ties of ritual laws which sanctify everyday life, and their whole life is permeated with the fulfillment of the command, "Love thy neighbour as thyself," which serves to give them a corporate life of ideal solidarity, and therefore of great resisting power.

The functionaries of the Jewish community are, on the one hand, scholars and teachers whose high task it is to preserve alive the God-idea and to work out the social-*ethical* meaning of Holy Writ—on the other hand, of officials who supervise the carrying out of the social-*hygienic* prescriptions of the ritual. It is the duty of every individual to practice the general precept of love and charity.

The absolutely equal interest of all for all gives a healthy democratic trend to the organization, but we must admit at the outset that this does not apply to women. The persecution of the adherents of the Jewish religion has for many centuries given a strange character to Jewish communal life, which has come to be generally recognized under the term Ghetto. The disappearance of the physical walls of the Ghetto has, however, not meant for all Jewish communities religious tolerance and freedom of conscience, nor the recognition of equality for other religious communities. Thus we see the communal life of the Jews in the Diaspora, though starting from the religious basis, developing on very different lines; varying with the culture of the people by whom it is surrounded and with the obstruction with which it meets. . . .

The Jewish woman accompanies the man in his general cultural development, yet the differentiation between the sexes *within the congregation*—and this is the subject under discussion—still remains very marked. Even for German conditions, with which we are primarily concerned, it would be unfair to judge her position by the standard of modern culture.

To understand that position aright, we must look back and consider that great conglomeration of law, tradition, and custom which exists subconsciously for the majority of Western Jews today as "Tradition"; which, for many, has a sort of historical value; while it is still observed by a minority in its entirety. Here is material for the Talmudist, the historian, the sociological student, and it may

seem to representatives of these branches of learning that I, an ignorant woman, presume too much in attempting to speak thereon.
But, in very fact, it is significant that there is no woman, nor ever
has been, who has thoroughly mastered the Jewish sources of study
necessary for a discussion of the question in its religious and historical aspect, or who has treated the material from a woman's point
of view, as we see women doing to-day in other branches of juristic
work. The house of study—the home and nursery of specifically
Jewish culture—has ever been closed to the woman, and wherever
Jewish learning is transmitted in the traditional way, so it will remain in the future. Thus, not only in the past, have we been referred
always to the male concept of the Torah, the commentaries, and the
tradition; but even now, when the feminine point of view could be
expressed in translations of the Hebrew text, and in reconsideration
of the subject-matter etc., the very possibility of individual critical
study of the original texts is denied us. We Jewish women must
take, unquestioningly, praise and blame, admiration and condem-
nation of the sex, as we get it scattered through the vast masses of
literature, through the spectacles of male scholars, who read into
Jewish literature their own personal opinion and personal experiences.

The purpose of this congress is therefore better realized by being
addressed by an unlearned woman who, however, has grown up
with the tradition, than by a scholar who, though he knew more,
would hardly represent the point of view we want to-day: to ascer-
tain the measure of woman's feeling and living interest in a state and
condition which has in part been fixed by history, but which must
now come into contact with the ever-flowing spring of all ethical
life.

In order to avoid any misunderstanding, I shall draw a sharp distinction between the importance of the woman and her position in
the Jewish community in olden and modern times. The old traditional Jewish conception of woman implies always the married
woman, since the Oriental notions of womanhood, which so largely
influenced Jewish legislation, did not embrace the idea of the female
as an individuality who might develop freely on her own lines without the sexual complement of the male. Woman is the bearer, the
guardian, and preserver of the nation, and only in so far as she carries out this, her primary function—on which depends the welfare
and continued existence of the people, Israel—does she come into
her own domain. The ordinances which enjoin the purity and holiness of marriage, the regulated intercourse between the sexes with
a view to rearing a numerous and healthy progeny—these gave
woman, in the eyes of the Law, a conscious value in ethical matters
and in the national economy, similar to that which she holds in the
scientific and practical sociology of to-day.

Be it understood that the married woman, and even as such, the
mother of children only, is the only woman held up for respect and
consideration in Jewish law. This respect is expressed not only in
poetical and theoretical sentiments, but takes very definite practical

shape in forms and precepts which, in our modern vocabulary, would be called "the safeguarding of motherhood on a foundation of ethics." This respect for motherhood is shown very clearly by the fact that according to Jewish law the woman is exempted from ritual observances which make demands outside the home. This means that for a Jewish woman nothing is of greater importance or urgency than her fulfillment of her duties as mother, which should demand all her time and attention.

It is not surprising to find that the old Jewish esteem for family life, and its healthy purity, its reverence for the married woman and legitimate mother, should engender a corresponding contempt for the unmarried mother and her offspring. This scorn, which within the narrow walls of the Ghetto may well have served as a protective check against harmful excrescences, becomes callousness in modern times and conditions, since freedom of thought and action, increased difficulties of living attendant on early marriage, assimilation of the good and bad elements of their new surroundings, have wrought changes in the sexual intercourse of Jews—a problem which demands our earnest attention.

The considerate exemption of woman from duties outside the home is not the only reason for her having become a sort of domestic recluse; the important precept of early marriage, and a certain fear of sexual passion in man, have cut the woman off from free intercourse with the male world, and thereby from all intellectual life.

For though the Jew was bound by law to exclusively Jewish study in the Hebrew language, this very training was the best school for sharpening the mind, and has rendered him, in every age, peculiarly receptive and responsive to other subjects of study. The women remained for the most part (less by law than by ancient custom) in total ignorance. Their deficient mental training tended to make them sexually and domestically so dependent on the male, that when political emancipation brought spiritual freedom to the man, it was not till much later that women began to develop themselves as individuals.

We have sufficient proof of the disregard of the woman in the Jewish service when we see that for purposes of prayer a woman is not counted as a member of the congregation; she is not called up to the reading of the Law, and she does not participate in the public ceremony of coming of age, as every boy of thirteen years of age is required to do. This last, the ceremony of Barmitzvoh, gives the boy early a higher status than the girl. By a religious privilege he feels himself from childhood superior to the female sex.

We see the same illogical disparity between the importance of the woman and her position in the congregation, when we consider the part she plays in carrying out the social-hygienic ordinances, and the all-important social-ethical precept of the sanctification of the Sabbath. The woman is entrusted implicitly with the carrying out of the dietary laws, which are still today of paramount importance wherever the communal supervision is unconscientious in its control of foodstuffs. More especially in the disinfection of meat by salting, and in the fulfillment of other seemingly unimportant precepts, the Jewish woman quietly and naturally fills the role of a sanitary official, and in times of epidemic, often unknown to herself, her loyal devotion has proved of incalculable service.

Still more important, because of its high ethical value, is her participation in the sanctification of the Sabbath. To the woman is given the symbolical ceremony of lighting the candles on Friday evening, the holy inauguration of the Sabbath; and it is her duty to see that in the Jewish home man and beast shall rest for twenty-four hours, and gather new life and strength for the coming six working days.

It has long been one of the most justifiable demands of women of all confessions that all working women who earn their daily bread should be allowed these hours of preparation before the day of rest, which Jewish law, saturated as it is with the social spirit, so judiciously and lovingly prescribes. It is especially for the trebly difficult and responsible duties of the woman, as housekeeper, mother and wage-earner, that this evening, which ushers in the day of rest, should be observed, in order to ensure the full religious, physical, and aesthetic enjoyment of the Sabbath.

There is only one domain which the Jewish woman shares equally with the man, and that is in the fulfillment of that command, which was said by one of our sages to contain the whole of the Jewish religion, "Love thy neighbor as thyself." This ancient Jewish affirmative command, the foundation of which is found in the Ten Commandments, holds good equally for both man and woman. But it must be practiced as well as preached. Feeding the hungry, nursing the sick, caring for the orphan, endowing the bride, performing last rites for the dead—all these works Jewish women can and should be ever willing to perform. . . .

[Yet] strangely enough women are largely absent from those independent social benevolent undertakings in which, according to Jewish law, both sexes should participate equally. The whole of Jewish philanthropy, that most admirable outward ethical expression of Judaism of the nineteenth century—I use the word philanthropy here deliberately, because the democratic element is lacking—has, since its inception, been carried on without the aid of women, and has been devoted almost exclusively to the good of the male section of the Jewish population. The Alliance Israélite Universelle, the great bequests of Baron Hirsch (directed to education and colonization), the widespread organizations of Freemasonry (B'nai B'rith)—all these have refused to fall in with the spirit of modern sociology, and jealously deny to woman their co-operation and co-responsibility. . . .

Had the Jewish woman been able to expend her energies and capabilities in communal work, and been given her rightful position and status in the congregation, we should not have had to lament the loss of so many, who in their justifiable longing for useful activity and self-development, have broken the bands which held them to their community, and have sought salvation elsewhere.

Full participation in all humanitarian objects is at once the final aim of the woman's movement and the meeting-point of all religions. The Jewish religion makes such demands of character and courage that the majority of Jewish women can find their high vocation anew within their own race and religion, and draw thence their truest inspiration. . . .

Prayers

Translated by Stephanie Forchheimer

· I ·

Time, thou ancient and revered, source of help and healing, Thou hast built and bestowed upon me so much; hast animated the heritage from my ancestors, which enriched my life, hast revealed to me pulsating filaments which bind together the very existence of things.

Time, thou all kindly, confer upon me, at the ripeness of old age, mildness.

· II ·

A Prayer for Women

Spirit of the universe, who has bound the world together through laws of justice, given us insight to comprehend them, a creative sense of work and readiness for deeds of love. We shudder—death stalks through the world: women are no longer able to bear children nor do they wish to do so. The organs of respiration and procreation are poisoned—fumes of egoism, hypocrisy and falsehood hover over the Jewish homes, which no longer differ from others to whom they are supposed to bring the great message of Mount Sinai.

Oh that the sound of the Shofar might rouse the congregation, that secular writings no longer obstructed the path of women, that the spectre of the great death would disappear, and that a generation would arise, born of strength and love and reverence for the holy Schechina [*sic*], who blesses those who live and govern with a pure heart. Amen.

· III ·

Malach homowes [Angel of Death], I have called Thee in days that were long for me. Nevertheless you approach me gently and unexpected. Your wing had grazed me softly, when you paused in your approach. What signal did you follow when, although conscious of your eternal and universal triumph, you yielded for awhile?

Is there still a mission for me to perform, which accomplished, shall complete the significance of my life? If so I shall rally and seek strength for it and pull myself together to accomplish whatever is commanded.

Malach homowes, Thy countenance is immobile and unfathom-
able. Envoy, Thou, and guardian of the great law, let me now await
Thee, idle and weak.

Oh, what a nice matchmaker
Eliezer is!
Oh, what gold and silver
He throws at her feet!—

No, you've read enough girls,
In the *Taytsh-khumesh*:
Something chases me out
Into the night tonight.

Longing is so lucid,
The night is ever dim,—
Throw yourselves at happiness, sisters,
Burst into silvery laughter!

Suddenly the evening
Arranges shadows verse by verse . . .
Perhaps messengers are waiting
For us, too, in the field!

Far away the distance trembles,
Twitches and flashes, and calls,—
I see golden jewelry
Glistening in the air . . .

Throw yourselves at happiness, sisters,
Burst into silvery laughter:
Rebecca's star will shine
Throughout the night.

**MIRIAM
ULINOVER,
Poland**

*Translated by Kathryn
Hellerstein*

**With the *Taytsh-
Khumesh*** (1922)

In one hand the old prayer book, tuition fee in her other,
And hanging from its string, the dangling pointer,—
As a child, my grandmother used to run quickly into the *kheder*
[school]
To repeat the alphabet, with the boys, in order.
Everything would have been fine; but the boys would hit her—
A girl's voice yowling can carry high as heaven.
Once long ago she nearly fainted, nearly perished
From the blows and benevolent slaps, what a horror!
But therefore a young wife is put in an ample chain,
With the same old prayer book, only now without a pointer,

The Old Prayer Book
(1922)

To lead the way through the entire *shtetl* [Jewish village] to the
    yard of the *shul* [synagogue].
How the new wife proudly takes up marching!
Wives stay mute, bashfully, silently, the women stare
At her mouth that does not rest from the Sabbath prayer,
As she, together with the congregation and the cantor,
Draws nearer the *Shekhine* [God's presence], praying, chanting.
In the *shul* an envious flurry, sweating, and brow wiping,
As wives, poor things, all engage in page-turning . . .
She flares up and throws herself afresh into the prayer:
For, of course, she is in her childhood home in the old *siddur*
    [prayer book]!

**KADYA
MOLODOWSKY,
Poland**

*Translated by Kathryn
Hellerstein*

Prayers (1927)

· I ·

Don't let me fall
As a stone falls on the hard ground.
And don't let my hands become dry
As the twigs of a tree
When the wind beats down the last leaves.
And when the storm raises dust from the earth
With anger and howling,
Don't let me fall.
I have asked so much,
But as a blade of your grass in a distant wild field
Lets drop a seed in the earth's lap
And dies away,
Sow in me your living breath,
As you sow a seed in the earth.

· II ·

I still don't know whom,
I still don't know why I ask.
A prayer lies bound to me,
And asks of a God,
And asks of a name.

I ask
In the field,
In the noise of the street,
Together with the wind, when it runs before my lips,
A prayer lies bound to me,
And asks of a God,
And asks of a name.

· III ·

I lie on the earth,
I kneel

In the ring of my horizons,
And stretch my hands
With an entreaty
To the west, when the sun sets,
To the east, when it rises there,
To each spark
To show me the light
And give light to my eyes,
To each worm that glows in the darkness at night,
That it shall bring its wonder before my heart
And redeem the darkness that is enclosed in me.

For poor brides who were servant girls,
Mother Sara draws forth from dim barrels
And pitchers sparkling wine.
Mother Sara carries with both hands
A full pitcher to whom it is decreed.
And for streetwalkers
Dreaming of white wedding shoes,
Mother Sara bears clear honey
In small saucers
To their tired mouths.
For high-born brides now poor,
Who blush to bring patched wash
Before their mother-in-law,
Mother Rebecca leads camels
Laden with white linen.
And when darkness spreads before their feet,
And all the camels kneel on the ground to rest,
Mother Rebecca measures linen ell by ell
From her fingers to her golden bracelet.
For those whose eyes are tired
From watching the neighborhood children,
And whose hands are thin from yearning
For a soft small body
And for the rocking of a cradle,
Mother Rachel brings healing leaves
Discovered on distant mountains,
And comforts them with a quiet word:
At any hour God may open the sealed womb.
For those who cry at night in lonely beds,
And have no one to share their sorrow,
Who talk to themselves with parched lips,
To them, Mother Leah comes quietly,
Her eyes covered with her pale hands.

Songs of women
(1927)

LILY H.
MONTAGU,
Great Britain

For Reform
Synagogue, Berlin[1]

It is a great honor for me to be allowed to speak before this distinguished assembly at the present time, when we are all gathered together to consider the spiritual possibilities of Judaism.

You have told me that you will forgive my many linguistic shortcomings, and I hope you will further make every allowance for an untrained preacher who would find it difficult to address so great an assembly, even in her own tongue.

You are present here as representing an organized religious community, but surely you feel with me that the relation of the individual soul to his God must always be in the foreground [of our thought]. The Psalmist brings to us his message as does the Prophet and the Priest. The relation between the universal man and his God is of such a holy nature that we do not often attempt to deal with it from the pulpit. And yet it is exactly this aspect of religion that is of supreme importance, and we have to consider how we can bring it home to ourselves and which way we want to demonstrate it to those for whom we are a leader. We, with all of our limitations, our hopes and our aims, seek to approach the perfect, infinite God. Without wanting to penetrate into the holy of holies of our co-religionists, we must strive to lead them to this communion with God [as well].

This morning, I want to examine only two aspects of this subject. I would emphasize that personal religion has a definite relation to organized religion and that personal religion must be given attention as it tends to become weakened and eventually ineffective. By "organized religion" I mean the external expression, the public observance by the religious community of the teachings of our faith. We know that it is the fashion today to decry organized religion. It is enough, we are told, for each person to lead a good life: outward observance is of little importance. It is conduct which matters supremely. "Why should a man attend services when he can lead a good life without doing so?" And who, in having this opinion, thinks himself thoroughly modern and we who think differently, old-fashioned. Let us examine the question more closely: Judaism is our religion, and we all want to lead a Jewish life.

The [organized] religious community to which we belong influences our opinions and gives our religion its characteristics: indeed, it makes it possible for it to exist.

As the great theologian, Baron von Hügel, said: Nobody would enjoy the sense of bounding health, racing along some dune on a balmy spring morning, without having eaten a good breakfast beforehand. There is a connection between the lump of camphor in our drawer and the odor which the camphor gives. Religious customs[2] are, in religion, the camphor and the breakfast, and the detached believers would have no camphor scent, no bounding liberty, had there not been from ancient times these concrete, heavy, primitive[3] things. There are certain things that we get out of organized religion which give our personal religion nourishment, but we should not get the influence of the past by a mechanical process; we must strive to make this assimilation ourselves.

If God, as we believe, is the God of life, then we must seek to harmonize our lives with His. The task is a difficult one. If God were not the moving force of all life but static, the approach would be less difficult. God demands partnership from us. We must move forward with Him in the creation of joy and righteousness. On account of modern inquiry, which we have no desire to ignore, our conception of God has somewhat changed. Yet modified or elaborated as it may be, the teaching of our ancestors that God is not only immanent in all things but is also outside of them since they cannot contain His perfection, urges us to seek direct communion with God at all times.

Our fathers taught that righteousness leads to God. If ours is to be a Jewish life, it is not enough to say that theoretically we believe in righteousness, truth, love and beauty. We must actually express these beliefs in our life.

Our fathers laid stress on irreproachable conduct, and it is that emphasis of theirs that directs our thoughts into activity today. It is because of the teaching of God's Unity which has been transmitted to us that we feel that all of life must be consecrated—body, mind and soul, because the Creator is One and indivisible and expresses Himself in His creation.

The conception of the immanence of God, derived from faith in His Unity, has grown stronger with the advance of modern thought. We believe in one moving force through which we and all the universe are created. God is manifested in us and in all our doings.

It is from the past that we have received the doctrine that sin separates us from God, but that we can turn at any moment from our evil doing and by our own efforts again come into contact with the spirit of goodness, which is God. We believe in the oneness of humanity, as all people are children of God. We believe that the spirit that comes from the eternal God is eternal, and that nothing can loosen this tie. We believe that we are a Brotherhood scattered over all of the world, but united and kept alive for the specific purpose of spreading belief in the One God, and this belief is expressed in all of the doctrines that we have inherited.

Now I suggest that these beliefs color our personal religion. They come to us in the first place through the study of our Bible and our history. But we must work on this inheritance before it can be of any real value to us. As Goethe said, we must "earn it to possess it." It must come to life through the activity of our own spirit. It must be adjusted to the needs of modern thought and modern life. [This process can be greatly facilitated through the observance of] Sabbaths and Holy Days [which] give us the opportunity to commune with God in fellowship. Moreover, the teachings contained in our ceremonials emphasize [the importance of] leading a good life. If they did not do this, they would be completely worthless. There would be no value in worship services and symbols did they not, preserved in their Purity and Beauty, serve as aids to right living.

Personal religion can thus be influenced and nourished through public worship,[4] but this result cannot automatically be achieved. An organized religion is made up of fractions of personal religion and each person must make his own contribution to the spiritual possessions which will form the inheritance for succeeding ages. Organized religion is a necessary background. I repeat, while we are children, our parents fit our lives into this background, but as we grow older, we once again adapt this background for ourselves. And yet there are numbers of people who say that they do not want organized religion.

What happens? I think this happens, and I say it with a full sense of responsibility: in nine out of ten cases, or in ninety-nine cases out of a hundred, ordinary people lose their sense of consecration. They lose their interest in prayer. They lose the consolation and stimulus of religion. They become indifferent and callous, and worship their own whims and fancies, their own material advancement. Of course there are rare souls who still lead the most intensely spiritual lives without any organized help whatever, and I have allowed for them in the one in ten. But I think they are really so rare that they should not be counted as more than one in a hundred.

I also freely admit that there are a number of average people who without any allegiance to the fellowship of Jews retain something of the religious side of life, even while they lose most of it. We would ask ourselves whether we dare say that we or those whom we wish to influence, belong to the class of exceptional souls who can do without any prop whatever. We ask, further, whether we would care to possess or to transmit a feeble, attenuated faith which lacks the blessing of virility which a living Judaism gives.

Now the second problem I want to suggest to you is: what can personal religion, which I prize as the most precious of all things, do for us? We must admit that there is a difference between a life touched by infinity and a life limited by that which is perceived by the senses by facts provable by the human mind. We want the unprovable, we want love, truth and beauty, and we can only find these on the spiritual plane. Personal religion can give us a standard of being. If we can admit nothing better outside ourselves, we do not bother to struggle for the best. Religion urges us to fight evil as contrary to the Divine Law. It urges us to combat abject misery, sin and disease because God is. In His name we can work, as we believe in co-operation with Him, since through Him goodness must ultimately prevail. Personal religion can give us a reason for trying to find a purpose in life. It gives us hope in moments of despair. Since we can actually come in contact with the God of Love, we cannot doubt the existence of love. Religion can consecrate happiness and intensify it. It can give consolation in times of sorrow. It can lift our lives out of dull monotony and give them a touch of poetry and romance. It can combat loneliness and give us increased dignity and self respect. It gives special beauty to family life and also to friendship. It can, in short, make life worthwhile.

Now friends, if we want personal religion I would urge in all sincerity that we must not cut ourselves adrift from organized religion;

if we do, we lose the best nourishment we can obtain. Organized religion has a part in the evolution of personal religion. It is the material upon which personal religion is grafted, but the process of grafting must be individual. Every human soul must, through thought, prayer, and study,[5] cultivate his own religion to suit himself. We Jews produce, each for himself, from the stock of Judaism, a living variety of the Jewish religion. We must work out and apply the doctrines which we receive from the past. We can find help if we seek it through prayer, by getting into contact with God. We must study and read, and we must not grudge the time that this study demands. We must try to acquire a religious view of life, to think as well as to pray. We have to ask ourselves whether each situation in which we find ourselves is right, if it is in harmony with Judaism. We have to ask ourselves whether the social conditions under which we live are based on righteousness, whether the pleasures we follow are good, whether our moods are worth bothering about, or whether they are unworthy. We must ask ourselves: are we living as if we were conscious of the presence of God and are we expressing every day something of His love? We must be sure that the books we read or write elevate our life's worth and that our friends have the same endeavor. We must know whether our relations with those whom we employ or with our employers are right, whether our work is honest, whether we are furthering the spiritual interest of our country, and whether we are working for the cause of international peace.

We have to answer all of these questions for ourselves. And many of us have also in our small, inadequate way to seek to persuade others to desire personal religion for themselves. I would venture to suggest that the only hope that we may influence others lies in the strength of our personal religion. If that is real and effective, it may here and there be our lovely privilege to kindle with the light of our enthusiasm some other wavering, seeking soul. Personal religion produces personality. We can only feed our bodies without it, but not the whole being, and personality, which is the whole being, depends on the evolution of religion [to make it strong and effective].[6]

It follows that if we want to live completely, we must have a care to bring our lives into touch with the Divine. In this union we may find the strength that we are seeking; for our eyes will be given the power of true vision. Perhaps too, the hope of immortality comes to us when the spirit finds itself in contact with God through religion, with God, with whom there is no death. Indeed, it was through communion with God that the idea of eternity first came to be felt in the human heart and each of us can attain personal beliefs through prayer and meditation. Then we shall feel that if we love, we can live forever; then we shall know that the search for truth calls us to a service which must endure forever. Thank God that we men and women are allowed the experience of love and the search after truth. Thank God that the only finality is in Himself.

Notes

1. Translated from the German by Ellen M. Umansky, with reference to Lily Montagu's early English draft on which this sermon obviously was based. Major discrepancies between the German and English translations are noted.
2. The English version says "the institutional" instead of "religious customs."
3. Though the German explicitly says "primitive," in the English draft Lily Montagu wrote "clumsy."
4. In the earlier, English draft she wrote "organized religion" instead of "public worship."
5. The English draft says "practice" instead of "study."
6. The bracketed words appear in the English draft, but not in the final, German version. They are added here for the sake of clarity.

SARAH KUSSY,
United States

Judaism and Its
Ceremonies

In reviewing the pages of history, and reflecting on the fate of nations, the continued existence of the Jewish race appears little short of miraculous. No other people has met with such varying fortune, none has encountered such grave vicissitudes; and yet to-day they stand essentially a nation, though scattered over every land where civilization has set its stamp. Various as are the conjectures regarding the causes of our stability, all will agree in assigning to the teachings of that greatest of law-givers the first real basis whereon our endurance is founded. Yet there were other influences built on that early structure, so solidly laid, which helped to strengthen in Israel that spirituality to which Judaism at its birth gave rise. When in the darkest hour of the Middle Ages the dreaded Inquisition was at work, our people were bound together by a tie which no fanaticism could sever. But not their monotheism alone, in the centuries of trial, upheld them; not only their faith in God, but also the manner in which that belief was manifested. And to-day, when we are inclined to chaff at the ritualism which Judaism still imposes, when old-time customs and ceremonies are regarded in the light of rubbish, from contact with which the purity of religion might receive a stain, let us consider a moment how they influenced the race in the past, and compare the results with our present state.

Because ceremonies are in themselves not an end, but a means to effect that end, too apt are we to underrate their full importance and significance. Religion, however, let us remember, is not always spontaneously active within us, and sometimes requires stimulating means from without to rouse it to life and enthusiasm. . . .

Today, when the West glows with the light which our fathers vainly sought in the East . . . the ancient faith, together with the exalted conception of the God it embraces, would be more firmly established in the minds of its so-called adherents were our ceremonies and observances, that arouse religious sentiment, a little more closely adhered to, for sentiment must ever remain an essential part of religion—a fact we are likely to forget in this materialistic age, where everything, even our creed, is being made more and more practical; when we no longer look for spontaneity in matters of faith, and are inclined to regard idealism in religions as a breath from the past, when seers prophesied, and nations blindly accepted the guide of a few zealous in the service of the Lord.

Well, perhaps this age is right. But let us not forget that it was the idealism of Judaism that sustained our race, and that, had facts alone been their mainstay, the cold, hard fact of nearly twenty centuries of endless suffering would long ago have terminated the temporal existence of Israel.

Yes, as a recent writer says, "religion is becoming more and more practical, but God forbid that it should not be also theoretical" and in plucking the weeds from the garden of our faith, in discouraging ignorance and superstition, let us beware that we encroach not too dangerously near the roots of the precious flowers planted by our early Jewish teachers, nourished but too often by the blood of their disciples. In our striving after truth, let us cherish, let us keep intact every custom and observance that may elevate the heart to a purer conception of the Divine Being, the Source and Essence of all Truth and Light!

INTRODUCTION
The National Women's League

From *The Women's League Handbook and Guide* (1947)

The National Women's League aims to stimulate and revitalize religious faith and the Jewish way of life among American Jewish women. It strives to attain its purpose by stressing the observance of Sabbath and Festivals, of Dietary laws and other traditional religious home ceremonials. It emphasizes Jewish education by means of educational programs and publications for women and children.

The Sisterhood

No modern congregation can function adequately without the aid of a well-organized women's group attached to it. This constitutes the Sisterhood. The Sisterhood too, has a goal. Its goal is, or should be, to accomplish locally, what the Women's League aspires to do nationally. It cannot do this alone effectively, but only if it works closely with and through the congregation with which it is affiliated. It must also work in close cooperation with the National Women's League, the religious school, adolescent and young folks groups, the community, and more especially, other Jewish women's organizations. In order to help the Sisterhood achieve its objectives the Women's League offers this "Handbook and Guide" for Synagogue Sisterhoods.

PART I: ORGANIZATION
How the Sisterhood Should Function

To function efficiently, it is necessary that the Sisterhood be governed by a code of generally accepted rules and regulations. A model constitution follows. If this constitution does not serve your purpose, amend it to suit your needs.

ARTICLE I
Name and Object

Section I: This organization shall be known as. . . .
Section II: Its object shall be to strengthen traditional Judaism
    a. By furthering the spiritual, material and social interests of Sisterhood and Congregation.
    b. By advancing Jewish education in the congregational affiliated groups.
    c. By emphasizing the Jewish religious practices of the home.
    d. By generally strengthening the religious life of the local Jewish community. . . .

SISTERHOOD GENERAL MEETINGS
The Meeting Room—Pictures and Posters

Give character to your meeting room. Let the environment indicate that this is the meeting-place of a religious group. The pictures on the wall should be appropriate. Select them carefully, with regard to beauty and theme. Artistic Jewish pictures are available. Make use of them. If you have a good group photograph, featuring a Sisterhood or congregational celebration, by all means display it. It will keep alive memories that will draw the children and grandchildren of those portrayed more closely into the congregational family.

Cardboard posters or placards are effective. They should bear brief quotations from the Bible, or other Jewish literature appropriate to the theme of the day. It is more interesting to display different posters at every meeting. They need be prepared only once by a competent person and may be used for years. Try to have them in Hebrew as well as in English. . . .

Conduct of the Meeting

. . . The business part of the meeting should be as follows:
Greetings
Bible Reading or Prayer
Minutes
Communications
Reports of Committees
Unfinished Business
New Business
[An] Educational Program. . . .

PART III:
PRAYERS FOR SISTERHOOD GATHERING
How Should a Prayer Be Delivered?

A prayer, whether original or not, should be delivered easily and naturally, indicating that it comes directly from the heart. Otherwise, it is not a prayer, but a recitation.

The prayers contained in this book may be simplified or re-written in your own language. Under no circumstances should a prayer be assigned to anyone at the last moment, without an opportunity to read it in advance.

OPENING MEETING

We thank Thee Oh God for the refreshing interlude of a summer of rest and recreation.

May it be the means of strengthening us in body and spirit. May it hearten us to battle with renewed courage, for Truth and Right, for Freedom and Justice, under Thy Law and guidance.

Keep us and our families in health and well being. Inspire us to live in accordance with the influence of the Synagogue, so that at home and abroad, our lives will reflect the teachings of Judaism. May these ideals be realized and fulfilled. Amen. . . .

BROTHERHOOD WEEK

We thank Thee, O Lord, for having blessed our country with a Lincoln and a Washington; men who fought for freedom, for justice, and who rated a man only according to his moral worth.

Thou who hast made and unmade nations, keep our America great and free; a land where men may enjoy the fruits of honest toil, and live in peace with their fellowmen, with none to make them afraid.

Banish want, fear, and hatred from our land. Enable us to rear our children in the knowledge and practice of those ethical principles that were revealed to man on Sinai's heights. May the moral discipline of Judaism enter into their character, strengthening it with that spiritual fortitude which America demands of all her children. Amen.

GRACE COHEN SHOHET,
United States

Prayer composed for dedication of Temple Israel Museum

Our God and God of our Fathers we open our hearts in thanksgiving to Thee, for the privilege here today of meeting as a Sisterhood in Israel in the name of Art. We thank Thee, oh God, for having brought us to this day of the dedication of a Jewish Museum, testimony to our love for the congealed poetry of our religious tradition.

Living as we do in the pressures of a materialistic world and a precarious peace, we are doubly grateful for that inner strength in man which grows out of his yearning for the creative life, and which Thou hast implanted within him. For the power to love the beautiful, to cherish and preserve it, we give Thee thanks.

Throughout history, Thy divine guidance has attracted Israel with an inspired magnetism to moral insights, to a preference for the good and the true. Thou hast strengthened the hand and endowed the mind of Thy people with the power to painstakingly and lovingly record the symbolism of these teachings. Ever protect us, oh God, from indifference to the good life or insensitivity to the aesthetic.

Thou hast, from earliest time, endowed man with the "will to form" and the coercion to create. We pause to give thanks that this spark is yet aflame in the world—that Jewish women are still fired with the desire to preserve thy testimony to this gift in their own religious tradition. Dear God, as thy spirit hovered over the face of the world and quickened it with the breath of life, so teach us to hover over our own world, that we may lift it out of the morass of the false gods of materialism. Sharpen our sensibilities that we may breathe into our world a tenderness toward beauty, an understanding of culture—the meaning of Art. Fire us with the zeal to keep green our Jewish vineyard, to give to our religious life artistic expression, to keep dynamic and flowing the good life, and the preservation of its symbols. That through this love of the good—the true—the beautiful, we "may build more stately mansions for the soul."

We are grateful today for the blessing of this pleasant hour that brings together people consecrated to the melioration of life, our dedicated Rabbi, esteemed Artists, and women in Israel who sustain its institutions.

For all these blessings, dear God, we give Thee thanks. Amen.

3 November 1953

HENRIETTA SZOLD, United States

Letter to Haym Peretz

New York, 16 September 1916

It is impossible for me to find words in which to tell you how deeply I was touched by your offer to act as *"Kaddish"* for my dear mother. I cannot even thank you—it is something that goes beyond thanks. It is beautiful, what you have offered to do—I shall never forget it.

You will wonder, then, that I cannot accept your offer. Perhaps it would be best for me not to try to explain to you in writing, but to wait until I see you to tell you why it is so. I know well, and appreciate what you say about, the Jewish custom; and Jewish custom is very dear and sacred to me.[1] And yet I cannot ask you to say *Kaddish* after my mother. The *Kaddish* means to me that the survivor publicly and markedly manifests his wish and intention to assume the relation to the Jewish community which his parent had, and that so the chain of tradition remains unbroken from generation to generation, each adding its own link. You can do that for the generations of your family, I must do that for the generations of my family.

I believe that the elimination of women from such duties was never intended by our law and custom—women were freed from positive duties when they could not perform them, but not when they could. It was never intended that, if they could perform them, their performance of them should not be considered as valuable and valid as when one of the male sex performed them. And of the *Kaddish* I feel sure this is particularly true.

My mother had eight daughters and no son; and yet never did I hear a word of regret pass the lips of either my mother or my father that one of us was not a son. When my father died, my mother would not permit others to take her daughters' place in saying the *Kaddish*, and so I am sure I am acting in her spirit when I am moved to decline your offer. But beautiful your offer remains nevertheless, and, I repeat, I know full well that it is much more in consonance with the generally accepted Jewish tradition than is my or my family's conception. You understand me, don't you?

Note

1. The *Kaddish*, a sanctification of God, is recited by children in mourning for their parents at synagogue services during one year. By tradition, only male children recite the prayer. If there are no male survivors, a stranger may act as a substitute.

Milan, 12 December 1909

Letter to Alice Seligsberg

It was a happy fortune that brought us from the East to this Christian pagan land. The Palestinian experience was tense. Here there are for us only things—no people. There, at Jerusalem and in the colonies, there was pulsating life, and life coupled with misery, poverty, filth, disease, and there was intellectual life, coupled with idealism, enthusiasm, hope. There was debate and demonstration, and argument and persuasion. And when I saw Jaffa recede from sight, I felt that all my powers had been called forth and kept alert during the whole of the four weeks I spent in Palestine. . . .

When I return I shall tell you much about Palestine and Zionism and the Jews. Briefly now only this: the prophecy of many of my friends that Palestine would unmake my Zionism has not been verified. I am the same Zionist I was. In fact, I am more than ever convinced that our only salvation lies that way. The only thing I admit is that I now think Zionism an ideal more difficult of realization than ever I did before, both on account of the Jews themselves and on account of Oriental and world conditions.

And do you know when that apprehension weighed upon me most heavily? When I listened to High Mass at St. Mark's Church in Venice, on the Feast of the Madonna Immaculate. There was the wonderful basilica, with its domes, its mosaics, jewels, and porphyry. There was the soothing music, the almost angel choir. There was the surpliced acolytes, the richly robed dignitaries, the cardinal-archbishop seated on his regal chair in vestments that beggar description, attended with pomp and ceremony. There was the crowd of decorous, devout worshipers, intent upon the (to me) unintelligible service. And I saw these symbols of a vast unseen power, and I thought of my poor little eleven-millioned people knocking at the door of humanity and begging only for the right to live. That was when I almost lost courage. If I have regained it, it was by means which you will call unfair—the more I see of Italy and her treasures, the more I see paganism in Christianity, and I feel that

Judaism can conquer it. But of this, too, more when I can speak with the mouth rather than the pen. . . .

Letter to Mrs. Julius Rosenwald

New York, 17 January 1915

Your night letter has come to hand, and you will receive a copy of all recent telegrams that have reached the Provisional Executive Committee for General Zionist Affairs concerning the situation both in Palestine and among the refugees in Jaffa. Most of our information at present concerning Palestine comes from a group of Palestinians who have taken up their abode in Alexandria, in order that they may serve as intermediaries between Palestine and ourselves. If it were not for them, we should lack information about many points, and we should not be able to get money to our people in Jaffa. . . .

The paramount consideration is that you are advancing the cause of Palestine. From my point of view, as I need not tell *you*, that is the cause of the Jew and, most important of all, of Judaism. In many respects the war catastrophe has left me bewildered and uncertain. In one respect I see more clearly than ever—that is in respect to Zionism. The anomalous situation of the Jew everywhere—the distress, misery, and in part degradation (witness Poland!) of seven millions, more than half, of our race; the bravery of the Jews who are serving in all the armies; the size of the contingent we are contributing to every front—means to me that the Jew and his Judaism must be perpetuated and can be perpetuated only by their repatriation in the land of the fathers. . . . It will yield sanctuary, refuge, and protection in the days of readjustment soon to dawn, we hope.

. . . If you succeed, in your appeal to the Federation of Temple Sisterhoods, in conveying to the Jewish women of America the need of such a sanctuary for the Jew, the need of a center from which Jewish culture and inspiration will flow, and if you can persuade them to set aside one day of the war as a Palestine Day, on which thoughts and means are to be consecrated to a great Jewish world-organizing purpose, you will have accomplished a result that will bring immediate blessing to those now in distress and in terror of life, and a blessing for all future times redounding to the benefit not only of those who will make use of their sanctuary rights in Palestine, but also those who like ourselves, remaining in a happy, prosperous country, will be free to draw spiritual nourishment from a center dominated wholly by Jewish traditions and the Jewish ideals of universal peace and universal brotherhood.

If you and they do not follow us Zionists so far, at least they will respond to the appeal for material help. . . . They may refuse to accept the whole Zionist ideal. But the wonderful vitality shown by the Zionist settlement in the Holy Land—the resourcefulness of the colonists, who could supply the cities with grain and food for months, and the usefulness of the Zionist bank in averting panic and the direst distress—they make of me a more confirmed and conscious Zionist than ever. I need not analyze the elements I have enumerated for you. You, who have been in the Holy Land, even if you do not—may I say, not yet?—agree with me, your mind will instinctively understand the leap mine makes in these troublous days to the Zionist conclusion.

. . . The Jew speaks of the first *Hurban*—the utter destruction of Solomon's Temple. He speaks of the second *Hurban*, the ruin of the second Temple by Titus. I feel that a future Graetz will speak of this war as the Jews' third *Hurban*.

There is only one hope in my heart—the effective aid being rendered to Palestine by all Jews without difference. In the first *Hurban* the Jews could not protect their sanctuary against the hordes of Nebuchadnezzar. In the second *Hurban* the Roman legions destroyed the Temple, leaving only the western wall, the last vestige of glory, now turned into a place of wailing. There is no third Temple on the hill of Zion to be destroyed in this third *Hurban*; but in Zion, nevertheless, there is a sanctuary, the refuge that has been established by Jewish pioneers, with the sweat, blood, and labor of those who believe. As American Jewesses they cannot possibly reject the centralized organization of Palestine, an endeavor for which Zionism stands first and last.

With cordial wishes for success, and, may I add this once only, with Zion's greeting. . . .

Letter to Adele Szold Setzer and Bertha Szold Levin

Jerusalem, 27 August 1938

On Friday a bomb exploded in the Jaffa marketplace killing as many persons as are killed, according to the newspaper reports, in a regular pitched battle in the Chinese or the Spanish war. Nevertheless, we are having "disturbances"—not a war—in Palestine!

In the afternoon my associate in the Aliyah, Mr. Hans Beyth, met a friend of his in the streets of Jerusalem. The friend had just arrived in town, his taxi having managed to escape from Ramleh. Ramleh is on the road between Jaffa and Jerusalem. As soon as the news of the bomb explosion in Jaffa reached Ramleh, the hoodlums there jumped to the conclusion that the dastardly deed was perpetrated by the Jews; and they stoned and shot at every taxi carrying Jews. Mr. Beyth's friend was covered with blood from top to toe, but not his own. He escaped unhurt, but the woman who sat next to him in the taxi was wounded in the cheek and her blood ran profusely.

And who was the woman? One of the Burgenlanders, the Austrians, seventy in number, who for months had been living on a raft in the Danube, not permitted to land in Austria (their home for centuries) or to take refuge in Czechoslovakia or Hungary on which their Danubian perch abutted, scourged daily by the Nazis who boarded the raft for the purpose, stung by swarms of mosquitoes by day and plagued by rats at night, their clothing dropping from them, undernourished by the food other Jews managed to get to them. For months all sorts of efforts were made to secure for them United States affidavits or Palestinian certificates. Two weeks ago some certificates were obtained; and she, this bleeding woman in the taxi, had been among the first to be released from her Danubian open-air prison, and promptly she dropped from the frying pan of the Nazis into the fire of the Arabs.

It's no use warning me not to overwork; it's no use telling anybody in Palestine to take care. One has to grit one's teeth and take a chance.

**ANDA AMIR,
Land of Israel**

Translated by Sue Ann Wasserman

Eve

Day after day was strung together
night after night—
they flooded me with pleasure and with joy.

From morning until evening the sun caressed me,
slipping its rays between the branches,
to kiss my curls.
The moist hyssop made my sleep gentle,
it pampered my dreams.

Until I'm satisfied,
Until I tire,
Until I become exhausted—
and can do no more.

The sun cooked my body,
the night aroused my bodily fluids,
but they have nowhere to go.
The whole span of my skin is heavy on me
as if it wants to burst forth
but it has no outlet.

Then I saw you, tree,
I recognized you by that apple,
you have stored it in the wisdom of all your juices.

And I knew the secret, for which you had grown,
for which you have grown tall, and even branched out,
I too have grown up,

I too have grown tall—
like you I carry my fruit.
So you have taught me, tree.

How is it that until now I have walked empty
between those who bear their fruit?
But I only hid my face

In a strange disgrace
in the presence of does whose bodies swelled,
bowed down from their weight.
Every little bird
Sits on her eggs,
fruit of her blood and innards.
She disgraces me.
Before her I am insignificant,
I who was created only for joy;
I who skipped from spring to spring,
and washed my feet in their crystal transparence,
I jumped from choice fruit to choice fruit,
whichever was sweet to my palate, to make myself happy.

And now I know,
and I am very heavy, yet happy;
I am sister to you,
swelling does.
Heavy she-wolves.
In a little while—we will bend down from our weight.
Like them—so I.

And I will no longer be ashamed before you—
the best of my blood, like the best of your blood,
will be crystallized into fruit.
I will surely accept it,
I will surely carry it,
even if it bends me to the ground,
like you.

I will no longer walk empty between you,
like an impulsive stream, it does not know
where its light waters are going.
You will be a blessing to me, magic spell that is in the heart,
for bringing me to the fruit,
through it I will be redeemed,
Though I will no longer know flighty pleasure.

Lot's Wife

To Zoar! To Zoar!—You called to me.
Do not look behind you,
do not turn to the left or to the right:
To Zoar!

Your voice was so harsh with its certainty about the future,
the quietude in your eyes is terrible.
For you every path is straight,
every road becomes smooth before your feet,
the road calls out and encourages you:
        tread on me and walk safely.

You—your whole past life, you have wiped it out from your very
   midst
without a sigh.
You have immersed yourself in the light of tomorrow,
you will be purified in it.
Clear and pure are the paths before you,
they are wide open to you, the one who crosses over.

How lucky you are,
you righteous and simple man,
when you called out: To Zoar.
But I—
I cannot;
please, do not call me
do not press me, my husband—
Surely all my blood has been given to him, to the one who
   vanished,
For him my very insides, for him my bowels burn.

I am drunk on yesterday.
Its murmuring is preserved with every pounding of my blood,
preserved its joys, its sorrows,
lasting within me, within me.
All of me is saturated,
there is no uninjured place in me, no place left untouched by
   them.
But how will I wipe them out from my heart?
How will I flee from their murmuring?
And they march with me,
with a thousand arms they catch up to me:
Turn back!
You are ours—
You are part of us—
Turn!

Then how could I not look behind me—
even if I am to be destroyed with Sodom?

A heavy fog is spread out before me,
it covers the mountain tops,
the expanses of the valleys,
every path at my feet distorts,
and dims what my eye sees.
I no longer see a thing except for the figures,
except for the life,
which you have commanded me to betray.

The road twists before me—
How straight it is for you,
my simple husband.

Turn back!
You are ours—
you are part of us—
Turn!

I will surely look behind me,

even if I am to be destroyed with Sodom,
even if only I surely know.
Here I will meet my end,
like a huge stone I will harden here,
at the foot of the doomed Sodom.

I will stand like a stone in my place,
forever will I look on the footsteps of my past,
I will look on their destruction—my destruction.

---

1 October 1938

**HANNAH SENESH,
Hungary, Yugoslavia,
Land of Israel**
Translated by Marta Cohn

From her diary

It is the Saturday before the Day of Atonement. I should have gone to synagogue, but instead I wrote a poem, and now I would rather attempt some self-analysis in my diary.

I don't quite know where to begin. That I made many errors this past year (though I don't feel I actually sinned) I know. Errors against God, righteousness, people, and above all, against Mother, and even against myself. I know I have many mistakes to answer for, and see them all clearly in my mind's eye. But I find myself incapable of enumerating them, of writing them all down. Perhaps deep down I'm afraid that someday someone might read what I have written. And I am really incapable of "confessing."

I would like to be as good as possible to Mother, to wear my Jewishness with pride, to be well thought of in my class at school, and I would very much like always to be able to believe and trust in God. There are times I cannot, and at such times I attempt to force myself to believe completely, firmly, with total certainty.

27 October 1938

I don't know whether I've already mentioned that I've become a Zionist. This word stands for a tremendous number of things. To me it means, in short, that I now consciously and strongly feel I am a Jew, and am proud of it. My primary aim is to go to Palestine, to work for it. Of course this did not develop from one day to the next; it was a somewhat gradual development. There was first talk of it about three years ago, and at that time I vehemently attacked the Zionist Movement. Since then people, events, times, have all brought me closer to the idea, and I am immeasurably happy that I've found this ideal, that I now feel firm ground under my feet, and can see a definite goal towards which it is really worth striving. I am going to start learning Hebrew, and I'll attend one of the youth groups. In short, I'm really going to knuckle down properly. I've become a different person, and it's a very good feeling.

One needs something to believe in, something for which one can have whole-hearted enthusiasm. One needs to feel that one's life has meaning, that one is needed in this world. Zionism fulfills all this for me. One hears a good many arguments against the Movement, but this doesn't matter. I believe in it, and that's the important thing.

I'm convinced Zionism is Jewry's solution to its problems, and that the outstanding work being done in Palestine is not in vain.

12 November 1938

I have so much to write about I don't even know where to begin. We have got back the Upper part of Northern Hungary.[1] From the 2nd of November until the 10th the joyous and enthusiastic entry of Hungarian troops took place from Komarom to Kassa. We had no school, and thanks to the radio we too felt involved in the entry. And this morning the four senior classes, in groups of ten, attended a special holiday sitting of Parliament which was very interesting. But I must honestly state that to me the road I am now following in the Zionist Movement means far more, both emotionally and spiritually.

I am learning Hebrew, reading about Palestine, and am also reading Szechenyi's *Peoples of the East*, a brilliant book which gives fundamental facts concerning the lives of all the people of the world. On the whole, I'm reading considerably more, and about far more serious subjects than hitherto.

I am determinedly and purposefully preparing for life in Palestine. And although I confess that in many respects it's painful to tear myself from my Hungarian sentiments, I must do so in my own interest, and the interests of Jewry. Our two-thousand-year history justifies us, the present compels us, the future gives us confidence. Whoever is aware of his Jewishness cannot continue with his eyes shut. As yet, our aims are not entirely definite nor am I sure what profession I'll choose. But I don't want to work only for myself and in my own interests, but for the mutual good of Jewish aims. Perhaps these are but the vague and confused thoughts and fantasies of youth, but I think I will have the fortitude, strength and ability to realize these dreams.

Mother is having difficulty accepting the idea that I will eventually emigrate, but because she is completely unselfish she won't place obstacles in my way. Naturally I would be so happy if she came too. The three of us must not be torn apart, must not go three different ways. . . .

20 November 1938

The thought that now occupies my every waking moment is Palestine. Everything in connection with it interests me, everything else is entirely secondary. Even school has lost some of its meaning, and the only thing I am studying hard is Hebrew. I already know a little . . . a few words. Eva Beregi is teaching me. She is remarkably kind, and won't accept any money from me, so I'm racking my brains to find some possible way of reciprocating. I have also joined a correspondence course. They send lessons, and it's quite good.

I'm almost positive I'll choose some sort of profession connected with agriculture. I'll probably study dairy farming and cheese production. A woman who was in Palestine, and enchanted by it, gave me the idea. She also told me all sorts of wonderful things about the Land. Listening to her was a joy. Everything that is beautiful, cheerful, and of some consolation to the Jews stems from Palestine.

Here the situation is constantly deteriorating. A new Jewish Law[2] is soon to be proclaimed. It will be the "most urgent" thus far. They are going to "solve" Land Reform by distributing the land at present in Jewish hands—and only that. The truly great estates won't be touched. But of course this was to be expected.

11 December 1938

It's nine o'clock in the morning but I'm the only one up—surrounded by paper streamers and an untidy mess. Yesterday I finally had my "evening"—or whatever one can call it, as it was 6:30 in the morning by the time I got to bed. Whether it was a successful party I can't say. I would be pleased to state it was, but to me the entire thing was, somehow, a disappointment. Perhaps one of the contributing factors was that I, personally, didn't enjoy myself very much. By this I mean there was no one with whom I spent any great length of time, or who really interested me. But there is something else: the times. And above all, my ideological point of view has so vastly changed since last year that I could not help but consider the affair frivolous, empty, and in a certain measure quite unnecessary at a time such as we're now going through.

There were nearly thirty people here, and only a few among them seriously interested me. I kept thinking how nice it would have been to have put all the money the party cost into the collection box of the Keren Kayemet.[3] Oh, dear, I would like best of all to go to Palestine now. I would be glad to forget my graduation, everything. I don't know what has happened to me, but I just can't live here any longer, can't stand my old group of friends, studying, or any of the things with which I've been familiar up till now.

I don't know how I'm going to bear the next half year. I would never have believed that I would spend my senior year this way. I see I haven't written anything at all about the party, but I just can't. A ship is leaving today with a great many Hungarian Jews aboard. I so wish I could have gone with them. I don't understand how I could have lived this way for so long.

I've just read what I've written. It's so pathetic. I see how greatly I've been influenced by Szechenyi's diary—his style is very noticeable in my own. But I can't help it. I think the sadness comes from deep within me, and I also like Szechenyi's work very much.

. . . This is a paper I read at a meeting of the Bible Society:

ROOTS OF ZIONISM OR
THE FUNDAMENTALS OF ZIONISM

When anyone in Hungary spoke of Zionism five or even two years ago, Jewish public opinion condemned him as a traitor to Hungary, laughed at him, considered him a mad visionary, and under no circumstances heard him out.

Today, due perhaps in large measure to the recent blows suffered, Hungarian Jews are beginning to concern themselves with Zionism. At least so it seems when they ask, "How big is Palestine? How many people can it accommodate?" and "Is there room for me in the expanding country?" Often the answers to these questions decide whether or not the questioner will become a Zionist.

But the question least frequently voiced is, "What is the purpose of Zionism, its basic aim?"

It is exactly with this seldom-voiced question I would like to deal, because I believe it to be the most important of all questions. When one understands and feels this and applies it to oneself, one will become a Zionist, regardless of how many can emigrate to Palestine today or tomorrow, whether conditions here will improve or deteriorate, whether or not there are possibilities of emigrating to other countries.

Thus, without relating it to the times and circumstances under which we are now living—in fact apart from all pertinent circumstances and situations—I would like to summarize absolute Zionism.

If we had to define Zionism briefly perhaps we could best do so in the words of Nachum Sokolov:[4] "Zionism is the movement of the Jewish people for its revival."

Perhaps many are at this very moment mentally vetoing this with the thought that Jews do not constitute a people. But how is a nation created out of a community? From a common origin, a common past, present and future, common laws, a common language and a native land.

In ancient Palestine these motives were united and formed a complete background. Then the native land ceased to exist, and gradually the language link to the ancient land weakened. But the consciousness of the people was saved by the *Torah*, that invisible but all-powerful mobile State.

It is, however, inconceivable that in the stateless world of the Middle Ages, when religion was the focal point of life, the self-assurance of the ghetto-bound Jew could have become so strengthened that he could have expressed his longing for a nation, or the restoration of his own way of life, or that he would have thought of rebuilding his own country. Yet the yearning expressed in the holiday greeting "Next Year in Jerusalem" is absolute proof that the hope of regaining the Homeland never died within the Jew.

Then came the Human Rights Laws of the 19th century and with them new ideas and concepts of national values. From the peoples of the greatest countries to those in the smallest Balkan enclaves, all attempted to find themselves and their rights. It was the time of decision. Did a Jewish people still exist, and if so, would it be influenced by the strength of the spirit of the New Movement?

The greater part of Jewry asked only for human rights, happily accepting the goodwill of the people among whom it lived, and in exchange casting off individuality and ancient characteristics. But a few hundred inspired zealots, young men from Russia, started off towards Zion, and shortly thereafter Herzl[5] wrote the *Judenstaat*. Thousands upon thousands endorsed the concept and ideals of Zionism, and suddenly there was a Jewish nation. He who feels there is not, let him speak for himself, but let him not forget those to whom Jewishness means more than the vital statistics on a birth certificate.

One of the fundamentals of Zionism is the realization that anti-Semitism is an illness which can neither be fought against with words, nor cured with superficial treatment. On the contrary, it must be treated and healed at its very roots.

Jewry is living under unnatural conditions, unable to realize its noble characteristics, to utilize its natural talents and capabilities. Thus it cannot cultivate its natural and immortal attributes or fulfill its destiny.

It is not true that during the Dispersion we have become teachers of the people, leaders. On the contrary, we have turned into imitators, servants, become the whipping boys for the sins and errors of those among whom we live. We have lost our individuality and renounced the most fundamental conditions of life.

How many great Jewish ideas and ideals died behind the walls of ghettoes during the Middle Ages even before seeing the light of day, or behind the invisible ghetto walls of modern Jewry?

If we compare the accomplishments of the 500,000 Jews now living in Palestine with the same number of Jews living in Hungary today, perhaps we will no longer voice the opinion that we can reach our aims only in the Diaspora. Thus Dispersion cannot be our aim, and certainly the sufferings of the Jews must be alleviated.

We don't want charity. We want only our lawful property and rights, and our freedom, for which we have struggled with our own labours. It is our human and national duty to demand these rights. We want to create a Homeland for the Jewish spirit and the Jewish people. The solution seems so very clear: we need a Jewish State.

"The Jewish State has become a universal necessity, thus it will become a reality," stated Herzl. Those Jews who want it, will create it, and they will have earned it, and deserved it. If we renounce Zionism, we renounce tradition, honour, truth, the right of man to live.

We cannot renounce a single one of our rights, not even if the ridiculous accusation were true—that Zionism breeds anti-Semitism. Anti-Semitism is not the result of Zionism, but of Dispersion.

But even if this were not so, woe to the individual who attempts to ingratiate himself with the enemy instead of following his own route. We can't renounce Zionism even if it does strengthen anti-Semitism. But amazingly enough, Zionism is the least attacked in this area. On the contrary, the only hope of lessening or ending anti-Semitism is to realize the ideals of Zionism. Then Jewry can live its own life peacefully, alongside other nations. For only Zionism and the establishment of a Jewish State could ever bring about the possibility of the Jews in the Diaspora being able to make manifest their love for their Homeland. Because then they could choose to be part of the Homeland—not from necessity, but by free will and free choice.

When the possibility of a new Homeland came up for discussion, the general Zionist opinion unanimously opted for Palestine. By so doing it gave assurance that its aim was not only to create a homeland, or haven for persecuted Jews in any spot on earth, but that it definitely wanted a Homeland, and that it wanted to create that Homeland on the very ground to which its history and religious heritage binds it.

I don't want to talk about the work which has been going on in Palestine for several decades, because that has nothing to do with the ideals of Zionism. That is, instead, a part of the realization of the Homeland. But one thing must be said at this time: that reality—that which is happening in Palestine—has justified and verified many times over the concepts and ideals of Zionism. The Jew has proved his will to live, his love of work, his ability to establish a state; and he has shown that the name of Palestine is so powerful that it is capable of gathering in Jews from any and all parts of the world.

This tiny piece of land on the shores of the Mediterranean which, after 2,000 years, the Jew can again feel to be his own, is big enough to enable the new Jewish life and modern Jewish culture to be attached to its ancient, fundamental ways, and flourish.

Even today, in its mutilated form, Palestine is big enough to be an island in the sea of seemingly hopeless Jewish destiny, an island upon which we can peacefully build a lighthouse to beam its light into the darkness, a light of everlasting human values, the light of the one God.

Notes

1. Following the Munich Agreement, Hungary was awarded 7,500 square miles of the Czechoslovak Highlands, with a population of 500,000 Hungarians and 272,000 Slovaks. This was originally part of Hungary and was lost in World War I.
2. Four to five percent of the land was in Jewish hands when the law of 1939 authorized the government to order the sale of Jewish agricultural properties.
3. Jewish National Fund.
4. Nachum Sokolov (1861–1936), Zionist leader and Hebrew journalist, President of the World Zionist Organization and Jewish Agency, 1931–35.
5. Theodor Herzl (1860–1904), founder of modern Zionism, devoted his life to the creation of a Jewish state.

You hold me now completely in your hands.

My heart beats like a frightened little bird's
Against your palm. Take heed! You do not think
A person lives within the page you thumb.
To you this book is paper, cloth, and ink.

Some binding thread and glue, and thus is dumb,
And cannot touch you (though the gaze be great
That seeks you from the printed marks inside),
And is an object with an object's fate.

And yet it has been veiled like a bride,
Adorned with gems, made ready to be loved,
Who asks you bashfully to change your mind,
To wake yourself, and feel, and to be moved.

But still she trembles, whispering to the wind:
"This shall not be." And smiles as if she knew.
Yet she must hope. A woman always tries,
Her very life is but a single "You . . ."

With her black flowers and her painted eyes,
With silver chains and silks of spangled blue.
She knew more beauty when a child and free,
But now forgets the better words she knew.

A man is so much cleverer than we,
Conversing with himself of truth and lie,
Of death and spring and iron-work and time,
But I say "you" and always "you and I."

This book is but a girl's dress in rhyme,
Which can be rich and red, or poor and pale,
Which may be wrinkled, but with gentle hands,
And only may be torn by loving nails.

So then, to tell my story, here I stand.
The dress's tint, though bleached in bitter lye,
Has not all washed away. It still is real.
I call then with a thin, ethereal cry.

You hear me speak. But do you hear me feel?

GERTRUD
KOLMAR,
Germany
Translated by Henry A. Smith

The Woman Poet

The Jewish Woman

I am a stranger.

Since no one dares approach me
I would be girded with towers

That wear their steep and stone-gray caps
Aloft in clouds.

The brazen key you will not find
That locks the musty stair. It spirals skyward
As a serpent lifts its scaly head
Into the light.

Oh these walls decay like cliffs
That streams have washed a thousand years;
And birds with raw and wrinkled craws
Lie burrowed deep in caves.

Inside the halls of sifting sand
Crouch lizards hiding speckled breasts—
An expedition I would mount
Into my ancient land.

Perhaps somewhere I can unearth
The buried Ur of the Chaldeans,
The idol Dagon, Hebrew tents,
Or the horn of Jericho.

What once blew down the haughty walls
Now lies in twisted ruin underground;
And yet I once drew breath
To sound its note.

Inside chests choked with dust
Lie dead the noble robes,
The dying gleam of pigeons' wings,
And the torpor of Behemoth.

Amazed, I clothe myself. For I am small
And far from ages glorious and strong.
Yet all about me stare expanses shining:
Shelter for my soul.

Now I seem strange, no longer know myself,
For I was there before great Rome and Carthage were,
Because in me the altar fires ignite
Of Deborah and her tribe.

And from the hidden golden bowl
A painful glistening runs into my blood,
And then a song rings out a name
That suits me once again.

The heavens call with colored signs.
Your face is closed:

And those who steal around me with the desert fox
Will never see it.

Enormous, crumbling columns of wind,
As green as nephrite, red as coral,
Blow across the towers. God lets them fall in ruin,
And yet they stand for ages more.

The night alone can hear. I love you, I love you, oh my people,
In my embrace I want to hold you warm and close
Just as a wife would hold her husband on the scaffold steps,
Or like a mother who cannot allow her son to die alone.

And when your throat is gagged, your bleeding cry suppressed,
When brutal shackles bind your trembling arms,
Oh let me be the voice that echoes down the shaft of all eternity,
The hand stretched high to touch God's towering heaven.

For the Greeks have struck white gods like sparks from mountain
    crags,
And Rome threw brazen shields across the earth,
Mongolian hordes whirled forth from deep in Asia,
And the emperors in Aachen gazed enchanted to the South.

And Germany and France hold high their books and shining
    swords,
And England wanders silver paths on ocean-going ships,
And Russia grew to giant shadows with a flame upon its hearth,
And we, we have proceeded through the gallows and the rack.

This bursting of our hearts, this sweat of death, this gaze without
    a tear,
And the eternal windblown sigh of martyrs at the stake,
The withered claw, the weary fist with veins like vipers
Raised against the murderers from ropes and funeral pyres of
    ages,

The gray beard singed in hellfires, torn by devils-grip,
The mutilated ear, the wounded brow and fleeing eye:
Oh all of you! Now, when the bitter hour strikes I will arise
And stand like a triumphal arch above your cavalcade of anguish!

I will not kiss the arm that wields the weighty scepter,
Nor the brazen knee, the earthen feet of demigods in desperate
    hours;
If only I could raise my voice to be a blazing torch
Amidst the darkened desert of the world, and thunder: JUSTICE!
    JUSTICE! JUSTICE!

We Jews

And yet my ankles are in chains; I drag a ringing prison as I go.
My lips are sealed in glowing wax.
My soul is like a swallow fluttering helpless in its cage.
And I can feel the fist that drags my weeping head toward the hill
  of ashes.

The night alone can hear. I love you, oh my people dressed in
  rags.
Now, like the son of Gaea who returned exhausted to his heathen
  mother earth,
So you must cast yourselves among the lowly and be weak;
  embrace your sorrow.
For one day your weary wandering shoes will stand upon the
  necks of all the mighty!

**TEHILLA
LICHTENSTEIN,
United States**

**God in the Silence
(1947)**

One of the most important goals which you can set yourself to achieve is the realization of God's presence in your life. I deem it so important because if you can attain to this realization, you will be lifted above all the cares and anxieties of life, you will find that life no longer has the power to hurt you, you will find that life assumes wonderful meaning and joy, you will find yourself safe and secure even in the midst of the greatest vicissitudes and storms, you will find a way out of your difficulties, you will find an assured way to happiness, an assured way to inner peace and serenity, a staff against the pitfalls and roughness of the road, a shelter against the four winds of heaven, a refuge from the storm of adverse circumstances, a shield and a buckler against your enemies, a rock to lean upon when your feet are weary, a mountain top to be lifted to when the tide of adversity is rising about you. All this, and more, much more than my poor pen can convey, will be yours when you truly realize that God is there, that He is beside you, that His love is about you, and His care is watching over you, and His strength is available to you. If the knowledge of the presence of God means all this, surely you must want to attain to this knowledge, to this awareness of God's presence. How shall we attain to such awareness? How shall we feel and recognize God's presence?

. . . When is a child most aware of his mother? When does he feel most acutely that she is there, and that she is the source of security and strength? When he needs her help, when he is in trouble, when his little heart is filled with woe, when his eyes are big with tears, when his own sturdy, independent little self has come up against an unyielding difficulty, then he calls out to her who has never failed him, then he turns to her who has always helped him in all his troubles, and it is then that he is most aware of her, most conscious of that great, wondrous, strong, unfailing presence. Before God, our Father, we are but children; we have our prowess and our power and our manifold resources, but above all we have Him; He is our greatest power, our greatest prowess, our greatest resource; and we have His help at all times, if we but knew it. . . .

There is a popular saying to the effect that "*Seeing* is Believing." Or in other words, that when a thing has been proven, when testimony has been offered that is satisfactory to the senses, conviction just naturally follows. If you can see it with your eyes, or feel it with your hands, or hear it with your ears, why, it is there, without a doubt. It is what might be considered common-sense, or hard-headedness; the kind of practical sense exhibited by the so-called man from Missouri, who says, "first show me." "Let me see, and I will believe." It is a sort of hind vision, which recognizes and accepts that which already has taken place, as opposed to *fore-vision* which sees that which is going to take place, and by seeing it brings it about. We *all* have hind vision; we all know that if we pull a lever, or press a button, a dark room will be flooded with electric light; because we have seen that happen again and again; *we have seen, and therefore we believe.*

But it is not hind-sight that makes the world go forward. Edison saw an electric bulb lighting up a room, *before* ever it had occurred, when the only artificial light was that of candle or oil or gas flame; he saw what was not there, because he believed it could be there, and he brought it about through his vision. He believed and he saw; because he believed, he saw it; he did not wait to see it, in order to believe it. The doers among men, the leaders, the discoverers, the bringers of light to men, are the privileged ones who see because they believe, and who see what they believe, and bring into existence that which they see, because they *see* it before it exists. And what they see, what they vision, or rather what they pre-vision, is not something that appears to their physical instrument of vision, but to the inner eye of the imagination. God has given us the physical eye, a miraculous instrument, with which to behold reality, the world about us, but he has given us the still more miraculous instrument of the imagination, he has given us the power of visualization, with which to create new and greater realities, a more perfect and happier world than the one we have experienced. . . .

. . . Visualization, the seeing of that which is not yet, which is not actually before us, as yet, is essential for the attainment of all the good that man may aspire to. This is true of the destiny of mankind, and it is true also of the destiny of the individual, with which we are at this moment particularly concerned. We would like here to indicate the way in which visualization may be come *your* instrument for the attainment of that which you need at this moment for fulfillment and happiness.

We should like to say, first of all, do not tie yourself down, do not *limit* yourself, to the meager testimony of your senses; do *not* follow the popular proverb, do not confine your understanding, do not *narrow* your belief to the small compass over which the physical eye can range. If you believe only what you see, your world will consist only of molecules and atoms, of inert matter, having little soul and meaning, you yourself will be but a moving mechanism, having neither significance nor permanency, nor connection with the central meaning of things. And where would God be in your consciousness, who is not to be seen except with the eyes of the soul, nor felt except by the sentient heart? But turn the proverb around, and see with your inner vision that which you believe; for *believing is seeing*. And I do not mean by that that faith makes you see, makes you imagine, that which is not and cannot be, and will never be; I do not mean that faith, that believing, will make you capable of deluding yourself, of mistaking illusion for reality, of being satisfied with illusion, with mere imaginings, and allowing them to take the place of reality. No, I mean that believing is the act of seeing, faith expresses itself in seeing; not seeing illusions, but seeing that which is sought, which is desired, which is to be attained.

Believing in God, for example, is seeing God; seeing Him in the form of those attributes that you believe Him to possess, seeing Him as strength, seeing Him as love, seeing Him as guidance, as shelter, as protection, as infinite loving kindness. Notice that the psalmist, who had in most remarkable measure, as great poets always have, the power of visualization, speaks of God as his rock, his fortress, his shield and his high tower. It was not that the Psalmist had a childish or anthropomorphic conception of God; on the contrary, it was he who gave us the most spiritual and utterly non-material and non-pagan conception of God; it was he who conceived of God as the Divine Mind, as the fount of infinite goodness and creativeness *within* the universe and *within* man. It was simply that his belief in God expressed itself in magnificently concrete terms; he saw a rock, a tower, a fortress, as symbols of Divine strength, and these visualizations created in him the sense of strength, of utter strength, of the unshaken and unshakable might which flowed from the very thought of God's presence, and which filled him, the Psalmist, with a sense of security and protection. . . .

We, in Jewish Science, through the wisdom of the Founder of Jewish Science, have seen the basic principle underlying this expression of faith, and have been enabled to adopt and adapt the uses of visualization to the act of prayer. Believing in God, as the Psalmist did, earnestly convinced, as he was, of the efficacy of prayer, we use the form of prayer that he found an unfailing instrument in his hours of difficulty, longing and distress. The Psalmist affirmed and visualized that which he desired God to bring about in his life; we in Jewish Science also use the declarative or affirmative form of prayer, and visualize the response that we are seeking through our prayer. We have not only found this form of prayer unfailingly efficacious, but can declare, without reservation, that unless your prayer is accompanied with a visualization of the response that you are seeking, it will fall far short of the optimum good of which prayer is capable. . . .

Because space does not permit the selection of more than one instance, among the countless that I could employ, I will try to show briefly just the power and effect of visualization as part of the prayer for health. . . .

God who is the source and fount of all good, is also the source of healing; it is from the Divine Mind that healing comes, when through wrong living or thinking or through ignorance of the laws of our being, we have impaired the natural health with which we have been endowed; and it is the healing power of the Divine Mind that we must invoke when we seek to regain our health. But the Divine Mind, and the divine attributes of God, have residence within man, they are within yourself, and therefore, healing, too, is within yourself; the healing that you seek is within yourself; you do not need to plead, you need not look for some foreign and perhaps reluctant power outside yourself toward whom to address yourself; you need only to declare, in full faith, without the hindrance of doubt or uncertainty, that which you know to be a certainty—that healing and renewed strength are flowing from within yourself through your whole being, (and incidentally, it is not a mere theory or religious hypothesis that the healing or recuperative powers are resident within man; any physician or physiologist will make the same declaration and verify it through the findings of scientific research) and your declaration will at once make you receptive to the unhindered flow of these healing forces.

We have said that visualization of a goal brings into action, or initiates the action on the part of the body, on the part of man's physical, mental and spiritual forces, which will achieve that goal; this is true in the field of material attainment, and it is equally, and even more true, in the evoking of divine action within man for the good of man. Therefore, along with your affirmation for health or healing, practice *visualization* of health or healing; affirm, "The Divine Mind is filling my being—my heart, if that is the organ that is suffering ill-health—with perfect health and renewed strength;" then see a stream, a stream of health, flowing from a divine fount, within or outside yourself, for God is both without and within yourself, see that stream pouring itself into your being, see that stream of health pouring into your heart and filling it, every nook and cranny and fiber of it, with renewed health and strength; see that stream clearly, hold it devotedly, knowing that that image is your prayer for the evocation of God's healing power, just as the Psalmist evoked God's strength in his behalf when he declared God to be his fortress and his high tower. We do not know whether renewed health comes in a stream or a force or a current like that flowing through an electric wire, but seeing it as a stream is a visualization of God's healing powers, just as seeing a tower is a visualization of God's strength; that image of a stream of health, stirs into action the divine forces of health within you, just as the image of a Divine fortress evoked in the Psalmist a surge of strength, and just as the visualization of rays of serenity will evoke within you the blessed experience of calmness and peace.

If you believe in God's goodness, then see God's goodness achieved; if you believe that God, the Divine Mind, has placed within you His own attributes of serenity and joy and power, then see those attributes of serenity and joy and power within you and expressing themselves through you; if you believe that God is the source of health and healing, and that He has placed the forces of healing within yourself, then see the divine flow of healing within yourself and see the divine flow of healing into whatever part of your being needs Divine help and recuperation. If you believe, you will see; believing is seeing; and seeing, visualizing, will bring about that which you visualize.

PAULA ACKERMAN, United States

Reserve Resources (Sermon)

The sudden and tragic events in my life that have catapulted me from the security of pers[onal?] worship to the solemn responsibility of this holy pulpit [have] left me somewhat dazed and bewildered and most subjective in my thinking. I hope you will bear with me patiently, then, for a few weeks until I can learn to think objectively—until I can [articulate] a clearer perspective of Judaism, not only its values for me, but as Deed and Creed—as Faith—as Way of Life.

To-night, I can speak to you only of its powerful reserve resources that have sustained and strengthened me thru [*sic*] my greatest need—that have lifted me from the Valley of the Shadow [of Death] to him again on the Heights with God.

When your congregational Board asked me to carry on the beautiful work that my beloved husband dedicated his life to, in utmost humility I asked your President what I could possibly give this Congregation. His answer was: "Let your lips speak the faith that is in your heart." How I wish, dear friends, that I could do just that for I know what it means to love the Lord with all my heart, with all my soul and with all my might and He who has always been my strength has truly now become my salvation.

Fitting God into the picture of our lives—living in His presence day by day, offering up to Him the passing moment, is perhaps the best prayer and the one formula for our happiness. More than that, it is the only way to build up a reserve resource in time of trouble, and need.

"How," you may ask? And where is our source material? Let me answer the second question first.

The primary source is, of course, our Bible. It is the basis of everything in Judaism. The first three words of Genesis: "Barashes Baroh Elohim"—"In the beginning God" have always been to me a tower of strength and refuge when the world seems so unstable and tottering. In the beginning God—He was, He is, He shall remain. It is my intention during the next few weeks to bring you some Book Reserves from the Bible's treasure chest—Dr. Ackerman has already given you Genesis and Ecclesiastes. I'd like to continue with the Book of Job, Psalms, Proverbs—many others in the hope that together we might discover an amazing direction for conduct in the word of God—a direction as valid and valuable today as when the words were uttered centuries ago.

Our second source is the Talmud. To be sure, the Talmud is a deep and comprehensive study to scholars who devote a life time to it but even a superficial gleaning of its contents such as I have had the privilege of giving to confirmands—studying and living with such great teachers as Rabbis Hillel, Akiva, Neir, Jehuda Ha Nasi—philosophers like Maimonides, Rashi, Spinoza—poets like Gabirol and HaLevi—all who made this veritable library of books have given me so much personal pleasure, courage and strength. They have become living personalities in my life (Beruriah[?]) and have helped me over many rough places. I should like so much to visit them with you and let you know your blessed heritage.

The third source and perhaps I should place it first because it is so readily accessible is my Prayer Book. I wonder if you realize what a precious small sanctuary you have in this little book. I wonder if you felt as I did tonight when we read this particular fourth service: what a very special meaning and significance it had for me—perhaps for you too. Had it been written for my own particular needs it could not have been more appropriately worded.

And therein, dear friends, lies the answer to my first question: How? How can we make God real in our lives?

There is no magic formula—it is simply training the ear and the eye to listen and perceive and receive. Let me illustrate: The watchword of Israel is *Sh'ma Yisroel Adonai Eloheinu Adonai Ehod.* Think for a moment of this sentence [with which] we're supposed to great and close each day, recite at every service and repeat with our dying breath. *Sh'ma*—Hear. Before we can hear we must train our ears to listen. Who? *Yisroel*—Hear, O Israel. What? *Adonai Eloheinu*—Listen, O Israel for the Lord our God—*Adonai Ehod*—the Lord is One. *Ehod* here means more than the number one—it means unity, universality, unique, incomparable, absolute—There lives a God! God is—He is One! In the *Adon Olom,* one of the great hymns that we have more recently neglected, we have the most classic expression of ethical monotheism as we understand it in Judaism. . . .

Prayer or meditation or Communion with God is vitally necessary if we are to build our spiritual resources for Reserve needs. I should like to tell you in the very near future why I believe so genuinely in God and prayer. But even before we can petition or commune we must condition ourselves—we must be prepared to listen and to receive. . . .

Dear Friends,

This past month has been full of such questions for me. This Holy Season has always been the Hi-Light [sic] of my year—but I find that there is a completely different perspective when viewed from the pulpit instead of the pew. It calls for an adjustment that bi-focals cannot clarify. I have spent the entire month in earnest and solemn soul-searching—in questioning and groping for answers. I hope you will be both patient and understanding with me as I lay bare my heart upon this altar, for the thoughts that I shall bring you,

Congregational address

as we embark on this New Year 5712 [1951], together tonight and throughout the Holy Cycle—are the findings of our inspired teachers who are helping me to find the answers, as I pray I may help you.

SONGS OF YEMENITE WOMEN, Israel

In the Name of God I Shall Begin

In the name of God I shall begin,
I shall begin with my Lord.
he will be my help,
from the moment I begin.

Said her father,
her father said,
"My daughter is young,
Do not frighten her."

Frighten her?
Why would you?
He already counted two hundred
Into her father's hand.

He already counted two hundred,
Counted two hundred
And took the beautiful one.
Oh, how wonderful!

The first word is,
And so it is:
I shall ask God
To watch over all of us.

Said his mother,
His mother said,
"My son is young,
No harm will come to him."

His sister said,
So she said:
"My brother is young,
His fortune will shine."

I Shall Begin to Sing

I shall begin to sing, of You O Lord,
Above all firmaments!
O Lord, my true support,
My heart is full of longing
And full of sighs.
O mother, I will not tell the sorrows,

Like a camel lying on my heart
And like daggers stabbing.
O my mother, my family,
How they abhorred me.
They sent me to a land
I do not know, nor am I known here.
To a distant land they sent me
And abused me indeed!
When I walked atop the roof
Others said: "How voluptuous and delightful!"
And when I came down to the yard
They said: "Who is this stranger?"

Part IV

1960-1990: CONTEMPORARY VOICES

Introduction

SINCE 1960, and even more so since 1970, there has been a great outpouring of material by Jewish women expressing their search for God, their understanding and, frequently, reevaluation of Jewish religious teachings, and their visions of Jewish community. While some of these works, particularly those by American Jewish women, have appeared in print in journals and anthologies and, in a few instances, in separate volumes by the authors themselves, most of this material has never before been published, and some of it was written especially for this volume. Some has been presented from pulpits and other public platforms, some has been recited or sung in performance or ritual settings, and some has previously been shared only with friends. This section reflects the astonishingly wide range of literary and creative genres on which Jewish women today are drawing to express their spirituality, including poetry, dance, song, ritual, *midrash*, prayers, blessings, spiritual autobiographies, sermons, and public addresses.

Much of the unpublished material in this section is written by American Jewish women because this is what we have greatest access to. While we hope that future works containing spiritual literature by Jewish women will include more material by women living outside the United States, it should be noted that the great size and vitality of the American Jewish community (in comparison to other Jewish communities throughout the world, with the exception of Israel), the growth of religious liberalism within the Jewish community and the many roles, including those of rabbi and cantor, open to women (unmatched by any other Jewish community anywhere),[1] and the great impact of the American feminist movement on Jewish women, as women and as Jews, all have contributed to what is becoming an increasingly vast corpus of spiritual literature produced by American Jewish women.

The first documents in this section are poems by Yiddish writer Malka Heifetz Tussman (1893–1987). Born on a farm in the Ukraine, she came to the United States in 1912, living in Chicago, Milwaukee, Los Angeles, and Berkeley, California. Married, with two sons, she taught Yiddish for many years. Her six books of poems, published relatively late in her life in the United States and Israel, appeared in print between 1949 and 1977. In 1981, she won the esteemed Manger Prize for Yiddish literature. The poems that we have included here were selected and translated by poet and feminist theologian Marcia Falk, who worked closely with Tussman, publishing the first English-language translation of her poems in 1977 (in a volume entitled *Am I Also You*), and has continued to translate Tussman's poetry. At present, Falk has translated over one hundred of Tussman's poems, many of which will appear in her forthcoming *With Teeth in the Earth: Selected Poems of Malka Heifetz Tussman,* to be published by the Wayne State University Press.

The first poem in this section, "Leaves," is a melancholy poem about life and death, revealing Tussman's strong sense of connection to the earth. Considered by Falk to be one of Tussman's most spiritual poems, it is written (and translated) in the form of a triolet, a musical French form that Tussman adapted to Yiddish. "Last Apple" again reveals Tussman's understanding of spirituality as an embracing of the entire world. Identifying with a fallen apple that no one wants to pick up, the poet kneels down to pick up the apple and in that moment feels a connection, not just to the apple, but to the tree, the leaf, the blossom, and, finally, the earth. Moving from self-pity to redemption, Tussman expresses a moment of transcendence rooted in a connection with and compassion for nature. At the same time, she separates her religious experience from philosophical and theological reflection. While embracing a tree may provide her with a sense of connection to creation, that embrace, she maintains, does not tell her about the nature of the tree itself (by implication, she seems to be cynically asking whether it can tell anyone, despite what some theologians have claimed).

In "Mild, My Wild," Tussman again talks of her close sense of connection to the earth, here using sensual, even sexual, language to describe the kinds of connections that she feels. Assuming a self-critical posture, she acknowledges her own abuse of the earth. Using sexual imagery—imagining herself as a male rider and the earth as a masochistic female who patiently accepts the rider's tantrums—she explores her own, complex relationship not only to the earth but also, presumably, to men and, more generally, to her own sexuality.

Finally, in "I Say," Tussman begins by addressing God directly. Although she calls God "the Almighty," she immediately assumes an intimate, even audacious tone, imagining God as a (male) wanderer whom she would invite into her bed if only her "heart were purer." If God, she seems to be saying, is indeed the almighty ruler depicted by Jewish tradition, her relationship with him must remain distant, for intimacy with such a God seems impossible. Thus, as many of her other poems suggest, it was through her connection to the earth, to other people, and to her own sexuality that Tussman explored and articulated most clearly her own sense of spirituality.

"The Coming of Lilith," a *midrash* written by feminist theologian Judith Plaskow (1947–) in 1972, uses the biblical account of creation, along with the rabbinic legend of Lilith, Adam's first wife, to express her own feelings both of anger at the patriarchalism of traditional Judaism and of exhilaration at the bonds of sisterhood created by the then-burgeoning feminist movement in America. Raising the question, "What would have happened if Lilith and Eve had met?" she imagines the great enthusiasm, creativity, and power they might have had as they began to rebuild the garden together.

Raised in New York in the Reform movement, Plaskow has long been active both in *havurah* and in Jewish feminist circles and was a founding member of B'not Esh (lit., Daughters of Fire), a Jewish feminist spirituality collective that has been in existence for ten years and of which several contributors to this volume are members.[2] One of the first women to earn a Ph.D. in theology at Yale University, Plaskow is the author of *Standing Again at Sinai*, the first Jewish feminist theological work to be written by a single author;[3] cofounder and coeditor of the *Journal of Feminist Studies in Religion*; and professor of religious studies at Manhattan College in New York. She is the mother of a son.

Following Plaskow's *midrash* are several poems by Hebrew poet Zelda Schneurson Mishkovsky (1914–84), who is known to her readers simply as Zelda. They have been selected and translated by Marcia Falk and will be included in Falk's forthcoming *The Spectacular Difference: Selected Poems of Zelda*. Authorized by the poet, this volume will be the first book-length collection of Zelda's poems to appear in English. An Orthodox Jew from a distinguished line of Hasidic rabbis, Zelda was born in Russia and emigrated to Palestine with her family in 1914. Educated primarily in religious girls' schools, where she later became a teacher, she also studied art briefly and continued to paint for most of her life. Married at the age of thirty-six, she devoted most of her married life to caring for her husband, who became ill shortly after their marriage. In order to do so, she retired from teaching and steadily began to publish poetry.[4] Her first volume of poems, entitled *P'nei* (Leisure), was published in 1967 and earned Zelda the prestigious Brenner Prize for Literature. Later publications led to her receiving the coveted Bialik Prize as well. In all, Zelda published six volumes of Hebrew poetry, the last in 1984.[5] In 1985, all six were collected into a single volume entitled *Shiray Zelda* (Poems of Zelda). Unique among Hasidic women in her writing of poetry, and even more so in her passionate, mystical, even sensual love of nature (what Marcia Falk calls her "visionary craziness"),[6] Zelda is one of Israel's most widely read poets.

In "I Am a Dead Bird," Zelda speaks of her faith as rooted in absolute trust in God and in her ability to hear music (i.e., to find beauty and to feel God's presence) even when surrounded by sorrow. "Yom Kippur Eve" reveals her remarkable use of images drawn from nature to convey her own religious experiences. Yet, as she writes in "Sun-Startled Pines," while she may discover great strength and beauty in nature, nature cannot reveal to her the secrets of the universe. As she maintains in "A Heavy Silence," it is God alone who knows these secrets, including the mysteries of life and death. Nevertheless, she views nature as a teacher of religious truths ("Moon Is Teaching Bible"), revealing both human and natural existence (again, inextricably linked) as intermingled with joy, hope, and sorrow.

"Mikva Dreams—A Performance" was first published by New York environmental artist Mierle Laderman Ukeles (1939–) in 1977. Giving written expression to a performance piece that she created, it focuses on the traditional commandment of *mikvah* (i.e., immersion into a gathering of running water) and, more specifically, on her monthly experience of *mikvah* as a married, Orthodox Jewish woman.[7] Ukeles compares *mikvah* to "a taste of heaven" because it enables her to feel as though she has undergone rebirth. In 1986, she performed "Mikva Dreams" at the Jewish Museum in New York City as part of a larger piece entitled "Immerse Again   Immerse Again," through which she expressed her longing for spiritual unification. Her husband, Jack, and three children, Yael, Raquel, and Meir, have all participated in her performance works. Artist in residence for the New York City Department of Sanitation since 1978, Ukeles has done a number of site-specific projects related to various aspects of sanitation. "Mikva (sic)," as a symbol of female purification, is related to her other works but "channels the theme into an extremely personal route that derives its form and actuality from the artist's profound Jewish consciousness."[8]

Poet Merle Feld (1947–) was raised in Brooklyn in a nonreligious Jewish family. After graduating from Brooklyn College in 1968— where she first encountered traditional Jewish observance and, by her own account, began her spiritual journey—she married, moved to Boston, and helped found Havurat Shalom, a small group of Jews who gathered regularly for worship, study, and celebration, which helped launch the proliferation of *havurot* throughout the United States. From 1984 to 1988, Feld served on the Board of Directors of the National Havurah Committee. Having dreamed of becoming a writer ever since she was a young girl, Feld finds that "writing is [her] deepest form of davening [praying]." During times of loss, pain, or experiences distinctly associated with mothering (Feld is the mother of two children), she writes to "comfort and visit with my own lonely soul."[9]

As the selections included here reveal, her poems are often about her body, about giving birth and mothering, about longing and affection, or about her Jewish self, all topics that demand, for her, a special effort to bring her own inner voice into communication with others. It is while writing that she feels most alive and most "uniquely" herself, so she turns to it during moments of unease. For Feld, writing these poems is an important supplement to her communal religious life, which is dominated by her activities as the wife of a Liberal rabbi. The poems enable her to express her private voice and to articulate a vision of spirituality clearly rooted in the realities of her own existence.

Following the poems by Feld is an autobiographical essay by Gail Berkeley (1953–), now Gail Berkeley Sherman, entitled "A Convert's Road to Prayer." Written in 1979 for a special issue of *Response* magazine edited by Ellen M. Umansky on Jewish prayer, it traces her personal religious journey, including her decision as a young adult to undertake what she described as a "new spiritual identity" as a Jew. Born and raised in upstate New York, Berkeley received her Ph.D. in English from Princeton University and has been a member of the English faculty at Reed College in Portland, Oregon, since 1981. The mother of two children, Ilana and Benjamin, she has recently remarried and is a member of a supportive Shabbat group.

The two short poems by New Yorker Constance Gemson (1948–) reflect a sense of pain and isolation, rooted in her own experience as outsider. The first poem, "All Alone among the Vikings," reflects her experiences in Sweden, where she lived in 1980. While many of the Swedes whom she met were curious about Jews, she sadly concluded that she appeared to them as little more than a "buried relic" or "ancient curio," the ongoing richness of Jewish history unimaginable and thus undiscovered. In "Lot's Wife," as in many of her poems, Gemson speaks of isolation and remembrance. Refusing to obey her husband's admonishments to forget her past, Lot's unnamed wife stands alone, punished by God for her actions.

There is a sadness in all Gemson's poetry. Yet she maintains that "there is also the power of continuity, strength, and fortitude [in the story of the Jew as outsider]."[10] Gemson identifies her spiritual journey with the search for this power. Raised in the Conservative movement, and still maintaining strong ties to Judaism, she finds a strong link between both her earlier professional work as a geriatric social worker and her current work as a staff trainer (conducting workshops on team building, communication skills, and time management) and Judaism's emphasis on social justice and on the kinds of personal and communal powers that she continually searches to discover.

Rivka Miriam (1952–) and Miriam Oren are contemporary Hebrew poets. Rivka Miriam was born in Jerusalem, the daughter of Yiddish writer Leib Rochman, and has been writing poetry since childhood. Her first book, *My Yellow Nightgown*, a collection of her poetry and sketches, appeared in 1966, when she was only fourteen years old.[11] Thirteen years later, she received the literary President's Prize. An artist as well as a writer, she exhibited her drawings at the Tel Aviv Museum in 1969.

Rivka Miriam's "A Song to Jacob Who Removed the Stone from the Mouth of the Well," translated by Sue Ann Wasserman, is one of her few poems to have been translated into English. Assuming the inner voice of the biblical Leah, it can be seen as a *midrash* on Genesis 16ff., the story of Jacob's being tricked into marrying the "weak-eyed" Leah instead of her sister, Rachel, and of Leah's subsequently bearing many children. The poem expresses Leah's sadness and sense of isolation. Everything she has, including her body and her children, has or will be taken from her. Her eyes have grown weak from crying, despondent at what has already befallen her and at what she knows lies ahead.

Miriam Oren was born in Tel Aviv and worked for many years as a literary critic for the Hebrew newspaper *Maariv*. The author of three books of Hebrew poetry, published between 1962 and 1977, she is now a translator of prose.[12] In "Eve," one of her only poems to be translated into English, she creates a *midrash* on the first few chapters of the Book of Genesis. Implicitly making reference to the biblical and rabbinic view that a married woman is entitled to food, clothing, and "conjugal rights" (i.e., sexual relations), Oren suggests that Eve ate the apple because life in the garden, a life in which all her basic needs were taken care of, was insufficient. While it is unclear whether Oren uses the garden here to symbolize childhood or patriarchal marriage, her poem seems to maintain that, to experience life fully, we need to reach out to the future, taking risks and making our own decisions. Implicitly referring to Proverbs 24:16—"Seven times the righteous man falls and gets up while the wicked are tripped by one misfortune"—when she writes, "Eve will fall seven times," the poet clearly admires Eve, portraying her as a model of righteousness, strength, and courage.[13]

Sheila Pelz Weinberg's "Campus Pilgrimage to Reverse the Nuclear Arms Race," delivered at a peace rally in the spring of 1983, was written on the occasion of a nationwide student march on Washington in protest of the American buildup of nuclear weapons. Then Hillel director at Haverford and Bryn Mawr colleges in Philadelphia and widely known as a Jewish peace activist and organizer, Weinberg was invited to participate in the march and to address the students at a Saturday morning rally. Turning to the weekly Torah portion for insight and inspiration, Weinberg emphasizes the importance of affirming and respecting the great diversity among those participating in the pilgrimage while at the same time clearly voicing those common concerns that had brought them together. Identifying God's presence with "the height of our hopes . . . our reason for trying, for caring, for loving," she enjoins her listeners to coalesce their feelings, thoughts, and actions and, keeping sight of their future vision, journey—like the ancient Israelites in search of the promised land—into the wilderness together.

Raised in the Conservative movement, Weinberg's own spiritual journey began with a rejection of traditional religious forms in favor of activist politics, feminism, and the study of Eastern spirituality and psychology. Later, she returned to Jewish sources and stories, finding them to be "abiding and meaningful vessels for [her] life experience and for [her] ongoing search for truth and peace."[14] She worked as a Hillel director in the Philadelphia area from 1977 to 1984, was ordained from the Reconstructionist Rabbinical College in 1986, and is currently rabbi of the Jewish community of

Amherst, Massachusetts. The single mother of a son and a daughter, she finds that the Reconstructionist movement, with its emphasis on the psychological importance of ritual and the equality of women and men, has helped provide her with a religious home. Nevertheless, she often finds herself turning to Hasidism, feminist theology and community, body work, and the twelve-step programs[15] for additional insight as her spiritual search for both world and self-wholeness continues.

The spiritual autobiography and the *midrash* on Sarah written by Ellen M. Umansky (1950–), both published in the mid-1980s, reflect her ongoing religious journey. Both these pieces give expression to her need to feel God's presence and to hear her voice, and the voice of her foremothers, within the Jewish tradition. Since she wrote "Reclaiming the Covenant: A Jewish Feminist's Search for Meaning," she has tried, with varying degrees of success, to eliminate references to the divine as "he" and simply to identify God as "God." In addition, she has come to recognize that the gender of God is less important than the *kinds* of images through which God is envisioned. There is a direct connection, she believes, between the ways in which we envision the human-divine relationship and the ways in which we actually relate to the world and its creations. To use images of hierarchical domination in imaging the divine— "King," "Lord," "Queen"—encourages us to view the human-divine relationship as one of domination and submission. God commands, and we obey. It establishes this relationship as a model of how things really are, encouraging us, even if unintentionally, to set ourselves over and against both the earth and other people (especially over those to whom we feel superior, by virtue of our race, sex, socioeconomic class, age, religious affiliation, nationality, etc.). At present, she is working to create new images of divinity that will encourage us to work *with* God rather than *under* God's authority.

Yet, when she is creating *midrash,* as her *midrash* on Genesis 22—the story of the binding of Isaac—reveals, her interest is less in reimaging the divine than in hearing the voice of her biblical ancestors, particularly those, like Sarah, about whom the Bible, and later rabbinic commentaries, tells us little. In reimaging Genesis 22 through Sarah's eyes (in the biblical text she is absent), she has tried to explore where Sarah was and how she felt when she discovered that her only son was missing and, later, when she realized that Abraham had almost killed him. To refer to God in this *midrash* as "he" seems—to her, at least—faithful to Sarah's own experience. What separates Abraham from Sarah is not their experience of God's gender but rather their experience of what this relationship with God entails.

Since writing these pieces, she has continued her spiritual journey, which has been greatly enriched by the birth of her three sons, Abraham, Ezra, and Seth. She has also come to reaffirm her identity as a Reform Jew—a process already begun in "Reclaiming the Covenant." She is a member of a Reform synagogue and, in addition to her continued affiliation with Emory University, is an adjunct faculty member of the Reform movement's Hebrew Union College–Jewish Institute of Religion in New York City.

Chicago-born dancer and choreographer Fanchon Shur (1935–) grew up in Los Angeles in what she describes as a "social activist Jewish family." As a child, she studied Hebrew and as a teenager Israeli and Jewish folk dance at the Los Angeles Jewish Community Center. While still young, she trained with Anne Lief Barlin at the Dance Center in Los Angeles, where she subsequently taught, choreographed, and performed dances based on world cultures, Israeli and Hasidic culture, and, more generally, Jewish legends. She also trained in the Dance Department of the University of California, Los Angeles, and is a Laban movement analyst certified at the Laban-Bartenieff Institute of Movement Studies and a movement therapist registered with the International Movement Therapy Association.

Since completing her training, Shur has raised six children and lived in Seattle (where she cofounded Dance Theatre Seattle) and Cincinnati, where she and her husband, Israeli musician and composer Bonia Shur, have lived since 1974. As her essay "My Dance Work as a Reflection of a Jewish Woman's Spirituality" (an expanded version of an essay originally written in 1984) makes clear, creative dance is for her the root of both her faith and her connection to other Jews. According to Shur, her most powerful sense of reality and what she considers to be "the tools for liberation" came from her natural childbirth experiences as well as from her visits to Israel and her ongoing creative work with Growth in Motion, her Cincinnati-based Movement Arts Center founded in 1978. Her most recent work includes "Sarah Speak!" (1986), a dance piece in which Fanchon, musically accompanied by Bonia Shur, counterpoints the story of the binding of Isaac with Sarah's determination to stop Abraham from killing their son, and "Purses, Pockets, and Family Secrets" (1990), for which she received a work-in-progress grant by the Ohio Joint Program in the Arts and Humanities.

Marcia Falk has been writing poetry for most of her life. Born in New York and raised in the Conservative movement, she received her Ph.D. in English and comparative literature from Stanford University, where she is currently an affiliated scholar at the Institute for Research on Women and Gender. She is also an affiliated scholar at the Beatrice M. Bain Research Group of the University of California, Berkeley. Well known for her poetry, her Yiddish and Hebrew translations (including the biblical Song of Songs, published by Harper San Francisco in 1990), and the Jewish feminist blessings that she has created, she now lives in Berkeley with her spouse and their son, Abraham Gilead.

Revealing a deep sense of connection with nature, many of Falk's poems have a mystical, almost dreamlike quality about them. In "Sabbath," a woman's observing a young girl running through a field provides her with a moment of transcendence. As in the poems of Malka Heifetz Tussman, Falk's poems are often sensual, even passionate (e.g., "Dialogues"), making an explicit connection between spirituality and sexuality. In so doing, she draws on images of human longing and of the longing to embrace nature fully.

Following Falk's poems are two short blessings that she has created, one a *kiddish* (the sanctification of wine), the other a *sheheheyanu* (a blessing for renewal). Both these blessings will appear in her forthcoming *The Book of Blessings: A Feminist-Jewish Reconstruction of Prayer* to be published by Harper San Francisco in 1992. Eliminated are traditional images of God as almighty Lord and King of the Universe. In their place are images taken from nature (God is the "source" and "flow of life"). God is envisioned as immanent process rather than as a transcendent, supernatural being. These blessings invite Jews to come together as members of a spiritual community and claim the power to bless that life force that gives birth to and nurtures all of creation.

Rabbi Laura Geller (1950–) merits the distinction of having been one of the first three women ordained as Reform rabbis. Receiving her ordination from Hebrew Union College–Jewish Institute of Religion in New York City in 1976, she served as director of the Hillel Jewish Center at the University of Southern California until 1990 and currently works as director for the Pacific Region of the American Jewish Congress. She is the mother of two children, Joshua and Elana.

In her address "Encountering the Divine Presence," delivered before an audience of several hundred Reform rabbis at the 1986 annual meeting of the Central Conference of American Rabbis, the professional organization of Reform rabbis in the United States and Canada, Geller explores her sense of Jewish self-identity, her reasons for becoming a rabbi, and her own understanding of God. Sharing with her colleagues her own experiences as a woman and as a Jew, she tells them that she has come to believe "that to be a Jew means to tell my story within the Jewish story." She emphasizes the importance of connection to ourselves, to the world, to others, and to God and, explicitly connecting spirituality with daily experience, reminds her listeners that, in addition to the Torah that was written down, "there is a Torah of our lives" to which we also need to listen.

The creation of new rituals has been an important step in women's reconceptualizing Judaism so that the experiences of both women and men are seen as central to both individual and communal Jewish life. Claiming the right to name themselves, God, and their religious communities, Penina Adelman and Savina Teubal are among those American Jewish women who, since the mid-1980s, have worked to create rituals that communally mark important moments or events in women's lives.

Penina V. Adelman (1953–) is a storyteller and social worker who lives with her husband and two children in Holden, Massachusetts.[16] Raised by parents who were born Jewish yet called themselves atheists, she nevertheless learned from them both a reverence for books and a love of learning for learning's sake (what Judaism traditionally has called *Torah lishma*). In Adelman's own words,

"After college, my hunger to have a heritage transferred itself from studying Native American ritual as an anthropology major to trying to find a way to make up for a nearly non-existent Jewish education. I attended a liberal Orthodox yeshivah in Jerusalem at age twenty-seven after first learning Hebrew and felt that I had come home. My level of observance now is much less intense than it was at that time. I consider myself to be a '*havurah* Jew,' I guess, one who tries to pick and choose knowledgeably and responsibly from the tradition, who feels most comfortable when the burden of transmitting the Jewish tradition is shared by all members of the community and is not mainly placed in the hands of the rabbi."[17]

"The Womb and the Word: A Fertility Ritual for Hannah" is a piece that Adelman wrote specifically for this volume, reflecting on how she came to write her "hybrid" *midrash*/ritual: a *midrash* on the biblical Hannah and how she felt when confronted with her own infertility and a ritual for miscarriage or infertility that can also "serve as a stimulus to anyone who has suffered the loss of a child, a parent, a spouse, a relationship, a pregnancy." Her reflection is followed by the ritual itself, first published in 1986 in her *Miriam's Well*.[18] Organizing the book around the theme of Rosh Hodesh (the New Moon)—which the ancient rabbis recognized as a women's holiday, although we have little information as to how it was celebrated—she creates a series of new rituals that can be enacted both at the time of the New Moon and on those occasions (e.g., pregnancy, miscarriage, the anniversary of a loved one's death) for which a number of these rituals are appropriate. Her ritual of loss, which Adelman first enacted with her own Rosh Hodesh group, enabled her to mourn her own miscarriage in a communal setting of women who offered her sympathy, compassion, and the reminder, as one woman tells her, that all those who "can't give birth to a live human being" can give birth to ideas and struggles.

Born in England, Savina J. Teubal (1926–) was raised in Buenos Aires, where she began her career as a short-story writer (in Spanish). Her family were Orthodox Syrian Jews. Religion, as she understood it in her youth, was a tribal affair. In Teubal's words, "Men officiated in the synagogue, where women prayed but took no active part. Women's religious activity centered in the home, particularly on the High Holy Days and the Sabbath. Aunts, uncles, cousins and friends lived in the same barrio. The women prepared for the Holy Days weeks in advance"—extending invitations, exchanging recipes, preparing the house, and cooking.[19]

Since 1959, Teubal has lived in the United States and is now happily settled in Santa Monica, California. The author of many essays and articles regarding the ancient Near East and its relation to the events in the Genesis narrative, she is also the author of *Sarah the Priestess* and *Hagar the Egyptian*.[20]

Her ritual "Simchat Hochmah" (the celebration of wisdom) was created in 1986 on the occasion of her sixtieth birthday. In reflecting on the events that led her to create this ritual, Teubal writes, "I think that [my] estrangement from my Syrian Judaism led me to seek a Judaism that has suited my increasing feminism. I don't know how conscious it has been, but in the past few years I have sought to create my own religious community (read tribe). We write our own prayers and Haggadah [used at the Passover *seder*], create rituals that are meaningful to our lives, cook together etc. Most of my religious activity today is almost exclusively with women. I think I resent not having been permitted to participate in male ritual and now balk at being 'allowed' to participate. It just doesn't feel authentic. This doesn't mean that I still can't, and do, feel very emotional when reciting the 'Shema' or see the Torah or sing the prayers to our ancient Arabic tunes. But I believe that is more nostalgia than spirituality. I think that my 'Simchat' sums up my present spirituality. Rooted in Judaism, its ritual and its history, it transcends traditional Jewish spirituality to include women's experience."[21]

Following Teubal's "Simchat Hochmah" ritual are sermons by two Reform rabbis, Shira Milgrom (1951–) and Sue Levi Elwell (1948–). Milgrom's, dated "Yom Kippur, 5749 [1988]," connects the sounds of the *shofar* (the ram's horn), blown on Rosh Hashanah and Yom Kippur, with the pain and joy of human existence. It reminds us, Milgrom asserts, that, to experience life in its fullness, we need to feel joy as well as pain, focusing not on our suffering but on those special moments that we accumulate—"experiences of surprise, of closeness, of great laughs, unexpected discovery, and unimagined joy." In this sermon, delivered to the congregation of the Jewish Community Center of White Plains, New York, the Reform Temple for which Milgrom serves as associate rabbi, Milgrom assumes a tone of familiarity, even intimacy, with members of the congregation. Drawing on her own experiences and the experiences of her family, she ends her sermon by sharing with the congregation her own understanding of God as "the transcendent moment [that runs] through all of life . . . always moving—ever-present and eternal."

Raised in the American South and California, the daughter of a rabbi, Milgrom completed an M.A. and predoctoral work in linguistics and language acquisition and worked for many years in the field of Jewish education before completing her rabbinical training at Hebrew Union College–Jewish Institute of Religion in New York City in 1986. She and her husband, Dr. David Elcott, are the parents of four children. In her work at the Jewish Community Center, Milgrom continually emphasizes the power of Judaism to bring people out of personal isolation by giving them a structure in which to express deep relationships. In her own life, she has found that the rituals of Jewish observance provide avenues for experiencing both the rewards of human relationships and the holy.

In her sermon dated Rosh Hashanah 1987, Rabbi Sue Levi Elwell similarly focuses on the sounds of the *shofar*. Addressing the congregants at Leo Baeck Temple in Los Angeles, she reminds them that the New Year is not just a time for remembering but a time for listening as well. Hearing the call of the *shofar*, she says, means hearing our own truths, paying careful attention to the cries, moans, and laughter of other human beings, and listening to the "still, small voice that inspires us towards acts of lovingkindness." Like Milgrom, Elwell brings to her congregants a leadership model of both teaching and friendship. She reaches out, not as one who seeks to exert authority over them, but rather as one who has become part of their religious community. Reminiscing about moments they shared together during the year, she also draws on her personal experiences, creating a sermon of both intimacy and power.

Raised in Buffalo, New York, in the Reform movement, Elwell received a Ph.D. in adult education from Indiana University and was ordained as a rabbi from Hebrew Union College–Jewish Institute of Religion in Cincinnati in 1986. After ordination, Elwell moved to Los Angeles with her husband and two daughters, Hana and Mira, where she served as assistant rabbi at Leo Baeck Temple. She is cofounder and director of the Los Angeles Jewish Feminist Center, a visiting lecturer at the University of California, Los Angeles, and rabbi of the Irvine Jewish community.

The two pieces that we have included by well-known feminist writer E. M. Broner (1927–) are meditations on the creation of rituals that celebrate female friendship. In "Sitting *Shiva* for a Lost Love," she describes the ritual that she and a number of friends created to help a friend of theirs mourn the end of a relationship with a man who married someone else, while, in "Body Memories," she describes how difficult it can be to use our bodies in expressing our emotions and, more particularly, in attempting to get in touch with the past. "Sitting Shiva for a Lost Love" describes the successful creation of a ritual; "Body Memories" describes the creation of one ritual that failed, only to be replaced by another.

Playwright, short-story writer, and novelist, Broner first explored the creation of female rituals in her memorable novel set in Jerusalem, *A Weave of Women,* published by Holt, Rinehart and Winston in 1978. Married to artist Robert Broner, she is the mother of four sons. The recipient of numerous grants and prizes (including the Wonder Woman Award in 1983), she has taught at Wayne State University and Sarah Lawrence College and continues to lecture widely. Raised in the Conservative movement, Broner retains strong ties to Judaism and for many years has been active in Jewish feminist efforts to reconceptualize Jewish teachings and celebrations.[22]

"We Learned from the Grandparents: Memories of a Cochin Jewish Woman," by Ruby Daniel with Barbara C. Johnson, provides a rare personal account of Jewish self-identity as seen through the eyes of a female member of the Cochin Jewish community. Here, Daniel describes to Johnson, an American cultural anthropologist, her own religious education as well as Jewish practices and values that she learned from her elders. She also speaks about holiday celebrations, spirits and the afterlife, and the importance of dreams in feeling the presence of the dead.

Barbara Johnson teaches at Goddard College in Vermont and has published several articles on the Cochin communities in Israel and India. She is currently writing a book in collaboration with Daniel, whom she describes as the unacknowledged guardian of Cochin Jewish history, stories, and songs. Included here are excerpts from the manuscript, chosen by Johnson to illustrate some of the ways in which Daniel's spiritual values developed in relation to the teachings and example of the women in her family. According to Johnson,

> Ruby Daniel was born in 1912 in Cochin, South India, into a community of Jews whose ancestors lived on the tropic southwest coast of India for perhaps two thousand years, enjoying friendly relations with their Hindu, Muslim, and Indian Christian neighbors. She learned as a child from her parents and grandparents to value her Jewish heritage and the special traditions associated with Jewish life in South India. Religious values were embedded in the particularity of her cultural context: in the Indian landscape and Malayalam language, in daily observance of Jewish practice, in the yearly rhythms of the Jewish festivals, and in the melodies and stories that she learned from her elders. She was one of the first young women from her community to move out into the wider world, by attending secondary school and college. As a single woman she supported her extended family, working as a clerk in the government service and then serving in the Indian Navy during World War II. In the early 1950s she made *aliyah* to Israel, along with most of the Cochin Jews. Today she is a member of Kibbutz Neot Mordecai in the Upper Galilee.[23]

For centuries, many Jewish women have found spiritual meaning in those ceremonies and observances traditionally encumbent on women. Yet, as Dvora Weisberg's "The Study of Torah as a Religious Act" (written expressly for this volume) and Susan Grossman's "On *Tefillin*" (written in 1986) reveal, some women have also begun to discover meaning in aspects of Jewish religious life from which women were previously prohibited or in which they were actively discouraged from engaging.

A doctoral candidate and instructor in the Department of Talmud and Rabbinics at the Jewish Theological Seminary of America, Weisberg (1960–) grew up in the Reform movement. In her own words,

> While I remember always feeling a sense of connectedness with the Jewish people and a belief in a personal God who was accessible through informal as well as formal prayer, I became interested in a more traditional Jewish life in high school and college. Fortunately (as far as I'm concerned), I also believed very strongly in the right of women to do whatever they felt capable of and interested in doing; it never occurred to me not to apply those values to Judaism. I've always approached Jewish tradition with the belief that it need not be sexist, that whatever bias against women we find in Judaism derives not from God but from men who shaped tradition after their values. Personally, I'm concerned with making my life meaningful within Judaism and making Judaism more accessible to others, especially to women, who tend to feel more alienated from tradition.[24]

Weisberg currently resides in Livingston, New Jersey, with her husband, Neal Scheindlin, and their son, Micah.

Rabbi Susan C. Grossman (1955–) was a member of the first class of women accepted into the rabbinical program at the Conservative movement's Jewish Theological Seminary (JTS). Ordained in 1989, she currently serves as rabbi of Genesis Agudas Achim Congregation in Tuckahoe, New York, where she lives with her husband, David Boder, and their son, Yonatan. The author of *The Teacher's Guide and Source Book to the Book of Jewish Belief,* she is also coeditor of *Daughters of the King.*[25] In reflecting on her Jewish background, Grossman writes,

> I did not receive any formal Jewish education when I was a child, although I was raised to believe in God and support the state of Israel. We were an average American Jewish family, celebrating the Passover *seder,* lighting the *menorah,* and eating *hamentaschen* [specially shaped cookies] on Purim. As part of my 1970s pilgrimage to San Francisco, ostensibly as a visiting student to study television for a semester at San Francisco State, I met Shlomo Carlbach and at his House of Love and Prayer there began to learn about Jewish observance. Several years of living in various upper New York State cities, on first jobs, allowed me to study with Conservative and Lubavitch rabbis. When I finally came to New York to study more seriously, I was already thinking of rabbinical school, but found that JTS was not open to women. I began studying for a masters in judaic studies at Brooklyn College, and working in the Jewish community during the day, hoping to become a scholar and communal leader if I could not become a rabbi since I have a deep seated feeling that God wants me to be working in the Jewish community.[26]

Deeply committed to the Conservative movement's ideology of an allegiance to observance and tradition coupled with scholarly investigation and *halakhic* (Jewish legal) change, Grossman waited to apply to rabbinical school until 1984, when JTS decided to admit women to the rabbinical program. She defines her personal goal as "helping to bring a thoughtful spirituality back into American Judaism."[27]

Also among the first class of women admitted to the rabbinical program at the Jewish Theological Seminary is Rabbi Amy Eilberg (1954–). Born and raised in a "nominally involved Conservative family" in Philadelphia, she entered the master's program in Talmud at JTS in 1976, earned a M.S.W. from Smith College in the early 1980s, and entered the rabbinical program at JTS in 1984. Completing the program a year later, she merits the distinction of being the first woman ordained as a Conservative rabbi (in the spring of 1985). Until her ordination, Eilberg was "passionately involved in . . . equal access feminism." Since that time, she has increasingly come to affirm women's experience on its own terms. Having served as a Jewish chaplain at the Methodist Hospital of Indiana, rabbi of Har Zion in Penn Valley, Pennsylvania, and, more recently, director of Yad L'Chaim, the Jewish Hospice Care Program in Philadelphia, Eilberg views her spirituality as shaped by a commitment to feminist and human empowerment.[28]

In the sermon that we have included here, dated 3 September 1988, Eilberg speaks personally about her daughter's second birthday. Reflecting on her own experiences of giving birth and of watching her child grow, she talks of their giving birth to one another: she by bringing her daughter into the world, her daughter by bringing "to life [within Eilberg] a long-buried side of [herself], that can rejoice and exclaim over life's everyday discoveries."

Following Eilberg's sermon is a poem by psychotherapist Barbara E. Breitman (1950–). Written for a friend, it celebrates their shared spiritual vision while acknowledging the great differences in their own religious journeys. Raised in an assimilated Jewish family, Breitman did not attend synagogue or religious school as a child. In her late teens, however, she experienced a spiritual awakening inspired by nature and poetry. Later, while coping with the depression that followed her father's death, she underwent a "consciousness-changing mystical experience that has informed [her] entire life." A graduate student in comparative religion at the University of Pennsylvania, she left the program after two years, later recognizing that she "had been suffering under the combined oppression of sexism in the male, Protestant academy and in the world of patriarchal Jewish scholarship." She subsequently pursued graduate studies in both social work and psychology. First finding a sense of Jewish community in the *havurah* movement, with which she has long been affiliated, she is also a member of B'not Esh, active in P'nai Or and the national Jewish Renewal movement, and a member of a Jewish feminist theology group that has been meeting regularly in Philadelphia since 1982.[29]

Itka Frajman Zygmuntowicz (1926–) carries within her two worlds: the culturally and religiously rich center of European Jewry and the nightmare world of the Holocaust. According to Holocaust scholar Sara Horowitz, whose in-depth interview with Zygmuntowicz is included in this section,

She was born in Poland during Passover, the Jewish holiday celebrating freedom. In 1941, the Frajman family was forced from their home and into the Nowe-Miasto Ghetto, and the following year they were transported to Auschwitz. In January 1945, Itka was moved from Auschwitz to Ravensbruck, a concentration camp in Germany, in a forced, six-day march. One month later, she was taken to a third camp, Malchow, where she remained until liberation. She was the only member of her family to survive.

The Swedish Red Cross brought Itka to a hospital in Sweden in 1945—eleven days after her nineteenth birthday. A year later she met her husband, Rachmil Zygmuntowicz—also a Holocaust survivor—and one month later they were married. Before leaving Sweden, Itka bore two sons and earned a degree in fashion design. The Zygmuntowicz family arrived in the United States in 1953 and settled in Philadelphia, where two more sons were born. Itka and Rachmil have two grandsons.

Inextricably intertwined with, and preserved through, her memories of her mother and grandmother is Itka's spiritual inheritance—a Jewish God, Jewish ethics, a connection with Jewish history and Jewish meaning. Viewed alongside the memoirs of other women who survived the Nazi genocide, Itka's narrative underscores the particular way in which women reflect back on the experience of atrocity and survival. While the testimonies of male and female survivors corroborate one another and verify the same set of historical facts, women remember differently—or they remember different things. In videotaped testimony, for example, many women survivors relate their final conversation with the mother who perished. In Itka's testimony, as in the tapes of other women, her mother's words give Itka permission to survive and to rebuild her life. The mother's words contain a moral imperative as well, both collective and personal. On the collective level, the daughter is enjoined to tell the story of the victims who cannot speak for themselves. On the personal level, the daughter is urged to retain her self—neither to imitate the Nazis nor to absorb the image they project of her.

For these Jewish daughters of Jewish women who perished in the Nazi genocide, their spiritual legacy passes to them along a chain of women. A sense of continuity with the Jewish past and with Jewish meaning is embedded in their memories of mothers, and often grandmothers, rather than articulated abstractly. Stretched to the breaking point yet not ruptured entirely, this inheritance enables many women survivors to develop a notion of responsibility to self and to community that acknowledges, rather than ignores, what they have seen and suffered.

Following Itka's testimony is Judith Kaplan Eisenstein's "The Spiritual Power of Music," written expressly for this volume. Born in New York City, the eldest of Rabbi Mordecai and Lena (Rubin) Kaplan's four daughters, Judith Eisenstein (1909–) developed an early interest in music. From the age of seven through the age of eighteen, she studied at the Institute of Musical Art (later to become Julliard), received a B.S. and an M.A. at Teachers College of Columbia University, and for twenty-five years taught music at the Teachers Institute of the Jewish Theological Seminary. In 1922, at the age of twelve and a half, Judith celebrated her bat mitzvah at her father's newly organized Society for the Advancement of Judaism (SAJ). An innovation created by Mordecai Kaplan to celebrate his daughter's reaching her religious majority and to underscore the SAJ's commitment to the religious equality of women, the ceremony consisted of Judith's being called to the Torah, reciting the appropriate blessings, and reading, in Hebrew and English, from the Torah itself.

Twelve years later, she married the SAJ's assistant rabbi, Ira Eisenstein, and subsequently gave birth to two daughters, Miriam and Ann. Moving to Chicago in 1954, Judith spent the next five years primarily as a *rebbetzin,* moving back to New York in 1959 with her family when her husband became president of the Reconstructionist Foundation. After studying for and receiving her Ph.D. in music from Hebrew Union College (HUC), she later taught at HUC and at the Reconstructionist Rabbinical College (RRC), which opened in Philadelphia in 1968. The author of many works on and of Jewish music, her publications include *Gateway to Jewish Song,* the first songbook written specifically for Jewish children (1937), *Songs of Childhood,* with Frieda Prensky (1955), *A Heritage of Mu-*

sic (1986), and five English cantatas written in collaboration with her husband. In 1981, following her husband's retirement as president of the Reconstructionist Foundation and Rabbinical College, the Eisensteins moved to Woodstock, New York, where she continues to write and, as the piece included here reveals, continues to find spiritual sustenance through music.

Marcia Cohn Spiegel (1927–) grew up in Chicago and was affiliated with the Conservative movement. When she and her husband, Sidney, moved to California, they joined the only synagogue near their home, a Reform Temple in Redondo Beach to which they belonged for twenty-five years. The mother of five children, Spiegel returned to school for a master's degree in Jewish communal service when her last child was entering junior high school. She is the author of *The Heritage of Noah: Alcoholism in the Jewish Community Today* (1979) and *Jewish Women Speak to God: The Poems and Prayers of Jewish Women* (1987), teaches courses in women's studies, and leads workshops exploring issues relating to changing roles and relationships in the Jewish family.

Spiegel's autobiographical reflection "Growing Up Jewish," written specifically for this volume, traces her spiritual growth. She reveals, with great honesty, the impact of her husband's alcoholism and the Jewish community's denial of his behavior on her life, leading her to Alanon (a support program for families and friends of alcoholics) and a new willingness to turn herself "over to God." Dissatisfied with the Christian setting in which Alanon meetings occurred, she subsequently joined together with others to found the L'Chaim Alcohol/Drug Workshop for Jews, a program in which she is still active today. Spiegel's essay tells of both a search for God and a search for religious community. Her path continues, having "twisted and turned unexpectedly" on occasion. Yet what she takes with her is a firm belief that it is only when we learn to trust our own feelings that we can discover "the power to open ourselves to healing," that is, to God, and thus become re-created.

Kathryn Hellerstein's "Tishe b'Av on 48th Street," which received an honorable mention in the Judah Magnes Museum Poetry Contest in 1987, reveals the poet's newfound sense of spiritual self-identity. Born in Cleveland in 1952, the eldest of six children, Hellerstein was raised in a secular Jewish family. Writing poetry since she was a teenager, she began studying Yiddish in graduate school and, since receiving her Ph.D. in literature from Stanford University, has published widely on such Yiddish poets as Malka Heifetz Tussman, Miriam Ulinover, and Kadya Molodowsky. Recently married and living in Philadelphia, she has since adopted what she describes as a "traditionally observant Jewish life-style."[30] Her poem (like others that she has written) both reveals and reflects on these personal and spiritual changes. Here, she expresses amazement and even a sense of thrill that, despite the fact that she is lying comfortably in bed, enjoying what appears to be a beautiful morning, the great sense of grief that she felt the evening before when she read by candlelight from the biblical Book of Lamentations, recalling the past sins of the Jewish people and the subsequent destruction of Jerusalem, remains with her. What she discovers here, and delights at, is her ability to find spiritual meaning within traditional observance, out of which she has gained a great sense of connection to the Jewish past, despite the realities of modern city living.

The personal narrative by Karen Erdos (1960–), the child of Holocaust survivors, details her lifelong sense of alienation from the American Jewish community and her own conflicting feelings about her Jewish self-identity. Raised in Long Island, Erdos grew up strongly identifying ethnically, although not religiously, as a Jew. She currently lives in Philadelphia, where she is a doctoral candidate in history at the University of Pennsylvania. Her dissertation is a study of the Jews of Louisiana from 1850 to 1910.

While in many ways Erdos feels a great sense of distance from the American Jewish community, particularly from those Jews who would label her or her parents as "lesser Jews" than those whose primary identification as Jews is religious, Erdos also feels inextricably bound both to Jewish history in general and, more particularly, to her family's history as Eastern European Jewish survivors of the Nazi occupation. While she describes her faith as amorphous ("I do believe, and yet I have nowhere to anchor that belief") and doubts whether religiously she will ever feel at home in the Jewish community, Erdos admits that she "still feel[s] tied to Judaism. My parents paid such a high price as Jews," she writes, "that Judaism will always be a part of me." Understanding spirituality as that which gives one a sense of connection to a community or, more generally, to the world, she has found that hearing the stories of other daughters of Holocaust survivors has given her that sense of connection. It has also infused her with the conviction that the validation of one's experiences is essential if one is to have the courage, the strength, and sufficient optimism to help create a better world.

While neither a survivor nor the daughter of survivors, writer and educator Blu Greenberg (1936–) has discovered that for her, as, she believes, "for all Jews, the Shoah [i.e., the destruction of European Jewry] has become a source of organizing one's spiritual life."[31] She has arrived at this conviction after years of contact and friendship with Holocaust survivors. Seeing the universe through their eyes, hearing of their experiences, she began to express their impact on her through poetry.

"Resisting Yom Hashoah 1985" powerfully reveals Greenberg's conflicting emotions. Steadily determined not to confront the Holocaust so as not to be overtaken by the pain caused by its remembrance and angry that the Jews' setting aside a day to commemorate the destruction may only give further victory to their "laughing tormenters," Greenberg finally overcomes her resistance, allows herself to mourn, and in so doing, feels both resignation and relief. The constant, although fleeting, intrusion of the Holocaust on her thoughts is evident in "The *Mikvah*." Alone in the *mikvah*, "soaking in a warm tub," she finds her sense of peace and relaxation suddenly shattered as she remembers how SS men would burst into the *mikvah* and kill the women who were there. A moment later, the image vanishes; alone again in the *mikvah,* she immerses twice, gets dressed, and goes home.

Born in Seattle, Blu Greenberg grew up in Far Rockaway, New York, in an Orthodox home. She studied in the *yeshivah* school system through high school, attended Brooklyn College and Yeshiva University Teachers Institute, and received master's degrees in clinical psychology (from the City University of New York) and Jewish history (from Yeshiva University). She has been writing and publishing poetry for almost twenty years and is the author of *On Women and Judaism* and *How to Run a Jewish Household.*[32] Married to Rabbi Irving Greenberg, she is the mother of five children— Moshe, David, Deborah, J.J., and Goody—and is a member of the Orthodox community in Riverdale, New York.

Following Greenberg's poems are two very different rituals written in late 1989 and early 1990. The first, by Rabbi Vicki Hollander (1952–), is a ritual of celebration; the second, by Laura Levitt (1960–) and Rabbi Sue Ann Wasserman (1960–), is a ritual of healing. Both are women-only rituals that affirm, as Vicki Hollander writes, the importance of making space "to come home to ourselves." Hollander's is a Rosh Hodesh ritual that celebrates life and all its blessings.[33] It celebrates womanhood and praises God, invoked as creator and compassionate being. Containing opening and closing ceremonies to be used each month, it also includes a special prayer for the particular month that is being welcomed. Here, we have included Hollander's prayer for Elul (the Hebrew month that comes in the late summer, early fall, just before the Jewish New Year). Turning to the teachings of both nature and Judaism itself, which sees Elul as a time of forgiveness, Elul, she tells us, "instructs us that the pieces that have died within us bear seeds of future possibilities."

Raised in Cleveland and ordained from Hebrew Union College– Jewish Institute of Religion in Cincinnati in 1979, Hollander has since served Reform, Conservative, and Traditional egalitarian communities. Having completed training in marriage and family therapy, she currently serves as spiritual leader to Eitz Or (a community that sees itself as part of the Jewish renewal movement) in Seattle. A single parent of one daughter, Hollander describes ritual development, spiritual renewal, and crafting poetic liturgical works as what form "the edge of her explorations."[34]

Laura Levitt was raised in Dover, Delaware, in the Conservative movement, received a master's degree in modern Jewish thought from Hebrew Union College–Jewish Institute of Religion, and is currently a teaching associate and Ph.D. candidate in constructive Jewish theology and women's studies at Emory University in Atlanta. Sue Ann Wasserman, many of whose translations of Hebrew poetry appear in this volume, grew up in Pound Ridge, New York, in the Reform movement, was ordained from the New York school of Hebrew Union College–Jewish Institute of Religion in 1987, and currently serves as assistant rabbi at The Temple in Atlanta.

The ceremony that Levitt and Wasserman have created draws on the image of *mikvah* as a symbol of rebirth, emphasizing its power of spiritual healing. Written by them together, after Levitt had been raped, it acknowledges the physical and emotional violation that Laura endured as well as her desire to rebuild her life without denying what had happened to her. Their appropriation of *mikvah*— like Vicki Hollander's use of Rosh Hodesh—reflects ways in which some contemporary Jewish women, particularly in America, are rediscovering, reappropriating, and transforming holidays and rituals that have traditionally held special spiritual significance for Jewish women.

The last piece in this section, an autobiographical essay entitled "God and Abuse: A Survivor's Story," was written expressly for this volume. Given the intensely personal and painful material contained in this essay, the author has chosen to publish it under the pseudonym Sophia Benjamin. Her story of physical and sexual abuse and of the connection that she has come to make between that abuse and her own spiritual journey is both enlightening and horrifying. It reminds us of the pain, loss, and abuse that is part of the spiritual heritage of untold numbers of Jewish women, a heritage that for many remains denied or unspoken. It reminds us of the power of healing and of the possibilities for creating a new understanding of and language for God. Finally, this essay reminds us that, while increasing numbers of Jewish women are claiming the right to name themselves, there are still many, like Sophia Benjamin, who cannot yet name themselves so freely.

Notes

1. While women are ordained as rabbis at Leo Baeck College in England, the seminary of the Reform and Liberal movements, these movements represent a minority of the affiliated Jews in England (out of a Jewish population that numbers at most 500,000, in comparison with the six million Jews living in the United States).
2. For a more detailed description of B'not Esh, see Martha Ackelsberg, "Spirituality, Community, and Politics: B'not Esh and the Feminist Reconstruction of Judaism," *Journal of Feminist Studies in Religion* 2, no. 2 (Fall 1986): 109–20. Other contributors to this sourcebook who are members of B'not Esh include Ellen Umansky, Barbara Breitman, Merle Feld, E. M. Broner, Penina Adelman, Sue Levi Elwell, Sheila Weinberg, Marcia Falk, Marcia Spiegel, and Barbara Johnson.
3. Judith Plaskow, *Standing Again at Sinai: Judaism from a Feminist Perspective* (New York: Harper & Row, 1990).
4. According to Marcia Falk, while the legend persists that Zelda's poems were not published until the 1960s, remaining in a drawer until her friends convinced her to publish them, this story is little more than a popular myth.
5. Those six volumes are *Leisure* (1967), *The Invisible Carmel* (1971), *Be Not Far* (1974), *Surely a Mountain, Surely Fire* (1977), *The Spectacular Difference* (1981), and *Parting from All Distance* (1984).
6. Conversation with Ellen M. Umansky, 26 July 1990.
7. While both women and men can and do go to the *mikvah*, *mikvah* is considered one of women's three special commandments (the other two being the kindling of the Sabbath lights and the baking of *challah* in a ritually prescribed way). According to rabbinic law, women are to immerse themselves in a *mikvah* before marriage, at a specified time following childbirth, and (for married women)

seven blood-free days following each menstrual cycle. Women who convert to Judaism also go to the *mikvah*—as do male converts—as part of the conversion ceremony.

8. From a pamphlet describing Ukeles's *mikvah* project (Jewish Museum, New York, 15–16 July 1986).
9. Letter to Dianne Ashton, 26 July 1989.
10. Letter to Ellen M. Umansky, 25 June 1989.
11. Her other books include *I Drowned in Dreams* (1969), *Seats in the Desert* (1973), and *Wood Touched Wood* (1978).
12. Those three books are *And It Came to Pass after These Things* (1962), *Man Is Fated* (1971), and *Land of Water* (1977).
13. See Sue Ann Wasserman, "Women's Voices through the Past and Present" (rabbinic thesis, Hebrew Union College–Jewish Institute of Religion, New York, 1987), 153.
14. Letter to Ellen M. Umansky, 13 June 1989.
15. For overcoming alcohol and/or chemical addiction.
16. She and her husband have adopted two children from Colombia.
17. Letter to Ellen M. Umansky, 3 July 1989.
18. Penina V. Adelman, *Miriam's Well: Rituals for Jewish Women around the Year* (New York: Biblio, 1986).
19. Letter to Ellen M. Umansky, 12 June 1989.
20. Savina J. Teubal, *Sarah the Priestess* (Athens, Ohio: Swallow, 1984), and *Hagar the Egyptian: The Lost Traditions of the Matriarchs* (New York: Harper & Row, 1990).
21. Letter to Ellen M. Umansky, 12 June 1989.
22. Such efforts include helping create and participating in an annual women-only, feminist *seder* at Passover and regularly attending the annual retreats of the Jewish feminist spirituality collective B'not Esh.
23. Information supplied by Barbara Johnson to Ellen M. Umansky, July 1990.
24. Letter to Ellen M. Umansky, summer 1989.
25. Susan Grossman, *The Teacher's Guide and Source Book to the Book of Jewish Belief* (New York: Behrman, 1989), and *Daughters of the King—Women and the Synagogue: History, Halakha, and Changing Realities* (Philadelphia: Jewish Publication Society, 1992).
26. Letter to Ellen M. Umansky, summer 1989.
27. Ibid.
28. Correspondence with Dianne Ashton, summer 1989.
29. Letter to Ellen M. Umansky, June 1990.
30. Conversations with Dianne Ashton, spring 1990.
31. Conversation with Ellen M. Umansky, July 1990.
32. Blu Greenberg, *On Women and Judaism: A View from Tradition* (Philadelphia: Jewish Publication Society, 1981), and *How to Run a Jewish Household* (New York: Simon & Schuster, 1983).
33. Like Penina Adelman, whose Rosh Hodesh celebrations are also excerpted in this volume, Hollander has taken Rosh Hodesh—traditionally viewed as a Jewish women's holiday, although we have little indication as to how this holiday was actually celebrated—and created rituals and prayers that reflect on Jewish women's lives today.
34. Letter to Ellen M. Umansky, 28 June 1990.

Leaves don't fall. They descend.
Longing for earth, they come winging.
In their time, they'll come again,
For leaves don't fall. They descend.
On the branches, they will be again
Green and fragrant, cradle-swinging,
For leaves don't fall. They descend.
Longing for earth, they come winging.

MALKA HEIFETZ TUSSMAN,
United States
Translated by Marcia Falk

Leaves

"I am like the last apple
that falls from the tree
and no one picks up."

I kneel to the fragrance
of the last apple,
and I pick it up.

In my hands—the tree,
in my hands—the leaf,
in my hands—the blossom,
and in my hands—the earth
that kisses the apple
that no one picks up.

Last Apple

The bird has a spark in his eye.
He bends his head sideways
and carries it to the sky.
Is he looking for heaven?
Does he need heaven?

Mild, My Wild

All my heaven-searching is heavy—
it cannot soar.
I hang all my heavy needs
on a bird's wing.
Actually I know nothing about birds
but I want to be like one.

The earth is mine
and I love her.
I want to fill my limbs with her strength,
bury my face in her fragrance.
I want to dig in my elbows
but I'm afraid of worms,
I'm afraid of the tiniest worm.

The earth is mine
and I subdue her.
I rode wantonly on her, my head high,
beat my feet on her heart,
tear out her ore,
wreak havoc,
and still I don't have enough.
She waits,
and accepts my tantrums patiently.

Go mild, my wild!
Or she'll inhale
and take me in,
open her mouth
and swallow me up.

Go mild, my wild!
Or I'll fall,
a glowing chrysolite,
into her pit.

Go mild, my wild!
There one must take small steps.
Nine times you roll it up,
layer by layer,
slowly you put out
your own light.
Humbly you close your eyes
and become as light as birds.

Go mild, my wild!
Slide silently into a sleeper's trance.
Dreamers say here
is the way to heaven.

I say to the Almighty:

Ever-homeless Wanderer,
I would—
if but my heart were pure—
invite
you in, to spend the night.

In the beginning, the Lord God formed Adam and Lilith from the dust of the ground and breathed into their nostrils the breath of life. Created from the same source, both having been formed from the ground, they were equal in all ways. Adam, being a man, didn't like this situation, and he looked for ways to change it. He said, "I'll have my figs now, Lilith," ordering her to wait on him, and he tried to leave to her the daily tasks of life in the garden. But Lilith wasn't one to take any nonsense; she picked herself up, uttered God's holy name, and flew away. "Well now, Lord," complained Adam, "that uppity woman you sent me has gone and deserted me." The Lord, inclined to be sympathetic, sent his messengers after Lilith, telling her to shape up and return to Adam or face dire punishment. She, however, preferring anything to living with Adam, decided to stay where she was. And so God, after more careful consideration this time, caused a deep sleep to fall on Adam and out of one of his ribs created for him a second companion, Eve.

For a time, Eve and Adam had a good thing going. Adam was happy now, and Eve, though she occasionally sensed capacities within herself that remained undeveloped, was basically satisfied with the role of Adam's wife and helper. The only thing that really disturbed her was the excluding closeness of the relationship between Adam and God. Adam and God just seemed to have more in common, both being men, and Adam came to identify with God more and more. After a while, that made God a bit uncomfortable too, and he started going over in his mind whether he may not have made a mistake letting Adam talk him into banishing Lilith and creating Eve, seeing the power that gave Adam.

Meanwhile Lilith, all alone, attempted from time to time to rejoin the human community in the garden. After her first fruitless attempt to breach its walls, Adam worked hard to build them stronger, even getting Eve to help him. He told her fearsome stories of the demon Lilith who threatens women in childbirth and steals children from their cradles in the middle of the night. The second time Lilith came, she stormed the garden's main gate, and a great battle ensued between her and Adam in which she was finally defeated. This time, however, before Lilith got away, Eve got a glimpse of her and saw she was a woman like herself.

After this encounter, seeds of curiosity and doubt began to grow in Eve's mind. Was Lilith indeed just another woman? Adam had

JUDITH PLASKOW, United States

The Coming of Lilith

said she was a demon. Another woman! The very idea attracted Eve. She had never seen another creature like herself before. And how beautiful and strong Lilith looked! How bravely she had fought! Slowly, slowly, Eve began to think about the limits of her own life within the garden.

One day, after many months of strange and disturbing thoughts, Eve, wandering around the edge of the garden, noticed a young apple tree she and Adam had planted, and saw that one of its branches stretched over the garden wall. Spontaneously, she tried to climb it, and struggling to the top, swung herself over the wall.

She did not wander long on the other side before she met the one she had come to find, for Lilith was waiting. At first sight of her, Eve remembered the tales of Adam and was frightened, but Lilith understood and greeted her kindly. "Who are you?" they asked each other, "What is your story?" And they sat and spoke together, of the past and then of the future. They talked for many hours, not once, but many times. They taught each other many things, and told each other stories, and laughed together, and cried, over and over, till the bond of sisterhood grew between them.

Meanwhile, back in the garden, Adam was puzzled by Eve's comings and goings, and disturbed by what he sensed to be her new attitude toward him. He talked to God about it, and God, having his own problems with Adam and a somewhat broader perspective, was able to help out a little—but he was confused, too. Something had failed to go according to plan. As in the days of Abraham, he needed counsel from his children. "I am who I am," thought God, "but I must become who I will become."

And God and Adam were expectant and afraid the day Eve and Lilith returned to the garden, bursting with possibilities, ready to rebuild it together.

ZELDA,
Israel
Translated by Marcia Falk

I Am a Dead Bird

I am a dead bird,
one bird that has died.
A bird cloaked in a gray coat.
A scoffer mocks me as I walk.

Suddenly Your silence envelops me,
O Everliving One.
In a teeming market, a dead fowl sings:
Only You exist.
In a teeming market, hobbles a bird
with a hidden song.

Yom Kippur Eve

On the eve of Yom Kippur,
we sailed
from experiences ended
to experiences begun.

For us, the eve of Yom Kippur
was the beginning of time
in the silence of an island
whose candles lit the sea.
There you held me to your sorrowing heart
in the presence of the Almighty,
before you went to pray with all the rest,
before you became one
of the flock in the chapel,
one of the trees
in the forest.

Sun-Startled Pines

Sun-startled pines
wafted a wild fragrance—
the same stunning strength
from the inmost flowering
made the world my home again
but did not reveal the core,
the divine intention
in budding and wilting plants.
And the point of my life
and the point of my death—
I will not know in this world.

A Heavy Silence

Death will take the spectacular difference
between fire and water
and cast it to the abyss.

A heavy silence
will crouch like a bull
on the names
that humans gave
to the birds of the sky
and to the creatures of the field,
to the evening skies,
to the enormous distances of space,
and to things that are hidden from the eye.

A heavy silence will crouch
like a bull on all the words.
And it will be as hard for me to part
from the names of things
as from the things themselves.

O Knower of mysteries,
help me understand
what to ask for on that day.

Moon Is Teaching Bible

Moon is teaching Bible.
Cyclamen, Poppy, and Mountain
listen with joy.
Only the girl cries.
Poppy can't hear her crying—
Poppy is blazing in Torah,
Poppy is burning like the verse.
Cyclamen doesn't listen to the crying—
Cyclamen swoons
from the sweetness of the secret.
Mountain won't hear her crying—
Mountain is sunk
in thought.

But here comes Wind,
soft and fragrant,
to honor hope, to sing
the heart of each flying rider,
each ardent hunter
swept to the ends of the sea.

MIERLE LADERMAN UKELES, United States

Mikva Dreams—A Performance (1978)

INTRODUCTORY NOTE

Into a particular sacred symbol of the primal water-womb MIKVA, I enter regularly during my life's span of natural fertility.[1] Here, I celebrate my own menses cycle, my personal holy body interface between the moon's tides and the earth's seasons.

Like most goddess traditions, MATRONIT-SHECHINA, the Jew's Female Divinity, has been pictured from ancient times as magically combining all these aspects: eternal renewed virgin, *and* eternal passionate lover, *and* eternal creating mother. Mikva is the site-intersection of all these holy energies.

My menstrual ritual is ancient, so ancient, from the very beginnings of my people's history. It has survived historic catastrophes, expulsions and wanderings. It has also survived—barely—these centuries' cultural hang-ups toward menstruation itself: superstitions which are really fear and loathing of woman body herself, woman deep mysterious fertile magic body and her times.

Like parasitical barnacles clinging to a truly nurturant source, misunderstandings have adhered to the concept and power of the Mikva. No. Mikva is not about woman as dirty. I don't know about you, but I get dirty many times a month. And when I do I take a bath.

Sisters! In this new time for all of us, I take this time to tell you of these private things.

The artist unfolds a white sheet, places it over her head, covering herself completely and continues the reading.

MIKVA DREAMS

In all the gentleness of continuing love, she goes to the Mikva. The Mikva waters hit above her breasts when she is standing up. The waters have pressure in them. She pushes into it as she comes down the steps. When she leaves, it seems as if the waters softly bulge her out, back to the world. No, she doesn't want to tell you about it. It is a secret between her love and herself. The Mikva is square. The water is warm, body temperature. Sometimes there are layers of cool water at the bottom. A square womb of living waters.

She goes in, naked, all dead edges removed—edges and surfaces that have come in contact with the world. Nails, loose hair. She has scrubbed herself. All foreign matter removed. A discipline. Is it possible to cleanse oneself completely? What if she looked into a microscope? Would she find foreign matter? The standard is the world of the naked eye. The Mikva is for her intrinsic self. Her self-self. Nothing else: no traffic with the world, no make-up with the world. The blood stopped flowing a week ago. She is the moon. The blood carried away the nest for an unfertilized egg. Her body gets ready every month—builds a nest come hell or high water. If the egg isn't caught and doesn't catch, the nest unravels bit by bit, and the body gets rid of it. Shucks it. A *non-life* has occurred. Shall she call it a death? She won't because of sister-friends who have had abortions for a million sorrowing reasons. What's one egg? She can't bear that many children. Overpopulation, desires for limits, human endurance, etc. etc. etc. etc. etc. Money, education, other kinds of life-giving to do.

But it *is* an event of non-life. An egg's funeral. A formal procession in measured amounts of time, not rushed; so-and-so number of days. Men don't bleed regularly. That's a simple fact. If they bleed, something is wrong. Women do bleed regularly. It's not an androgynous fact. Much as the artist loves androgynous facts. It is a separating fact. Also children. Only women bleed regularly. Regularly they are involved in either new life or non-life. The Mikva separates one from the other.

In all the glory of continuing love, the Mikva is a taste of Heaven. She tumbles down into the water, like a fetus, and is reborn to life. Old surfaces gone, non-life gone. Life is holy, to be understood as holy and separated from Death, from dead parts. She is always holy—but she causes a separation to be made between life and non-life.

Choose life the Holy One tells her and she does.

If Heaven is the home of eternal life, in all the caring of continuing love, the Mikva is a room in Heaven. This is what Heaven is like, she thought. How outrageous. This? Tiles, steps, a light. What did she expect? The *Shomeret,* the guardian, is this Heaven's angel. A real angel who maintains the balance between this secret place and outside, mysterious, telling no tales. The *Shomeret*'s job is to watch. To see that no foreign bodies are on her. That she has twenty new edges on her twenty tips—nails and toes—that meet the world, that grow and die always. Mostly, the *Shomeret* watches silently that all of her is drawn into the water—nothing sticks out when she contracts back into the womb of warm waters. Every part must go into the waters or it's not "*kasher.*" "*Kasher*" means okay, proper. The girl-woman-lifebearer, who has passed through a time of non-life, enters wholly into the living waters one time. "*Kasher*" says the *Shomeret.* She praises G-D, life-death maintainer, who was-is-will-be forever. Twice more she enters the waters. Sees her fingers through the waters, spreads her limbs; the waters press against her openings; she opens herself to the waters. "*Kasher,*" says the *Shomeret.* Then she is reborn. The living waters return her to life alone.

Her cells begin to die again immediately. Her womb begins to build its blood-nest again. Foreign matter makes contact and sticks to her, silently, right away. But she has a chance to start again.

She moves into another time period. Month to month, how many months, how many contacts does the girl-woman have on this bridge between herself alone and the future?

Say she starts menses at thirteen and reaches menopause at forty-eight. That's thirty-five years of possible fertilization times twelve months a year equals four hundred-twenty eggs she grows within her. Say she gets married at twenty-eight and goes to the Mikva from that time on. That gives her twenty Mikva-going years times twelve months a year, or two hundred-forty times to go to the Mikva. Say she has one, two, three children. That means twenty-seven months of no menses—round off to thirty months "off" because of afterbirth bleeding. That means roughly two hundred and ten times to go to the Mikva during her life; two hundred and ten times to separate from events of non-life in her life. Two hundred and ten times to immerse, to go down into, be swallowed by the people's womb of living waters, to come back to life just as her people's women have done for so many thousands of years.

In all the maintenance of continuing love, her own specific, particular kind of moon-blood body in nature dies in those waters and is born again. And immerse again.

[*Spoken while inhaling and exhaling: no pauses for breath.*]

Note

1. "Mikva is a sacred water immersion place. Both men and women use the Mikva, but differently. It is referred to in the Bible as 'mayim chayim,' meaning living waters. Running water, not stagnant water. Any natural gathering of running water or requisite amount constitutes a natural Mikva: lake, river, sea. In cities, the Mikva is built using an approximation of natural water, that is, water collected through the force of gravity, usually rainwater. The rainwater is gathered into a huge container called the 'bor' or pit. A building is constructed around this *bor.* The building contains small individual sunken pools for private immersion. Each pool shares a wall with the *bor.* Each shared wall has a hole cut in it which can be plugged up or left open. In order to make the adjoining pools into legally valid *Mikvaot,* they are 'seeded' with *bor* water and then filled with regular heated tap water. When the hole between this pool and the *bor* is unplugged so that the waters are touching (or, as the sources put it, 'kissing'), the pool becomes a valid Mikva" (Ukeles's definition of *mikvah* is paraphrased from Rachel Adler).

I'm not feeling it a blessing to be
a   woman   in   her   prime
the cells inside me rioting
about   to   explode
black   moods
depression
rage
the   aching
the waiting
a victim
brought
low
that's
me

Do I ever rejoice in how I am made?
Yes   with a baby at my breast
and   in   lovemaking
alive with pleasure
throbbing
glowing
triumphant
free

But   then   again   this   monthly   assault
the undertow,   the   tide that   pulls
mercilessly dashing me against the rocks
this pounding   of rage,   overwhelming
overpowering   poor   cowering   me
How   shall I   not   curse   the   tide
as it   pulls   my soul   at will?

A prayer:
some day, some month
perhaps   this   month
let my   body and   its blood
at long last teach me the lesson
I struggle so   against   accepting—
let go   let go   let go   give up   control
surrender   to the   flow of   life   within.

MERLE FELD,
United States

Meditation on
Menstruation

Healing after a
Miscarriage

Nothing helps. I taste ashes
in my mouth. My eyes are flat,
dead. I want no platitudes,
no stupid shallow comfort.
I hate all pregnant women,
all new mothers, all soft babies.

The space I'd made inside myself
where I'd moved over
to give my beloved room to grow—
now there's a tight angry
bitter knot of hatred there instead.

What is my supplication?
Stupid people and new mothers,
leave me alone.
Deliver me, Lord,
of this bitter afterbirth.
Open my heart
to my husband-lover-friend
that we may comfort each other.
Open my womb
that it may yet bear
living fruit.

We All Stood Together

for Rachel Adler

My brother and I were at Sinai
He kept a journal
of what he saw
of what he heard
of what it all meant to him

I wish I had such a record
of what happened to me there

It seems like every time I want to write
I can't
I'm always holding a baby
one of my own
or one for a friend
always holding a baby
so my hands are never free
to write things down

And then
as time passes
the particulars
the hard data
the who what when where why
slip away from me
and all I'm left with is
the feeling

But feelings are just sounds
the vowel barking of a mute

My brother is so sure of what he heard
after all he's got a record of it
consonant after consonant after consonant

If we remembered it together
we could recreate holy time
sparks flying

How good to stop
and look out upon eternity a while;
and daily
in the morning, afternoon, and evening
be at ease in Zion.

CHARLES REZNIKOFF

GAIL BERKELEY,
United States

A Convert's Road to
Prayer

My ears filled with the melodies of *Birkhot ha-Shachar* (morning prayers). On my first Shabbat at the *minyan* (worship community), I'd been too nervous to accept an eagerly offered *aliyah* (public blessing of the Torah). A year later, I was the *shaliach tzibur* (prayer leader, cantor). After a struggle that had begun years before, the prayers of my chosen people were finally mine: I was at ease in Zion.

A friend's mother best expressed the reason for my conversion when she remarked that somehow, through some dreadful mistake, a Jewish *neshama* (soul) had been matched up with the wrong body. Such a soul finds satisfying expression through Jewish prayer, as I eventually discovered. But growing up, I knew only that the melding of God and humanity seemed to me an unnecessary theological complication; that the state of the world gave me little assurance that the Messiah had ever come; and that, for me, neither ethical action nor prayer was rooted in *imitatio Christi*.

Prayer for me as I grew up was an uncomfortable, prophylactic, often mournful drama—dramatic in the sense that it was an impressive church spectacle, and also that I felt only tangentially involved in the central action. Starkly solemn Good Friday services evoked a frisson of terror, but no feeling of communication. Home rituals included prayers whispered for protection through the night, or grace mumbled by an embarrassed child while the rest of us squirmed through this rarely-heard prelude to a holiday dinner. At home or in church, the relationship between worshiper and God seemed indirect; though my mother, a classic (Christian) reformer, reminded us that we didn't pray to images of saints (unlike Catholics), Jesus seemed equally intermediate to me. Prayer was intensely personal, strengthening the link between God and a human being only by cutting off from the rest of humanity one kneeling figure, eyes tightly closed. Posture and dogma seemed equally unlikely to me.

In short, I had a sublimely Protestant conversion. When once I'd discovered Jewish teaching, prayer, and *halakhah*, I rejected one set of beliefs and metaphors for another on the basis of my own personal religious inclinations. Only after years of living as a Jew do I feel that I've made a Jewish conversion. Perhaps this process is a necessary one; but it means that the convert's road is filled with pitfalls. I left a tradition which damned me for doing so, and whose observances had left some emotional residue nonetheless in the person I am. Would Judaism ever feel as familiar to me as the religion I'd left? I knew I was unwilling to phrase religious questions in Christian terms, but would I ever master the Jewish idiom? Feeling within me a Jewish *neshama* guaranteed only a vague recognition of my own language, not control over grammar and syntax. In addressing *Avinu Malkeynu* (Our Father, Our King), how would I know that I wasn't addressing the God of my childhood—whom I'd disavowed? How would I heal the split between my two selves—pre- and post-conversion?

Somehow, the answer to all these questions had to be found in establishing a new spiritual identity. Whether converts leave their traditions in anger, bitterness, indifference, or disappointment, in our conversions we promise to wrestle with new terms in defining our lives and our relation to spiritual absolutes. Prayer must be a part of such experiential conversion, and rabbis who require attendance at a variety of Jewish services are wise. Yet experience of prayer surely ranks below historical and Hebrew education, Torah study, and even fundraising as a focus of interest and energy in many Jewish institutions. Avenues of spiritual growth are sparsely marked. Where can converts turn during the time they are traveling toward a new identity?

For me, the avenues were various. Before conversion, I lived through a Jewish year, participating through Hillel in warmly communal, emotionally intense Shabbatot. Friends wrote creative services; I puzzled over the *siddur* with them. *Kabbalat Shabbat* (prayers welcoming the Sabbath) evoked creation, exodus, and spiritual reanimation: history and creative rest. Instead of a focus on personal salvation, I found *tikkun olam* (obligation to improve the world), the outgrowth of a covenant between God and a people. In place of petitions to "Our Father," I found the emphatic declarations of the *kaddish* (prayer extolling God's holiness). *Brachot* (blessings) dignified the everyday actions of creating light, washing, eating, and drinking; together, a family brought the Shabbat queen to life. A congregation did not merely collect the individual supplications of souls in varying states of grace; a community reaffirmed the existence of God to whom praises are due. And when I heard Levi Yitzhak's "Din Toyre mit Gott," I knew my place was in this tradition of argument and responsibility.

I am the veteran of many lessons. In my first conversion classes, little was said about prayer. Although I am sure that many rabbis instruct proselytes in more than the *Sh'ma* (central prayer), the *Sheheheyanu* (thanks given for new events, possessions), the blessings over Shabbat candles and after *mikvah*, I know that many converts feel, in synagogue and in their own homes, just as I did in those first few years of being Jewish: lost and inadequate. More than the language has been pulled out from under our feet, and by our own action: no wonder our progress is unsteady. Fortunately, I found at least one *rav* (rabbi) at every stage of my journey. In Helsinki, early in my Jewish life, a lonely figure in the *ezrat nashim* (women's section) one Shabbat after another, I was determined to discover the congruity between the Hebrew chanted below and the unhelpful *siddur,* whose facing pages of Swedish and Hebrew were alike almost incomprehensible to me. Yes, the *gabbai* (sexton) tried, almost literally, to chase me away when he discovered that my parents were Christian Finns, not Finnish Jews; but in the following weeks, Rabbi Lanxner, the only rabbi in Finland, supervised my struggles through the *Sh'moneh Esre* (central prayer) on many Shabbat afternoons. (This patient man's time-consuming teaching comments sadly enough on Finnish Jewry, depleted by assimilation and *aliyah.*) And then Israel: "If I forget thee, O Jerusalem" rang in my ears with special poignancy during a short visit before I returned to the U.S.

The New York Havurah, my next Jewish community, did not include in its goals the education of inexpert *davenners* (worshipers). Yet as members explored and interpreted the traditional liturgy, some with love and some in anger, I began not only to recognize the sequence of prayers whose words I'd learned with Rabbi Lanxner, but to appreciate the varying tempos of *Kabbalat Shabbat.* Another place, a new struggle: *Shaharit l'Shabbat* (Sabbath morning liturgy) was the gift of the Murray-Dodge *minyan.* The efforts of a few encouraging people realized an oft-voiced *minyan* goal, the gradual involvement of neophyte *davenners* in all aspects of the service. It all began with helping to dress the Torah, an honor almost anyone could feel confident in accepting. Next came leading the Torah discussion: wrestling meaning from the history of the Jewish encounter with God. From such a position the step to that of *shaliach tzibur* was a short one.

The women of a congregation with which I was affiliated for several years provided the next part of my education. Yes, prolonged silence greeted the discovery that the rabbi's wife was a convert; but the silence opened into varied conversations. When the *Imahot* (matriarchs) were added to the *Avot* (patriarchs) in certain parts of the service, some women woke up to other exclusions. Ironically, I found myself teaching Hebrew, more privileged than many whose Jewish educations had stopped short of the *Alef-Bet* (Hebrew alphabet). I heard echoes of my own feelings of inadequacy from years past, and realized that my journey was not unique. Prayer? Many found the idea unsettling. Our problems and conflicts and joys as Jewish women today gave rise to a women's service for *Kabbalat Shabbat,* in which the device of women speaking disparate lines from various points in the sanctuary mirrored the different directions from which women come to Jewish worship.

Yet if not unique, my journey, I see now, has been highly privileged, for I have been accompanied by many whose ability to decipher—or, indeed, discover—almost hidden signposts I cherish.

Those times, and they have been many and painful, when it seemed I had given up one inadequate spiritual identity only for uncertainty and doubt, could have left a much greater residue of conflict and struggle. And so I wonder what the paths of those converts who appear less and less frequently at services have been like. I wonder, and worry—about them, their children, and the Jewish community.

Learning to pray involves more than just studying Hebrew or memorizing melodies and movements, but developing the desire and ability to pray with *kavvanah,* with gladness of heart. In seeking to be at ease in Zion rather than leaving prayer behind me in my childhood or continuing to feel lost in the synagogue, I chose the road less traveled. How many Jews explore the byroads of prayer? How many of our institutions support such quests? A convert's needs are often no more urgent than those of many other Jews, and the convert has the great advantage of an easily-expressed reason for seeking instruction and a variety of experience.

CONSTANCE GEMSON, United States

All Alone among the Vikings

I am surrounded by blue eyes, rows of identical marbles.
People ask do Jews have a native dress
or say Passover is just like our Easter.

I smile a five second summary of Judaism standing on one foot.
Offering my Reader's Digest version, I explain
life is more than Portnoy's complaint.

I am a buried relic, an ancient curio
a discovery of a Swedish Margaret Mead.
My life is not monochromatic. I bloom in the darkness.

I see Jewish topics in the book store.
Are they found by a wandering Swede?
The facts and fiber of my history is beyond his fantasy.

In his pale life, can he dream in vivid color of the shtetl in Poland?
Can he believe Chagall's flying fiddler and dancing fish?

Lot's Wife

Her name is nameless,
known as his wife, wearing his title,
draped by his desire.

To be Lot's wife was her mission
By lot, by chance, by error,
she followed him with conviction, a sleep-walker weaving in a
    dream.

Then she is asked to leave this land
where there was fire she tamed and food she grew.
Her calling is to forget,

He hurries her to pack for the family, to leave this old land,
place her thin memories in a bundle she will not need them.

The future waits vast but violent.
The new colors are vivid and burn her eyes.
The sun is harsh in its power.

She wants to hold the past, ripe as first fruit.
For this she looks back to remember,
and slowly turns to salt.

He did not know that I am Leah
and I—was Leah.
Rachel, he said, Rachel, like a lamb that strips the grass bare
thusly in you are stems stripped.
A flock of sheep made noise between our blankets,
the tent flies were dragged in the wind.
Rachel, he said, Rachel—
And my eyes were weak
like the bottom of a gloomy egg.
To the egg whites of my eyes the whites of my eyes melted.
The tent ropes strained greatly
to join the ground.
While the wind is blowing from the palm of my hands.

And he did not know that I am Leah
and a flock of children burst forth from my womb to his hands.

RIVKA MIRIAM,
Israel
Translated by Sue Ann Wasserman

A Song to Jacob Who Removed the Stone from the Mouth of the Well

---

Not by bread alone
does Eve live
   nor by her garments
     her conjugal rights
     and the light of her eyes

Eve will fall seven times
and between her teeth
one small bite
from the fruit of the tree which was
as green as wormwood
not the tree of knowledge
only the tree of life
itself.

MIRIAM OREN,
Israel
Translated by Sue Ann Wasserman

Eve

**SHEILA PELZ
WEINBERG,**
United States

**Campus Pilgrimage
to Reverse the
Nuclear Arms Race**

I am very pleased to be here today and to have this opportunity to wish you well on your journey of peace. Today is the seventh day, and the practice of the Jewish people is to gather on this day to remember creation—creation occurred in six days, according to Genesis, and, on the seventh day, God rested. We human beings mirror the divine act. We work all week, and on the seventh day we remember creation and pause, so that we can look around and feel more, take in all the wonders around us that we often miss the other six days. Your pilgrimage draws its inspiration from this same love of creation, love of life—and fear that creation is threatened. (It is curious to note that two of the major symbolic and political acts for peace are marches and encampments—an effort to transform the military system into acts for peace.)

On Sabbath morning it is customary to read from the Torah, which is divided into sections, one per week. In this way, we can complete one cycle in a year. This week's portion begins the fourth of five books, which is called Numbers—in Hebrew, *B'midbar* (In the wilderness). Our portion begins with a census count, carefully numbering the members of the various tribes and also giving their names and the names of the chief families. The major theme is the leading of the people, their system of journeys and encampments. Perhaps this great forty-year march of preparation—where a motley crew of slaves starts out and prepares to enter the land of promise as a free and holy people—can offer us some inspiration and insight as we set off on another march for freedom and life.

I read the Sabbath portion with this event in my mind, and I would like to share a few thoughts that emerged for me from the ancient text.

There is an interesting mixture of numbers and names in the census count. The numbers tend to be cold and distancing, and yet they are crucial. We *do* care about budget figures and statistics of deployment. We do need to pay attention to polls, positive and negative media reactions. You will be thinking in terms of numbers: how many joined us, how many miles did we walk today, how much money have we collected. An awareness of statistics, figures—numbers—is crucial to any serious endeavor. Sometimes we would like to ignore this dimension of our struggle, but we do so only at a cost to ourselves.

However, the most beautiful names are mentioned along with the numbers. Reuel, "God is a friend"; Elishamma, "God has heard"; Nethanel, "God has given"—most of the names contain a divine name as well. We would be missing something essential if we didn't learn each other's names and if we forgot to notice what this amazing experience is awakening in each of our own souls and in each of the other individuals whom we encounter along the way, all with special names and stories.

Another teaching: the text tells us, Every person shall camp with their own standard according to the ensigns, by their parents' house. Then it tells us, As they camp, so shall they march.

We find a wonderful description of how the camp was organized and how that organization was carried forward through the wilderness journey. We learn that the twelve tribes were divided into four groups corresponding to the four directions, North, South, East, and West. Each cluster had its own standard, unique color, motto, and insignia. Later commentators loved to further embellish the account in the Torah text. One version has the different colors of the flags corresponding to the colors of the precious stones that were set in the breastplate of the high priest on which were engraved the names of the twelve tribes.

We see in this formation a consciousness of diversity and an emphasis on each person or group bringing to the whole undertaking their fullest selves in their splendid uniqueness. The peace movement in recent years has been composed of myriad organizations representing diverse professions, religious groups, neighborhoods, various women's organizations—all affirming their individual identities while voicing common concerns. We trust that this affirmation and respect for difference is integral to the pilgrimage.

The camp organization according to the four directions reminds us of something else. We need to acknowledge each direction. We know the painful and terrifying truth that violence may erupt at any moment in any part of the globe. We know that the world lives with deep tension along the lines of the compass—East and West glare at each other; the North-South axis reflects the First World–Third World chasm filled with resentment and fear. The turbulence is acknowledged. But the four corners of the encampment and march also represent the four elements, earth, air, fire, and water, four aspects of reality that are alive simultaneously—the worlds of thought, of feeling, of action, and of mystery. The task of peace, the journey in the wilderness that you are on, is a gathering from the four corners and a bringing to wholeness, which means *shalom,* which means peace.

So we learn in our Torah portion that in the center of the encampment, in rest and in motion, was the *mishkan,* and around the *mishkan* were the priests who took care of it. The *mishkan* was the portable Mt. Sinai, the sanctuary, the "lost ark"; the *mishkan* was where the presence of God could be experienced. The *mishkan* is our vision, the heights of our hopes, the best we can dream, our inspiration, our reason for trying, for caring, for loving.

So, I close with a hope and a prayer for us all. May we be able to call on the identity and clarity of our own unique standards, may we receive protection from and give reverence to all the four corners. And, most of all, may we know what is the holy center of this journey for peace. May we orient ourselves always toward the *mishkan.*

ELLEN M.
UMANSKY,
United States

Reclaiming the
Covenant:
A Jewish Feminist's
Search for Meaning

Up until high school, being Jewish was something I took for granted. I didn't think about it much. I lived in a Jewish neighborhood [outside of New York City], had Jewish friends, belonged to a Reform Temple, liked "Jewish" food, and celebrated Jewish holidays with the rest of my family. . . .

As a child, I never tired of the stories my grandfather used to tell me: his family fleeing from Russia, the dangerous boat trip to America, the move from New Orleans to New York, boxing to earn some money, fighting his way up from poverty, the successes and failures of his life. Most of all, I loved the songs and imaginary stories he taught me. They spoke of Eastern European Jewish immigrants trying to "make it" in America—poor but proud, clever, and determined to succeed. My grandmother told fewer stories. Yet it was from her, I think, that I first felt the beauty of Judaism. She and my grandfather (my father's parents) lived with us, just as my parents and older sister had lived with them for the thirteen years before [my younger sister] Amy and I were born. I remember coming home from school late Friday afternoons, walking into the house and finding the Shabbos candles already lit, casting a soft and sacred glow.

My grandmother and mother always made us a special dinner on Friday nights: chopped liver, chicken soup, pot roast or roasted chicken. It was the one night, too, that we ate bread—fresh *challah* from the neighborhood bakery. There was something special about Friday nights. . . . Though we ate in the kitchen, as we always did during the weekdays, the lit Shabbos candles and the special cloth on the table transported us to another kitchen, a "Jewish" kitchen, where bacon and pork chops weren't served (as they were in my home though never on Friday nights), where words like *kreplach* and *knaidlach* rolled off the tongue, and where meat and milk were never mixed together (one might eat a cheeseburger in my house but never on Friday evenings). Moreover, the vast quantity of food we consumed helped to create a feeling of sacred time. On other nights of the week we often ate quickly, but to get through our Friday night meal took time and effort (stopping frequently to rest and begin eating anew). Thus, for the hour or two that we sat around the kitchen table, we forgot about homework and television and talking on the phone to our friends. Friday night dinner became our Sabbath celebration. It helped us unselfconsciously to affirm—all of us—the fact that we were Jews.

There were other things we did as a family that also affirmed our Jewishness. We went to Rosh Hashanah and Yom Kippur services together, gave each other gifts at Chanukah, had two large Passover Seders conducted by my father, and attended weddings and Bar Mitzvahs of relatives and family friends. When my grandfather died, we sat *shiva* for a week, with ten men saying *kaddish* for him in our living room. I remember thinking it strange that my father felt it necessary to get on the phone in order to "round up" extra men for the brief worship service. At the time, the word *minyan*—

prayer quorum—was foreign to me. As a Reform Jew, I had learned that public worship could begin as soon as one person arrived, male or female, and that the prayer of one Jew was as important as the prayers of a thousand. Thus, I couldn't understand either why we needed ten people or why all of those people needed to be men. We had plenty of women in our family. Why was it, I wondered, that the participation of my mother, grandmother, and aunts somehow didn't count?

None of us, however, questioned my father's actions. Perhaps my aunts were too grief stricken to notice; more likely, they had simply reverted to the kind of Judaism in which they had been raised. Traditionally, they knew, only men said *kaddish*. Women could grieve, but only men could pray. Perhaps I would have articulated my own feeling of strangeness concerning my father's behavior had I been able to separate in my mind the notion of spiritual quest from that of Jewish self-identity. To me, however, being a Jew simply meant being part of a particular historical and religious community to which I, my parents, and ancestors belonged. It was my responsibility to understand Judaism's teachings and to follow them, not to question why we believed certain things but to accept those beliefs as my own. Spiritual quests were for Abraham and Moses. The covenant of which I was a part was a covenant that *they* had made. The ground rules had already been set. They had defined what it meant to be a Jew. It was my task to embody this definition. . . .

Yet what did the words *Jewish faith* mean? To me, I think, they meant the teachings of Reform Judaism. . . . [Indeed,] during the ten years in which I attended religious school, I was taught ideas that I now can identify as part of the ideology of [classical Reform]. Although to my knowledge my religious school teachers never used the word *mission,* I learned that it was my responsibility as a Jew to follow the ethical teachings of the prophets and to be a witness to the reality of God. At my Confirmation ceremony, I made a pledge of allegiance "to the Torah of Israel and to the Faith for which it stands—one God, Father of all men, exalted through Righteousness, Brotherhood and Peace." I vowed dutifully to obey the Ten Commandments and to "hallow my life, in the name of the Eternal God, to the religion of Israel" and with the rest of my class formally entered into the covenant established between the Jewish people and their God.

As a member of that covenant, I struggled to find meaning in both private and public prayer. If I had indeed entered into a covenant with God, I wanted to be sure *who* He was and *what* He demanded. In religious school, we learned that God is the "highest and the best that we know and can say," a Being who reveals Himself in nature, in history, and as the "still small voice" of conscience within us. I remember once, in high school, questioning God's reality. As an experiment, I tried *not* to pray, telling myself, in John Lennon's words, that God was merely a "concept by which we measure our pain." Yet over and over again I found myself turning to the Divine, asking Him for strength, guidance, comfort, and protection. I wasn't sure whether God existed as I/we imagined Him to be. In college, I became convinced (through the influence of Immanuel Kant) that God-as-He-really-is would *always* be inaccessible to me. But from the age of sixteen on, my *belief* in God became stronger. I believed that the Divine, though universal, had entered into a special relationship with the Jewish people and that I was obligated—in behavior and thought—to prove myself worthy of that relationship. Without realizing it (and despite my earlier belief that spiritual quests were for Abraham and Moses), I had begun my own spiritual journey. . . .

[At Wellesley College, my Jewish complacency was irrevocably shattered. Encountering anti-Semitism for the first time, particularly among some of my peers, I began to] study the New Testament and the history of early Christianity in an attempt to understand why my being Jewish was so important to those that continued to challenge my religious upbringing. . . .

By the time I left Wellesley, I was determined to pursue my study of religion further. While I had enthusiastically embraced philosophy as an undergraduate major, the study of religion had become an obsession. In learning more about the Bible and the history of Christianity (I would have taken history of Judaism courses, but none was offered at Wellesley then), I felt that I was learning more about myself and those around me. . . . I honestly don't think I began graduate school to ask my *own* questions. Yet as my study grew—and deepened—the questions I began to ask most often were those I came to recognize as my own.

Unsure about whether I wanted to enter a Ph.D. program (and ignorant of the fact that women had recently been admitted to Hebrew Union College, the Reform rabbinical seminary), I decided to enter a two-year-master's program at Yale Divinity School. During my first year at Yale, I continued to explore the relationship between Judaism and Christianity, becoming particularly fascinated with the development of anti-Semitism in the early church. By the second year, however, my studies had shifted focus. Having begun to understand Hebrew and taking a variety of courses at the Divinity School, the Graduate School, and Yale College, not in Old Testament but *Hebrew Bible,* Jewish history, rabbinic literature, and the history of Jewish ethics, I felt my intellectual and emotional selves begin to merge and for the first time began to see myself not simply as Jewish but as "religious."

My earlier vow to remain faithful to God's covenant with Israel took on new meaning as I began to understand the uniqueness of that covenant within the ancient Near East. The development of Israelite religion from polytheism to henotheism to monotheism gave me a new and richer insight into the teachings of the Hebrew prophets. For the first time, I began to recognize the importance of ritual observance and ways in which the rabbis of the Talmud had succeeded in making Judaism an all-encompassing way of life. Perhaps most importantly, my study of Jewish ethics convinced me that even modern problems could be examined from a Jewish perspective. It wasn't enough, as I had imagined, simply to be a "good person." Through my courses at Yale, and later Columbia, I began to explore ways in which I could become a "good Jew."

When I moved into my first apartment, in the spring of 1973, I decided to observe *kashrut* (the Jewish dietary laws). A few years later, I joined the New York Havurah, an alternative Jewish group, with whom I celebrated Shabbat, holidays, and *simchas* (joyous occasions). I especially looked forward to monthly retreats, when we spent two days away from the city together. Most memorable were late-into-the-night discussions on being Jewish, our feelings toward prayer, the significance of observance, and the political situation in the Middle East. I'd been in Israel during the spring of 1972 and again, to study Hebrew, during the summer of 1974, but it was only within the Havurah that I felt "safe enough" to discuss both the pride and disappointments I felt during my trips to Israel. The Havurah became the first Jewish community of which I truly felt a member. While as a group we were far from homogeneous, all of us, it seemed to me, were engaged in a common struggle. All of us were trying to live our lives in personally and *Jewishly* meaningful ways.

Yet at the same time I was struggling to redefine my Jewish identity, I found myself engaged in another struggle relating to my identity as a woman. The feminist movement, whose impact I'd first felt at Wellesley, slowly but radically began to reshape how I saw the world and how I viewed myself. I began to question my father's assumption that for a woman a career was only something to "fall back on." As a college freshman, I saw my intelligence as a future source of frustration. I tried to convince myself that somehow I would learn to stifle my questions, put aside my abilities, and remain content with the life that a future Prince Charming would carve out for me. Four years later, having found a number of important role models in my female professors, two consciousness-raising groups that set scores of "clicks" going off in my head, and a boyfriend (later to become my husband) who encouraged me to carve out a life of my own, I began to explore *my* needs and expectations.

Consequently, many of the papers I wrote in graduate school focused on women's role in Judaism . . .

Comparative essays that I wrote on the position of women in ancient Israelite, Mesopotamian, and Egyptian societies forced me to recognize that in many significant respects, women's lives were more restricted within Israelite society than in the other ancient Near Eastern cultures out of which Judaism emerged. The misogynism of the rabbis, made clear in legal and nonlegal material, the development of a liturgy exclusively focusing on male images of the Divine, and the exemption of women from important religious obligations, including study and communal prayer, led me to conclude, with great reluctance, that perhaps women were more peripheral to Jewish life than I had wanted to believe. The more I read, the more I came to identify Judaism as a religion created by and for men. My own doctoral research on nineteenth- and twentieth-century Jewish women seemed to verify the sense of alienation and exclusion that I had begun to feel. Many of the modern Jewish women about whose lives I read had undergone a struggle that seemed to echo my own. They too had sought to find a place for themselves within Judaism without sacrificing either self-fulfillment or personal growth. Yet many, like myself, had found themselves confronted with a seemingly insoluble dilemma. . . .

Within the last few years, my own struggle to reclaim the Jewish covenant as a bond between God and *all* of the Jewish people—male and female—has been both challenging and frustrating. At times, I have almost abandoned my struggle. The continued exclusion of women from positions of secular and religious leadership within the Jewish community, the extent to which women's spirituality—past and present—is still ignored, the lack of formal ceremonies celebrating important life-cycle events of women, and the liturgical description of God as "God of our Fathers" (but not our mothers) make me angry and sad. At first, I directed my anger toward Judaism itself, ready to write it off as hopelessly patriarchal. But more recently, I've come to redirect my anger. It's not Judaism itself that angers me but those who seem to have forgotten that Judaism has never been monolithic and that in every period of Jewish history Judaism has developed and grown.

Those who argue that liturgy cannot be changed have lost sight of Judaism as a living religion. How meaningful today are images of God as King, Lord, and Shepherd? And why, if both men and women have been created in God's image, should we not address the Divine as Father *and* Mother, Master and Mistress of Heaven? Martin Buber envisioned Judaism as arising out of a We-Thou dialogue between the Jewish people and God. I'm beginning to suspect, however, that my forefathers did most of the talking. Consequently, Judaism as we now know it was largely fashioned by generations of men who decided what *they* wanted Judaism to be.

Yet even the rabbis of the Talmud admitted that the covenant established at Sinai was given to men *and women*. Perhaps my foremothers were content to live out their membership vicariously, through the rituals and prayers of their fathers, husbands, and sons. Vicarious membership, however, will no longer do. As a feminist, I have begun to reclaim my voice; as a Jew, I am ready to activate my membership within the covenant and to reopen the dialogue with *our* God.

As I think about my spiritual journey, I realize that my search for meaning may never end. What I've learned in the seventeen years since I took my Confirmation vows is that the ground rules are *not* preestablished, that it is my obligation as a Jew to help create a Judaism that is meaningful for my generation. Three thousand years ago, Moses stood at Mt. Sinai and received the Ten Commandments from God. When he came down the mountain and saw the Israelites worshiping a golden calf, he broke the tablets in anger. Perhaps he did so not only to warn us against idolatry but also to make it clear that not even God's words are irrevocably carved in stone.

It was morning. Sarah had just awakened and reached over to touch her husband, Abraham, to caress him, but Abraham wasn't there. Neither, she discovered, was Isaac, her only son, Isaac, whom she loved more than anyone or anything in the world. She quickly dressed and went outside, hoping they'd be nearby. But they were gone, and so was Abraham's ass and his two young servants. It wasn't unusual for Abraham to take Isaac somewhere, but never this early and never without saying good-bye. And so she waited, and wept, and screamed.

Hours passed. It was hot and Sarah thought about going inside to escape the heat of the sun. But what if I miss them, she thought. I want to make sure that I catch the first glimpse of them, even if they're far away. And so she stood and waited . . . and waited . . . and waited. She felt anxious, nervous, upset. "Where could they be?" "Where has Abraham taken my son?" The sun began to set. She started to shiver, partly from the cold, mostly from fear. Again she cried, and wailed, and moaned. Isaac had been God's gift to her, a sign of His love and a continuing bond between them. She had laughed when God told her she was pregnant. She was old and no longer able to bear a child. But God had given her Isaac and filled her breasts with milk and for the first time in her life Sarah was happy.

She looked around her and saw the fields, now empty, and in the distance saw the mountains, sloping upwards into the sky. And then she saw them . . . Abraham walking with his ass and his servants and Isaac far behind, walking slowly, his head turning from side to side, his hands oddly moving as though he were trying to make sense of something, and Sarah knew in that instant where Abraham and Isaac had been and why they had gone. Though she could barely make out the features of Isaac's face, she could tell from his movements and his gestures that he was angry, that he wanted nothing to do with his father who had tried to kill him. Abraham was almost down the mountain by now and soon would be home. He'd try to explain, to make her understand *his* side of the story. But Sarah wanted no part of it. She was tired of hearing Abraham's excuses and even more tired of hearing what *he* thought God demanded. And so Sarah turned and went inside and prayed that if only for one night, Abraham would leave her alone.

FANCHON SHUR,
United States

My Dance Work as a
Reflection of a Jewish
Woman's Spirituality[1]

I am always asking, What is the unique wisdom and knowledge that women share? In a world controlled by patriarchal values perhaps another question will help. Why have the great cultural innovators in the art of movement all been women: Isadora Duncan, Martha Graham, Sarah Levi-Tanai (director of Israel's national dance theater INBAL)?

I believe that women find stronger connection and meaning through a fusion of intuition, feeling, sensation, and thinking. This integration is vividly revealed in the expressiveness of movement.

This is because the art of movement does not deny or separate the life force from its bodily component. As a dance artist, I have intuitively charted a path free of patriarchal influences, both in leadership and in creativity. The dance traditionally fuses the feminine and masculine elements of experience. It emphasizes the truth and power of the physical body to house and express spirit.

Once we get in contact with this power, we must open up our rituals to the experience of that energy. It will become very clear how acceptance of the power of our physical selves to express the spirit affects personal spiritual involvement, interaction with others, and our sense of community. Inevitably, that power will stimulate a desperately needed HOLISTIC LITURGY.

I moved to Cincinnati in 1974, when Bonia Shur became director of liturgical arts at Hebrew Union College–Jewish Institute of Religion [the rabbinical seminary of the Reform movement]. For twenty years, he and I have collaborated in merging music and motion with Jewish themes. As a part of the HUC community, I became more involved in Reform Jewish liturgy and ritual. Consequently, I found a growing dichotomy between my modes of experiencing spiritual connection and those offered in Reform Jewish prayer services. I became aware that, except for the lighting of candles and other rites traditionally celebrated in the home, there was no ritual within the synagogue to express women's sacred lives.

In a piece that I created entitled "*Tallit:* Prayer Shawl," I attempted to bring together a ritual acknowledging the spiritual power of women, the physical life rhythms that move us into living worship, and the power of long, wordless experience. After all, we women were UNDERNEATH the *tallit* all the centuries when men *davenned* [prayed]. We were living, caring, dying, burying, washing, raging, nursing, being burned and defiled, scapegoated and yearning, meeting intimately. So I choreographed a half-hour silent meditation within a synagogue service.

Taking place in the social hall of the synagogue where the service is held, the *tallit*, like a Torah, is ritually unrolled during the *Barechu* (the call to worship). Its white stretch texture 40′ × 25′ × 20′) with two blue stripes on one side has openings for the heads of five women. The women enter the fabric on the *Sh'ma*. None touch, yet each is moved by the pull of each other's movement.

The dancers in the cloth reflect, meditate, *daven,* whirl as the huge cloth rustles in the air, blowing pages of prayer books resting on laps of the congregation. The sound track weaves the laughing giggles of children with motives from Bonia Shur's "L'Cha Dodi." The women listen to each other through time and space; some leave the shawl and fly to be free of its connection, yet are caught in its folds at the moment of suspension—finite yet sacred.

After the silent meditation in motion, the dancers in the *tallit* become still. The entire congregation is invited to join the edges of the *tallit* silently. The dancers slowly sway, as energy moves in and through the congregants' hands and fingers, as they hold strongly to the fabric. All chant the adoration together and the *kaddish* [the memorial prayer]. Then, from the earth-bound acceptance of our own death and our connection, all women and men of our multifaceted faith, we move the edges of the *tallit* around this center of women.

Spontaneous interaction implies that we all sense nonverbally exactly WHETHER WE CAN TRUST ANOTHER PERSON. We do this through how we carry ourselves, the flow of our expression, the rhythm of our phrasing, and the synchronicity of our gestures. When we ignore human movement we ignore our innate ability to perceive and respond to the process of becoming. We are naturally expressive through our bodies, and our rituals either build spontaneity or inhibit that option.

Experience has taught me that congregants are usually *numbed* in worship services. Each person has unique responses that need to be exchanged in public because they are the very essence of spiritual vitality. I don't mean blind enthusiasm, but acknowledging that what happens on a physical level IS communication.

Perhaps the choreographic process in "Jewess in the Renaissance" will help clarify. This dance is both a historical piece and a metaphor, telling of a woman whose spirit has been marked by anonymity, a woman who has worn the badge of shame during the history of the Jewish people. She reenters the synagogue to lead in the return of spontaneity to Jewish rituals. As the dancer enters in a long Renaissance dress with a swirling cape, down the aisle in regal celebratory exuberant promenade, the congregation as audience witnesses her experience of separation as she is marked and cast out of the mainstream Renaissance culture. Two readers from the audience proclaim papal edicts commanding all Jews to wear badges, and her cape becomes transformed into a *tallit*.

By theatrical illusion, variously shaped badges are revealed and disappear from her costume. The last badge revealed by surprise is a red heart on her breast. With it, she dances a love offering, offering herself to the congregants, to the witnesses, and to the world. Confident of the audience's encouragement, she dons her Renaissance cape of celebration and, swirling her way through the congregation, engages the seated congregants in an exchange of hand gestures and eye movements. The fourth movement brings the dance to its climax as I throw a "gift" in motion to the congregation, which is prepared to catch "it." Through silent gestures, the congregation perceives that they can give and take energy from each other. Congregants look at each other, send movement across space to be gathered across aisles, balcony to *bima* [pulpit], back to front. Those near each other feel their aliveness within a "sermon" in motion. The Jewess, having ignited them, leaves.

As these brief reflections reveal, dance serves for me as a form of prayer, meditation, and connection with life forces. It has also seeded some of my deepest relationships with people. As a movement therapist, I work with many women clients. Their life stories emerge out of rigid bodies moving, changing, becoming connected and whole. Their stories reveal an overwhelming amount of sexual and emotional abuse. The effect is *detachment of body from mind*. This phenomenon has verified my own reasons for a life work pursuing the marriage between *spirituality and changing matter through embodiment.*

Our tissues, our cells remember . . . re-member when the traumas were so persistent and messages were so mixed, so confused within our tissues and our cells. I see a relation between the detachment from our body messages and the way feelings and experiences are objectified and then abstracted in a patriarchal, word-based religious system. I am often aware of the way in which a male god image must reflect the way males experience insemination, followed by detachment, stepping back and then judging. In just that way, our bodies detach from our minds and forget. We live in a state of denial. Unquestioningly, we worship with male, dominating images of God.

It is through the miraculous process of experiencing deep movement that I began my questioning. Faith in the constancy of change and the miraculous ability of our bodies never to be the same taught me to be real, and *I learned of Faith by touching earth, I learned of faith by listening to breath move through me, I learned of faith by feeling my ribs and chest soften when the spasms of releasing past traumas brought with them the images of abandonment and sexual abuse and betrayal from my own early life and early family. The faith I found was in my own body as spiritual truth, and my felt "thought" or symbol creation has me imaging my own body as goddess, as earth, as shechinah . . . not an invisible shechinah, but experientially perceived energy systems relating me to us all.* It is "down to Earth" spirituality, but not, as it is commonly misnamed, concrete! "Earthy" does not mean frozen and made of the same hardened stuff that covers up our very earth herself/himself!!! I would call concrete an image of stress and trauma, hardened into our body's tissues.

Since I first created many of my dance works, including "*Tallit*" and "Jewess in the Renaissance," they have expanded into full ceremonial works. "*Tallit*," for example, now weaves ancient God/dess images with earth-centered incantations into the fabric of the *tallit;* and we become a dancing community for one and one half hours as the *tallit* becomes a snake, an umbilical cord, an ocean (*mayim*), earth (*adama*), breath (*ruach*), fire (*esh*), Jerusalem, the inclusive prayer shawl a wedding canopy (*huppah*) lifted over our head on ten foot poles, enabling us to marry all to all and dance in unabashed ecstasy—a tree of life, a newborn, a living Torah!

My dances are my liturgies. All my family are collaborators, my family life events the stuff of dances. And all my work is infused with a deep concern for social justice and political as well as personal change. I have broken so many taboos in this work, reappropriating exclusive religious symbols and REAPPROPRIATING HOW TO PRAY AS WELL,

> WITH BODY AS SPIRIT,
> WITH COMMUNITY AS THE "BIGGER DANCE,"
> MOVING ENERGY AS AUTHENTIC INDIVIDUALS
> IN EVER LARGER COMMUNITIES.

As a movement therapist, I have found that we are the embodiment of our society. We are all victims of disembodiment as our people were victims in the Holocaust's literal, genocidal disembodiment.

I am no longer afraid to do what is taboo. Jewish spirituality for me is creation centered, womb-heart-word centered, giving us the potential power to heal our fragmented, dismembered, disembodied, ABSTRACTED, ALIENATED worship.

The same healing modes that infuse my therapy with clients and students and with my Ceremonial Dance Company have infused my spiritual life as a mother of six children, including four from my own womb. The challenge of raising these children in a society whose school system is filled with abstractions and disembodiments helped me develop a way of teaching what I call "curriculum in motion." Especially challenging for me was to raise five boy children and to find how movement awareness touched and kept alive their spirituality. In teaching the same concept in Jewish religious schools to many boys who had been bored and turned off, as they say, I shared faith, bending dogma into flesh-filled, passionately moving, kinetically and visually interactive relationships.

"*Tallit*," which for many years has been touring the United States, has this as its dedication:

> "*Tallit:* Prayer Shawl" is dedicated to the Jews of Bonia Shur's hometown, Dvinsk, Latvia, where eleven thousand Jews were killed in the Holocaust. Shortly after receiving Grandmother Raise Mere's blessing, Bonia, with his father and brother, escaped.
>
> To the eleven thousand and to all marginalized people we resolve that their lives were not taken in vain:
> *We will uproot violence by facing it in ourselves;*
> *by letting heal what we have repressed;*
> *by rejecting the religious, philosophical*
> *and political beliefs that permit us to subordinate,*
> *exclude,*
> *isolate,*
> *oppress,*
> *and kill others.*
> It is our purpose to open up the matrix of myth, legend, and history:
> to include hidden, silenced sources and images needed to balance us
> so there will be no more Holocausts. Never again!

I have realized that my works must voice not only our private prayers but also our communal intentions. To this end I must envelop myself in loving, empowering symbols and ceremonies.

Note

1. This piece has been adapted from an earlier essay, commissioned by the women's rabbinic organization at Hebrew Union College–Jewish Institute of Religion in Cincinnati in 1984 for a journal that was never published. It was revised and greatly expanded by Fanchon for this volume in 1989.

**MARCIA FALK,
United States**

Sabbath

In the green and yellow grass of the broad field
fringed by greening trees,
leaves flapping,
birds talking and flapping,
a young girl disappears.
She lies down in her bright shirt
into the soft green grass
and disappears.

Later, the girl rises from her bed in the grass
and lifts her head among the white-topped stalks of clover.
She rises and walks off,
wading down into the field,
which waves around her like a lake—
so that soon she imagines she is sailing on a summer lake,
her body light as a sail in the fresh cold breeze.

All this is seen by the woman who sits on the roof.
She sits on the sun-warmed roof
and watches the tree-ringed field rock and sway
around the bobbing head of a girl wading through the weeds.

This is the picture the woman sees:
field, girl, bluejay, trees.
No matter what happens outside of this,
the girl will always be part of this.

Then, for a tiny instant,
the woman is weightless in the galaxy
which floats around her, blue and indifferent
and fierce as a winter sea.

Dialogues

The waving blue arms of the elm
and the agitated answer of the green fig,

the fat globes of yellow sugarmum
where bees suck love,

and you, in the morning's shade,
sipping hot coffee—

the darkbrown taste of the beans
and the milky froth—

say:

Indulge: the world
is abundant,
and ceaselessly dying—

This loving, dying world
to which we are given,
out of which we have come—

O body of the world,
eat with joy
the body of the world!

Introduction to New Blessings

The following new *berakhot* (blessings), excerpted from my *Book of Blessings: A Feminist-Jewish Reconstruction of Prayer* (San Francisco: Harper San Francisco, 1992), are examples of the new liturgy that I have been composing for the past several years. For a long time before I began to write my own blessings, I struggled with the traditional Hebrew prayers, attempting to make them work for me, wanting to have them articulate what I believe as a practicing feminist Jew. I finally had to acknowledge that, unlike Humpty Dumpty, I could not make words mean whatever I wanted them to. Although my private *kavvanot* (meditations) could help me focus to pray, they could not stretch the meanings of the liturgy beyond certain limits: I simply could not trick myself into believing that the traditional Hebrew prayers expressed the theology out of which I live. Nor did they express the values of the Jewish communities with which I identify, especially those of the Jewish feminist community.

Nonetheless, I feel (as I have always felt) strongly connected to my history as a Jew and, in particular, to the Hebrew poetic tradition—the tradition that produced the liturgy that appears in our prayer books today. But tradition implies process and change, the movement of the past into the future, the continual forging of links on an unending chain. The liturgy was not always "fixed"; the old prayers were once new creations of individuals living in particular cultures and times. Prayers changed as communities changed; they evolved as Judaism itself evolved. I believe that the challenge for heterodox Jewish communities today—and especially for those that embrace feminist values—is not just to study and preserve the classic texts but to create new ones, just as we create new practices and customs, to keep Jewish tradition moving forward into the future.

My *berakhot* do not bless a "Lord God King of the Universe" or, indeed, any "sovereign" at all. Instead, they point toward a divinity that is immanent, that inheres in all creation and nurtures all creativity. Because I believe in a monotheism that does not deny diversity but instead celebrates differences, I use a multiplicity of images to point toward an underlying unity—the unity that embraces all creation. Thus, no single formula replaces the "Lord God King" in my *berakhot;* rather, I vary my metaphors for divinity to reflect the particular moment being marked by the blessing. All my images have their roots in classical Jewish sources—Bible, *midrash, piyyut*—although, of course, most are turned and shaped to reflect my own poetic sensibility.

The first blessing below is a new *kiddush* (sanctification) over wine, to mark the festival of *Rosh Hodesh* (New Moon), which was traditionally designated as a women's holiday. Although in the past there have been no special blessings for women to say on *Rosh Hodesh,* today Jewish women are creating new rituals and celebrations for this monthly occasion. My blessing is intended for use in these rituals as well as in other new events and occasions that Jews wish to mark as a community. Following the *kiddush* is my *sheheḥeyanu* blessing, to be used for all new occasions as well as movements of renewal.

Kiddush (Sanctification) for New Holidays and Occasions

אֶת עֵין הַחַיִּים מַצְמִיחַת פְּרִי הַגֶּפֶן וְנִשְׁזֹר אֶת שָׁרִיגֵי חַיֵּינוּ בְּמָסֹרֶת הָעָם. נְבָרֵךְ

N'varekh et ein ha-hayyim matzmihat p'ri ha-gafen V'nishzor et sarigei hayyeinu b'masoret ha-am.

Let us bless the source of life that nurtures fruit on the vine as we weave the branches of our lives into the tradition.

Sheheḥeyanu (Blessing for Renewal)

נְבָרֵךְ אֶת מַעְיַן חַיֵּינוּ שֶׁהֶחֱיָנוּ וְקִיְּמָנוּ וְהִגִּיעָנוּ לַזְּמַן הַזֶּה.

N'varekh et ma'yan hayyeinu, sheheheyanu, v'kiyy'manu, v'higgianu, la-z'man ha-zeh.

Let us bless the flow of life that revives us, sustains us, and brings us to this time.

LAURA GELLER, United States

Encountering the Divine Presence (1986)

My letter from [Central Conference of American Rabbis] Vice President and Program Chair Gene Lipman extended the invitation to speak on the theme, "Encountering the Diving Presence." A few days later another letter followed, explaining that although we were gathering in a resort in Florida, the topic of the panel was not the "Diving Presence" but the "Divine Presence." But then, maybe they are not so different after all.

What drew me to Judaism had little to do with encountering the Divine Presence. Raised in the Reform Judaism of the 1950s and early 1960s, I learned that being Jewish meant being concerned with *tikkun olam,* although I didn't learn the Hebrew expression until much later. My earliest Jewish memory is not of candle lighting or *kiddush* or even the Four Questions. It is, rather, a memory of sneaking down to the living room after I had been put to bed and overhearing my mother and father discuss with members of our Temple's Social Action Committee the propriety of buying a house as a "straw." I was five or six. To me, a "straw" was something you drank chocolate milk with. The next morning my parents explained to me about racism and segregation, that black families couldn't buy houses in certain neighborhoods. "Buying a house as a straw" meant buying a house in a segregated neighborhood in order to sell it to a black family. We should do this, they explained, because we are Jewish. Being Jewish meant being involved with *tikkun olam*.

Years later, when I was already in rabbinical school and was struggling to learn the most basic Jewish skills, I became friendly with Jews who had grown up in traditional homes, Jews who knew how to *daven* [pray] and *lain* [sing the verses of the Torah] and were fluent in Hebrew. I was jealous of their comfort with the tradition, angry at how little I had learned in my Reform Jewish upbringing. But I had learned one thing that many of them had not learned— that being Jewish meant being involved with *tikkun olam*. One shouldn't have to choose between Jewish skills and Jewish values, but I realized through my jealousy that as an adult one can learn how to *daven* and *lain* and speak Hebrew, but it is much harder as an adult to learn that being Jewish means being involved with *tikkun olam*. Still, it had nothing to do with encountering the Divine Presence.

Like many of my generation, my years in college were caught up with the political struggles of civil rights and anti-war activities. Freshman year I joined a sit in for fair housing in the State Capitol Building. It was during the week of Passover. I didn't eat the donuts being passed around. I remember thinking that civil disobedience was a good way to celebrate Passover. The summer after my freshman year I went to Memphis to a convention of the Southern Christian Leadership Conference. The convention was very Christian and very black; I felt acutely out of place. My discomfort was obvious enough for our local SCLC organizer to take me aside and say, "You're right; you don't belong here. Go home and work in your own community."

So I went home—to the Jewish community. I organized through the local synagogues, canvassed door to door in the Jewish neighborhoods, did draft counseling for Jewish young men. I also began to study religion. I majored in ethics. I wanted to understand the connection between ethics and theology, to explore whether one must postulate a God in order to be good. I thought a lot about God, but I never encountered anything. [At Brown University,] I struggled with H. Richard Niebuhr's God, Paul Tillich's God, Karl Barth's God, and finally, in my senior year, Abraham Joshua Heschel's God and Martin Buber's God.

I knew it was important to be involved in *tikkun olam* and I sensed *tikkun olam* had something theoretically to do with God. And all this inchoate thought had something to do with being Jewish.

So I went to rabbinical school to learn to be Jewish.

The first year of the program, the year in Israel, was not an easy year for me. For the first time I encountered traditional Judaism and its attitude toward women. I went with my classmates to Mea

She'arim [an ultraorthodox section of Jerusalem] on Simchat Torah and watched *them* dance. I wrestled with a Torah that was on the one hand exhilarating and on the other hand excruciating, texts of liberation and texts of terror. I felt like I was sinking in quicksand, that I would have to choose between my heart and my liver, my sense of self as a woman and my evolving Jewish commitment.

In my second year at [Hebrew Union College], in a wonderful old classroom overlooking 68th Street [in New York city], we learned *Berachot* with our teacher Rabbi Julius Kravitz. I had never learned about all the occasions for a blessing—new clothes, new fruit, seeing the ocean, seeing a rainbow, being in the presence of a scholar, on hearing good news or even bad news—I was exhilarated! God is present at every moment; it is up to us to acknowledge God's presence. We do it through saying blessings. Rabbi Kravitz said, "There is no important moment in the lifetime of a Jew for which there is no blessing." I remember thinking, "Yes! There is no important moment in the lifetime of a Jew for which there is no blessing." And then I realized that it was not true. There had been important moments in my lifetime for which there was no blessing . . . like when I first got my period. There in the classroom overlooking 68th Street I became again the thirteen year old girl running to tell her mother she had just got her period. And I heard again my mother tell me that when she got her first period my grandmother slapped her. I could almost feel the force of my grandmother's hand on my mother's face, the shame, the confusion, the anger. I remembered my grandmother's explanation when I asked her why; she answered, "Your mother was losing blood, she was pale, she needed color in her cheek, the evil eye, poo poo poo." And, as I thought back to that time, I understood that there should have been a blessing—*sh'asani eisha, she'hechianu* [Thank you, God, for having made me a woman]—because holiness was present at that moment.

God had been present all along but I had never noticed. Perhaps I wasn't looking, or perhaps I was looking in the wrong places. If I had been looking I would have looked to a great and powerful wind to tear the mountain and shatter the rocks, to the earthquake or to the fire . . . but instead, I needed to listen to the gentle whisper, the still small voice, the Presence one encounters by diving deep and surfacing. As the playwright Ntozake Shange wrote: "I found god in myself / & i loved her / i loved her fiercely" (Ntozake Shange, from *for colored girls who have considered suicide/when the rainbow is enuf*).

A blessing would have gently taught me what it means to be a woman, would have invisibly instructed me how miraculous the human body is, would have drawn me closer to my mother, my grandmothers and all the women whose lives made mine possible. A blessing would have named the divinity present in this moment of transformation, this moment of connection. On 68th Street I suddenly realized that my experience is Jewish experience. There is a Torah of our lives as well as the Torah that was written down. Both need to be listened to and wrestled with: both unfold through interactive commentary.

I have come to believe that all theology is autobiography, that to be a Jew means to tell my story within the Jewish story. I had understood on some level even as a child that the Jewish story had shaped my story, the story of *Yetziat Mitzrayim* [the going out of Egypt], *matan Torah* [the giving of the Torah], and *tikkun olam* had formed the core of my sense of my self and my purpose in the world. But now I believe that my story also shapes the Jewish story. My experience propels me to ask different questions of Torah, to uncover different voices that more closely resemble my own.

When my son was eighteen months old, it was time to wean him. I was ambivalent about it; working full time as a rabbi meant I didn't spend much time with him. Nursing was a special bond that only he and I shared. I talked with a much older woman friend, a woman in her sixties, about my ambivalence. She said, "You're going to have to wean your child many times in your life. You might as well learn to do it now." I needed help so I turned to tradition, exploring Jewish images of nursing and weaning. Some of the images were stunning and empowering. In Pesikta de Rav Kahana 12:2, a psalm verse (Ps. 18:20) is interpreted to mean "God took out her breast to give Israel Torah." That image, of God as a mother cradling her infant child, nursing her child, with Torah the milk she gives her child, gave me words for the "stirring of wonder" I felt as I was nursing my son. That image opened up my experience of God, of Torah and of self. Some other Jewish images of nursing were problematic—images of men breastfeeding children, images on the one hand liberating because they suggest a different vision of men nurturing children and on the other hand irritating because they describe men appropriating women's birthgiving and sustaining functions. Most important, though, I recognized in the stories of Isaac and Samuel's birth the core of a weaning celebration, a ritual probably celebrated by our mothers over the generations. So we celebrated the weaning of my son with a ritual, a Jewish ritual of celebration and transformation. In the words of novelist Monique Wittig: "There was a time when you were not a slave, remember that. You walked alone, full of laughter, you bathed bare bellied. You say you have lost all recollection of it, remember. . . . You say there are no words to describe this time, you say it does not exist. But remember. Make an effort to remember. Or, failing that, invent" (Monique Wittig, *Les Guerilleres* [New York: Viking Press, 1969] 89).

There *are* no important moments in the life of a Jew for which there are no blessings. God is present at all times; it is up to us to notice God, to feel God's presence, to celebrate that which is holy in our own experience. Sometimes we are remembering, uncovering, discovering—exploring Torah with new eyes, different questions. But failing that, we invent.

Not long after I began my work as the Hillel rabbi at [the University of Southern California] a young Jewish woman came to me to ask: "Rabbi, what is the ritual after one has had an abortion?" She had chosen to have an abortion and yet she was filled with grief and deep in mourning. Years later a much older woman asked for help from Jewish tradition in working through her childhood experiences of sexual abuse at the hands of her father. The agony of infertility, the confusion connected to menopause, the anger and sadness connected to divorce—these are all moments that Jews have come to me for help in uncovering the healing power of God and Jewish tradition. God is present in these moments as well: the acknowledgment of God's presence is the beginning of healing.

So we remember rituals; and failing that, we invent. We invent carefully, because, as my teacher Barbara Myerhoff has said:

> All rituals are paradoxical and dangerous enterprises, the traditional and improvised, the sacred and the secular. Paradoxical because rituals are conspicuously artificial and theatrical, yet designed to suggest the inevitability and absolute truth of their messages. Dangerous because when we are not convinced by a ritual we may become aware of ourselves as having made them up, thence on the paralyzing realization that we have made up all our truths; our ceremonies, our most precious conceptions and convictions—all are mere inventions. [Barbara Myerhoff, *Number Our Days* (New York: Dutton, 1979), 86]

We remember and we invent because rituals teach people that God is present in their experience and that encountering the Divine Presence is the beginning of empowerment, of wholeness, of personal *tikkun*. Personal *tikkun* is the beginning of a process that can lead to *tikkun olam*.

Prayer remains very difficult for me. I make the mistake of taking literally what should be taken seriously. I feel alienated from the Father, the King.

I try to remember that when the tradition speaks of God as father, it doesn't mean that God is really a father. It means that there is something in my relationship with my father that opens me up to God and that there is something about my encounter with God that opens me up to my father. But I learn something different about God through my connection to my mother, my husband, my son, my teachers, my students, my friends. God is the Thou I discover through my encounter with the human thous in my life, people of whom I can say "for seeing your face is like seeing the face of God." I ache to find prayers that speak toward the totality of divinity, words I can use that can bind me to other Jews as they connect me with God.

I haven't yet found a way in communal prayer to speak toward the God I encounter in my experience. I want to affirm the messianic vision of the *birchat hamazon* [the blessings after meals], that we can help create a world where there is enough food for everyone, that how I eat and what I eat does link me to other people—the farmers who grew the food, the migrant workers who picked it, the ones who carried it to the stores. . . . I want to pray after I eat but I can't sing about the *brit sh'chatamta b'vsaranu* [God's covenant that is sealed in our flesh]. I whisper about the *brit* [covenant] that is sealed in my heart, but I feel lonely, cut off from the community.

Rabbi Eugene Borowitz taught me that study is a form of prayer. Study is easier for me, especially study in *chevrusa*. In wrestling with texts I feel less lonely. Wrestling with Torah is like making love. I get close enough to be wounded—and the texts often hurt. But I've gotten close enough to be blessed—the astonishing moment of blinding insight when the world suddenly looks forever different, when we discover wholeness in what had seemed to be disparate and unconnected. Divinity is clearly present in those moments. And so, like my teacher Rabbi Borowitz, I always say a blessing before I learn.

Denise Levertov's extraordinary and often-quoted poem "The Thread" best articulates my experience of encountering the Divine Presence. . . . In her poem, Levertov speaks of an invisible, silent thread or "net of threads finer than cobweb and as elastic," pulling or tugging at her each time that she feels a "stirring of wonder." Those moments when I, in Levertov's words, "feel the tug of it" are sometimes moments of transformation, always moments of connection. They are moments when I sense the wholeness in what so often seems fragmented and broken. Sometimes they are moments of joy, other times of intense anguish. Through the joy or sadness, through the wonder or the tears I feel the thread, the net of threads linking me to other people and the world around me. It is this web of connectedness that the encounter with divinity illuminates—a vision of wholeness, of *tikkun olam*.

Encountering the Divine Presence is a blessing. It is also a challenge. Diving deep and surfacing, remembering and inventing, wrestling and loving, being wounded and being blessed is a beginning. It pulls at me, sometimes gently, invisibly, silently, and sometimes with the force of a command. It calls me to imagine a different kind of world where wholeness is real, a world where every human being can live as though he or she really were created in the image of God. And it empowers me to work with other people to repair the world.

PENINA V. ADELMAN, United States

The Womb and the Word: A Fertility Ritual for Hannah

Conceiving a child did not come easily to me. Neither did the words to convey my frustration, despair, and uncertainty to those who might have helped. But, stories have been a source of strength and nourishment to me since I was a little girl. I devoured the books of the Brothers Grimm and Andrew Lang like hills of chocolate chip cookies. Myths of the Greek gods and goddesses were more substantial, like roasted meat with gravy. In later years, I began to feast on the tales of my biblical ancestors. When my life has presented a problem or paradox, I have sought a solution in close study of the sacred text.

I learned to do this by studying the Midrash, collections of rabbinic interpretations and parables which aim to clarify particular aspects of the *Tanakh* (compiled as early as the fifth century c.e.). One of my teachers, Judah Goldin, explained that when the rabbis found something in the text which disturbed them, from a grammatical deviation to a perplexing character flaw, they responded with a *midrash*.

When I lost my first pregnancy after trying to conceive for a prolonged period of time, my sense of living harmoniously with Nature was sufficiently disturbed to impel me to make a *midrash* in response. This *midrash* would be a hybrid creature, part-story, part-ritual.

Nobody I knew well had ever lost a baby. I had heard horror stories of friends of friends and their pregnancies-turned-nightmares, but these were remote occurrences. When Death came to our household, my husband and I had only each other. Our parents (the grandparents-to-be) seemed puzzled and overwhelmed by this tragic break from the norm. They wanted to help, but how could they give us a live child? While I was in the hospital recovering from the laparotomy which removed the Fallopian tube where the pregnancy had been trapped, phone calls and visitors kept coming. But when I was finally settled once more at home, I looked at my husband, Steve and asked: What do we do now? How do we start to live again?

What nobody could tell us was that we had experienced the real death of a potential being. We were grieving, but we could not put words to it, we could not invite people over to sit *shiva* for our dead baby. Then I remembered all those disgusting dead baby jokes I used to hear in fifth grade. Humor fills the vacuum caused by taboo. Talking about and mourning for the death of an abstract being, one that was never held or touched, was taboo in our society and in Judaism.

This was intolerable to me. I had to find a way to mark this death or I would be grieving for the rest of my life. In the works of Elizabeth Kubler-Ross I discovered the notion that one's own experience with Death is the instructor to follow. I would look into my tradition to find what to do. I remembered the story of Hannah and Peninnah in the First Book of Samuel.

Hannah was the favorite wife of Elkanah, but she was unable to bear him any children. Peninnah, her co-wife, less favored, bore one healthy child after the other. Through much suffering, deliberation, humiliation, and prayer, Hannah was finally blessed with a son whom she named Samuel.

Here was my model. Hannah had lost hope and self-esteem. She even displayed symptoms of severe depression: she stopped eating and wept constantly (1 Sam. 1:7–8). This indicated how deeply she was mourning for the child she might never have.

Like Hannah I was paralyzed—by infertility and by my recent pregnancy loss. The Rabbis considered Hannah the paradigm of heartfelt prayer and unceasing faith. Therefore, I would consider her story to be a kind of prayer, an inspiration to survive this overwhelming period of loss and despair which was facing me. Accordingly, in the year following my pregnancy loss, I sat down daily with the story of Hannah and studied it from every possible angle. Each day I read another verse and pondered it. Then I read commentaries on the story, mostly in *Pesikta Rabbati,* to see what the Rabbis thought about Hannah and her rival, Peninnah. Finally I wrote a new version of the story, a synthesis of the original text, its commentaries, and my identification with Hannah through the experience of infertility.

The ritual of studying Hannah's story became a *kaddish* which I said each day for my dead child. In this way I was able to live through the loss instead of being consumed by it. Incidentally, my husband's response was quite different. Whereas I turned inward to find strength and renewed faith by studying texts, he used activity to overcome the loss and became a Jewish Big Brother. One year after the death, we created a joint ritual. [Their ritual is described in Penina V. Adelman, "Playing House: The Birth of a Ritual," *Reconstructionist* (January–February 1989).] Before this could happen, however, we needed to do some individual preparation.

The more I studied, the more convinced I became that there was a ritual hidden there if I could only see it. However, this ritual lived between the lines of Hebrew text. No older wise woman was going to teach the ritual to me. Thus, part of the interpretive process would be uncovering this ritual for infertility.

My need to look into the sacred texts of my tradition in search of solace and hope echoed my desire to look life straight in the eye again after losing my baby and to find meaning in the experience. Magical thinking led me to believe that by studying Hannah intensely I would ingest some of her strength and that this strength was contained in the very letters of her story. Similar reasoning often lies behind the activity of Torah study. The *wachnact* or "night of watching" before a *brit milah* when there is communal study all night long to protect the newborn from the Angel of Death is a folk custom which illustrates the notion of study as a form of Jewish worship just as Torah readings in the synagogue during the week, on the Sabbath and holidays do. In addition, the *tefillin* and *mezuzah* which contain Hebrew prayers may be seen as types of amulets protecting those who use them. Thus, I believed that the study of Hannah's story might protect me from further loss and offer some guidance in becoming a mother.

Hannah's silent prayer became the basis of the ritual. It represented the silence of all those who had experienced such losses and could find no place within Judaism to mark them. By studying Hannah and identifying with her, I became another link on a chain of women who had had difficulty in conceiving or had lost children. This chain included all the matriarchs and extended back as far as Lilith (Adam's first wife, who was condemned to lose all her babies as they were born because she refused to submit to Adam's will). In this ritual, giving voice to the silence would be my goal.

I first sang and told the story of Hannah in my Rosh Hodesh group composed of women only, a safe forum for the initial public exposure of my experience. Then on the one year anniversary of the pregnancy loss, I performed the story as the *haftarah* on the first day of Rosh Hashanah, the time when Hannah's story is traditionally read.

Presenting my *midrash* in public before a group of men and women meant the experience was no longer my burden and my husband's alone. At last, I understood my compulsion to develop a ritual where there had been none. Ritual places personal experience in the public realm where it may be witnessed, dealt with, and shared. The loss of a child, potential or real, becomes bearable when the person sitting to your right and the person sitting to your left experience it with you and can say, "Finally I understand."

A Ritual of Loss (1986)

For Rosh Hodesh, Tammuz (June/July): A Time to Mourn

BRING: Copies of the story of Hannah; an object of good fortune or protection (a *hamsa* or *mizrach*) [good luck charm, used as protection for the home] which could be jointly made/given by members of the group to support and strengthen the woman who is the subject of the ritual. (As preparation, read the myth of Tammuz;[1] and the story of Hannah in 1 Sam. 1:1–2.)

SETTING: At the home of the woman for whom the ritual of healing is intended. Since this ritual will touch upon the very painful issues of loss and grieving, care must be taken to assure that its location is a safe place, free from distractions or noise. Selecting an outdoor area is not encouraged.

THEMES OF TAMMUZ

Keeper: The name of this month, *Tammuz*, recalls an ancient myth of death and rebirth—when a descent into the depths is made as a means of fructification. To find traces of the rituals of *Tammuz*, we look in the Book of Ezekiel:

> Then he brought me to the door of the gate of the Lord's house which was towards the north; and behold, there sat women weeping for Tammuz. [Ezek. 8:14]

According to Sumerian tradition, Tammuz was a beautiful young god or god-like man who died and was then brought back to life with the aid of his sister, Innini. The myth of the dying and rising god, Tammuz, became transformed in Judaism into the destruction and rebuilding of the Holy Temple, the cyclical annihilation and rejuvenation of the Jewish people. This rhythm pervades the history of the Jews.

Several historical events occur in *Tammuz*, making this month as a time of despair and mourning for the Jewish people. On the 17th of *Tammuz*, Noah sent a dove from the ark to scout for land, but the bird found no place to rest (Gen. 8:9). On the same day, when

Moses returned from the top of the mountain, he broke the Tablets of the Law after finding his people worshipping the golden calf (Exod. 32:19). During the time of the First and Second Temples, the walls of Jerusalem were breached by the enemy. The 17th of *Tammuz* signifies the beginning of a three-week period of intense mourning which culminates in the Ninth of *Av, Tisha B'Av,* the date when both the First and the Second Temples were destroyed. That day has since become a minor fast day.

SIGN OF TAMMUZ

Keeper: The sign of this month is *Sartan,* the Crab. The crab echoes the major theme of *Tammuz* for it scrapes away at the earth in its search for food, remains buried for a time, and later returns above ground to continue its journey.

KAVANNAH

Grieving for pregnancy-loss or infertility.

The reader should be aware of the potentially broad applications of the following ritual. In the one presented, the loss is that of a fetus through miscarriage. Our ritual might serve as a stimulus to anyone who has suffered the loss of a child, a parent, a spouse, a relationship, a pregnancy. Society regularly marks the death of a human being, but not necessarily the end of a period of grief. The end of a marriage in divorce, the death of an unborn child, the abortion of a fetus, and the loss of a lover—all require a period of mourning. These events are seldom ritualized. We believe time must be set aside for this.

The following *Avedah* ritual is one example of a woman dealing with a loss which society does not recognize or validate.

> Keeper: Tonight, with your help, I would like to perform a ritual to acknowledge an important event in my life. One year ago this month, I lost a pregnancy. My personal loss is reflected in the very character of the month of *Tammuz* during which the life force is snuffed out in the person of the god of vegetation, *Tammuz*. It is also the month in which began the destruction of Jerusalem, the spiritual center of the Jewish people. I, too, lost my spiritual center when I lost my potential child. My very womanhood seemed to be in jeopardy since I could not continue to carry a child.
>
> There are no rituals within Judaism to mark the loss of a pregnancy. For my own spiritual survival, I had to dip into Miriam's Well to create one—based on the story of Hannah in the Bible, in the First Book of Samuel.
>
> Every day since I lost my baby, I have turned to the Book of Samuel to study the story of Hannah, who suffered because she was unable to bear a child. I found solace, inspiration and meaning in her story.
>
> The story of Hannah forms the basis for the *midrash* I wish to share with you as part of my *Avedah* ritual. This *midrash* is about creativity, individual and communal. It illustrates the idea that an individual is

often unable to express innermost emotions or thoughts unless other sympathetic people witness them.

I was able to grieve and soul-search on my own, and then felt I needed to come to you with what I discovered, to make a statement as a group about this loss. My hope is that this ritual will heal wounds all of us bear as the result of losses we've experienced.

(A woman starts the ritual by singing a *niggun* and the rest join in. The music sets a mood of sadness, longing, quiet pain and underlying strength. The songs that follow contribute to this mood: *A mol iz geven a mayseh (Yiddish folksong); Gesher Tsar Me'od.*)

Keeper: Let's read the story of Hannah together.

(Copies of 1 Sam. 1–2 are given. One woman reads the story aloud as the others silently follow. Then a discussion ensues, using these questions. Each group may frame their own or proceed.)

—What is the deeper meaning of the repeated biblical motif of two wives—one is fertile and one is barren, one is beautiful and one is ugly, one is righteous and one is unsavory? Examples are pairs such as Eve and Lilith, Sarah and Hagar, Rachel and Leah, Hannah and Peninnah, Esther and Vashti.

—Why is Hannah's prayer considered by the Rabbis to be the ideal form of prayer? Is this justified? What are your notions of prayer, ideal or mundane?

(After the women have discussed the story, the Keeper explains how she created a *midrash* from her own understanding of the text.)

Keeper: The stories in the Bible tell of many women who were infertile—they could not conceive a child. Infertility need not necessarily denote a physical state but rather a spiritual, emotional or mental state of barrenness. This is the teaching of Hannah, with its hint as to how one may change the barrenness to creation.

What I did with this story can be applied to any story in the Hebrew Bible. First, the reading of Hannah's story became for me a daily ritual of comfort and exploration. Each morning for a year I sat with this story and digested it, studied it, and was inspired by it. Each day I read another verse and pondered it, asking questions, struggling with it. Then I read commentaries on the story, mostly in *Pesikta Rabbati,* to see what the Rabbis thought about Hannah and her rival, Peninnah.[2] Finally I wrote my own version of the story. It was a synthesis of the original text, its commentaries, and my own answers to questions about it. Hannah began to speak to me through her ancient story, through rabbinic teachings, and through my own experience.

This ritual of studying Hannah's story became a *kaddish* which I said each day for my dead baby. In this way I was able to live through the loss instead of being consumed by it. The process I have described may be applied to any story which speaks to you in your own situation.

TORAH STUDY

Keeper: When I looked carefully at Hannah's story, I noted that the turning point was her prayer. She can no longer tolerate her infertile state and is driven to "pour out her heart" before God. The text says,

Now Hannah was praying in her heart; only her lips moved, but her voice could not be heard. So Eli thought she was drunk (1 Sam. 1:13).

Of course, the priest who represented the religious establishment could not understand such heartfelt prayer and misinterpreted her behavior as inebriation and decadence.

Here, in Hannah's prayerful silence, the text demands of the reader an active imagination. What is Hannah saying to God? The silent narrative is an invitation for the reader to open up emotionally, as Hannah did, in order for inner healing to occur.

This is the basis for the *Avedah* ritual. I'll sing the ballad of Hannah and when I reach the part about her prayer, I shall stop and invite all to imagine what Hannah might have expressed.

What would you give to Hannah to help her focus her *kavannah* for this prayer to God, to help her shape her words after her long silence?

This ballad has a chorus with just two words, *Rachem Aleinu,* "have compassion for us." In Hebrew the word for compassion, *rachmanut,* and for womb, *rechem,* come from the same root. I've always thought that the wombs of women form a secret, silent network of communication all over the world. Every woman knows what it means to menstruate, to bear a child, to experience menopause. Every time a woman tells a story "from her womb," other women hearing the story feel it in their depths as well.

Ballad of Hannah[3]

(TUNE: "SCARBOROUGH FAIR"; TRADITIONAL ENGLISH FOLKSONG)

1. Once there lived a man named
      Elkanah,
   "God has gotten" was his name,
   He got two wives, this Elkanah,
   Bitter rivals all the same.

   The first one's name was
      Peninnah,
   Precious pearl, Pe-nin-nah,
   Mother of pearls, Pe-nin-nah,
   Pearls in her womb, Pe-nin-nah.

   The second one's name was
      Hannah,
   Full of grace, Hannah
   Full of love, Hannah
   Full of longing, Hannah

   Chorus: *Rachem aleinu* (in
      cantorial style)
         Rachem aleinu
         Rachem aleinu

   For Peninnah had children while
      Hannah had none,
   Peninnah had pearls while
      Hannah had none,
   Peninnah had hope while
      Hannah had none,

   Peninnah gave life while
      Hannah gave none.

   Every morning, every day
      Peninnah would taunt
   her rival and say,
   Have you fed your children
      breakfast?
   Have you dressed them for
      school?
   Have you taught them well the
      Golden Rule?

2. Hannah spoke not a word in
      return,
   But deep inside, her heart did
      burn,
   She thought, there must be more
      than this to life.
   Than being a mother and a wife.

   Chorus . . . *Rachem aleinu,* etc.

   Years rolled by like unstrung
      pearls,
   Peninnah kept having more boys
      and girls,
   Hannah kept waiting for one
      seed to grow,

But her belly was filled with
darkness and woe.

Hannah could not eat and she
could not sleep,
All she could do was sit and
weep
And mourn for the children who
might have been.
She felt like a sinner without
a sin.

Chorus . . . *Rachem aleinu,* etc.

Elkanah tried to understand
Why Hannah felt like a barren
land.

"Am I not better than ten sons
to you?
Let's count our blessings though
they seem few."

That very year when they went
up to pray
To the Lord of Hosts to bless
their way,
Hannah did remain behind,
She had words in her heart, she
had things on her mind.

Chorus . . . *Rachem aleinu,* etc.

(The Keeper stops singing at this point and invites the other women
to give voice to Hannah's prayer in whatever way feels natural.)

Woman: Hannah, I'd like to give you some words from another
woman who knew how to speak from her heart, Emily Dickinson.
(She reads "Hope is the thing with feathers.")[4]

Woman: I have a "tune without words" for you, Hannah.[5] My
mother used to sing it when she lit the candles on Friday night. I never
heard her sing it—she died when I was two. My grandmother, who
was not observant, who brought me up, sang it for me as she lit the
Sabbath candles. And each time she would say, "I'm only lighting
these candles and singing the tune for your mother, because she
would have wanted you to know these things."[6]

This is important for you, Hannah, because the Rabbis read into
the letters of your name—*chet, nun, heh*—an acronym for the three
basic *mitzvot,* commandments, which are incumbent upon women.
They are *hallah,* which starts with the letter *chet,* signifying the portion of bread which is to be set aside for the priest each week; *niddah,*
which begins with the letter *nun,* meaning the laws of ritual purity a
woman is to observe; and finally, *hadlakat nerot,* which begins with
a *heh,* lighting candles on the Sabbath, which is the duty of the
woman of the household (She sings the remembered tune.)

Woman: I brought you this purple cord from Rachel's Tomb, Hannah. Brides and new mothers derive strength from the matriarch,
Rachel. She also intercedes on behalf of women who have great difficulty bearing children.[7]

By coming together at this time to honor Hannah and Rachel, to
think about their infertility and to remember their strength, adding it
to our own, we become the "thirteenth stone" for the Tomb of
Rachel.[8] This thirteenth stone, forgotten until now, represents the sisters of the Twelve Tribes, the daughters of Rachel and Leah who are
here in spirit with us. As the *Midrash* states, "To each of the twelve
tribes was born a sister, and to Benjamin were born two sisters."

Now is the time to reclaim the lost stone, the lost words of Hannah, the lost stories of Rachel and Leah and all our foremothers, the
lost Torah of the Thirteen Sisters! Let their words resound throughout the land!

(The women take turns in reaffirming the meaning of the story.)

Woman: Hannah, wisdom grows in your womb like a child. We tell your story on the New Moon of *Tishre,* the greatest *Rosh Hodesh* of the year.[9]

Woman: The Rabbis saw in the letters of the words *Roshei Hodshim* the word *rechem,* womb. The circle of the year is a womb in which the seasons, the earth, the festivals, the sacred stories are born anew, again and again.

Woman: Life can be seen as a series of impregnations, labors, births, growths and then new conceptions, maturations over time. Each "impregnation" may be another coming to consciousness.

Woman: "Pregnancy" may be the stage of carrying an "issue" within, experiencing grief and growth. This is a time of change, confusion, fear, movement.

Woman: "Labor" is the period of struggling with resolution. That may be a painful time or a carefree one. If the birth is healthy, growth continues happily. If the stage of resolution or "birth" is not reached, one may have to begin again.

Woman: Hannah, this way of thinking has helped me. If I can't give birth to a live human being, I can give birth to the ideas and struggles within me.

Woman: Hannah, remember our foremothers, Sarah, Hagar, Rebecca, Rachel and Leah; how they, too, wrestled with barrenness and fertility. Let them teach us how to gain strength through our common struggle.

(After the women have offered words to Hannah, the Keeper concludes the story by way of prose narrative and ballad.)

Keeper of *Tammuz:* Eli, the priest, was incensed by the myriad voices he heard in the sanctuary. He told Hannah to be gone, to take her drunkenness elsewhere.

But Hannah explained to him that she had not been drinking, saying, "I have been pouring out my soul before God."

Then Eli was struck by her sorrowful, heartfelt words. He had not been able to pray for years and her words opened his heart so that he felt like praying. Her words were pearls, stringing themselves from her heart to his ears. He told her to go back to her husband and tell him what she had just said. Soon, promised Eli, she would have a child.

Hannah returned to Elkanah and told him all she had told the priest. Her husband was overcome by sadness. "Hannah, I never understood your agony at not having children. Tell your story to Peninnah." This was done, and Peninnah, too, was touched by her rival's pains. She embraced Hannah. Soon after Hannah bore a son. Word of Hannah's marvelous gift spread quickly. When people came to tell her their problems, she responded with words which were pearls reaching from her heart to their ears.

Ballad

So Hannah bore many words,
She only spoke what she heard.
Inside her grew numerous pearls
Those words became her boys and girls.

The first one's name was Shmuel,
"His name is God"—Shmuel,

Every word a name of God—Shmuel.
Every word a pearl—Shmuel.

Now my story has come to an end
As Peninnah and Hannah on each other depend,
For pearls are formed in the womb of grace
Where the fertile and the barren learn to embrace.

Chorus . . . *Rachem aleinu,* etc.

The women are visibly moved by Hannah's tale. One woman introduces the concept of group wailing.

GROUP WAILING

Woman: I feel that the tears of Hannah are palpable in the air here and so I would like to try weeping together as did the professional mourning women of old.

(She sings a mournful *niggun,* a wordless tune. It is not necessary to have a specific tune in mind. One can begin the group wailing simply by moaning over and over again. This often opens one up to weeping as does the sound of others' moans. This activity will not suit everyone. Those who are uncomfortable with it should be encouraged to remain silent or sit outside the circle. For those who are willing, group wailing is a way to express bottled-up grief in a safe environment. Each group intuitively finds its own rhythm of wailing, rising to a crescendo, a high intensity, and then fading to a *niggun* and to relaxed breathing. A *niggun* in the "blues" mode is very appropriate to this activity. The group wailing ends and there is silence for several moments.)

SINGING

The Keeper now sits in the center of the room. The women stand, circling around her, singing songs of fruitfulness and compassion, restoration and rebuilding. As they sing, the woman who is marking her loss may become the center of a final ritual of healing. The women place their hands on her womb, heart and head.

Suggestions for songs: *HaNitsamim; Yibaneh Ha Mikdash; Rakhmana D'Anyee* (Liturgy—Hasidic melody); *Yerushalayim, M'Harbanotayikh Evneh;* The Water Lily.[10]

When they have finished singing, refreshments are served. The Keeper has completed the Ritual of Hannah, the climax of a year of mourning.

Notes

1. Variants of this myth are found among peoples of the ancient Near East as well as the Greeks and Romans. Tammuz is also known as Attis, Adonis, Dammuzi, Osiris, and Persephone. Innini is known as Cybele, Vanus, Ishtar, Isis, and Demeter. The myth has several possible origins. One may stem from the practice of child sacrifice during a time of distress or disaster, when a ruler might offer up his child to the gods as a means of appeasement. Or the muth of Tammuz may originate from the cycle of nature, as crops die during midsummer and resume in the rainy season, so does Tammuz descend to the underworld, reemerging

later as a living being. The myth of Tammuz may be found in Stephen Herbert Langdon's "Tammuz," included in the collection *The Mythology of All Races* (Boston: Marshall Jones, 1931), 7:336–51. See also Diane Walkstein and Samuel Kramer, *Inanna* (New York: Harper & Row, 1983).

2. *Pesikta Rabbati*, Piska 43, pp. 752–68.
3. *Midrash*/Ballad of Hannah by P. V. Adelman, 1983.
4. From *The Complete Poems of Emily Dickinson*, ed. Thomas H. Johnson (Boston: Little, Brown, 1960), 254.
5. Ibid.
6. Story collected from Maia Brumberg at a Rosh Hodesh celebration in Boston, 1981.
7. For a different use of the cord from Rachel's Tomb, see the *Adar Aleph*.
8. For more on the custom of adding a stone to a gravesite during a visit to honor the dead, see *Encyclopedia Judaica* (Jerusalem: Keter, 1972), S.V. "Holy Places," 8:922.
9. The story of Hannah is read each year as the *haftarah* for the first day of *Rosh Hashanah*.
10. Folk song on the album *The Water Lily* by Priscilla Herdman.

Create a tradition? A tradition is based on accumulated experience, handed down from ancestors to posterity. Well, I believe I did just that! I created a ceremony, a rite of passage from adult to elder, to establish my presence in the community as a functional and useful human being. The ritual also served some personal needs: that of facing my mortality, for instance. Calling my ritual a *tradition* may be a misnomer since my ritual has not been "handed down to posterity." Nevertheless, I felt that a crone ceremony filled a significant need in our society. Subsequently, others have created similar rites of passage based on my own, and I have been asked to speak and write about this experience on various occasions. I think I can consider that I have "handed down" my experience.

I decided to have a ritual on the occasion of my sixtieth birthday. Sixty seemed to me an appropriate age because I had just begun to feel the physical changes that come with age, changes that required a modification of my life-style. However, the reason I was drawn to assume my new status with a ceremony was inspired by the Genesis narratives I have been so involved with for the past decade. I came to realize that the biblical stories that dealt with Sarah, Hagar, and Abraham were, in most cases, rituals. Each time a ritual was performed, the life of the protagonist changed radically. Ostensibly, the main theme dealt with in the Bible is succession: Sarah acquired a son; Hagar acquired a son; and Abraham acquired two sons. But the overall theme is the spiritual journey our ancestors set out on. Both Sarah and Abraham are advanced in age at the time of their calling, so I thought that their summons was a propitious one for us to follow. I therefore included in the ritual elements from the Genesis narratives: a blessing, a change of name, a covenant, a reconciliation with death, an affirmation of life.

A ritual must fulfill a communal need as well as a personal one. That is the reason why I decided to have other women, whom I

SAVINA J. TEUBAL,
United States

Simchat Hochmah

consider to be a part of my spiritual community, create the ritual with me.

I have been asked on various occasions why I chose to have the ceremony at temple instead of having it at my home. I did this for various reasons: the temple symbolizes community, but, more than that, it symbolizes Jewish community; it represents the substance of my roots; furthermore, I was able to perform the liturgy denied me as an orthodox Jewish woman. I included portions of the Sabbath service because I envisioned Simchat Hochmah to be a truly Jewish ritual that springs from specifically Jewish roots. The highlights of the Sabbath service include carrying the scrolls and reading the weekly Torah portion. Carrying the scrolls and reading from Torah were a deeply moving experience for someone who had been allowed on the *bimah* [the platform facing the Ark where the scrolls are kept] only on her wedding day. It was as though I had been accepted as a full Jewish person for the first time in my life!

Unlike the terse sentences that report the deaths of the patriarchs, there is an entire chapter in Genesis dedicated to the death and burial of the matriarch Sarah. One of the reasons for this exceptional treatment is because of Sarah's status as mother of a people, of a life reflected in death; but I think it was also symbolic of the magnitude of mortality in the life cycle. I believe that the detailed description of Sarah's death and burial established her position in life, her mortality, and the wisdom of the immortality of her essence. Genesis 23, then, teaches us the internalization of death in the life cycle.

How to face mortality in one's own ceremony is a difficult proposition, to say the least. It was feminist scholar Drorah Setel's inspiration that led me to consider wearing a *kittel*. The *kittel* is a white ceremonial robe worn by some congregants on solemn occasions such as Rosh Hashanah and Yom Kippur, during one's lifetime, and serves in death as the shroud. In this way the body is clothed in the same manner in the sanctity of life as well as in the sanctity of death. It is symbolic, in the larger scheme of things, of the cycle of life and death in harmony with the cosmos.

I began the ceremony wearing an ancient robe, woven and made by women of Macedonia, which I had bought some years ago in Yugoslavia. Halfway into the ritual, I changed into a white linen *galabie* that I had brought with me from Jerusalem, where I had been that summer. The *galabie* is a simple garment, like a long shirt dress, the customary attire of Middle Eastern men and women. This garment was particularly meaningful to me because my cultural background is Syrian and the *galabie* was worn by my ancestors. I think that anyone seriously considering taking part in a Simchat Hochmah ritual should include the experience of wearing a *kittel*, the garment they will be buried in. It is a sobering occurrence and was, perhaps, the most moving part of the ritual.

Another element from the Sarah and Abraham story that I chose to include in the ritual was a covenant or a promise. A covenant is a solemn commitment that binds two parties to fulfill an agreement in which each is rewarded by the action of the other. A promise is an assurance by one person to fulfill an agreement, perhaps give a reward, but the rewarding is not reciprocal. God made covenants with Abraham and made promises to Sarah. I elected to make a pledge in memory of the promises made to Sarah. I offered my community a Beth Chayim Chadashim grant to anyone who would continue my work in feminist Judaism.

I ended the ritual with the planting of a tree. Trees were a significant spiritual symbol for our ancestors: Sarah lived in *elonei mamre,* a grove of sacred terebinths at Mamre; Deborah, Rebekah's nurse, was buried under an oak in Beth-El; Abraham planted a tamarisk at Beer-sheva, etc. Trees symbolized the connection between the depths of the earth, where life is quickened, and the canopy above, where life becomes visible.

I brought a young tree (in a pot) to temple and symbolically planted it with handfuls of earth and enjoined those who wished to partake in the planting.

I am indebted for the success of my Simhat to the incredible talents of cantor and composer Debbie Friedman and feminist rabbinic student Drorah Setel. Drorah encouraged and helped me create the ritual. It was her brilliant idea also that I wear the *kittel,* a moving experience for me. Debbie wrote the theme song, "lechi lach," specifically for this occasion. Debbie also created the melody for a blessing written especially for this ritual by Marcia Falk, "shir la-shem v'lanshamah."

My Simhat was not only a success but a moving experience for myself and all who experienced the special spiritual qualities of these two young women who also led the service. I cannot express how fortunate I was to have Drorah Setel and Debbie Friedman, dedicated as they were, to my rite of passage.

SIMCHAT HOCHMAH: A CRONE RITUAL

TEMPLE BETH CHAYIM CHADASHIM,
LOS ANGELES, CALIFORNIA
(NOVEMBER 1986)

I. *Pesukei de Zimra* Congregation (songs)

Welcoming Song: B'ruchot Habaot (music: Debbie Friedman; words: Marcia Falk and Debbie Friedman).
LECHI LACH [Go, take yourself] (Theme Song)
(Music: Debbie Friedman; words: Savina J. Teubal and Debbie Friedman).

II. *Introduction* (read by Community Elders)

We celebrate Simchat Hochmah to mark an outstanding event: the beginning of a new phase in our lives, different from all others. It is a rite of passage that honors one of the many stages in life between the time of birth and the time of death. Like many other celebrations (bat/bar mitzvah, graduation, wedding), Simchat Hochmah validates the part of life already lived, and empowers the portion of our future.

Every celebration/initiation brings with it the promise of a new and exciting future; *Simchat Hochmah* is no exception: it marks the beginning of the *Joy of Wisdom,* the long-awaited reward of a full life. Because Simchat Hochmah marks such an exceptional transition in life it is necessary that the ritual be highly symbolic.

It seems especially fitting that Simchat Hochmah should be celebrated in the month of Heshvan because the Torah portion to be read today is the awe-inspiring *lech lecha,* the call of divinity that has come down to us through the ages, a call made to Sarai and Abram, a call to the quest for a new spirituality.

> LECH LECHA, Go, take yourself
> . . . to a place that I will show you
> and I will bless you;
> I will make your name great
> and you shall be a blessing
> I will bless them that bless you. . . . [Gen. 12:2]

This oracle was very likely uttered by the priestess Sarah and was directed to both herself and her brother-husband, since the subsequent story is a detailed account of the changed visions of both these people.

This call of initiation into a new life was given as a great blessing to Abraham and Sarah, not in their youth, but when they were both already older. Why did God select a time later in life for their spiritual journey? Does a spiritual quest require a certain maturity?

We have a wonderful lesson to learn from Sarah and Abraham, and Hagar also. On one level, all three of our ancestors are "barren" throughout their young, adult, and middle-aged lives. Ostensibly the yearning of all three is to produce offspring. Each ancestor does achieve this reality but not without supernatural intervention. Sarah acquires a son, Hagar acquires a son, and Abraham acquires two sons. On a metaphoric level it is significant that we know nothing of the ancestors' lives before the process of realizing their vision begins, as though all prior experience is but a prelude, a leading up to the most monumental and enigmatic task. But each ancestor has faith enough to press forward against all odds, because the quest is not for biological descent but for spiritual heritage.

Because the greatest portion of their spiritual life commences in their old age, the physical beauty of old age is also stressed in the biblical narratives: Sarah is beautiful to her husband, to kings, and to God. Although Sarah's distinction is placed in the context of sexual desire in the biblical passages, the true nature of the stories has little to do with sexuality; rather it emphasizes the beauty of the matriarch's innermost being; a time when physical beauty acquires a new dimension; when the core nourishes and glows through the exterior. It was not only the birth of a child that was of utmost importance to our ancestors but the inner vision of forging a destiny and establishing a legacy.

It is this vibrant beauty from within that marks, not only an elder's accomplishments in life, but the inner enlightenment we call wisdom.

Wisdom is the process by which visions are realized.

Wisdom is not an end result but a process acquired through faith in the future reality of one's own vision(s), whether subliminally or supernaturally guided.

It is in the context of vision becoming reality that we celebrate Simchat Hochmah, by including in the ceremony some of the steps taken by our ancestors:

A title or change of name.

A blessing.

A covenant or promise (individual or communal).

A reconciliation with death; an affirmation of life.

A rejoicing, in which the individual and the community celebrate the occasion, perhaps by recounting past and future visions.

I have included portions of the Sabbath service in the ritual because I want Simchat Hochmah to be a truly Jewish ritual that springs from specifically Jewish roots. The highlight of the Sabbath morning service is the reading of the Torah portion. The Torah is a religious symbol of Judaism, and without Torah, at least to me, there would be no Judaism.

We dress Torah, we carry her, we care for her, we crown her. The Torah, the actual scrolls, are as close to an image of goddess as we have left to us from antiquity. Torah is the source of Jewish wisdom (*hochmah*), whose roots are our foundations and whose branches spread out to infinity.

III. *Birchot Hashachar* (Morning Blessings)

These are the obligations without measure:

> To honor mother and father
> to perform acts of love and kindness
> to attend the house of study daily
> to welcome strangers
> to visit the sick
> to rejoice with lovers
> to console the bereaved
> to pray with sincerity
> to make peace when there is strife.

And the study of Torah is equal to them all, because it leads to them all.

IV. *Kaddish D'Rabbanan* (Scholar's Kaddish)

(Music: Debbie Friedman)

SHEMA

Shema Israel: you are ancient and ever changing
Shema Israel: The Holy Name is the Name of many

Shema Israel: find comfort beneath the wings of Shekhinah
Shema Israel: the sacred way is before you.

V. *Tefillah* (prayer)

Congregants talk about people who are or have been significant in their lives.

Silent period.

VI. *Ritual and Torah Portion*

1. The participant leaves the sanctuary to change into the *kittel*.
As she changes, she recites the *Birkat Hama'ayan* (based on a traditional prayer):

> I bless the wellspring of life and death
> that sanctifies me with *mitzvot* [commandments],
> and commands me to enwrap myself in a comely garment
> and find peace and rest
> beneath the wings of the Shekhina.

Then she returns to the *bimah* while the congregants sing LECHI LACH.

2. Naming ceremony
In recognition of our status as elders of the congregation, with a vision and destiny for our community, the new elders will receive their title and a blessing from the congregation.

People who do not feel that the name given to them by their parents represents the essence of their being may at this time ask the congregation to recognize them with a new name.

Since the service honoring the elders of this congregation is Simchat Hochmah, the joy of Wisdom, the title we have chosen to bestow on our elder is *Hachamah* (Wise Woman) and *Hacham* (Wise Man). A *tallit* [prayer shawl] is held up over the *bimah* where the elders congregate, and a blessing (written by Marcia Falk) is given by the officiant and then sung by the congregation.

3. *Aliyah*
The Torah is taken from the ark and welcomed with song. The participants read the portion "Lech Lecha" (Gen. 12:1–2, 17:15) with Commentary.

WHY LECHI LACH?
SOME THOUGHTS ON THE TORAH PORTION

Go, leave, leave your home, leave your family, everything that you know, love, and are familiar with, leave it all behind, and set out on a journey, with no particular destination. Know only that, if you do this, a future awaits you of recognition and blessing. This is how this section of today's Torah reading begins.

Traditionally, as well as literally, these first couple of verses are addressed solely to Abraham, as though Sarah were simply the patriarch's adjunct. In fact, in this particular section, right at the beginning of the narrative, the text even mentions the name of Lot before it records the name of Sarah. Although this incongruity has never to my knowledge been brought to our attention by biblical scholars, I think it is important to note that the verse mentioning Lot is an interpolation. Nevertheless, the subsequent narratives deal as much with the matriarch as with the patriarch. I therefore address this sequence as having (originally?) been addressed to Sarah as well as to Abraham.

In what way is this calling of value to us today? I think it is particularly important to think of *lechi lach/lech lecha* as a divine admonition to a radical change in one's life-style, to permit one's own true essence to become apparent. It is a time to discard the unwanted pressures left by our parents or the culture of our tribe or clan. It is truly the time we can, and must, make the effort to give to the next generation the benefits of our vision with its realities and its dreams.

The second section that I read is intimately connected to the first and comes close to the end of Today's Torah portion. God says to Abraham: Sarai, your wife, you will not call her name Sarai, but Sarah is her name: and I will bless her and also I will give her a son for you and I will bless her so she will be as nations; kings of peoples will come from her.

The story is told quickly in Genesis, but it actually took twenty-five years from the time of the promise of a blessing to the actual fulfillment of that blessing. It seems to me, then, that a blessing, once promised and then given, should not be taken lightly. A blessing, when promised, is a vision; when given, it becomes a reality.

Today, as we celebrate wisdom, I would like to talk about the promise and the vision. They are still there. What we have to do is recognize them. Promises and covenants and visions were not the prerogative only of the ancients. The difference between our ancestors and ourselves is that they took visions and miracles as a matter of course, as proof of the existence of the supernatural. Omens exist only if you believe in them. We have lost the capacity to recognize an omen or a vision.

But now, when I look back on my life so far, I feel that I received an oracle that I did not recognize. In my case I don't think it made a difference whether I understood it at the time or not.

I have said on many occasions that my life seems to have paralleled Sarah's to a certain extent. Like Sarah I am a stranger in a strange land (as opposed to being in the land of my birth); I married but had no children; I spent many childless years honing my profession as a writer and educator. In much later years, I lived with a woman who had a child and whose child became like my own. Sarah acquired Ishmael, a son; I acquired Maria, a daughter. And now, in my later years, I have embarked on a whole new world, the study of Torah.

I ask myself two questions. When did I get the calling? Where am I on the journey? I believe I got the calling at a spiritualist meeting in England. The medium told me that someone was calling me and that her name was Sara. She said the woman was very old, very beautiful, and was holding a flower out to me. Her message was, "Don't despair; keep to your path, it is all right." I thought it was my grandmother Sara who had come to me, to console me about my broken marriage and to tell me to go on with my life. Now I think it was the matriarch Sarah, who perhaps is the same as my grandmother. I think the priestess Sarah was apprising me of another destiny, not that of a wife and mother, but that of an educator. Not an educator of one sole child, but of a tribe or clan or people.

And that answers my second question, Where am I on my journey? I am fulfilling the oracle of Sarah. I did not despair. I think now that my vision was that of the matriarch Sarah either offering the way or directing me on a path that would bring her back to her people. That, presumably, was my destiny.

I was very young when Sarah appeared to me, and I forged ahead knowing that I had a destiny but not knowing what it was. It is because I was not able to get in touch with the supernatural or the cosmos that I spent a great deal of my life spinning my wheels. But now I think I fulfilled my destiny, that portion of it anyway that Sarah attempted to reveal to me.

And now I am here again, open to a new calling. I hear somewhere in the cosmos, *lechi lach,* Go Savina, go toward the culmination of your life. Go toward what you will leave behind, the legacy of your essence.

Today you witness, each one of you, the beginning of the cycle that reintegrates my being with the cosmos. The cycle that reaffirms life. Like the *kittel* I wear, the ceremonial robe that unites and affirms the two aspects of the new cycle: a festive garment and a shroud.

The matriarch's destiny was to have a child. I am going toward this new phase in my life with faith, and courage, and excitement . . . and I said earlier that my life has in a strange way paralleled that of Sarah . . . but I hope the Shekhinah will not let me have another child in my old age!

VII. *The Covenant and the Promise*

Note. Either a promise or a covenant may be elected by the participant in memory of the promises and covenants received by our ancestors.

A covenant or promise serves as a bond between the participant and her community both during her lifetime and after her death. The congregation surrounds the participant as she announces her legacy to them. They then bless her, specifically, in song or recitation.

VIII. *Elonei Mamre* (The terebinth grove of Mamre)

The ceremony ends with the symbolic planting of a tree by the participant.

When I came, I tended the trees my ancestors had planted
Now I plant the trees for those who come after me.
I plant this tree so that its roots will mingle with my ashes
so that those of you who come after me will be blessed in its shade
find nourishment in its beauty and comfort under its canopy
May this tree grow to be filled with the presence of the Shekhinah.

Congregants file by the tree singing LECHI LACH.

End of Ceremony.

In South Wales, there is a species of caterpillar—a "moth with no mouth"—"that lays its eggs and then changes into a moth that has no digestive system, no way of taking in food, so that it starves to death in a few hours. Nature has designed this moth to reproduce, to lay eggs and pass on the life of the species. Once it has done that it has no reason to go on living, so it is programmed to die" (Harold Kushner, *When All You've Ever Wanted Isn't Enough*, 19).

Are we like that moth? "Do we live only to produce children, to perpetuate the human race? And having done that, is it our destiny to disappear and make way for the next generation? . . . The need for meaning is not a biological need like the need for food and air. Neither is it a psychological need, like the need for acceptance and self-esteem. It is a religious need, an ultimate thirst of our souls" (Kushner).

So we come here. A nearly palpable sense of expectancy fills the air as Jews gather in their synagogues to commence this awesome time—this awesome search—this awesome expectation to satisfy our deep thirst. . . . If logic tells you that life is a meaningless accident, don't give up on life. Give up on logic. Don't deny the thirst. Don't deny the powerful thirst inside of you that urges you to ask the question in the first place.

Drink! When Russians do it, they say "Nazdarovia—to health!" When the French do it, they say "a tes amours—to your loves!" When we drink, we say "l'chayim!—to life!" A flower that will fade? A cloud passing by? A dream soon forgotten? I come here to drink—not of insignificance, not of meaninglessness or worthlessness—I come to drink of life. . . .

These things do I remember, calls out the afternoon Yom Kippur service—"the oppressed, the afflicted, like lambs led to the slaughter" (*Gates of Repentance*, p. 431).

The martyrs of the Hadrianic persecutions, the slaughtered of the Crusades—even now we stumble out of the wreckage. How long will we continue to remember the times of our suffering? And on this day? This day I have come to drink of life!

Others have shared this anger—the resentment of carrying the *pecklach*, the burden, of Jewish suffering on bent shoulders. And many intelligent Jewish students have asked, "If this is true, if Judaism is a long chain of suffering—if Jews have always suffered—

SHIRA MILGROM,
United States

Sermon, Yom Kippur,
5749 (1988)

why on earth would I want to perpetuate this pain? Why be Jewish?"

And those of us who didn't leave Judaism left that kind of Judaism. And in its place we have reasserted that Judaism is life affirming—Judaism is meant for joy. We celebrate freedom, victory, birth, renewal, festival, and song. Our newer congregations name themselves: Chayim Chadashim, House of Renewed Life; Shir Hadash, A New Song.

A colleague and close friend is rabbi of the Reform Temple in Suffern, New York—a new and growing congregation. As part of the expansion of their facilities, the congregation sent away for catalogs of office and school furniture, among them church furniture. The church catalogs arrived promptly, addressed to the Reform Temple of Suffering.

Whoa! A mistake. No suffering here. We've had it with suffering. The first heralding blast of the *shofar*—the blast that catapults us into the New Year—is the *tekiyah*, sounded throughout the biblical period to announce times of joy! Joy—first and last.

But in between? The call of the *shevarim*. The three-part wail of the *shevarim*.

Sometimes, I reason that if pain and sadness make me unhappy, if I don't let myself feel the pain, then I'll be happier. I still remember the man I saw two years ago, lying on a southern California beach. He was clothed in a long, hooded terrycloth robe, covering all of his body except for his feet and his face—which was hidden behind wide sunglasses. A large beach umbrella was propped up over him; his head was outlined by earphones connected to a large tape recorder, and he lay on one side, facing away from the ocean. His skin couldn't feel the rays of the sun, his body was shaded from its heat, his ears couldn't hear the roar of the ocean, his eyes couldn't see its waves.

If I don't let myself feel the pain, then I'll be happier. So I choose to feel no pain. And I won't. But when we stop ourselves from feeling pain, we stop ourselves from feeling. From feeling anything. And we become like that man in the sun—not hearing, not seeing, not touching, not feeling. . . .

We have hurt. We do experience pain. It is the price and privilege of living and growing older. And it is true that as a people we have suffered. We are a very old people. We have lived to recount tremendous pain—and incredible joy.

During the Rabbinic period, two joyous times were set aside to match up young men and young women—times of rejoicing and celebration. One was Tu B'Av, the fifteenth of the month of Av. And the other time?—it's amazing—the afternoon of Yom Kippur. It was known and understood that the deep experience of pain is requisite for being able to experience deep joy. To let myself feel the pain, yes—but to emerge from it. Traditional Judaism still mandates set amounts of time for mourning, periods of lessening intensity: *shiva,* 7 days; *sheloshim,* thirty days, and eleven months, then once a year. There must be a limit to our grief. Yes, it is life affirming to allow ourselves to feel—to feel pain. But it is antilife to mourn without limit—to consume one's life in sadness. The *shevarim*—the mournful wail of the *shofar*—is an essential life-affirming part of feeling, but it is surrounded—limited on both sides—by the call of the *tekiyah*, the blast of joy.

There are three calls of the *shofar*: the *tekiyah*, the blast of joy; the *shevarim*, the mournful wail; and a third. Rosh Hashanah is known by another name. It is not known as Yom Tekiyah, the Day of the Tekiyah—not as Yom Shevarim, the Day of Shevarim. The third call of the *shofar* is the *teruah*—the nine-staccato call, the call of alarm. "Awake, you sleepers, from your sleep!"

The voice of Maimonides rings through the *shofar* service: "Rouse yourselves, you slumberers, out of your slumber. Examine your deeds, and turn to God in repentance. Remember your Creator, you who are caught up in the daily round, losing sight of eternal truth; you who are wasting your years in vain pursuits that neither profit nor save. Look closely at yourselves; improve your ways and your deeds . . . every one of you" (*Gates of Repentance*, 139).

. . . Learn to live the moment, even if it does not last. In fact, learn to live it because it is only a moment and will not last.

Many years ago, the mother of friends was dying—and, for reasons somewhat mysterious, she asked that [my husband] David spend time with her. The time was transforming for each of them. A few weeks later—and two weeks before her death—she asked that her friends and family celebrate Shabbat in her hospice room, the first Shabbat she had ever called for in her life. David told me afterward that she had said to him when it was over, "I will remember this forever." Forever. I still am overwhelmed. She was not denying her imminent death. She spoke of her readiness to die. Yet she said, I will remember this forever. . . .

If we think of life as a limited resource—a given number of years to live, x million breaths or heartbeats before our bodies give out—then every passing year uses up the remaining amount of what little is left. And I read this High Holiday liturgy, and it fills me with resentment and anger and disappointment.

But suppose we viewed life not as using up our limited supply but as the accumulation of moments—moments like treasures, experiences of surprise, of warmth, of closeness, of great laughs, unexpected discovery, and unimagined joy. Agatha Christie's second husband was the archaeologist Lord Mallowan. When asked what it was like being married to an archaeologist, Agatha Christie replied, "It's wonderful. The older I get, the more interested he is in me." You don't have to be an archaeologist to feel that way. The older we get, the more extraordinary life becomes—and the more amazing our capacity to experience its fullness.

I have come to drink of life, and I am reminded that life needs the *shevarim*, the capacity to feel pain, the pains of my life, of my people, and the hurts of others. That this is a time of *tekiyah*—the opening blast of Rosh Hashanah and the closing blast of Yom Kippur will be the *tekiyah* of joy—life is meant for joy.

But these days are not known by those names. Its other name is Yom Teruah—the day of *teruah*. Life is . . . like a flower that will fade, like a cloud that vanishes. But the call to alarm sounds—don't let that get you down! Only let it remind you that this is your chance. This is it. This is life. It is made up of infinite eternities—innumerable moments that will last forever.

There is practically not a person who has visited San Francisco who has not ridden its fabled cable cars. But most don't get down on their hands and knees—no, not to kiss the ground—to peer through the metal guides that run along the center of the street to the cable down below. The cable always runs—and, in order for the cable car to climb and descend the steep streets of the city, it latches onto the powerful cable below the street, and the cable pulls it up. I often imagine God in that way. It is the transcendent movement through all of life. It is always moving—ever present and eternal. But it is not out there or over there or way up there. It runs through everything. Every potential moment is imbued with the transcendent. Every potential movement is imbued with the eternal. In the language of Judaism, every regular moment can be *kadosh*. *Kadosh* is when you grab onto the cable—tap into the transcendent. Biting an apple can be a reflexive, nonthinking, instinctual thing to do when you're hungry and holding an apple. Or it can be a moment—bracketed by a few words, a blessing—in which we choose to let ourselves be aware of the wonder of life, of body, of color and taste. A moment. Not to rush through the world, race from appointment to meeting, rush through dinner so the kids have time for homework, rush them through bed time so you have time for yourself . . . wondering why we don't have time. A moment.

Yes, the genius of Judaism is that it is the magnificent architect of time. Like a brilliant space planner who walks into a huge empty space—and by adding furniture, shapes, dividers, and all kinds of structures creates more space—so it is with Judaism. Each of us is given this seemingly endless expanse of time—a lifetime—and how often we feel that we have no time—and that life is running out. Judaism, in its brilliance, creates more time out of this expanse of time. Time to be with and bless our children, time to celebrate births and growing into adulthood, time to become sensitized to the slavery and abuse of others while we reexperience our own, time to remember and to heal, time to tell our husband or wife that we need and love them, time to bless being alive, time to look inward.

Moments.

Teruah! The call to alarm cries—don't be fooled. Life is like a flower that will fade, a cloud passing by. But the moment, the moment fully lived, has tapped into the transcendent, the Eternal.

The *shofar* service comes to a close with a single verse:

אַשְׁרֵי הָעָם יוֹדְעֵי תְּרוּעָה
Ashrei ha'am yod'ei teruah
Happy is the people who knows the sound of teruah

God, in the light of Your Presence

ה׳, בְּאוֹר פָּנֶיךָ יְהַלֵּיכוּן

Adonai, b'or panecha y' haleichoon

Your Presence—embedded, available within each moment
God, in the light of Your Presence they will walk.
Happy is the people who knows the sound of the teruah.

Rosh Hashana: A time for remembering. It was just one year ago that I stood before you for my first High Holiday sermon at Leo Baeck. This has been an extraordinary year for this congregation, and for me as well. This year has been one of welcome and farewell, of great joy and delight, and of great sadness and pain. I have shared this *bima* with bar and bat mitzvah students, who have delighted us all with their competence and confidence as they chanted our people's ancient story. I have basked in the glow of achievement of our confirmands, who completed a rigorous year of study and service with a ceremony of power and beauty. Together we at Leo Baeck have welcomed new life and, on one occasion, thanked God for the recovery of a child whose life was saved by an organ transplant. One memorable moment came after the Consecration service in January. As we welcomed new members into the congregation and new students into our religious school, each school-age child received a small Torah. I noticed one small child, whose older sister had been consecrated, crying bitterly. When I approached him, I heard his muffled, tearful words, "I want a Torah too." I assured him that next year he, too, would be consecrated. But his tears reminded me of the care with which we parents and teachers must nurture our children's delicate yearning for and love of Torah. He made me remember what it is I want to teach him to remember.

This year I have sat with some of you in hospital rooms, speaking with hope, whispering with anxiety, silent in shared pain and anguish. I have wept with some of you as we buried loved ones and friends. I have stood with some of you at the gates of the encampment of the homeless in the shadow of LA's skyscrapers, and remembered with shame the internments of other innocent Americans at Manzanar and Heart Mountain. When will we learn that isolation is *not* the answer to our fear of difference, that separation is not how we must treat those who embody our own greatest fears of isolation and alienation? We, of all people, must remember the basic right of each human being to dignity and to justice.

The Torah portion that we read today begins *V'yhe ahar hadevarim ha eleh,* And it came to pass, after these things, that God tested Abraham. This is a day of new beginnings, but our Torah portion for this day bids us turn back. *After these things.* The difficult, haunting story of Abraham's attempted sacrifice of Isaac begins in the middle. The story assumes, and indeed depends on, previous action and interaction.

SUE LEVI ELWELL, United States

Rosh Hashanah Sermon (1987)

So it is for us. We begin a new year today, on Rosh Hashana, this birthday of the year. But, like our ancestor Abraham, none of us begins with a clean slate. We stand at the threshold of this new year, which we count as 5748 since creation, carrying the baggage of the months and the years that have come before. Some of us have spent many long and lonely hours unpacking this luggage during the month of Elul, the period of *tshuvah,* of self-examination, that precedes this day. With trepidation but determination, we have opened each battered bag and box, and have been flooded with joy and pain as we have sorted and turned the memories and mementos of the past year—the glorious graduation, the excitement of a new home, the joy of the birth of a first grandchild, the shock of an unexpected death. We wince with pain at the memory of a conversation that still haunts us; we flush with pleasure when we recall the vacation from which we wished we did not have to return. We turn back— and reclaim our pasts, with all their contradictions. One of the names for this day is *Yom haZikaron,* the day of memory, the day of remembering. And, as Jews, we must deliberately resist amnesia and nostalgia and claim memory and connectness.[1] On this day, we begin to remember who we are.

Our Torah portion continues. *V'haElohim nisah et Avraham,* And God tested Abraham. Another name for this day is *Yom ha Din,* the day of judgment. Surely, Abraham was judged on this day. And tradition teaches us that we are all judged on this day. But it is not God who judges us. We must judge ourselves. That is the essence of *tshuvah,* this time of turning. We ask ourselves where we have failed, and where we have hit the mark.

Our sages asked, Why does the Torah teach that God began to create the human race with *Adam,* one human being? To teach that, if any person causes another to perish, it is as if that person has caused the destruction of the whole world. And, conversely, when a person saves a single soul, that person is treated as if he or she had saved a whole world.[2] That is, I believe, what being a Jew, and a human being, is all about. Each of us is in the business of *saving human lives.* And we do that best by being ourselves, by saving our own lives.

How do we save our own lives? By taking risks, by pushing against the boundaries and limits that others have established, by being fully present. By stretching. By paying attention to the small acts of kindness that make up our everyday lives. Robert Frost puts it well. He writes, "Something we were withholding made us weak / until we found that it was ourselves. . . ." The beginning of wisdom is the ability to know oneself, and to judge oneself. And once we know how to judge ourselves, to save ourselves, we can become among those who save others. "Only once one is connected to one's core is one connected to others."[3]

I'd like to tell you a story. Once there was a seamstress who lived alone in a small house on the edge of the town. She was very poor and owned little except a rough bed, a small table, a chair, and the lamp that enabled her to sew once the sun had set. She was a quiet woman who kept to herself. But she was a woman with a special light in her eyes. In spite of her outward poverty, she seemed to possess an inner strength, a richness of spirit.

Her only visitors were her customers, who arrived at her door laden with bolts of fabric to be made into garments. Ever since anyone in the town could remember, the seamstress provided the clothes for the children in the local orphanage. She seemed to take special delight in creating simple shirts and trousers out of remnants left by her wealthier customers. And the children were excited to receive the clothes each year before Rosh Hashana. The director of the orphanage assumed that their delight was because these were the only *new* clothes the children ever received.

The seasons came and went, and one year, just as the new moon of Elul appeared, the seamstress died. Her death was hardly noticed in the town.

Many years later, the little town became a bustling suburb. The orphanage closed down, and the little *shul* became a grand synagogue. As Rosh Hashana approached, the congregation needed to raise funds for their operating costs. The president of the temple remembered that a very successful industrialist had spent his childhood in the local orphanage. "If he would come and worship with us for the High Holidays, perhaps he would share with us the secret of his success."

So the famous one, who now lived many miles away in the capital, was invited back to the town that had been his childhood home. And, because he was a sentimental man, he accepted the invitation.

"So," said the president of the synagogue, in a self-important voice. "Tell us. What is the secret of your success? From rags to riches, eh?" And he laughed the rich laugh of those who are used to a full stomach.

"It is actually very simple," replied the industrialist. "When I was a child, as you know, I lived in the local orphanage. Now you must understand the loneliness of an orphan. All too many nights my pillow was wet with tears, tears of longing for my poor, dead parents, tears of anger for my blighted future. In spite of the kindness of the staff and the company of the other children, I often felt very alone.

"So every year, I waited impatiently for the New Year to come. For, in honor of the holiday, each child was given a new set of clothes. Now, simply receiving a set of clean, never-before-worn clothes might have been wonderful enough. But, for me, the new clothes held a special secret: each year, in one of the pockets, was a small note. The note was just for me. And I savored its message throughout the year. It reassured me that I was *not* alone and that I would not spend all the days of my life in longing."

"But," said his host, "but what was written on the notes? What words could have made it possible for you to rise from *that* to *this*?"

"That's not what is important. Someone, and I never learned who, sent those messages just to me. And that made all the difference."

Such acts of loving-kindness, of life saving, are not only found in fables. The parents of a fatally injured infant offer their child's liver for transplantation and thus help save a life. Most "life saving" is less visible, less public, but not less important. A recent issue of *Newsweek* featured the stories of fifty-one individuals who, through their lives and their works, have saved a life, or the life of a community. These "plain folk" are unknown, uncelebrated heroes whose vision of the possibility of a better, more just society has led them to create and staff shelters and training centers for battered women and their children, to organize support groups for the victims of tragedy, to establish soup kitchens for the homeless and hungry, to develop hospices for AIDS patients, and to organize day care for the elderly. Some of these men and women have been recognized and rewarded by the Carnegie Commission's "Hero Fund."[4] But most are ordinary people, people who, like many of us who sit here today, know the power of simple acts of loving-kindness.

We reach out to others through our own pain, both in spite of it and because of it. We reach out to realize the true meaning of *rachamim*. *Rachamim* is from the same root as the Hebrew word for womb, *rechem*. *Rachamim* is usually translated as *compassion*. Com-passion; passion with, passion for. The passion of a mother for the fruit of her womb. The one-to-one caring from which some us have grown too distant. For many of us, it is easy to write a check, to send a donation, to reach into our pockets to support Jews at home and abroad, to aid any who lack the essentials of life, regardless of who they are or where they live. But have we lost the power of direct connection? Do we have difficulty translating our commitment to *tikkun olam* into everyday acts?

"One can always find warm hearts who in a glow of emotion would like to make the whole world happy but who have never attempted the sober experiment of bringing a real blessing to a single human being. It is easy to revel enthusiastically in one's love of humanity, but it is more difficult to do good to someone solely because that person is a human being." These are the words of Leo Baeck. How can we embark on "the sober experiment of bringing a real blessing" to those with whom we live and work every day? How can we fulfil Hillel's charge: *Ba'makom she ain anashim, tishtadel l'hiot ish,* In a place where no one behaves like a human being, each of us must strive to be human?[5] How can we help realize *Yom haDin* as a day not only of judgment but as a day for justice?

Rosh Hashana is *Yom haZikaron* and *Yom haDin*. It is also the only day on which the *shofar* is blown for more than a single blast. But this day is not only *Yom Teruah,* the day of the sounding of the *shofar.* It is also the day for hearing that call. God calls out, "Abraham!" and he answers, immediately, "*Hineni*," Here I am. Isaac, frightened by his father's silence as they climb the mountain together, calls out, "Father!" Abraham again responds, "*Hineni*," Here I am. Does his terse answer soothe his distraught son? And then, at the moment when we are sure that Isaac's life is lost, as Abraham lifts the knife to slay his son, the voice of the angel explodes from the heavens: "Abraham, Abraham!" Stunned, the dazed, or perhaps crazed, Abraham answers once more: "*Hineni.*" I am here, listening, and, please God, hearing.

This exchange reflects the importance of listening. This day is a day of listening, perhaps with a new severity, a renewed attention. Can we listen to one another with the same attention that we accord to the *shofar*? Will we let the raucus *shofar* blasts startle us out of our complacency? Might we be able, maybe for the first time, to listen to our own voices and hear our own truths? For when we can hear our own breathing, our own heartbeats, the sound of our own blood pulsing through our veins, then we can begin to hear the essential humanity of those around us. Their cries, and moans, and laughter, will no longer be muted by the cacophony of our daily lives. If we listen, carefully and deliberately, we may, in the words of theologian Nelle Morton, "hear others into speech." Will we hear those around us who have been silent and silenced? Will we hear those who have been forgotten? Will we hear those who call for justice?

This afternoon my family and I will drive to the beach to perform the ancient ritual of *tashlich*. We will walk across the sand to the water's edge and cast what my daughter Mira calls our "bad feelings" into the surf. We have stood together in many places over the years: along the banks of Alewife Creek in Medford, Massachusetts; below the crashing waters at Pretty Boy Dam in Northern Baltimore County; in the silence of Griffey Lake outside Bloomington, Indiana; along the banks of the Ohio River at Cincinnati's riverfront park. Last year was our first *tashlich* at the Pacific Ocean.

This year, like so many Jews before us, we will gather at the water's edge and empty our pockets. We will cast out the crumbs of last year's deeds, the memories of wounds sustained and inflicted, the remnants of conversations that hurt instead of healed. Standing on the shore of the ocean, we will repeat some ancient words and add some of our own, grateful to the Source of Life who enables us to distinguish between what must be cast off and what must be cherished and preserved. On this day of remembering, we shall remember. On this day of judgment, we will seek to become bringers of justice. On this day of listening, we will try very hard to listen to the still, small voice that inspires us toward acts of loving-kindness. And through such acts each of us can save the world.

Notes

1. I have adapted these words from Adrienne Rich, "Resisting Amnesia: History and Personal Life," in *Blood, Bread and Poetry: Selected Prose, 1979–1985* (New York: Norton, 1986), 145.
2. Sanhedrin 4:5.
3. Anne Morrow Lindbergh.
4. *New York Times* (5 July 1987).
5. *Pirkei Avot* 2.6.

E. M. BRONER,
United States

Body Memories

I had a friend who had heavy troubles. They sat firmly on her chest and pressed her back to bed every morning. Sometimes they would grab her head and squeeze pain into it. Sometimes they made my dancer friend clumsy and caused her to stumble.

Sometimes they would squeeze her eyes until tears fell.

Sometimes they entered her mouth and when she would speak wheezes and whistles sounded.

She said, "Be part of my life."

Which says, "Help me."

Since she is a dancer, I could see her either at her bedside or in the dance studio.

I am not a dancer. I have warts and calluses on my feet.

I have shortness of breath and a flabby stomach.

But I went to the studio to dance.

She would sit still.

"Give me something to do," she whispered.

I would come to the community dance class with poems, stories, journals about women and their lives.

There wasn't much interest. These women never thought they had a life.

Or the life was preparing to go on holiday.

One day, while my friend was speaking to her troubles, I said to the women, Use a body memory—a woman's body memory. Think back to the times of cradling, nursing, loving, quarreling; think of the mother and daughter and daughter and mother, that clanging chain of a relationship.

I said the most terrible thing of all, what they feared more than trouble, Think about aging.

I fixed them with my eye: "Any questions?"

"Yes," they asked. "Will I look awkward?" "Will I look clumsy?" "Will I look foolish?"

These well-to-do suburban women wanted the rehearsal mirror to reflect eternal youth. They did not want a frown to appear from strenuous effort, or there would be a line between the brows. They did not want sorrow on stage, or the mouth would sag.

They could not be angular.

They could not be awkward.

They could not be angry.

Or their bodies would look ungraceful.

And why else take dancing? As their mothers told them long ago, forty, fifty years ago.

In spite of themselves, they thought.

And performed.

One did a composition called "Period Piece," entering menarch, with the red scarf of bleeding, with the tribal women welcoming the young woman.

They softened, they rocked, cradled. They bristled and did quarreling abrasive compositions.

But it was hard enough to do something on their own. It was worth less than something mimetic.

And they hated the costumes my friend rose wearily to order. Grey, long simple dresses. Not pretty and colorful. And what would their husbands say to that?

But, for a scared moment, there was strength and pride.

They did not want me to work with them again.

And I did not.

It was a ritual in spite of itself.

My friend healed. She began to push her troubles off her chest. They became smaller. Sometimes she could fit them in her pocket. Sometimes she could pluck them from her arm and keep them from burrowing into her skin, and squash them like ticks on her dog.

The ritual of friendship was the one that succeeded.

My darling friend has a broken heart.

Teresa Bernardez, the psychiatrist, has explained to me that the heart develops lesions when it loses love and that it actually breaks.

My friend has had a love for nine years and he has gone. He, sixty-three, has gone to find a woman twenty-three. My friend was forty-three and thinks life is over, unfair, it's a man's world.

She cannot cease from weeping.

Her features are dissolving in the salt water.

Her coloring has changed to boiled red.

She, a great beauty, has dulled her eyes, her hair, her soul.

So, we gather to sit *shiva* on the day her lover has married the young woman.

There are several of us there—editor, medical school student, community worker, psychologist, writer. We bring two things with us: a tape-recorder and a cooked chicken.

We sit in a circle and speak into the machine.

We remind the bereaved of truth.

We remind the bereaved of her lost self.

We correct memory.

We reclaim the past.

The friend has been swept away. We must regather her, sweep her up, bring her back to us.

We remind friend of who she is, how she is still whole.

We each remember the lost love. We correct our friend's memory.

We embrace in holy circle.

We drink wine to the reunited wholeness of the friend.

We acknowledge amputation, separation as part of life.

We cook and eat together. Ordinary routines go on.

We speak of work, of dreams, of visions.

The friend weeps and is embraced, and the tears wash away the loss.

Sitting *Shiva* for a Lost Love (1986)

Our friend may wear a sign of mourning, besides her reddened eyes and heaving chest.

We cut a black arm band and give it to our friend with a finite time in which to mourn . . . and to end it.

DVORA WEISBERG, United States

The Study of Torah as a Religious Act

When I was sixteen, I decided, after a summer in Israel, that I wanted to know more about Judaism. I went to my rabbi and asked for help. He told me to read the Bible. I went to the temple library, took the first volume of the Hebrew Bible off the shelf, and began to read. My modern Hebrew was decent, but my knowledge of biblical Hebrew had been confined to memorizing twenty verses for my bat mitzvah. The English translation sounded archaic. I wasn't in the position to evaluate the commentary. I simply read—a verse in Hebrew, the English translation, the commentary—from Genesis through 2 Kings. I was enthralled.

Two years later, I took my first Talmud class. The language and the terminology of the text were confusing. The subject matter—the differences between adjudicating capital and monetary cases—was even more removed from the Judaism with which I grew up than were the narratives of the Torah. I spent the first weeks of the class praying that the professor would not call on me. But again, I was enthralled.

Why was I so captivated by texts that were so far removed from my own religious experience? I certainly cannot discount the intellectual challenge presented by the Talmud, the sense of accomplishment I felt when I was able to decode a difficult text. But I was not responding to Talmud simply as an academic discipline; I was discovering a new approach to Judaism. I felt more passionate about the texts of Judaism than I had felt about any aspect of Judaism I had previously experienced. Talmud was complex and demanding. Despite the apparent lack of relevance, I cared about the Talmud I was learning. Studying itself became as important as understanding the material; through the Talmud I felt connected to generations of Jews stretching back two thousand years.

What makes studying Torah religiously meaningful for me? What makes it more moving than *kashrut* or Shabbat or even prayer? The answer given in the texts themselves is a pragmatic one, that study makes all the other commandments possible, but that doesn't explain my fascination with a page of Talmud that may discuss ancient rituals that I find less than compelling. While I acknowledge that I chose to pursue the study of Jewish legal texts in part to understand Jewish practice better, that alone is certainly not what motivates me.

Torah is sometimes referred to in Jewish textual tradition as a path. Study of Torah is for me an attempt to follow that path, which I believe leads toward God. One twentieth-century scholar, when asked why he favored brief *davenning* [praying] in order to return more quickly to his studies, is reported to have responded, "When I pray, I talk to God; when I study, God talks to me." God's voice echoes through the texts I study, but I don't see study as a one-way street. Studying Torah leads me into a dialogue with God; if God is offering questions and answers, then I too am countering with my own concerns.

Studying Torah not only allows me to engage in dialogue with God; it is also a component in my attempt to emulate God. One of my favorite passages in the Talmud relates that a certain rabbi, Rabbah bar Nahmani, was studying Torah and became aware that a dispute was taking place in the heavenly academy. God was arguing one side and all the other participants were arguing the other. It was agreed that Rabbah bar Nahmani should decide since his expertise in the matter exceeded that of the disputants. Rabbah bar Nahmani ruled in favor of the position espoused by God. Only then was opinion of the creator accepted; God could not prevail over the heavenly academy without human assistance!

For me this story transmits several messages. Torah is not studied for purely practical reasons; God and the heavenly hosts surely have no fear of the type of ritual impurity with which the dispute dealt. Rather, *talmud torah lishma*, the study of Torah for its own sake, is so valuable that it is an appropriate occupation even for God. Furthermore, humans play the central role in the study and interpretation of Torah; even God, who is the source and giver of Torah, requires human aid to understand the text. The statement of Rabbi Joshua that the Torah is not in heaven not only gives humans the authority to decide Jewish law; it makes them responsible to continue studying and creating Torah. When I study, I feel that I am an active participant in a process that began with the Jewish people, an ongoing search for God's will and our place in the universe.

I have been a student of Talmud for ten years and a teacher of Talmud for five. On the one hand, I am in the best of situations; the learning and teaching that I experience as a religious act also pay the bills. This situation, however, is potentially a problem. What is religious about what I do if I do it professionally? If I am asked to teach in a secular setting, does my work cease to be religious, or am I somehow bringing religion into a place where it is not meant to intrude? Can I be a dispassionate scholar and at the same time be passionately religious if the same text is the focus of both my professional and my personal labors?

I think it is dishonest to pretend the Talmud is not a religious work. At the same time, it is possible to present the religious message of the Talmud without imposing it on students. The results of scholarship cannot be tailored to the needs of religion, but scholarship that has as its impetus the desire to understand Jewish texts better may also be the *talmud Torah* that rabbinic Judaism lauds. I believe that my learning becomes a religious experience as a result of some interaction between me and the text, some transformation that I can't verbalize or even pinpoint in time or space but that I know occurs.

Like many other religious activities, the study of Torah has been the province of men throughout most of Jewish history. The texts of rabbinic Judaism are the work of men, and the views of women that they offer are frequently disturbing. Furthermore, while women are studying Torah today more than at any other time in Jewish history, the idea of women as students and teachers of Talmud is still bizarre to many and offensive to some. How can a woman find religious meaning in these texts? Where are the role models for women who wish to become *talmidei chachamim,* students and teachers of Torah?

How do I grapple with Torah? I begin by approaching the text on two levels. On the simple level, the Talmud is a human product and thus articulates the beliefs of its authors. I may agree with some of these beliefs and disagree with others; some may move me, and others may disturb me. While these men may have seen their work as an attempt to understand the will of God, I do not have to accept their understanding as infallible. Love of Torah need not be blind love.

On a more complex level, Torah is an expression of the will of God. As a religious statement, is Torah accessible to women? A *midrash* that expands on the story of the daughters of Zelophehad in the Book of Numbers may provide the answer. When the daughters of Zelophehad heard that the land of Israel was to be divided only among the men, they came together for consultation. They decided to appeal for justice, believing that "the compassion of humans is not like that of God, for, while humans may show more feeling for men than women, that is not true of the One who spoke and brought the world into being. . . . [God's] compassion is for all, as it is said. . . . 'The Lord is good to all, and His compassion extends to all His creations.'" Their belief that God does not play favorites was no doubt confirmed when God ruled in their favor.

We sometimes feel that rabbinic Judaism shows more concern for the feelings of men and ignores those of women. The author of the *midrash* I just mentioned understood that and tried to show that women are no less dear to God than men. I refuse to believe that God avoids women. I believe that God is willing to enter into a relationship with anyone who seeks such a relationship. I also believe that Torah is accessible to all who wish to study it. I am not willing to dismiss texts because parts of them upset me. Traditional texts form the basis of the Judaism of which I want to be a part; can I leave their interpretation to men and then protest that my concerns are not dealt with?

I have always found it easier to love the Talmud than to be taken seriously as a student of Talmud. When I went to purchase a set of Talmud on New York's Lower East Side, one salesclerk suggested that I "bring [my] fiancé in to make his own selection"; it was inconceivable to him that I was buying such books for myself. One of my cousins asked me to come and meet a friend of his, a Hasidic rabbi, and demonstrate my knowledge; the rabbi refused to believe a woman was capable of studying Talmud, and my cousin had made a bet with him! I was furious with both of them, the rabbi because he thought Talmud was beyond women and my cousin for treating the whole thing like a joke. I refused.

Incidents like these are frustrating but probably inevitable when a woman enters the previously all-male world of Talmud study. For the most part, my teachers and fellow students have been supportive of my studying. The compensation for having had few women as role models is the satisfaction that comes with charting new territory. I had no women as teachers and few as classmates in graduate school, but now half my students are women. If people are surprised when I tell them what I teach, they are also excited and enthusiastic. I feel no need to apologize for or defend my decision to devote myself to the study of Talmud to those who believe that the Talmud is still beyond the comprehension of women or to those who feel the Talmud is beneath the consideration of Jewish feminists. I do what I do out of love.

For years I've been asked how a young woman from San Francisco with a modest Jewish background came to be an observant Jew and a Talmudist. I've never formulated a good answer. I keep thinking back, looking for the specific event or person that influenced the decisions that made me who and what I am today, but I cannot pinpoint it. Perhaps in one of those early encounters with Torah I found something more powerful than I expected, some religious experience that I still can't describe. Torah is a path that, having been chosen, seems to draw me further and further along, convinced that every twist and turn of the road brings me a little closer to God.

I used to suffer from *tefillin*-phobia. It was an embarrassing condition, one I found difficult to explain to friends or strangers. They saw me comfortably wrapped in my sky blue *tallit* and would ask, "And do you wear *tefillin* too?" "No," I would answer, invariably shrugging my shoulders and looking down. I sometimes mumbled something about not yet looking into the *halakhot* (Jewish law), but that was not the real reason. I was simply terrified of those thick, black straps I perceived of as *tefillin*.

To me, *tefillin* seemed to epitomize the antithesis of spirituality. They seemed to bind their wearer to earth, to *mitzvot* in the world, when I wanted to fly up in search of *devukut*, spiritual union with God. This was one of the apologetics made for why men needed to wear *tefillin* and why women did not. Men, the argument went, need a physical link with the natural order of the world, a link women inherently feel through their monthly menstrual cycle.

My avoidance of *tefillin* seemed to confirm this argument. Now, after wearing *tefillin* in daily prayer for more than five years, I can honestly say that this argument is little more than a *tzedie meise*, a "grandfather story," that helps discourage anyone with spiritual leanings from performing a very important *mitzvah*.

SUSAN C. GROSSMAN, United States

On *Tefillin*

But I have jumped ahead of myself. How did I overcome my *tefil-lin*-phobia? In part, I felt I had little choice. When I was interviewed for entrance into the Jewish Theological Seminary Rabbinical School, as part of the first class to accept women for ordination, the interviewers reminded me that acceptance into the program also meant acceptance of all *mitzvot* on my part; *all mitzvot,* even those I might previously have not felt obligated to observe as a woman. The morning after my interview, I took down my husband's *tefillin* and a book explaining how to put them on. I slipped the *yad* (the hand *tefillin*) over my arm once, twice . . . seven times. . . . I placed the *rosh* (the head *tefillin*) on my head. . . . Everything felt strange and constricting until I began wrapping my fingers with the straps of the *yad.* As I wound the straps around my second and ring fingers, I read from the prayer book this excerpt from the prophet Hosea:

> I will betroth you to Myself forever,
> I will betroth you to Myself in righteousness and in justice, in
>   kindness and in mercy,
> I will betroth you to Myself in faithfulness and you shall know the
>   Lord.

It is with great wisdom that the Rabbis compared the relationship between God and Israel to that of a husband and wife. As someone who had not been raised religious but had become religious only after college, I had experienced the great joy and passion one feels in serving God during those first years of great growth in Judaism. I would do any *mitzvah* I learned about, and I would search to find more *mitzvot* to do. I felt like a bride who selflessly sought to discover and then fulfill any desire of my groom. This honeymoon period, with its intensity of feeling and selflessness, is hard to match. Between husband and wife this feeling is rekindled monthly at the end of the woman's menstruation when she returns from the *mikveh* and husband and wife resume relations anew. Wrapping myself in *tefillin* now provides a daily rekindling of my feelings for serving God, a rededication of the actions of my hands, the desires of my heart and the intentions of my mind to do God's will.

This idea, of course, is not new. It is explicit in the paragraph said before putting on the *yad*. Yet, until I began saying this paragraph as part of my observance of the *mitzvah* of *tefillin,* I could not understand it in a way that was meaningful to me. I learned a second very important lesson in accepting the *mitzvah* of *tefillin*: one cannot always wait to understand a *mitzvah* or even wait to be attracted to observe a *mitzvah* before actually observing it, for often the understanding comes only through the observance. By doing, I was able to appropriate the act, internalize it, and synthesize a relationship to the act that had meaning for me, a meaning certainly within the bounds of traditional interpretation but on which I added an extra, feminist, significance.

For all the rich meaning I found in the traditional liturgy, I still felt the need to add a particularly female aspect to this *mitzvah,* maybe because of the overwhelming history of rabbis denying women the right to wear *tefillin*. One day, after completing the winding of the *yad* strap around my fingers and hand, I found myself winding the end of the *yad* strap four times across my palm around the rest of the strap wound around my hand so that the strap would not unravel while I recited the prayers. While doing this I spontaneously added this meditation, one line for each extra wrapping:

> May you imbue me with wisdom,
> and let me serve you with all my actions,
> all my intellect,
> and all my emotions.

Then I realized I had made four windings, which could represent each of the foremothers of Judaism. Since then I have continued to add the four securing windings on my plan to hold the wound *yad* strap in place, reciting the short meditation above but thinking about how each line relates to each of the matriarchs:

> "May you imbue me with wisdom," as you filled Sarah with wisdom, for she was your prophetess with whom you did speak; "and let me serve you with all my actions," as did Rivka, who ensured that your will was followed in determining who would next lead Israel; with "all my intellect," as did Leah, whose eyes, according to *midrash,* were weak, weak from studying so hard, and you assured that she was blessed according to the values of the society in which she lived; and with "all my emotions," as does Rachel who weeps and pleads before you for mercy on her children, us, the people of Israel.

I have since looked at the seven windings around the arm to find personal significance in them as well. To me, the seven windings reflect a unification of the heritage passed on to us by the three patriarchs, Abraham, Isaac, and Jacob, and the four matriarchs, Sarah, Rebecca, Leah, and Rachel. It is only when we combine the strengths and contributions of both our male and our female heritages, and only when we recognize and rejoice in all our individual strengths and talents—those defined traditionally as male or as female—that we are truly serving God as individuals and as a community.

The choice to observe is, in effect, a privilege for those in the process of becoming observant. Having grown up with little Jewish education, it is often wiser to do a little at a time and keep adding observance than to accept everything at once and become overwhelmed. This is an important process, for we must make each new observance our own, just as I have made laying *tefillin* my own. For women, even those raised religious, the question of whether to take on *mitzvot* that were not traditionally observed by women raises similar questions as well.

There is a line all *baalei teshuvah* (returnees to observance) cross, a point not marked by any rite of passage, yet an important watershed in the life of becoming observant. It is the point when one's Jewish life-style is essentially settled. One knows how to observe.

One organizes one's life around the Jewish calendar. One knows where on the spectrum of observance one falls and is comfortable with that decision. This is the point of critical juncture, for the honeymoon is potentially over. Observance can become rote. Although satisfying, the thrill and sparkle of observance is gone. It is almost difficult to remember God amid all the rules and bustle of everyday Jewish life. We have appropriated Jewish observance so well that we take it for granted, just as we often take the ones we hold most dear for granted because we are already comfortable with them.

It is hard not to pay attention when one goes to *mikveh*. From the inconvenience of leaving the house at night to the warm flush of water against one's skin during the immersion, *mikveh* demands attention and awareness. So does *tefillin*, with its macramé of windings and pressure on the skin. *Tefillin* is our daily reminder of God and of our relationship with God.

I no longer see heavy black straps when I look at *tefillin* today. Instead, I see glistening ebony wedding bands that reflect in the morning sunlight for a service of the heart, my morning prayers.

AMY EILBERG,
United States

The Gifts of First Fruits (1988)

Generally my work as a rabbi and as a modern Jew is the work of translation, the work of finding ways to bridge the gap that separates me and my community from the Torah, the *siddur* [prayer book], the ancient texts of Judaism. I need to find ways to make ancient texts come alive in the context of our modern lives, to make meaningful connections between modern life and ancient text, between us and our ancestors who lived centuries and millennia ago.

Given this general perspective, I was stunned to open the *parasha* this week. I was stunned because this week's Torah portion, Parashat Ki Tavo, begins with words that could have been written about my own life, words that describe the central event in my family's life this week just as well as they describe the life of ancient Israelite society. The twenty-sixth chapter of Deuteronomy opens with the *mitzvah* of bringing first fruits to Jerusalem, as a sign of gratitude to God for the many gifts that life has to offer. This week, my family celebrated the second birthday of *my* first fruit, my firstborn daughter Penina.

The Torah speaks of the obligation to give the first fruits as a gift to God, in recognition of the fact that all the land's produce, all our offspring, all our meaningful blessings, come to us through powers beyond our control. This is part of a broad system of Torah law, whereby first fruits, firstborn animals, and firstborn male children are symbolically given to God, in metaphoric repayment for all that we are given. Through this system we are helped to cultivate gratitude, appreciation, a sense of wonder for the workings of our lives, and we are helped to be clear about the boundaries between that which we control and that which is out of our hands.

This week my family had a party to celebrate Penina's second birthday, and the feelings that arose for me around this celebration could not be more closely related to the Torah's themes this week. Since I have you captive for the next few moments, I'd like to share with you some of those thoughts and feelings, giving me a valuable opportunity to do my own work of translation, my own Jewish reflection on this event in our lives.

Birthdays are always special. It seemed to me this week that the second birthday had a special magic, a special connection to the day of the child's birth. For just as surely as there was magic and awe and joy on the day that my child was born, so too, now that she stands on the verge of meaningful speech, she is being reborn—psychologically and cognitively, emerging yet again as a real person, as a human being, a creature of my creation and yet—extraordinarily—quite separate and different from me and from my husband. It is extraordinary how much this little computer, scientist, explorer child has absorbed and learned in the past two years. In fact, she may have taught me nearly as much as I have taught her, and it is those learnings that I would like to share with you today.

First and foremost, having a child brought for me the gift of wonder. How clearly I remember the moment of Penina's birth—the moment of intense fear and then intense relief, the hushed silence as the medical staff examined her, then the explosion of noise as she cried, as they cried out in joy, as she was pronounced healthy and whole and brought to me. As long as I live, I do not expect to encounter a moment of such intense wonder and joy—except, God willing, on the birth of future children—as I experienced on that day. Yet the wonder did not end then. I remember watching the development of wonder in her—that most incredible quality of childlike wonder that I have, through Penina, found reborn in myself—the joy of discovery, as I introduced my daughter to her first dog, her first firetruck, her first elephant, her first Hanukkah candle. By her second year she was actively seeking out her own discoveries and teaching me—reteaching me what I, in my oh-so-sophisticated adulthood, had forgotten about the magic and wonder of discovery—as she exclaimed over a bug, a new tricycle, music, the stars, or the joys of companionship with a new friend. As surely as I gave birth to her, Penina has given me a sense of rebirth, as she brought to life a long-buried side of myself that can rejoice and exclaim over life's everyday discoveries. What a wonderful gift from my child.

As she grows inevitably through toddlerhood, I am increasingly aware of the way in which she teaches me patience. I remember in her infancy how I struggled to believe that "this too shall pass," through sleepless nights and colic, through the sense of a permanent appendage attached to my left arm, through the exhaustion of needing to be the prime source of stimulation and comfort for another human being. Then came toddlerhood, and with it came autonomy, control, dawdling, choices, what she wants to wear and to eat and who must give it to her, following her orders about meals and toys and schedules, and letting go of things I thought were important—like how neat my house was and when dinner was supposed to be eaten. Many of these things have fallen by the wayside as I have struggled, with Penina, to learn what is really important. She has taught me patience that I never thought I had.

Most of all, she has taught me about control—and the lack thereof. From the moment of conception onward, even a high-powered professional feminist type like me had to begin to learn that what was really important was no longer entirely in my control. My husband and I laughed at two dear friends of ours who planned their date of conception to the day, were fortunate enough and fertile enough to conceive exactly as planned, only to have their baby born four weeks premature. Thank God, the baby was fine, and the parents learned a much-needed lesson (I hope).

From the moment of conception to the nature of the labor and delivery experience to the nature of the child herself, I grew to admit that these things were not mine to arrange, to manipulate, to control. I began to learn, laughing as all new parents must, that my control over my life was gone, and I began to learn that the control I had always thought I had was an illusion, a destructive one at that. That fantasy of control was a burden and a setup for overresponsibility and self-blame, a block to true self-knowledge and an impediment to deep intimacy. The loss of control at first felt like a terrible loss but has begun to emerge as a blessing and a gift, as I am free to appreciate that which is mine and to accept the things I cannot change or affect. What a wonderful rebirth, and what a wonderful gift.

All these are spiritual learnings, but Penina's birth taught me something special in my relationship with God as well. I will never forget the first time I was able to *daven* [pray] after my daughter's birth. In my recovery from a surgical delivery, I was too weak to *daven* for a full week after the baby's birth—a very long hiatus from *davenning* for me. When I was able to hold the *siddur* in my hands once again, on the second Shabbat of my daughter's life, I found myself reaching out to a different God than ever before. I found myself talking not to an image of God as the God of law and command and blame, an image I had known so well throughout my childhood and my rabbinic training. At that moment, I called out to God as the giver of life, the God of mothers and children, of love and care and nourishment, a God who would understand that there was sanctity in nursing and diaper changing and rocking and comforting as surely as there was sanctity in my encounter with the *siddur*. That night, for the first time in my life, I encountered a feminine image of God, who rejoiced in the birth of my daughter and my own rebirth as a mother. This is a gift that will be with me forever.

To close this reflection, permit me to share with you something that my husband and I read at Penina's birthday party, above her gentle protest, a segment of the ceremony that we created to celebrate her birth two years ago. It is from Psalm 8, a psalm that speaks of creation and wonder, of first fruits and gratitude, of the extraordinary partnership between parents and God.

> O Lord, our Lord,
> How majestic is Your name throughout the earth,
> You whose splendor is celebrated all over the heavens!
> From the mouths of infants and sucklings
> you have founded strength on account of Your foes,
> to put an end to enemy and avenger.
> When I behold Your heavens, the work of Your hands,
> the moon and stars that you have set in place:
> what is humanity that you have been mindful of us,
> the human person to cause you to take note?
>
> You have made the human little less than divine
> and adorned us with glory and majesty;
> you have made us master over Your handiwork,
> laying the world at our feet,
> whatever travels the paths of the seas.
> O Lord, our Lord, how majestic is Your name throughout the earth!

May this week's *parasha* and its echoes in your lives, as in mine, guide us all in learning to appreciate the many fruits and gifts that are ours, that our lives may grow richer not only in tangible blessings but in gratitude and in joy. Amen.

Dear friend,
with you I feel seen
I am recognized
and somehow, no matter how far from each other
we seem to stray in time and space
when I look again in your eyes
I am known.

It is a mystery to me
that we arrive so often on similar terrain
when our journeys
seem so different.
You married young,
became a mother young.
You left your husband
as the saying goes,
with babes in arm
and ventured forth into the wilderness.
You became a Rabbi.

I have watched you stride
I have watched you bleed
I have watched you fall
and then I watched you sprout wings and leave the ground.

BARBARA E.
BREITMAN,
United States

For Sheila

I have marveled always at your grace.
I tell friends you have the energy of a young stallion
and I see you, even in your pain,
like a young lioness
moving swiftly through the grass,
and leaping for the stars.

I have taken a solitary path,
walked through the caves and valleys alone,
sung out my song
in an open field
facing the wide sky alone.
I have borne no children
and married no man,
but when we traverse the starry night together
all these different facts of our lives
drop away.

We walk the same path
for it is a path to God
and when I see you
and know you
and when you look at me
it is the shared vision
we recognize
in each other's eyes.

I walk this journey with you
not knowing where it leads,
but knowing
that with you on the journey
I am never really alone.

You are moving away from me now
in time and space
farther than you have ever been before.

I will expand my heart
to keep you in its fold
and so I will grow with you
as we always do.

ITKA FRAJMAN
ZYGMUNTOWICZ
with SARA
HOROWITZ,
United States

Survival and Memory

I was born, raised, and lived with my family of blessed memory in Ciechanow, Poland, in a world that unfortunately no longer exists, except in my memory. Ciechanow was a small town located about ninety kilometers north of Warsaw. The total prewar population of Ciechanow was about 15,000, a little less than half of that was Jewish. However, both my peaceful prewar childhood world and my horror-filled teenage world are still as real for me as the world that I live in at the present.

Four Centuries of Jewish Women's Spirituality

My parents, Simo and Eljo Frajman, named me after my maternal great-grandmother Ito. My legal name is Itka. My beloved family used to call me Itkolo, endearing for Itka. I love to be called Itkolo. I was only thirteen years old, the oldest of three children, when my world collapsed and nineteen when Hitler's did—but I vividly remember the stark contrast of my world before, during, and after Nazi destruction. Everything that I experienced I compared to what my parents taught me and to what my Hebrew teachers in school taught me.

When I was young, we did not have electricity, and we used to store food in our food cellar—I can almost see it before my eyes. There was a square in the floor, and it had an iron ring. You pulled up the ring and opened it up. There was a long ladder—it wasn't built in, it was put in. It was dark with a dirt floor, no windows, and you had to walk down this ladder each time you had to bring up some food or take something down.

All the children took turns bringing things up from the cellar. One time, I was supposed to take something down, and my mother saw that I was afraid because of the dark. She took a candle and put it in my hand and she said, "Go, Itka. God is in the cellar, too." And she told me that she'd wait for me. I went down. Somehow, her confidence in me and knowing that she was waiting for me made me not afraid so much. I took the candle, went down, and brought up the butter. Afterward, I wasn't so afraid of the dark cellar. Just a few years later I would have to go down to the darkest cellar that there is, and I would be all alone. In my wildest imagination I could not imagine this.

We didn't have built-in closets like we have now. Then we had what was called a French armoir. It was a tall chest that reached from the floor almost to the ceiling, and it had two doors. The right side was used for the wardrobe, and the other side had shelves and was for linen. The very highest had hats laying there. But, for some reason, the part where we had the wardrobe was always locked. When I was a child, still a preschooler, I used to be so curious about what was in that closet. Why was it locked? I never saw it open, and I couldn't imagine what was in it.

I used to play all kinds of games trying to guess. Maybe a treasure, or maybe a skeleton. I even sent so far as to think that maybe I was adopted and they locked up the papers because they were afraid that I would find out. One day my mother said, "Itka, come, I want to show you something." And I remember I was so excited with anticipation and curiosity and so frightened simultaneously to find out what was in that closet. She took out the key and opened it. "Look, my child." It was old leather-bound books—a whole closet of books. My mother was afraid the children might tear the books. She took out a book, and she said, "When you learn to read, you will discover a treasure here. You will be with the greatest minds. You can sit in Ciechanow, Poland, and you will see the whole world, and you will travel through the ages."

She took out a book. She took me on her knee. I can remember today—we sat near the window on a chair, and she started to read stories, and this became a daily ritual. And this gave me so much closeness to my mother. Because when we read she held me on her lap and I felt the warmth of the relationship and the story. I was a very curious child, and my mother always encouraged that curiosity.

Once my mother read me a story about a man and his horse and buggy. He had a lot of children to feed, so he thought, if the horse didn't eat so much, he'd have more to feed the children. He got the idea that he would wean the horse from eating so much. And a horse is a horse is a horse, and he didn't complain. He ate less. One day, the man came into the stable, and the horse was already dead. He said, "What a stupid horse! He was almost weaned, and now he went and died!" I asked, "Mother, what does this mean?" And she said, "It is the same with a Jewish person. If you don't stay true to your religion, if one day you say to yourself 'I'm just not going to do this one little thing that is required of me,' before you know it, you will not be doing anything. And if you don't show loyalty and devotion to God and men, you are no longer being true to what you stand for."

Every morning when I got up, my grandmother would say prayers with me, along with grace after every meal, and every evening. From early childhood on, my parents and grandmother stressed the importance of *menschlekhkeit*—which in English means acting humanely. Whenever I did something wrong, my parents or grandmother always used to correct me by saying, "This isn't *menschlekhkeit*, Itka."

What I liked most about my grandmother was that she never took me for granted. I remember that whenever I did a little errand for her she would thank me many times over. Then, when I would say, "Grandmother, it is just a little thing," she would say, "Yes my little child, but kindness and *menschlekhkeit* are not little things."

I remember once I came home crying bitterly because, as I was walking home from school, a group of non-Jewish kids who I did not even know attacked me. When I came home, my mother asked me, "Why are you crying, Itka?" And I told her. She tried to comfort me. Later, she looked at me, and she asked me, "What did you do, my child?" And I said, "Nothing." And my mother said with assurance, "Well then, you have nothing to cry about. Your *menschlekhkeit* does not depend on how others treat you but on how you treat others."

That was very comforting to me, but, when I look back, it was also very confusing. I believed that I must never hurt or shame anyone. Therefore, I was not sure how I should defend myself when somebody hurt me. That was a big conflict. It took many years after the Holocaust to work this out within me. What I didn't realize— what my parents did not make clear but in retrospect I can understand—is that there is a difference between hurting someone and defending yourself. This I found out much later. Whatever I said or did, my family measured our behavior by the yardstick of *menschlekhkeit*. Is it just? Is it correct? Is it the proper, moral way to behave? They always used to say, "It is not *menschlekhkeit*, Itka." I used to cringe when they told me this, but as I grew older, as I realize now, I started to measure myself by this yardstick.

I recall when I was a little girl a poor man came one day to our door and asked my grandmother for alms. My grandmother gave me a few coins and asked me to give them to the man waiting at the door. I looked with curiosity at the money in my hand and asked my grandmother with astonishment, "Grandma, so much money?" My grandmother smiled and said, "My child, you only have what you choose to give away." My grandmother was a very warm, caring, and compassionate woman, and was very religious. When I questioned her proverb, "You only have what you give away," she answered, "My child, I only give away what God and my parents have given me. We are all givers and takers of life."

My grandmother of blessed memory has been dead for many years, but I can still feel her, sweet and loving. Death is only a physical separation, while love and remembrance are a spiritual union. Only the flesh is mortal, but words and deeds like God are immortal. The words and deeds of every person who has walked this earth before us is still influencing our destiny even though we can no longer influence theirs. Since Adam and Eve, people influence each other for both good and evil.

Four groups of people dramatically influenced my destiny: my beloved family, who knew me and loved me and empowered me with positive energy; the Nazis, who didn't know me but hated me for being born Jewish and in one single day murdered in Auschwitz my entire family; the world that stood silently by, indifferent to my profound level of suffering and grief; and the caring people of the Swedish Red Cross, who didn't know me but liberated me and brought me to a hospital in Lund, Sweden. I am one and the same person, yet four different groups of people viewed me differently and treated me differently. I was loved for who I am, and I was hated for who I am. The more my tormenters tortured me for who I am, the more I became determined never to become like them or to view myself through their eyes. There are those who claim that love is blind, but it seems to me that hatred is blind. Love builds bridges of communication, and hatred builds walls of isolation. Hatred divides us and destroys us, and love protects us and unites us. In union, there is strength, there is brotherhood, there is blessedness, and there is heavenly peace.

I became aware that there is a destiny that others choose for us and a destiny that we choose for ourselves. We can choose how to live, and we can choose to protect life or destroy it. For nearly six years, chronic hunger, terror, and death were my steady companions. I am one of a handful of Jewish Holocaust survivors of Auschwitz concentration camps and the sole survivor of my murdered family of blessed memory. The only member of our household in Ciechanow, Poland, who was privileged to die of old age and have a proper Jewish burial was my maternal widowed grandmother. I was grief stricken when my beloved grandmother died, but now I am grateful that she was spared all the suffering that I had to endure.

All on earth that I loved and held sacred I lost in the Holocaust, including nearly six precious years of my life. All on earth that I had left after liberation from Malchow, Germany, was my skeletal body minus all my hair, minus my monthly cycle, a tattered concentration camp shift dress without undergarments, a pair of beaten up unmatched wooden clogs, plus my "badge of honor," a large blue number 25673 that the Nazis tattooed on my left forearm on the day of my initiation to Auschwitz inferno. I was homeless, stateless, penniless, jobless, orphaned, and bereaved. I could not speak or understand Swedish, I had no marketable skills and only seven grades of public school and several grades of Hebrew school. Unlike my non-Jewish fellow survivors, I could not go back home to my beloved family, relatives, and friends and resume my former life as they did. Jewish homes, Jewish families, and Jewish communities were destroyed. I was a displaced person, a stranger; alive, but with no home to live in. I had no one to love me, to miss me, to comfort me, or to guide me. My childhood world was gone, but not from my heart and mind. Nothing dies as long as it is remembered and transmitted from person to person, from generation to generation. Or, as my beloved grandmother used to say, "My child, you only have what you choose to give away!"

**JUDITH KAPLAN
EISENSTEIN,
United States**

**The Spiritual Power
of Music**

In all the many years of my life, I have not actually verbalized whatever faith has sustained me, yet I have often felt sustained and comforted. Now that I pause to think about it, I realize that there has always been a sense of belonging, of being part—indeed, *just* a part—of something larger than myself. A good deal of the time it was an unidentified feeling. As a child, the "something larger" was probably family. As I grew, it was a congregation of people who came together weekly, and on holidays, who did things together. Then the belonging stretched beyond the immediate things and people that touched me, back into the past, out into the world, and in hope for the future. It also became a more conscious phenomenon—one that I could invoke when I needed it.

The sensation of being just part of a greater whole came in two ways. One way was through such knowledge as came my way of a long ancestry. Not necessarily knowledge of my family. Indeed, I knew and still know very little of that beyond my own grandparents. But knowledge of my Jewish people. True, I was born in America and have been very much part of American life. But my particular ancestry led all the way back, so to speak, to Abraham and Sarah. The knowledge increased as I grew and studied. Details were filled in. This larger family extended farther out into the world and provided a greater whole, of which I was, consequently, a smaller part. Somehow, especially in times of distress, that smallness was comfortable; it made it possible for me to merge into the ongoing stream of history, into what was out there before me and would continue after I would be no more.

The other way of becoming part of an ongoing living entity came, perhaps even more powerfully, through the senses: sights, smells, and, above all, sounds. While I could enjoy the awesome mountain, the fragrance of a new spring, the magnificence of man-made beauty in architecture and painting, for me the transcendent experience came with music, and it came at different levels as I matured. When I was a child, it came with singing in the little synagogue my family attended summers, in Long Branch, New Jersey. There, in the women's section on the left side of the center aisle, I sat next to a wonderful lady named Sarah Epstein, who had a robust contralto voice. From her I learned to "harmonize." We sang parallel thirds and sixths to almost all the melodies, and it was my ten-year-old first joy in choral singing. As I grew up and studied music, I listened to the music of the giants—Bach and Mozart, Haydn and Beethoven. Just listening was all I needed to lose myself in a universe beyond anything I had ever known. Above all was the sensation of singing in a large choral group, singing Handel's *Messiah,* Bach chorales, medieval carols.

Alas, there was a fly in the ointment! There was always the niggling awareness that I couldn't really sing the Credo of the B Minor Mass comfortably. Even Isaiah's words, "He was despised and rejected of men," were clearly intended by Handel to describe Jesus. Such glorious music, and I was outside it. I longed for a setting of our own *Kedushah* that could move me as did Bach's Sanctus with no holding back, no reservations.

In response to this tormenting need, perhaps (among other needs), I began to explore the music of my own people. There, indeed, was the raw material for great creation. I learned the ancient tunes, the chants of prayer and Scripture, the great leitmotifs of the high holy days and festivals. In their unembellished state they were stirring. Hearing them did provide a deep sense of continuity with my people—which I felt must extend to generations to come. Singing in a synagogue choral group conducted by Chemjo Vinaver intensified the emotional impact—he was a fine musician, with a deep knowledge and love of the tradition. Learning the music of Jewish communities other than my own—the Sephardic community, the Yemenites, and others—I found even more raw material that could be drawn on to expand the sense of belonging to a far greater entity. I sought out the compositions for the liturgy produced by skilled composers in many different ages. Frankly, none of them could match the magnificence of the Christian works, but they were the works of people who had, only late in our history, emerged from the restrictions of the ghetto and the poverty of the *shtetl.* I knew, or thought I knew, that, given time and effort, we Jews, too, would have a great transcendent religious music.

In this sense, my own devotion to the cause of music for Jewish life is my own religious search. It may sound presumptuous, but I hoped to help preserve the treasures of the past and see them transmuted into the monuments of the future. There were a number of composers in the earlier half of this century who were groping to find the way to a great musical liturgy. I hoped to be able to encourage younger aspirants and to lead them to that wealth of raw material that I had found. I felt that surely the day would come when the *Kedushah* and the *Hallel* would be sung in glorious soaring tones, when people of the congregations would be able to join their voices to the choirs by reading from notation fine melodies and even fine harmonies.

It was beginning to happen. There was, of course, the magnificent *Avodat Hakodesh* of Ernest Bloch. There were many other fine works, certainly many individual passages of great beauty by other composers. There were also congregations that were encouraged to sing from written music and to sing simple two-, three-, and four-voice arrangements, to sing the choice melodies of all times and all communities.

All this development has been suspended today—I pray only temporarily. Neither the gems of traditional chant nor the best of composed religious music is given a hearing except in a very few synagogues, and congregations sing and clap and stamp their feet to camp songs and Klezmer tunes. For me, there is no way to find the particular sense of transcendence that I once did in the music of the synagogue. I'm grateful if it is not actually painful. I believe that not only I but many others who cherish their Jewish identity and have a deep love of music are suffering a great loss.

MARCIA COHN
SPIEGEL,
United States

Growing Up Jewish

There was a time, not too long ago, when all that was expected of a nice Jewish girl growing up in America was that she marry a nice Jewish boy and have nice Jewish children; if she was an especially good Jewish girl, she would also keep kosher, or at least have two sets of dishes. That is the world into which I was born. My parents had already moved out of the ghetto in Chicago into a middle-class neighborhood where Jews could acculturate along with second-generation Greek, Irish, and Italian families.

I was eager to learn everything, a voracious reader who was never without a book, so starting Hebrew school was anticipated with great excitement—at last I could share the mysteries concealed in the strange letters and words. But eagerness quickly turned to boredom when I found that studying Hebrew was not too different from learning the piano, lots of scales and exercises but no pieces. We learned the alphabet and began reading prayers, prayers with no meaning, with no translation, just reading.

Boredom turned to anger when the boys began to leave the class in a group and returned grinning and smirking and giving the few girls in class the covert glances of a group who are sharing some kind of secret joke. I knew that they must be doing something magical, mystical, and sexual down in Smoler Hall, but I couldn't imagine what it could be. However, I knew that it was private, and I knew that I was left out. (I was a grandmother before I realized that the boys were learning to put on *tefillin* preparing for bar mitzvah.) It was hard to be a good Jewish girl after that. I became restless, played hookey, misbehaved, got sent back to class. A cycle that repeated itself for years.

Religious school and Hebrew school remained a tedious chore until my early adolescence, when I realized that there was an advantage to being where all the boys were. Lots of boys. Not many girls. So I joined the youth group that led the junior congregation and put on high holiday services for the kids. Of course the major role for girls in this group was to sing in the choir, just the thing for an off-key nonsinger. But I was diligent in attendance, learned the prayers and the melodies, and became comfortable with the ritual—although with little more understanding than when I cut class years before. While I formed a powerful bond with the group, it was a social connection, a Jewish connection; religion was only the structure in which the bonding took place. There was certainly no recognition of spirituality.

However, I didn't miss what I didn't know. I had certainly envied my non-Jewish friends their Christmas trees and Easter bunnies, but the routine of catechism and Mass was as tedious to them as Hebrew school had been to me. There was no sense of wonder, of mystery. Just one more thing you had to do for your parents.

My perception of religion changed when I became the token Jew at Rockford College, a small girls' college with ties to the Congregational church. Twice-weekly chapel attendance was required, as were Vespers on Sunday evening. The annual Christmas celebration was a major focus of school life, with drama, music, services, wassailing, and carols. I was emotionally touched by the simple, direct service, the sweet harmonies of the music, the message of peace and hope and serenity. For the first time I believed that God might be present. A far cry from my childish tests of God by sneaking a candy bar on Yom Kippur or eating a potato chip during Passover. I was often moved to tears by the music and the message of love. I yearned to be part of this culture but felt cut off and alienated because I was Jewish. This was not mine.

During the early years of my marriage to Sidney and the birth of our children, religion remained only a social activity. We belonged to a synagogue and observed all the appropriate life-cycle rituals, our core social group was Jewish, and our family connections remained strong, even when we lived in an environment where there were few other Jews. I was active in scouts, the PTA, Junior Great Books, and many community activities, but I was always nervous, always waiting for the anti-Semitic slur, the joke, or the remark that put me on the defensive. Becoming involved in the creation of a synagogue was a comfortable social answer for me. I could be active, I could be busy, I could be safe, and I could be Jewish.

The confluence of three experiences changed my life. During the 1960s, I was in charge of the religious school and youth activities at our synagogue while my own children were growing up. The impact of contemporary folk music, the influence of Eastern mysticism, and the exposure to Jewish summer camp activities began to be felt in our synagogue. Children who had been exposed to new ways of doing things wanted services to be meaningful to them. They spoke up for change. In the summer, when the rabbi was away on vacation, my children had an opportunity to shape these changes. Their creative services were filled with music, with dance, with poetry. They created services that spoke to the heart, not the mind, that moved one to tears, and often to a sense of wonder. Again, I felt the stirrings remembered from my college days, vague and faint, unnamed feelings of yearning and hope.

At this same time I was forced to recognize that my husband was an alcoholic. The denial of his behavior by the Jewish community to whom I turned for help left me feeling isolated and alone. The rabbi assured me that Jews weren't alcoholic. My parents assured me that it was all my fault. The therapist to whom I turned reiterated that Jews don't drink. Eventually, I found my way to Alanon, a support program for the families and friends of alcoholics. At the very first meeting in the social hall of St. Peter's by the Sea Presbyterian Church I found help, comfort, solace, and assurance. More than that, I found a godliness and spirituality that I had never felt in the synagogue. In order to survive I had to reach out to a higher power, to God as I perceived God. I never knew that Jews were allowed to give over control of their lives. I had gotten a message that the power was yours alone to act. I never knew about faith ("That is a Christian concept," I was taught).

My attendance at frequent Alanon meetings caused me anguish and confusion about religion. I prayed to God for help and was filled with a sense of light, of peace, of release. As I turned my life over to God, I gained the freedom to act on my own behalf. That epiphanic moment of illumination began my recovery from my coaddiction. However, I identified that life-changing moment with the Christian setting in which it took place. Each week, as the group rose to recite the Lord's Prayer at the close of the meeting, I squirmed in discomfort, but I joined the circle with thanks for the spiritual healing that I had found. I never saw another Jewish face at these meetings. I felt as if I was part of a secret world that somehow contradicted my Jewish beliefs.

The third event happened simultaneously. As Sisterhood president I had the task of preparing the annual Sisterhood Service for Shabbat. I decided to use quotations about women from the sages and found a wonderful source in *Famous Jewish Quotations* where I read, "It is better to burn the Torah than to teach it to your daughters." The old feelings of anger and bitterness that my six-year-old self had felt in Hebrew school returned with a vengeance. I determined to use only the words of women, to have a service in which only women participated, only women chanted, only women read from the Torah. In 1976 that was not very easy. Very few anthologies had women's poetry or prayers, but I found enough to create the service. When I couldn't find anyone to read from the Torah, I learned to do it myself. That moment when I took the Torah into my arms and held it and then read from the scrolls was a magic moment, filled with awe and a vast sense of wonder. I wept with joy.

Since I have always universalized from my own experience I decided that other women might also want to use women's writing for services or programs, so I thought a nice little Sisterhood project would be to put together a collection of such poetry and prayers.

For the next few years I searched the archives of Hebrew Union College, of the University of Judaism, of the University of California, Los Angeles. I joined a women writers group. I wrote to women all over the world. After gathering poetry by over two hundred women I started to put together an anthology—much more than the little collection I had first imagined. I typed the poems and prayers of women from across the centuries and around the world— Jewish women, like myself, yearning, hoping, praying. As I typed I took their words into my soul: their yearnings were my yearnings; their hopes were my hopes. I knew that I was not alone. Jewish women throughout the ages have struggled with the same emotions, have felt isolated and alienated, have also felt joy and a powerful connection to God.

I had experienced Jewish ritual that was spiritually uplifting; I had learned that God can play a role in our lives and that the words of women bond me with other women through the act of sharing our lives and feelings. I had come to a crossroads; I changed the direction of my journey and started on a path with no signs or directions or warnings. My second life had begun.

As I worked on the poetry collection, I was eager to meet some of the local poets whose poetry had become so important to me. Our first public poetry reading became the first step on my new journey. Tremendous energy was generated by this group of strangers as they read their poetry to each other, shared their ideas, their feelings, and their lives. It was a connection that we did not want to break and that we continue to this day. What we shared in common was the creative urge that often appeared to threaten those close to us; we needed to validate our feelings and expressions in a safe, uncritical place. We explored together the impact of our lives on our writing and the impact of our writing on our lives. We explored the process of artistic creation, and we examined the role of Judaism in our art. As we strengthened each other as individuals, each of us grew in power, both personally and spiritually. The Creative Jewish Women's Alliance became an ongoing force in our development.

The second step in my new life was an act of serendipity. I learned that Marcia Falk, the wonderful poet, had moved to the Los Angeles area. I was eager to meet her and invited her to visit the Creative Jewish Women's Alliance. Marcia expressed her interest in Jewish feminist spirituality and wanted to meet other women who shared that interest. Until that conversation I had never used the word spirituality. I had certainly not considered myself a feminist. At once I had a new identity. I didn't know who the other women involved in Jewish feminist spirituality might be, but I am a compulsive community organizer, practiced in years of school, Scouts, and synagogue, and I knew how to put on a conference. I knew that, if we were clear enough in describing our program to the public, we would get the women we wanted to meet.

"God, Prayer, and the Jewish Woman" was all we had hoped it would be. With only minimal publicity over one hundred women showed up. The women ranged in age from eighteen to eighty-five; every religious segment was represented, from the most radical to the most orthodox. We created a safe space where our beliefs were not questioned, where we could explore and try new things and talk about new ideas and sing new songs. Elderly women put on *tallit* and wept. I accepted my spiritual identity and appreciated that it was deeply grounded in Judaism. I learned that all of us there that day shared these feelings, which had been expressed differently in each of our lives. Exclusion and alienation had affected each of us. I have participated in many conferences, conclaves, and retreats since then, but my life changed forever when I could finally name my feelings.

The third step on this new path was confronting the Jewish community on their denial of alcoholism and chemical dependency. I returned to school to get a degree in Jewish communal service from Hebrew Union College–Jewish Institute of Religion. My thesis was a study of recovering Jewish alcoholics ("The Inheritance of Noah: Alcoholism in the Jewish Community Today"). I learned that my story was not unique. Other Jews also struggled to reconcile their addiction and their Judaism. I was not the only Jew attending a twelve-step program (such as Alcoholics Anonymous and Alanon) with discomfort. Again, I figured the way to attack the problem was to put on a conference.

Hebrew Union College School of Jewish Communal Service and the National Council on Alcoholism cooperated to present an educational forum. As the afternoon progressed, several of the prominent panelists told the audience of assembled rabbis, social workers, and educators their own stories of struggles with addiction and the Jewish community. The most dramatic moment came when a tall, stately woman in the audience arose and said, "I am a Jew, and I am an alcoholic. I am a better Jew today because I am an alcoholic." Moved by her words, other professionals stood up and identified themselves as recovering alcoholics. The community could no longer deny the reality. It was time to begin the work.

The formation of the Alcohol/Drug Action Program brought together many of those who were in the audience at Hebrew Union College that day. As we shared our stories of wrestling with feelings of isolation and separation, we began to plan a support system in which to reconcile our Jewish spirituality and the twelve steps of our anonymous programs. What evolved was the L'Chaim Alcohol/Drug Workshop. Our meetings are attended by Jews who recognize that they have problems with addiction or compulsive behavior but are uncomfortable with what they perceive as a Christian bias in the nondenominational anonymous meetings. At L'Chaim, they learn that these ideas have their roots in Jewish religious values. They meet other Jews who are in similar recovery programs and are encouraged to join them at their meetings. At one of our first retreats, a small group discussion began with participants sharing their feelings about Judaism and addiction. One at a time the speakers began to tell their stories, only to be overwhelmed with tears as they expressed their sense of relief in being able to talk about one without concealing the other.

Also attending the L'Chaim meetings are Jews who have successfully participated in recovery programs and, having developed a strong sense of spirituality, are looking for a Jewish place to bring together their recovery programs and their Jewish roots. People in recovery have tremendous spiritual power. They believe in God because they see God at work in their lives. They deal every day with a higher power. For many of them the synagogue does not address their deep spiritual needs. L'Chaim members come together in a Jewish spiritual setting where they can be whole. They no longer have to segregate their Jewish identity to confront their addiction.

Women that I met along the way have opened themselves to me and told me their stories. In many of their lives I began to recognize bits and pieces of my own life that I had kept hidden even from myself. Just as I took in the words of the poets as I typed, I took in the emotions of the stories that I heard: stories of violence and incest and family dysfunction hidden behind a facade of *shalom bayit* (peace in the home). Addiction and compulsion are only a part of the story. Each additional secret pushes us further out of the circle of Jewish spirituality and community, makes us feel different, ashamed, stigmatized. As I search for a loving, healing, nurturing, protecting God who allows me to be a partner in creation, I wonder how many others who join me in the search are seeking to heal similar bitter scars.

I am fortunate to be part of a spiritual sisterhood, B'not Esh, that allows me to explore new ways of doing things Jewishly, a safe place to ask the difficult questions, a safe space to try new prayers and new rituals, a place to feel holy, a place to feel the presence of God, to experience the Shechina. A place to be a Jew and to take the new experiences back into the world to share with others. I have learned with another group of women, the Mikvah Ladies, that we have the power to heal each other's wounds with blessing and with prayer. From all these women I gained the courage to create a croning ceremony for my sixtieth birthday—a ceremony to mark the passage to aging and eventual death.

As I shared with others, my own strength grew. I discovered a skill in organizing for outreach that empowered others through conferences and retreats. I developed a passion for teaching, teaching the texts that changed my life, discovering new texts that deepen our understanding of women's lives and feelings. I have learned to trust my feelings. As I participated with others in the creation of new ceremonies and rituals, I found that we have the power to create the transcendent moment, that moment that brings us each closer to God, the power to open ourselves to healing. We begin together as we each begin alone, to name, to describe, to share, and finally to touch. We re-create ourselves in community and spirituality.

My journey has begun. The path has twisted and turned unexpectedly. Serendipity has led me along. God has provided what I needed when I needed it. Yet the old yearning for the comfortable social contact is still there, and I seek out my community synagogue, a familiar place, with neighbors and friends, a place where not much has changed. We call women to the Torah now and count them in a *minyan* (prayer quorum). We add a few new responsive readings and a new melody now and again. The old melodies feel right, the old words seem comfortable—I still don't think about what they mean. On Shabbat I sit in the sanctuary alone and find comfort in the familiarity. But the six-year-old who rebelled at B'nai Israel in Chicago sits inside me in California and feels the same discomfort and isolation.

RUBY DANIEL, with BARBARA C. JOHNSON, Israel

We Learned from the Grandparents: Memories of a Cochin Jewish Woman

It has been suggested that I should write down everything I have heard from my grandparents and from other old people who have heard stories from their own grandparents. So I make myself bold enough to put pen on paper to say what I can remember from what I heard, mostly from my grandmother Rachel (Docho), the daughter of Daniel Haim and the wife of Eliyavu Japheth, both of whom were learned in Torah. They were very orthodox people, but she was a foot above them.

In the city of Cochin on the Malabar Coast of South India, there is a street called Jew Town or Jews Street because for many centuries only Jews lived there. The houses are built on both sides of a narrow road as a block. There are only two or three openings to get in and get out of this Town. When I was growing up there were three synagogues in that street, one at each end and one in the middle. At the northern end is the Palace of the Maharaja with the Hindu temple. Next to the temple wall is the Paradesi synagogue, where my ancestors worshiped for hundreds of years, and Jew Town reaches from there to the Kadavumbagam synagogue at the southern end of the street, near the small house where I lived with my family.

We celebrated our feasts and Sabbaths and other ceremonies with great freedom. The Jews got on well with the Hindus, Muslims, and Christians, one helping the other in case of emergency. One never interfered with the religious practice of the other. The women lent one another jewelry for weddings and feasts. All the festivals were celebrated two days, as is customary for Jews in the Diaspora. It was the Sephardi prayer books that we used, imported from Vienna, Amsterdam, etc. The tunes for a given prayer vary for different feasts. Unless people hear the correct tune, they don't feel as if they are celebrating that particular feast.

On Friday night all our family sat together and sang the Sabbath songs. On Saturday night we lit the lamps very late, waiting for the light to be brought from the synagogue. The servants lit the light from the synagogue after the evening prayers and brought home the lighted candles to every house in the town.

LEARNING FROM THE ELDERS

The author lived with her brothers and sister, parents, maternal grandparents, and an aunt. Other aunts, an uncle, and cousins lived nearby. She first learned Jewish practices and values from the elders of her family, both at home and in the wider ritual life of the community.

When I was a small child, most of the time I was with Grandmother Docho and my Aunty Seema. They, especially Grandmother, taught me tunes of prayers, and Grandmother told stories she heard from her grandmother. The neighbor women liked Grandmother very much. Sometimes they came for advice, if a child was ill or about many other things, or to gossip and talk about ghosts and spirits. When the ladies came to visit, I always sat in a corner and listened to their stories, while the other children went out to play with their friends.

Grandmother was a very good-looking woman, with long hair that fell in curls like rolls when she left it down. One time after a bath she was sitting at the table copying songs when a friend came to visit. That woman took a ruler and put it inside one roll of Grandmother's hair, and the hair was so heavy she didn't feel it until she moved her head and the ruler fell out. Of course women who have such hair are pretty.

She was a perfect wife, keeping up all the traditions for Shabbat and the holidays, and keeping *kashrut* [the dietary laws] in the house. I learned all this from her. That's called domestic culture; you talk about things, just as when I am telling about something and I suddenly think of a story, so I say the story. We all learned from the grandparents to keep Shabbat, to keep *kashrut*. Even now, if I do a mistake, I know I am doing a mistake, and if I have to do it, still I feel guilty.

Rosh Hashana and Yom Kippur

Beginning on the first day of the month of Elul everyone prepared for Rosh Hashana and Yom Kippur with forty days of *selichoth*, special prayers that were said in the night. Every night (with the exception of Sabbath nights and Rosh Hashana) we would get up at three o'clock and read the *selichoth* prayers. I remember hearing the *shamash* of the synagogue as he went from house to house in the street calling out the names of the older men to wake them and call them to the synagogue. The youngsters wanted to hear their names called too, so sometimes a boy would give the *shamash* a bit of money, asking him to also call out his name for *selichoth*. The synagogue was a little far away, so the women prayed in the house. My Grandmother's tunes and the way she read were much better than a *hazan*. So we the grandchildren liked it, and all of us got up with her at three o'clock and read the prayers with her in a high pitch.

Rosh Hashana or New Year's Day is supposed by the Jews to be a day of reckoning. One should not sleep on that day as the spirit will then go to heaven and sign the document of the reckoning of one's sins. Then it would be impossible to change it, and it will be an established fact. The Cochin Jews referred to this day as *Yom Hadhin*, the Day of Judgment. Grandmother used to drive us mad saying, "Rosh Hashanah is coming. Yom Hadhin. Take care of the children, that they don't get sick." As if God is coming or something, Yom Hadhin is coming. She makes the whole town shiver.

The days between the New Year and Yom Kippur are supposed to be days of repentance (*Yeme Tshuvah*). Before going to the synagogue, people would go to one another's house in the neighborhood and kiss the hands or bend to kiss the feet of the elderly or those who are older than themselves, begging to be forgiven. Everybody dressed themselves in white attire, and women wore white clothes with tinsel work and adorned themselves with jewelry. Some people wore the embroidered white clothes that they had prepared for their death, in which they were to be buried.

On the Eve of Kippur, before beginning the twenty-five hours of fasting, we had a sumptuous meal prepared with chicken and rice and the rest of it, like a feast day. From that time we would not eat or drink until the next night. Even very old people were carried to the synagogue on their beds, and they also fasted. They bade the people not to give them drink or food, even if they happened to be unconscious and cry for food.

Yom Kippur was said to be the day when the dead were wandering about, especially in the synagogue. Many stories are told of ghosts that were seen in the town at that time. I have heard one story about my Grandmother Rivka, my father's mother, who died long before I was born. The Paradesi synagogue was a little far away, at the northern end of the town, while our house was in the middle of the town. On Yom Kippur eve, everyone was rushing to the synagogue to be in time for the Kol Nidre prayer. Unless we are in time to hear this prayer, we feel as if we did not observe Yom Kippur. We are not released from the previous year's vows. After sending the children and the grandchildren to the synagogue, Grandmother Rivka was the last to leave the house, as is usual with the housewives. In those days, there were only Jews living in the neighborhood, and all of them had gone to the synagogue. There were a few shops of non-Jews, and during Yom Kippur they had no business, so they closed up earlier and went home. The town was practically deserted.

It so happened that, on that particular day, when my Grandmother Rivka arrived at the synagogue, she found out that she had forgotten her spectacles. It would be a tragedy if she cannot read the prayers. Then she saw there was time enough to run to the house and get her glasses. So she went in a hurry to the house, opened it, and found her glasses on the table in the hall where she had put them. She took them, and, when she turned to go out, she saw a woman in a white dress at the doorway, as if going to kiss the *mezuza*. Grandma was so frightened that she could not even scream. It would not help her anyway. There was no one in the vicinity to hear her. So she collected all her courage and pleaded with the phantom, "If you stand like that, how can I go to the synagogue? How can I hear Kol Nidre? It is getting late." Then the woman moved on one side and disappeared, and then Grandmother ran back to the synagogue. She did not meet any human beings on the way back.

For Yom Kippur day, the morning prayer starts at 5 A.M. and continues till one o'clock, and people sit reading *pizmonim* till 2 o'clock, when the afternoon prayers start. This ends at 7 P.M. There were people who didn't sit down the whole day. It is very hot on that day inside the synagogue. A gentile servant used to pour water over the granite pavement around the synagogue to keep the heat down the whole afternoon. No snuff or smelling salts were used unless someone felt very faint.

The five prayers during the day of Yom Kippur were conducted by five elderly men with two youngsters to help them with those parts recited in tunes. We did not have a rabbi or a hired *hazan* to sweat it out the whole day, and the prayers are too long for one man to conduct it. We had special tunes for this feast. Very often the youngsters learn the tunes from the women, who could sing better than the men. The women also sang in high-pitched voices together with the men, though they always sat separate, either upstairs or on a veranda or in a separate room of the synagogue. If they had been given the green light, these ladies would have confidently climbed up the pulpit to conduct the service.

DEATH, AFTERLIFE, SPIRITS, AND DREAMS

From her grandfather, Ruby Daniel inherited a certain skepticism and a "scientific attitude" about death and the afterlife. At the same time she loves to hear and recount stories of dreams and spirits and messages from the beyond. A sense of mystery and wonder pervades much of her writing.

My grandfather Eliyavu Japheth was a very learned man in the Torah. Elders from all the Jewish communities used to come and learn *Halachah* and *Gemara* from him. Grandfather was the *schochet* who slaughtered chickens and animals for all of Jew Town, according to the Jewish law. He was not a cabbalist like some of the other learned men in the town, including my other grandfather Daniel. It is said that the two of them used to argue about their different beliefs. Both of them were Rabbanim. These people were not fools like the present generation. At that time everybody was interested in learning Torah and all the things connected with it.

Grandfather did not believe in ghosts and spirits. He had a scientific attitude about death. Once he said, "Suppose a candle is burning. You put out the fire. Where does it go? Death is like that." Once when he was not well, we sent for the doctor, who was our relative. As she was leaving he blessed her, saying "May you live to 120 years." She said she didn't want to live like that, as she was already fed up with life. Then he replied, "Don't say so. Even if you are in great difficulty, no one wants to die. Why do you want to die? Our body and soul are made out of a combination of different elements, like everything else in the world. When one dies, those elements will be integrated into the other elements from which they came. Then a part might become a worm or a frog or such things. Even one's soul, what we call the *neshama,* is the same. After death the components join their own elements. That is why I think people say there is no heaven or hell. Everything is in this world itself."

Well! I am not qualified to discuss this thing. But I don't think Moshe Rabenu has said anything about the other world. Everywhere he said if you follow the precepts of the Torah your life will be prolonged in the land that I give you, and you will have a good life. I don't think he said you will go to heaven when you die, or to hell. You will get the reward of your good deeds toward the end perhaps, if you deserve it.

Nevertheless, after Grandfather died, some people felt his presence. My brother Bingley had his bar mitzvah only four months before, and he had to do the last rites for him because my father was so ill. We were all shaken at the time. We all slept on the floor, one next to the other. My Aunt Rebecca and her daughter were staying with us at that time, so we sent Bingley to sleep in the next house, where my Aunt Sippora and her children lived. Putting a mat under the bed that stood in the front of the room, he slept off. Suddenly in the middle of the night he opened his eyes and saw Grandfather standing at the door of the room, looking at him. He closed his eyes and slept again, and didn't tell anyone what he had seen. The next night my Aunt Dolly dreamt her Father. She cried to him, "Why are you not visiting us?" Then he replied, "Yes! I did come last night, and I saw Bingley and I waved to him." When she told us about the dream, Bingley said yes, that was what happened.

Not long after that, Grandmother dreamt that Grandfather came and told her, "If you will go with me, then I will take you straight to Paradise." She asked him, "How can I go to Paradise?" and he said, "I will carry you on my back." She said, "If I go away, people will talk when they don't find me in the morning, and say I eloped with someone." Then he said, "What do you care, I am the one who is taking you away. You are going with me!" She said, "Why should I go just now? When I die, will I not go to Paradise?" He said of course she will go to Paradise, but if she waits it will be a little painful. She said anyway she would wait and go when she died.

Many people in Cochin had dreams that came true in time. People dream so many hundreds of things that are not important, but there are also important dreams, in which they feel the presence of someone who has died. Usually it is the women who talk about these dreams. Most of the men don't speak about them, even if they see something. Sometimes it's a good dream, and sometimes it is not. Sometimes the dream comes when a person is worried, as when someone is ill or has a great problem, but sometimes such a dream comes when one is not thinking about anything in particular. I don't know; who can explain all these things?

Once my father's mother, Grandmother Rivka, was saved from danger by a dream. She was a young woman at the time, and she was lying down at night feeding the baby. The double door was open, and the kerosene lamp was burning. Her husband Daniel always used to come late because he was learning and teaching with people in the town. Anyway, she slept off and dreamt that her mother, who had been dead for a long time, came and called her by name. "Rivka, are you sleeping? The door on the top floor is open." It was a one-story building, and there was no door on the top, only a window. Suddenly she woke up and saw that it was midnight and the door in front of her was open. She was so frightened from the dream that she got up and closed the door. Just as she was drawing the iron bolt, there was a very loud noise of someone from the other side hitting on the door with both hands. Grandmother said perhaps somebody was waiting there to rob her, and she woke from the dream just in time.

There is also a remarkable story about Benaya Benjamin, my grandmother Docho's uncle, who was a businessman in Bombay. He was once arrested on false charges. The only way he can escape is to tell a lie. His advocates advised him to do so, but he would never tell a lie. Anyway he was shut up in prison, even though he had friends among the famous Sassoons and Ezras who were ready to swear of his innocence. His nephew Williams, who was only a boy then, used to bring his meals to the prison three times a day because Benaya ate only kosher food. Back in Cochin all his relatives were very concerned about him.

The night before the trial Benaya was so worried, as no one could predict the result. He was sitting on his bed when he heard the sound of someone opening the iron doors, which had been locked by the jailors a while before for the night. He was wondering who could come in the middle of the night when he saw his mother, who had died a few years before, coming through the door. She said, "Why are you wearing this prisoner's cap, my son?" She pulled off the cap from his head and threw it on the floor and said, "Your case number 9 is dismissed," and then disappeared. He did not even know the number of his case. When Williams came the next morning, he asked him to find out the number of his case, and it was indeed number 9. The next day the case was dismissed.

That same night in Cochin my grandmother Docho dreamt that she went out of the house. She saw a light. When she looked up she saw a door open in the sky from where the light was coming. I don't remember if she saw anyone. She woke Grandfather and told him about her dream. This Eliyavu Japheth, the man who never believed in dreams and ghosts, listened to her. He said, "That is salvation for Benaya."

There are so many stories of ghosts and spirits seen by people in Jew Town, one would think that when the body of the dead is taken out through the front door, the spirit enters by the back door. Jew Town has a definite attraction. The Jews who lived there for so many hundreds of years did not want to get out, even though most of us have now come to Israel. The ghosts and spirits of the dead were not willing to leave entirely. Their presence is still felt by those living in their houses or in the streets or in the synagogue.

KATHRYN HELLERSTEIN,
United States

Tishe b'Av on 48th Street (1987)

Last night, eve of the Ninth of Av, we remembered
To mourn
The sins of that city, "now lonely as a widow,"

Like a virgin daughter,
Now taken,
Like a woman made unclean,

Like a ruined garden,
Its paths stoney,
Its starving inhabitants

Devouring their own petted
Children
Like the cruel ostrich.

Millennium after millennium,
Today
Jerusalem has fallen

Right here, in our new house,
At our
Season of coming together,

In the midst of all our scattered
Things,
Our selves not yet in order.

A bride with broom and scraper, I am
Commanded
Not to clean, not to build, not to love,

But to lament. My stomach growls
At the memory—
Bread, an egg, and ash—stale on my tongue.

That utter destruction,
Khurbm,
Will repeat until Messiah comes.

Pigs' blood flooding the Holy of
Holies,
Rapes, fires, torturous deaths of martyrs

Are words to mourn. My lips refuse them.
I lie
Here in our sunny room.

In through the window, the breezes bring
Morning.
A cicada chitters in the birch tree,

A boy comforts a baby, cajoles it,
"*Que pasa!?*"
And the baby wails from the heart,

Its wet diaper a sorrow. A neighbor
Complains,
"The screen door locked, man!"

And I am locked out, cold, on the outskirts of
Summer morning,
Foreigner with a hand on the garden gate,

Pausing where bees rise from roses, where lavender
Goes to seed
With thyme and healing mint.

My toes stretching against smooth sheets
Celebrate
My exile. And I sing a terrible prayer:

"Without the Destruction,
Would
Be no Dispersion.

"Gathered in, I shall be
Homeless,
In der fremd away from *goles.*"

Last night we crouched on the floor and by
Candles
Read *Lamentations.* And I wept.

"Aicha!"—"How!" We began by
Exclaiming
Amazement at grief. I begin with

A thrill of loss, a wonder that mourning
Abides
This morning, this feeling at home.

**KAREN ERDOS
with DIANNE
ASHTON,
United States**

A Personal Reflection

In the fall of 1989, I attended a gathering of daughters of Holocaust survivors for the first time. For me, the gathering held tremendous spiritual support. We were all daughters of Jewish survivors. We intended, not to invalidate the experience of non-Jewish survivors, but to validate our experience. All our families suffered because they were Jewish. This was an experience we needed to validate, and share, with one another.

A workshop on grief and mourning began with the lighting of the *yahrzeit* [memorial] candle honoring those who had died and also acknowledging our sense of loss. After everyone had spoken, a woman recited a feminized version of the *kaddish,* the traditional Jewish prayer for the dead [presumably one in which references to God grammatically took on feminine form]. It was said very slowly, very deliberately, and then the English was read. Previously, when I had heard it read, it seemed that the faster one could read it the better. To hear it said in a way that allowed me to think about it was a real change. Although I had heard the prayer many times before (my mother recited it for her father, my grandfather recited it for his various relatives, and so on), I never really knew what it meant. That day I not only understood the words of the *kaddish* but also, for the first time, felt my own personal loss connected to that traditional Jewish prayer. It was no longer just an old rite. It acknowledged our loss and suggested that we don't have to give up on our own lives. I felt less isolated. Hearing the prayer feminized was very important to me because I could connect to it much more directly.

Ironically, my family was never oriented toward the religious side of Judaism. We identified very strongly as Jews but didn't go to synagogue very often. My mother's parents were Orthodox, but my father's family was very irreligious. After my mother died, my father and I had a falling out over how she should be buried. I thought she would want to have a religious burial; my father disagreed. He wanted her buried in a dress, not in a burial shroud, as I insisted. I desperately wanted to do the right thing, although I had no idea what Jewish tradition really demanded. In the end, my father yielded to my desires because the type of funeral we had seemed to matter so much to me, although, again, I wasn't sure why. We sat *shiva* [the proscribed period of mourning] in our house and had the mourning ribbons, and I wore them for the entire time, even though people constantly asked me, "What does that mean?" Their question irritated me. I thought I should wear the ribbons, but really didn't know why. It felt comforting to do the mourning rites, to do what was expected. My mother's death left me with such a profound sense of loss that somehow, just performing these rites, even though I didn't understand their meaning, provided me with a sense of comfort.

My faith has always been amorphous. I still hope that I will come into contact with my mother in some way again in the future. Still, when I think about death, I have a very mixed sense of it. On the one hand, I don't perceive it as a nothingness into which everything just disintegrates. On the other hand, I don't have a well-defined sense of heaven and hell, just a strong sense that there is a spirit out there and that it is possible that I will connect again with my mother and other members of my family. But I lose that sense when it comes to those who have done horrible things. I don't really know what to do with them. I think of entire families who died during the war, and it makes so much sense to think that they will be reunited. It makes the loss easier to bear. But I don't know what to do with the other end of the spectrum—those who created all that havoc. What happens to the evil people? What happens to the Hitlers? Are they still around in some capacity?

This is one of the questions about the Holocaust that has always perplexed me. How did the people who survived, who came back almost from the dead, have children and have very productive, although very scarred, lives? How does a person find great meaning after the Holocaust? Some people came out of that experience clinging much more tightly to their beliefs. My family was very Jewish culturally but not religiously. They were never part of a community of Jews. In part, this was not a conscious decision. My father was a psychiatrist employed by a state psychiatric hospital and given housing. Most of his colleagues were not Jewish. On the other hand, my parents' decision not to join a synagogue seems to indicate a conscious decision to remain apart from the organized Jewish community.

My mother and my grandfather, her father, seemed to retreat more into Judaism when they were very ill. My grandfather had been very religious. For the last couple of weeks of his life he didn't speak and showed very little emotion. But, when the rabbi came to his hospital room and began to pray for him, my grandfather cried. He obviously felt a sense of real connection to the rabbi. My mother read more popular religious books. She was very saddened by Harold Kushner's *When Bad Things Happen to Good People*. She kept it in her night table and spent many hours lying in bed reading and crying. She was very scared and saddened by the whole prospect of dying, having come through as much as she did. She was sixty when she died. One of her final memories was of the war. When she was in the hospital, just before she lapsed into a coma, she said, "Oh the Nazis are coming, what's going to happen to my daughter?" At that point I was twenty-one. I was an adult.

While in some ways I find the depth of human evil impossible to comprehend, in other ways I find it to be understandable. The fact is, people do hate those who are different. There are some Jews who would say that my parents are not Jews, although they suffered so much for their religion. I find that to be a travesty. It is one of the things that has put a great deal of distance between me and the Jewish community. I may not have been raised religiously, but I grew up strongly identifying as a Jew. To have people tell me that I am something of a lesser person or that my connection to Judaism is not as important or as real as theirs has always made me very angry. Their response is not evil, but intolerance can be easily magnified. So in a way it doesn't surprise me that six million Jews and six million others were killed. If I am going to have any sense of religious faith, I have to think that human beings are responsible for the universe they create. Perhaps, coming together after death is the way that goodness can be reached.

My father's father and his family really thought of themselves as Hungarians, ethnically Hungarian, not Jewish. The Jewish part was not important to them, being Hungarian was. They didn't go to synagogue and did not keep the dietary laws. In fact, they raised pigs themselves. Despite the stories he told about their anti-Semitism, my father still feels very betrayed by the Hungarians. He'll still say, "They were my people, they turned on me," even though his people chased him through the streets throwing rocks at him. There was a schizophrenic sense that they were part of Hungarian culture, yet different. I'm sure that everyone who suffered during the Holocaust felt betrayed. Yet, for many, it was a betrayal by humanity; for my father, it was a betrayal by a particular country and people of which he intimately felt part.

I think my mother had less of this sense of schizophrenia because she grew up in a very religious home. The first time her mother broke the dietary laws was in the cattle car on the way to Auschwitz. Someone had some ham, and people had to eat whatever food was available. People convinced her to have a little. I think that there was a sense of increasing hostility from crowds gathered outside of the train. It started with stones being thrown and ended up with, as my parents said, people coming to the train stations and bringing picnic lunches to watch as the Jews were herded onto the cattle cars.

Because of all that my parents went through, death is the fundamental spiritual issue for me. I think that many women decide to have children because they are going to die. They want to pass on to their children their values and their possessions. Certainly, many people felt that way after the Holocaust. Many survivors began to have children almost immediately after the war. In fact, some of the women I met at the gathering in 1989 were born in 1946. Many of the women were significantly older than I or had parents who had survived as children who couldn't have children immediately or were the last of a long line of siblings. This sense of bringing life out of death, which might push people to have children, was particularly profound, I think, for Holocaust survivors.

My mother wanted a child but had seven or eight miscarriages before I was born. She had an abortion in Germany because she could not come to America if she were pregnant. Either that or pregnancy made it more difficult to get on a list to enter the United States, but my impression is that if she were pregnant she wouldn't have received permission to come here at all. After her abortion she had many miscarriages. She got pregnant very easily and didn't give up trying to have a child once she was in America. She never thought the miscarriages were linked to anything that had happened to her in the camps, although the women were given medicine to stop their periods.

Once I was born it was very important to them that I know and accept their experiences, that I make them a part of my life and a part of the lives of people with whom I interacted. Many of the women at the gathering said that the Holocaust wasn't mentioned as they were growing up and that only recently had they come to see how they were shaped by being children of survivors. But for me it was different. I was supposed to mention to people that I was a daughter of survivors. In fact, it was supposed to be one of the first things I said. On the few occasions when I didn't, or if I seemed reluctant to do so, my father got very angry. Once, for example, a friend who was a Hungarian Christian was coming over. I didn't want my father to go on and on about how terrible the Hungarians are, particularly because my friend's father had been a political prisoner during the war. When I asked my father not to say anything, he got extremely angry at me. He said I was a ghetto Jew who was not willing to stand up for what was really important, that is, Jewish survival. While in general I agree with my father that it's important to make sure that people are aware of the Holocaust, I didn't think that it was necessary in that specific situation. I realize that my father is driven by motives that I cannot feel because the experiences of my life have been so different from his. Yet I know that he doesn't see my experience as a child of survivors as peculiar in any way. It was his experience during the war that was unique and important, and I have no right to that experience. He has no idea why I would want to go to the gathering of daughters of survivors.

I think that I am too tied up in the whole survivor legacy ever to escape it very much. The truth is, I feel very different from my American-born Jewish peers. I was born here in America fifteen years after the end of the war. By the time I was cognizant of anything, my parents had been out of the camps for twenty years. There was a great deal of temporal distance between me and their experience. Nevertheless, I feel very different from most Jews. I have had very few friends who are Jewish. Almost all my friends have been Christian. I have never been romantically involved with a Jew. Yet, at the gathering of daughters of Holocaust survivors, I found comfort in being with others who were Jews.

I have always felt alienated from the Jewish community. While I have been searching for a community of which I can feel part, the Jewish community does not seem to be the right one. Part of the reason is that many Jews are uncomfortable talking about the Holocaust. Another part is that I didn't go to Hebrew school or

receive any religious education. Some Jews have been really conde-
scending when I've told them that. If the Jewish community were
right for me, it would be more accepting of me as I am. In turn, I
would be able to be more accepting of the Jewish community. It
does trouble me that I am caught in a weird, uncomfortable place. I
do believe, yet I have nowhere to anchor that belief. I don't know
exactly how to form a coherent belief on my own without a community. The children of survivors whom I met have provided me,
for the first time in my life, with a community with which I think I
can feel at home.

What is spirituality? To me, spirituality can include hiding Jews
who are being persecuted, being moved by any kind of religious
event, choosing your life's work, praying to God, or simply caring
for your mother at her death. For me, at least, spirituality has a
great deal to do with a sense of connection to a past and to a future:
to a past that so profoundly shapes my own future and the future of
the world. In my view, one has to allow people to define their own
spiritual experience. One also needs to validate that experience,
whatever it may be. Validating a person's experience allows him or
her to nurture a sense of spirituality and connection to a community
or to a world that is outside of oneself. It legitimizes people, makes
them feel whole. Spirituality, then—at least for me—needs to grow
in relationship to community. Finding the daughters of survivors
group and reciting *kaddish* with them profoundly moved me. I felt
linked to their stories and thus more connected to Judaism than I
ever had before.

I still feel confused and conflicted about my Jewish self-identity.
Despite my frustration with many of my Jewish friends, and despite
my feeling different from most American Jews, I still feel tied to
Judaism. My parents paid such a high price as Jews that that will
always be a part of me. I recognize that I need to work through my
feelings. Judaism was forced to play a major role in my parents'
lives. It is now up to me to understand its role in my life and in the
feminist and political commitments that I already have made to
help create a world that, finally, can live with itself.

BLU GREENBERG,
United States

Resisting Yom
Hashoah 1985

A purple crocus thrusts up
Near the ancient oak
The morning dove coos
Its velvety call
As the street comes alive
With the tinny beep
Of car pool caravans
Carrying gay young children
To their refreshed teachers

Dawn's dew dampens
The rolled and rubber-banded *Times*

Tossed from a speeding van
Onto the greening grass
A blue-crowned jay
Flits from oak to mulberry to maple
In silence

No matter
I hear the song
In my heart
This fresh spring morning
Dreamt of months ago
In January's bone-chilling grayness

Morning's work becomes a blessing
All clichés are true
'Tis good to be alive
Healthy, safe, loving, working
The ink flows, the pen chases
Its shadow across the page
Seldom does the phone ring
Interrupting thought
Few are the descents
To the refrigerator
My spirits soar
Then level
Then soar once more
It is a day
For which women who write
In their homes
Are born

Midday, the spring sun
Moves forward and backward
Slipping in and out of
Feathery clouds
Midday, and a speck of gloom
Barely noticed
Settles round the joyous edges
Spreading ever so slowly
As the seconds inexorably race
Toward the newly sacred day
That will begin at dusk

Late afternoon
Like a spreading stain
The heaviness
Creeps unwelcome
Toward the heart's lining
Not yet piercing
Yet not unknown

I long to hold the lightness
Lengthen the cheer
One moment more
But I cannot
Soon I will be overtaken
By memory's pain
My people's woe

Now anger lurches in
Fury and rage explode
Why must I give them
Victory anew
The laughing tormentors
In their graves
Who rise to assault my calendar
Why must I pay
An eve of sadness
Limbs weighted down
By close horror
That sharpens with time
No I shall not go
No heartbreak for me tonight
No one will pummel my spirits
Not tonight
No!

Seven-thirty
Time for *maariv* [evening worship]
And I leave for Loehmann's
Faintly excusing myself with
"I remember all year long"
"Good girl, I've always gone"
Tonight no one is home
To chastise
To raise an eyebrow
As I drive away
From setting sun
The song cranks up again
Slightly off-tune
And fighting for space
Inside the lining

Tonight at Loehmann's I shall find
A beautiful dress
A party dress
A Yom Hashoah victory dress
I laugh perversely
Sweeping through the racks
I load my aching arms
For the journey

To the try-on room
Where a darting-eyed salesgirl
With fresh pimples calls out
"Only six garments at a time"
"Over the head, ladies"

Tonight only a few wigged women
From Boro Park
Have trekked to Loehmann's Bronx
Among them Hungarians
Who ache all year long
Amid silver and crystal
But brook no change
In Sinai's calendar

In time, I find it
A beautiful Norma Kamali
This season's colors
Yellow and black
No matter
I shall wear it

At nine, the intercom vibrates
Assistant manager's staccato voice
With a hint of desperation
After ten hours on her feet
Enmeshed in fabrics, hangers, racks
Half-naked ladies
Cash registers that bleep
Instead of ring
Harsh fluorescent lights
Mindless, gossipy packers
"This store is closing
In thirty minutes
Please
Take your final solutions
To the cash register"

Giving up the ghost
I fling Norma Kamali
Yellow and black
Over the rack
And rush out

I reach shul
Just as the faithful—
Half of them survivors
Purged once more—
Begin to file out
Dispersing sooner than usual

A few linger, somber and subdued
On the concrete plaza
Beneath the street light
A few laugh, softly, self-consciously
Catharsis working

I sit in my car
Across the street
Until the last soul has
departed
Knowing
This is where I belong

The *Mikvah*

Renewal of the cycle
Expectation and arousal
Women leaving clean and shiny
Young brides and premenopausals.

Alone, at peace, relaxed
Soaking in a warm tub
Before the *tevilah*
Suddenly
I tighten
Remembering that the S.S. would gun
Their motors
Burst into the *mikvah*
Those pure women . . .
Those poor women . . .
Those poor, poor women . . .

My lady-of-the-lake
Checks to see
If I've cut my nails
Removed my lipstick
"Kosher," she says to me
Kosher again, after the second dip.
A motor slows down outside
My husband coming to take me home.

**VICKI
HOLLANDER,
United States**

**A Rosh Hodesh
Ceremony (1990)**

AN OPENING CEREMONY

Like the moon,
we shed our layers.
Leave them at the door.
We who caretake life.
We who are healers.
We who are doers.

We who mother
the world.

   It's time for us.
   This time is for us.
   We step inside the sacred circle.
   We make
   space for ourselves
   to be.

The moon now glides toward darkness,
toward rest.
She retreats
in order to emerge
whole.
She quiets
in order to
and fill night
with light.

   So too shall we
   make a space for ourselves.
   A space of renewal.
   So we who nourish life
   can emerge as the moon,
   bearing
   our light
   our touch
   to better repair our world.

Like the melting of ice,
the moons boundaries
slowly fade.
She merges with sky
and air and stars,
and sings her nightsongs
sweetly.

   So too we make this space
   a space away.
   A time to come home to ourselves
   and sing of our journeys,
   and tell of our stories,
   and stretch,
   and laugh,
   and touch,
   and renew,
   as does the moon.

She sings songs of praise
to the One who shaped her.

She dances joy,
gratefulness
for the gift of life,
to the One who sculpted her.

> So too do we sing songs.
> So do we give voice.
> So do we rise in joy
> at our being
> in this world,
> at our being
> in life,
> at our blessings.

And so we ready
to leave the world at the door,
to make a special place for our
selves
to let down that which separates us,
to make a space for us.

> To sing and
> to dance,
> to touch and
> to play,
> to laugh and
> to cry,
> to listen and
> to share,
> to make sense out of confusion,
> to grow and
> to ignite,
> to weave and
> to mend,
> to renew and
> to touch life.

We are bidden
to cry the unshed tears,
to loosen jaws which clench,
to open the closed recesses within,
to scour that which has solidified,
   like calcium deposits in the inside of a kettle,
   staining the inner parts of our being.
We are bidden
to wash ourselves clean
that we might be fresh again,
that we might shine again,
that we might stand restored,
   pure as first made.

HaRahaman
support us as we tread this path
for the way is most arduous.
We lie exposed and open as a freshly cut fig
raw, naked, succulent.
We face choked words, and mottled histories
   tortured sculptures of intentions that missed the mark
   overgrown gardens of emotions that grew awry
   all which have served us
   cankeriously,
   leaving their marks etched without and within.

Help us learn Elul's lessons.
Help us wash.
Aid us scrub away the rings.
Enable us to pass through
cleansed,
renewed
so that we might sing our songs
and bear the flame
higher.
Be with us as we walk forward,
as we walk forward
HaRahaman.

We, who are made of earth and heaven, body and spirit,
We, who are filled with water,
so as to merge with the world
and simultaneously,
with flame,
which lights our soul with fire.
We praise You
for breathing into us the breath
of life.

   Barech Atah Adonai Eloheynu Melech Ha-olam She-asani Ishah
   Praised are you, Holy One, who made me a woman.

Praised are You, Holy One, Who sculpts the moon and sprinkles
the stars above, who shapes the world, and life, and time.
Who plants wonder in the world each day.
Who wipes our brow when we are weary, and
gives us drink when we are dry.
Who lights our soul with dance and hope.
Who blows upon the flame within us,
And delights in our glow.

PRAYER FOR THE NEW MONTH
Rosh Hodesh Elul

HaRahaman,
O One of loving warmth,
be with us as we walk with
and learn from Elul.

The month of Elul
awakes each dawn,
to the voice of shofar,
and rouses each midnight,
to the music of prayer.
The month of Elul
bears
scent of wild rose and
sound of the departing wings
of turtle doves.

The month of Elul
time of readying
time of shaping understanding
time of picking ripe figs.

Elul stands
holding
remnants of summer heat and
hot desert winds which
scatter shards of thistles, grasses, and vegetable seeds
wildly into the air.
Elul stands
holding
new born autumn fog and
freshly woven dew which
shoos scent of carob and tamarisk blooms
mischievously into evening breeze
driving insect life afrenzy.
Thus Elul instructs us
that the pieces that have died within us
bear seeds of future possibilities,
and that when parched,
rains of restoration follow.

Elul bids us learn from the earth,
who moves gracefully into season of ripening
who readies for her winter.
Elul bids us follow in her wake
and take stock of our vintage,
and review our winter larders,
and examine our cupboards' wares,

our storage of woolens,
to check both inner and outer resources, and
to move one step
beyond.

Elul enjoins us to forgive.
For she, wisened with age,
knows that accounts unsettled act
like the small tear in a sack of flour
from which a steady stream of wheat pours
surreptitiously
until the sack lies depleted,
thus too do unforgiven deeds and words
drain and alter our form.

Elul calls us
to forgive,
to forgive others whom we have wounded
wittingly and unwittingly
by words, and by actions.
She bids us speak words,
which stick in our craw like
    leftover morning gruel clings to the pot, and
        to ask forgiveness, and
        to grant forgiveness.

Elul calls us
to forgive,
to forgive ourselves whom we have wounded
wittingly and unwittingly
by words, and by actions.
She bids us look at ourselves,
which stings like lemon juice in an open wound,
and to ask forgiveness, and
    to grant forgiveness.

Holy One
as the new month nears,
renew us.
Gift us with length of days,
a life of peace,
of goodness,
a life of blessing,
a life which can sustain us,
a life we can face with vigor,
a life where we touch awe,
a life where we struggle,
    aware of when we get off track,
a life without shame,
a life of richness,

of honor,
a life wherein we feel Torah's light,
    where we seek Your Presence,
a life where the inner questions of our heart
    will know response,
    and peace.
So may it be.

(We rise and make a circle, arms encircling,
    We speak words of departure, of peace)

Hum and sing:

    U-frose aleinu su-kat, su-kat shlom-mecha (2)

    (Spread over us your tent of peace)

CLOSING CEREMONY
(LIGHT CANDLE)

The moon sheds her light
like a robe.
She moves into the darkness.
The darkness,
where it is still, . . .
quiet.
It's there she finds
rest.

A space to renew.
A place
to come home to.
It's there she washes her weary feet
drawn from the tides' warm evening waters.
It's there she
sings love songs to the stars
which echo in, and nourish her soul.
In the dark
she returns
to herself
once more.

So we too return to ourselves once again.
We become children inside
and celebrate,
and laugh,
and refresh our souls,
and feel our light within,
flicker, and rise, and dance.
Our flame which burns and reaches upward and beyond
longing, yearning for union

with the One Who Spoke
and the world came into being.

We celebrate our having been shaped as a woman.
We praise HaMakom for our curves
and our cycles,
for our feminine and
our masculine,
for our warmth, and for our fire.

We praise HaMakom for enabling us to give birth to
ourselves,
to form newness
to release uncontrollability, wildness, and dance
into the world.

INTRODUCTION

LAURA LEVITT
and SUE ANN
WASSERMAN,
United States

Mikvah Ceremony for
Laura (1989)

LAURA: The ceremony that follows was put together for me by
my friend and my rabbi Sue Ann Wasserman after my rape in November 1989. The ceremony marks my particular experience and
desire to heal. It is a ritual that speaks to the specific place I had
come to in my healing on November 24, 1989. I went to the
mikvah[1] with Sue Ann and my mother a few days after my first
period after the rape. It was the day after Thanksgiving during my
parents' first visit. It was erev Shabbat. Since November I have had
other ways of marking time since the rape. My body has overcome
a multitude of diseases punctuated by visits to doctors. This has
been ongoing. I just took my second HIV test.[2] I have had to wait
over six months for definitive results. Although I have maintained
my professional life from the beginning, both teaching and studying, it has taken much time to recover other aspects of my life. I
have slowly resumed having a fantasy life and a sex life, but I still
long for a time when I will be able to live alone again.

SUE ANN: Although I grew up in a religious Reform Jewish home,
mikvah was not a part of my background. I became interested in
mikvah and the laws of family purity[3] while in rabbinic school. My
interest stemmed from my need and desire to find parts of my tradition that spoke to me as a woman. I read and wrote and thought
about *mikvah* as a woman's ritual both past and present. My practical knowledge of *mikvah* has come through my work with people
who are converting to Judaism. I became convinced of its power to
provide a meeting place for people and God, through listening to
my students speak about their experience and how significant the
mikvah was as a conclusion to their formal study for conversion.[4]

LAURA: Healing is a process. This *mikvah* ceremony is distinct in
that it represents one of the few ways that I have been able to attend

to my spiritual as well as my physical and emotional healing. Sharing this ceremony with other Jewish women is part of this healing. It is a way for me to give something of myself to other Jewish women, especially those who have been sexually abused. I want them to know that they are not alone. I also want them to know that there is a place for us and even our most painful experiences to be commemorated in Jewish community/ies.

My body was violated by rape. The *mikvah* offered me a place to acknowledge both that violation and my desire to heal. My need for ritual was very real. I needed to do something concrete to express my psychic and physical pain as a Jewish woman among other Jewish women I am close to.

For me, healing is not simply a return to some "wholeness" in the past; it is an experience of growth and change. Healing is the careful rebuilding of a life in the present that does not deny what has happened.

SUE ANN: When Laura was raped, I wanted to find a way to support her as her friend. As a rabbi, I needed to find a way for Judaism to respond to her. The *mikvah* seemed to be the most appropriate ritual for several reasons. (1) It was predominantly our foremothers' ritual. (2) It requires the whole body. (3) Its waters flow in and out—representing continuity and process. (4) Its waters symbolically flow from Eden, a place of wholeness. (5) The natural waters remind us of the constant intermingling presence of the Creator in our own lives. (6) Finally, water itself is cleansing, supportive, and life sustaining.

The task then was to find words that would give this ancient ritual meaning in the context of Laura's experience. I drew on the sources at hand and included my own words as well as asking Laura to bring whatever readings she thought would be healing for her.

LAURA: The poems I chose to read during the *mikvah* ceremony reflect these feelings. Like the narrator in Irena Klepfisz's "Di rayze aheym" (The journey home),[5] I too wanted to return "home" but knew that the home I knew before the rape was no longer accessible to me. Nevertheless, I still needed a home. Healing has meant that I have had to rebuild a new life where I can attend to my scars while also experiencing joy again. I have had to rebuild my life "even from a broken web."[6] These words, the poetry of contemporary Jewish women, have helped me articulate some of these feelings, but to speak them at the *mikvah* made them physically tangible.

Historically, the *mikvah* is a sacred space for Jewish women and our bodies. Through this ceremony, I was able to enter into that tradition. Sue Ann helped me reconstitute this place to attend to my own physical needs for healing. In a steamy room overlooking a pool of running water in a synagogue in Atlanta, we recited these words and I entered the water. In so doing, the violation of my Jewish female body was attended to. It was neither silenced nor ignored.

SUE ANN: We stood together at the *mikvah*, the three of us, reading a liturgy that had been created in a day, to prepare us to perform a ritual that has existed for centuries. It was a powerful and empowering experience, but it was only a first step in the creation of a new liturgy that will speak to those who seek healing after a rape or any form of sexual abuse.

"*MIKVAH* CEREMONY FOR LAURA"

SUE ANN: According to the Talmud, the ultimate source of all water is the river that emerged from Eden. By immersing ourselves in the *mikvah*, we participate in the wholeness of Eden. Natural water is required for a *mikvah* because water is a symbol of the life forces of the universe. Fundamentally, *mikvah* is not about "uncleanliness" but about human encounters with the power of the holy.[7]

To be read around by paragraph:
"In our tradition, water has always played a pivotal role. There is something elemental about it. Before the world was created, there existed the presence of God hovering over the surface of the water.

When, in the times of Noah, God wished to make a new beginning of life on earth, the fountains of the deep were opened and waters came forth, returning the earth to its pristine beginnings.

Our patriarchs and matriarchs met at the well, for the source of water was the center of community life. Thus the well, the source of water, marked the promise of new beginnings in their lives.

Water is also a sign of redemption in our People's history. It was the waters of the Red Sea that parted and allowed us to go forth from bondage into freedom.

Water is also a symbol of sustenance. Miriam, the sister of Moses, was deemed to be so righteous, that during her lifetime, when the Israelites wandered in the wilderness, God caused a well, Miriam's well it was called, to accompany the people and sustain them with water."[8]

LAURA: "Anger and tenderness: my selves.
And now I can believe they breathe in me
as angels, not polarities.
Anger and tenderness: the spider's genius
to spin and weave in the same action
from her own body, anywhere—
even from a broken web."[9]

(*Laura reads*)
"Di rayze aheym" (The journey home), by Irena
Klepfisz[10]

SUE ANN: This ceremony is to help bring closure to your physical healing and cleansing. Your physical injuries are fading. You've done much cleaning; your apartment, your body, with soaps and masks, and miraculously your body has cleansed itself through menstruation.

This ceremony is also an attempt to help you begin the spiritual and emotional healing you must do. I see these *mikvah* waters as symbolic of two things. First, the tears you have yet to cry. Perhaps being surrounded by them from the outside will release them from the inside. Second, we do not sink in water but rather are buoyed up by it. It supports us gently. This is like your community of friends and family who have kept you afloat and sustained you. We, like the waters, are messengers of the Shechinah.[11] The Divine Presence is made present in your life through our loving and embracing arms and through the warm caress of these living waters.

LAURA: Now, as I immerse myself, I being a new cycle in my life. May my entry into the waters of the *mikvah* strengthen me for the journey that lies ahead.[12]

> "Water is God's gift to living souls,
> to cleanse us, to purify us,
> to sustain us and renew us." [13]

SUE ANN: "May the God whom we call Mikveh Yisrael, and God who is the source of living waters, be with you now and always."[14]

the immersion

Immersion and then recite:

בָּרוּךְ אַתָּה יְיָ אֱלֹהֵינוּ מֶלֶךְ הָעוֹלָם אֲשֶׁר קִדְּשָׁנוּ בְּמִצְוֹתָיו ,וְצִוָּנוּ עַל הַטְבִילָה.

Baruch ata Adonai Eloheynu Melech Ha-olam asher kid'shanu, be-mitzvotav vitsivanu al ha'tevilah.

Praised are you, Adonai, God of all creation, who sanctifies us with your commandments and commanded us concerning immersion.

Immersion and then recite:

בָּרוּךְ אַתָּה יְיָ ,אֱלֹהֵינוּ מֶלֶךְ הָעוֹלָם. שֶׁהֶחֱיָנוּ וְקִיְּמָנוּ וְהִגִּיעָנוּ לַזְּמַן הַזֶּה.

Baruch ata Adonai, Eloheynu Melech Ha-olam she-hehiyanu vihigianu vikiamanu lazman hazeh.

Blessed are You, Lord our God, Ruler of the Universe, who kept us alive and preserved us and enabled us to reach this season.

Immersion for a third and final time.

Following the imersion

Read around by stanzas:

"God give us the strength
   to transcend setbacks and pain
   to put our difficulties into perspective

God give us the strength
   to fight against all forms of injustice,
   whether they be subtle or easily apparent

God give us the strength
   to take the path less traveled
           and more disturbing

God give us the strength
   to persevere
   to reach out to those in need—
       may we abandon none of your creations

May we never become callous or apathetic because
   of our own disappointments

May our personal pain never be used as
   an excuse to stop heading your call

God give us the strength
   to continually strive to do more

   Let us always strive to give, even if we,
   ourselves, feel alone or impoverished

For we must always strive to reach beyond
                   ourselves."[15]

Notes

1. *Mikvah* has many meanings in Hebrew. It is a confluence of water, a reservoir, a pool, or a ritual bath. *Mikvah* is also understood to be a source of hope and trust, another name for God. The *mikvah* ceremony refers to the ritual of immersion in such a place for purposes of ritual purification. According to *halakhah*, Jewish law, the ritual of immersion is required for conversion to Judaism, but it is most commonly associated with "laws of family purity." Within monogamous heterosexual Jewish marriages, "as menstruation begins, a married couple halts all erotic activities. A minimum of five days are considered menstrual, then seven 'clean' days are observed with the same restrictions. After nightfall of the seventh day, the woman bathes herself . . . and immerses herself in a special pool built to exacting specifications" (Susan Weidman Schneider, *Jewish and Female: A Guide and Sourcebook for Today's Jewish Woman* [New York: Touchstone, 1985], 204; see pp. 203–13 for an extended discussion of the ritual and its revival).
2. HIV, the human immunodeficiency virus, is believed to be the cause of AIDS, acquired immunodeficiency syndrome. HIV is a blood-borne virus transmitted through the exchange of bodily fluids.
3. See n. 1 above.

4. *Mikvah* is a part of the traditional conversion process. To convert to Judaism one must engage in formal study of the tradition and, having done so for a significant period of time, must agree to take on the obligations of the tradition. According to *halakhah*, the ceremony that marks this transition is *mikvah*. Immersion concretizes the transformation that has already been achieved through study and obligation. In Reform Judaism, ritual immersion is an optional part of the conversion process.

5. Melanie Kaye/Kantrowitz and Irena Klepfisz, eds., *The Tribe of Dina: A Jewish Women's Anthology* (Montpelier, Vt.: Sinister Wisdom 29/30, 1986), 49–52.

6. Adrienne Rich, *A Wild Patience Has Taken Me This Far: Poems, 1978–1981* (New York: Norton, 1981), 9.

7. Anita Diamant, *The New Jewish Wedding* (New York: Summit, 1985), 151.

8. Jeffrey Perry-Marx, "A Ceremony of Tevilih," unpublished manuscript used in a Senior Rabbinic workshop on Outreach given by Rabbi Nina Mizrachi at Hebrew Union College–Jewish Institute for Religion, New York, spring 1987.

9. Adrienne Rich, *A Wild Patience Has Taken Me This Far: Poems, 1978–1981* (New York: Norton, 1981), 9.

10. Melanie Kaye/Kantrowitz and Irena Klepfisz, eds., *The Tribe of Dina: A Jewish Woman's Anthology* (Montpelier, Vt.: Sinister Wisdom 29/30, 1986), 49–52.

11. The Shechinah is the Divine Presence in the world, the in-dwelling or immanent presence of God. Jewish mystical literature describes this presence as female. In the mystical tradition, the Shechinah is the feminine principle of God to be found in the world.

12. From "A Bridal Mikvah Ceremony," written by Barbara Rossman Penzener and Amy Zwiback-Levenson, in Diamant, *The New Jewish Wedding*, 157–58.

13. Ibid.

14. Perry-Marx, "A Ceremony of Tevilih."

15. This prayer was written by Angela Graboys and Laura Rappaport. It is found in a daily service they edited, "ROW Service," an unpublished manuscript, Cincinnati, Hebrew Union College–Jewish Institute of Religion. ROW is an organization for women rabbinical students at Hebrew Union College–Jewish Institute of Religion in Cincinnati.

SOPHIA
BENJAMIN,
United States

God and Abuse:
A Survivor's Story

"God is like sugar in a glass of water: you can't see it, but you know it's there." I am six years old. It is my first year of religious school, and I am being "consecrated." The rabbi's words are the first I remember hearing about God. They seem ridiculous. Even if you can't see sugar, you can taste it, feel it. I don't remember ever talking to anyone about God before, but I already know he doesn't exist. I am scornful of people who think he does. It's just like Christian kids believing in Santa Claus or Jesus. Why is our "God" any different?

This is also my first memory of being in a synagogue. My mother has just remarried, and all my new cousins go to religious school, so I want to go too. In a few more weeks I'll find out why they complain about it so bitterly, but by then it will be too late to change my mind; I'll be told I no longer have a choice. Meanwhile, I want to belong despite this absurd talk about God, and I like some of the other aspects of the ceremony, especially receiving a miniature Torah scroll and an enamel pin depicting the tablets with the Ten Commandments.

"God is like sugar in a glass of water; you can't see it, but you know it's there." I am six years old. For the past two years—per-

haps longer, although I don't have memories going back that far—
I have been sexually abused.

Before my mother remarries we live with my grandparents. My
cousin baby-sits for me. When I lie down on the couch under my
favorite blanket, she teaches me a secret game. It feels funny but I
sort of like it.

A neighborhood boy, the older brother of a friend, comes over to
my house and takes me into my closet. It's dark, I'm frightened.
What he does hurts. I hate going over to my friend's house because
I never know what his brother is going to do. He doesn't touch me
when I'm over there, but he exposes himself—while I'm watching
television or calling to me from the bushes on my way home.

I'm afraid to go to sleep by myself. I insist on sleeping in my
mother's bed and want her to stay in the room with me until I fall
asleep. When I sleep in my own bed, I wake in the middle of the
night in terror and run to her. Sometimes I wet my bed. Sometimes
when I wake up there is a man leaning over me, touching my geni-
tals. His face is blank in the darkness.

The only man who lives in our house is my grandfather. I love
him very much. He teaches me how to put my winter jacket on by
putting my arms in while it's spread on the floor and lifting it over
my head. He likes to tease me. We play a game where he tells me to
go away and then pulls me back when I do. I squeal with delight.
When he's not playing with me, he doesn't like me to make noise. I
watch television with heavy headphones on. He has strict rules
about a lot of things. When I set the table, I have to lift the dishes in
a pile and put the bottom one at his place without touching it. My
grandfather is an old man with white hair, and everyone is afraid of
him. He is an atheist, so we are all atheists. He is an alcoholic, and
he is dying of cancer.

He doesn't get really sick until after my mother remarries. Sometimes he baby-sits for me, and I don't want to go near him. I know
there's something wrong, although none of the adults tell me he's
dying. I'm never taken to visit him in the hospital. When he dies, I
feel bad and guilty that I avoided him. I feel I did something wrong.
His body is cremated. There is no funeral or memorial service.

I am six years old. The last time I remember seeing my father was
when I was four. He lives in Europe, where I was born and where
my mother and I used to live too. He came to visit once after we
moved to my grandparents' house. He and my mother came together to see my nursery school. He read me a book about Indian
chiefs. That's all I remember about him. No one ever talks to me
about him.

My mother has just remarried. The wedding takes place four
days before my sixth birthday, and then my mother goes away on
her honeymoon for a week. When she gets back, the man she has
married tells me to call him "Dad." He will be my father now.

The first morning we have breakfast together my mother serves
grapefruit. I ask for maple syrup to put on mine, the way I always
ate it at my grandparents'. My new father is furious; he doesn't

think people should put maple syrup on grapefruit. I don't understand. I cry. He yells. Soon I will learn that when he gets angry like that I will get beaten. Sometimes I do everything I can to try to get him not to hit me. Sometimes it seems so unfair, and I get so angry I yell too, even though I know I'll get hit. I feel bad and guilty. I feel I must have done something wrong. I know that the only power I have against him is the truth: "You're not even my real father." I only remember saying that once. When I do I'm told I've done something awful, that I'm ungrateful, that I shouldn't say such things, that I've hurt him.

I am adopted by my new father. He, my mother, and I go to court. The judge tells all three of us to come into his chambers. He asks me if I love my new father. I feel frightened and confused. I know what I'm supposed to answer. I say "Yes."

A few months later I am at a huge Hanukkah party with an overwhelming number of new relatives. My new father is angry at me and literally throws me out into the snow. Years later one of those cousins tells me this story and how no one could believe it was happening. I guess that's why no one did anything.

"God is like sugar in a glass of water; you can't see it, but you know it's there." I am six years old. How can I possibly believe God is there?

I am in fourth or fifth grade. My best friend, a Unitarian, and I are discussing which of the ancient Greek goddesses we like the best. We don't describe them as "ancient Greek goddesses"; we perceive them as real and present in our lives. We read everything we can about them, write stories about them, draw endless pictures of them in our school sketchbooks, imagine ourselves living in ancient Greece, where we would be allowed to worship them openly.

My favorite is Athena because she is the goddess of wisdom. I have learned that my intelligence is my most important quality. It is really the only good thing about me. I am always among the best students in school. My parents are always pleased with my reports, although they laugh and tease me when my fourth-grade teacher describes me as "a delicate plant." Perhaps she writes that because I often cry for no apparent reason. My stepfather teases me for that too. When I get more upset and ask him to stop, he says, "But you're so much fun to tease."

I'm also embarrassed about the phrase my teacher uses because the word "delicate" seems to draw attention to what I consider the very indelicate size of my body. Soon after my mother remarried I began to overeat compulsively. Of course no one calls it that. They call it being fat. My mother takes me to a nutrition clinic at the local children's hospital, where I'm put on a diet and weighed every week. I feel humiliated. I don't stay on the diet. I feel bad and guilty. I feel I've done something wrong. Consciously, at least, I don't pay much attention to the fact that my beloved Athena is also a warrior.

A few years later I have moved to Christianity for my religious images. Female saints, most especially Joan of Arc, and nuns now populate my interior world. I read everything I can about them. I long to hear voices like St. Joan. I memorize the Hail Mary and say it to myself, half hoping and dreading a response. I cry over *The Nun's Story*, horrified and thrilled at the descriptions of self-flagellation. I read those sections over and over, knowing I should be ashamed, not understanding why they hold such fascination for me. I long to be like these women. I envy the holiness of their suffering.

"God is shit as well as sparrows." I am twenty-one years old. I am in my first year of rabbinic school. The whole college is on retreat at a monastery—probably, the students agree, because of the wonderful food (one of the monks is a former professional chef) and an excellent billiards table in the monastery library. For the first time in my life I am talking with other people about God. I am absolutely terrified.

We have been given a list of five topics and asked to write our beliefs about them. God is one of the topics. After we write for a while we are divided into small discussion groups. This is the moment I've been dreading: when everyone's going to find out I'm a fraud and don't believe in God and don't belong in rabbinic school. As I listen to the others an astonishing thing happens. What they say makes sense to me. There is doubt and confusion expressed. There is a desire for belief with which I identify. There are experiences of connection that actually seem possible for me too.

When we gather the small groups back together, one of our teachers tells us of his spiritual struggles. He tries to teach us about the difference between spirituality and sentimentality: "God is shit as well as sparrows." Not just sweetness and light. Not just goodness, as endless numbers of well-intentioned religious school teachers have tried to convince me. God is not a person. God is power, and in power there is the potential for danger and destruction. Mystery and manners are incompatible. "There is no virtue in predictability" is another lesson I will learn from this teacher. I experience a thrill of recognition, although I've never heard anything like it before.

Later in the day I stroll through the monastery with him, and we stop in the book shop. Although he is a rabbi and it is Shabbat, he buys me a St. Theresa medal because, he says, the inscription suits me. It reads, "I will spend my heaven doing good upon earth." I am both ecstatic and scandalized.

In a hallway of the monastery is a large poster depicting the Virgin Mary. The caption reads, "Mary, the selfless space." I am outraged. For the past five years feminism has been central to my life; my admiration for suffering, selfless women has long vanished. It will be another two years before I regain any memory of my own sexual or physical abuse, and, as my teacher has realized, I have identified the pain of my own experience with injustice done to others.

As I begin rabbinic school I am deeply confused about being a feminist and wanting to be a rabbi. Since the age of fifteen, when I decided to enter the rabbinate, I have seen it as a form of community organizing. When I discuss this with my feminist friends, most of them denounce all historical religion for being patriarchal and oppressive to women. I feel angry that black and Hispanic women who choose to work within their particular communities are praised and supported but that the message given to me is that my tradition is not worth nurturance and struggle. I see the women developing what is beginning to be called "feminist spirituality" as rootless. To join them I would have to disconnect myself from a rich heritage of ritual, liturgy, life-cycle celebration, as well as the elements of material culture, such as dance, music, food. At the same time I am appalled and equally outraged by the sexism I experience within Judaism and among Jews, the exclusion of women's experience from what is considered authentic tradition. I enter rabbinic school thinking I will give myself a year to decide between feminism and Judaism.

There is another reason I think I might not become a rabbi. Since last spring I have been in a lesbian relationship. The issue of what constitutes a "real" lesbian and whether I am one occupies a good deal of time in discussion with my partner and other lesbian friends. I have been heterosexually active since the age of sixteen. The following year, in Israel, I fell in love with a woman, but she was married, so we did not become lovers. (In retrospect I find it funny and rather wonderful that the only moral issue for us was adultery, not homosexuality.)

I have no sense that there is anything wrong with lesbianism. On the contrary, being with a woman as part of a community of women has brought an enormous sense of joy, even exuberance, into my life. I feel known and understood in a way I never have before. The first time my partner tells me I am beautiful something miraculous happens: I believe her. I feel that because she is a woman she perceives things about me that male lovers had not, perhaps could not. Touching her body, smelling her, tasting her, I come to imagine my own body as pleasurable. While making love there is an astonishing sense of wonder. It is not the loss of self I have heard about so often but rather a gaining of self, a sense of belonging and connection with who or what is beyond me. I experience a tangible presence I will also learn to call God. Or, more appropriately, Goddess.

A year later I am still in rabbinic school. I begin to see a coherence in my work that I had not expected. I barely notice myself using words like "spirituality," although I stumble once again, for a different reason now, over "God." In Bible Class we are studying Jeremiah. I am angered but not surprised by the misogyny of the text. What confuses me is that such hatred of women should exist side by side with such a moving passion for social justice. It strikes me that this is really the key issue for me as a feminist: not to decide which texts or traditions are "authentic" because they affirm women's experience but to understand, or at least to explore, the relationship within the same tradition and even within the same text between oppressive and affirming beliefs. I am not yet aware of why I care so deeply about this particular issue, why I need to understand how hate and love, injury and attachment, shit and sparrows, can coexist in this way.

As I write this I am two months short of my thirty-third birthday. For the past three years the central concern in my life has been to heal from the effects of growing up in a dysfunctional family and surviving physical and sexual abuse.

Ten years ago I began to recover the memories of those experiences. I was working with a therapist and found myself describing the last time my stepfather beat me. I was fifteen. We were in the kitchen. I remember him screaming at me and slamming me into the cupboards. I used the word "temper" for my father's behavior, as in, "We always had to be careful of his temper." It was another two years before I used the words "rage," "beaten," "battered," or "abused." I was sitting with two new friends after dinner. We were telling each other about our lives, and one of the other women began to discuss the fact that her father had battered her. Until that moment it had never occurred to me that what had happened to me happened in any other Jewish family. It had never occurred to me that there was a connection between the way I had been hit and what people meant when they talked about battered women and children.

Around the same time I first recalled the sexual violence. The memory that came back to me concerned the neighborhood boy. In the moment I first remembered it felt like it was happening all over again: I was that four-year-old girl being violated. Afterward, I was able to tell the story in a calm, detached way, as if describing a photograph or a historical incident.

I was still in therapy and would be, on and off, for the next six years before anyone suggested that family dysfunction and abuse had any relationship to later developments in my life. Meanwhile, I was working in the Jewish community and never felt able to discuss these issues with any of my colleagues. I never heard them mentioned in a Jewish context. If it hadn't been for my friend, I would still have thought I was the only Jew who had been physically abused within her family. I didn't realize I knew any other survivors of sexual abuse.

Three years ago, just before Rosh Hashanah, I was having a fight with my partner. I don't even remember how it started, but how it ended changed my life. We were screaming at each other and, enraged, she took a drawer out of her dresser and threw it at my head. I pushed her to the ground. Both of us froze in shocked silence. I knew I had to leave. I knew I couldn't go on living this way. Somehow I knew just the right friend to call. She told me to pack a bag and come stay with her. After that, she suggested, I might want to go to an Alanon meeting.

In Alanon and, later, in Adult Children of Alcoholics (ACoA) and other twelve-step recovery groups I met rooms full of people, including many Jews, who shared my experience. At first it was just astonishing to hear stories that sounded so similar to my own; now

I almost take it for granted, although I retain a strong sense of gratitude for the ability to feel a sense of connection with others after so many years of separation. In that regard, entering recovery was similar to becoming a feminist: in breaking through isolation and seeing the relationship between my experience and others' I began to perceive everything else about my life in a different way. Like feminism, recovery has also rewarded me with community and hope.

About a year and a half after I began recovery I went to an ACoA meeting at which there were close to two hundred people. Toward the end of the meeting a man spoke about the significance of the support he received through the group. Looking around he said, "You are all my angels." Later, as we said the closing prayer, I felt surrounded and held by all the voices around me. There was a wonderful sense of lightness and love, a metaphoric rustle of wings.

While the Hebrew word *mal'ach* could mean any sort of messenger, I'm not surprised that angels have been associated with human forms. That is certainly the way I experience them in my own life: human beings have been the most apparent bearers of such divine gifts as love, wisdom, nurturance, and vision. The teacher who gave me the St. Theresa medal is one. So is the friend who led me to Alanon.

About a year ago I met two others, a man and a girl, father and daughter. He was in the process of getting a divorce. She was just about four. When I first spent time with both of them I felt unexpected waves of jealousy and grief. I realized that there was something wrong about what had happened to me when my parents got divorced. It wasn't normal and all right that my father had disappeared and no one had said anything to me. I began the agonizing process of mourning a child's loss of a parent.

The girl's fourth birthday was ten days before I turned thirty-two. Around that time I found myself weeping for apparently no reason, feeling disoriented and afraid to be alone. This time I was working with a therapist who recognized the signs. She recommended a book on healing from sexual abuse. I bought it that afternoon. Since then I have been remembering with my emotions and my body what only my intellect had been able to recall about what else had happened to me when I was four.

As I worked on my healing and recovery I quickly understood why it was so important for me to develop an understanding and language for God that did not rely on human images. Having grown up in households in which I was abused by the adults responsible for my care, it was not surprising that I never found satisfaction or security in a God depicted in the roles of a human caretaker. Having survived a childhood in which I was powerless to defend myself or fight back against adult abuse, I see no reason to recast myself in the role of helpless child in relationship to an omnipotent parent. The overwhelmingly prevalent images of God as a human male and especially as a father were and are completely untenable for me as a survivor of abandonment, sexual violence, and physical abuse by the father, grandfather, and stepfather present in my life.

I found that the static inequalities of power expressed in relationships such as king/subject, shepherd/sheep, judge/accused that run throughout biblical and rabbinic theology were equally injurious. They assume a separation between divine and human in which the former has absolute power over the latter. In addition, they replicate the destructive power relationships of domination and subordination that provided the framework for my abuse. As both a feminist and someone struggling to heal my own victimization, I realized that it was essential for me to claim divinity as something inherent in my nature as a human being. I no longer see the traditional images of Jewish theology as merely outdated or sexist in a discriminatory way. I believe that they both reflect and help support a society in which power is abused, in which women and children of both sexes are battered and raped.

This perception has allowed me to solve the "Jeremiah dilemma" of how justice and oppression can coexist. As a victimized people Jews have learned the injustice of abusive power relationships. But because they also participated in those relationships they learned to reenact them. Until recently, the limitations of Jewish power meant that such reenactment was limited to domestic, sexual, and class violence within the Jewish community. As Jews have acquired power in the state of Israel they have also replicated the patterns of their oppression on a political level in their relations with Palestinians.

Like my family of origin, I now see rabbinic Judaism as passing down traditions of abuse as well as giving me gifts of life. To heal and remain healthy I need to transform those traditions, but in doing so I do not need to reject all connection with my past.

Perceiving a relationship between being a victim and learning to victimize has also altered my perception of female power. For some time I felt a sense of joy, affirmation, and protection in female images of divinity. Such images did not stir up the memories and emotions that male images did.

Recovering memories of my sexual abuse, however, I began to struggle with the fact that a woman was among my abusers. I worked to resist the impulse to excuse her, just as I excused my mother for failing to protect me from my stepfather. In ACoA meetings I found myself reluctant to remain attentive as I heard story after story of children, boys as well as girls, who were physically, sexually, and emotionally violated by their mothers. I was ashamed to acknowledge that it was in lesbian relationships that I replicated familial patterns of psychological and, finally, physical abuse. Once I broke through my denial of women's violence I could no more feel at ease with female/mother images of deity than I could with male/father ones.

It was in rejecting God as a person that I came to an experience of a personal god. Another way of describing this is to say that, previously, my spirituality was intellectual and abstract. It involved concepts and general categories of experience such as "connection," "well-being," or "the power of life and death." Since coming into recovery I have begun to have specific and personal definitions of divinity in my life: friendship, acceptance by and for others, caring for and about myself, recognizing and feeling my emotions, healing my personal "public/private" split and presenting myself honestly.

I also continue to have many questions, doubts, and confusion. I do not see my own or anyone else's experience of abuse as part of a "larger plan" that is somehow, ultimately, for good. Sometimes I experience myself as grotesquely disfigured by the emotional and physical scars created by those who abused me; when I forget that they were not my choice or my fault, it is easy to despair that they will ever fade. I find it excruciatingly difficult to trust that things can continue to go well in my life, that I will not be abandoned and abused over and over again, and that the forces of love and care I identify with God are as real and present in the world outside of me as are forces of destruction.

I used to try to explain my understanding of God as power and process rather than a person by saying that instead of calling God "Creator of the universe" I would prefer to say that the power that creates the universe is what I also call God. Now I can point to concrete events and behaviors in my own life that lead me to know God is present, both in the world and in who I am as an individual human being. God is not only a source of healing and redemption in the abstract; I have experience of a healing and redeeming power in my own life. God is like sugar in a glass of water: I can't see it, but I know it's there because I can taste—and can add to—the sweetness.

Sources

ACKERMAN "Reserve Resources" (2 February 1951) and short address (1951), by Paula Ackerman. Private Collection, William Ackerman, Jr., Thomaston, Georgia.

ADELMAN "The Womb and the Word: A Fertility Ritual for Hannah," by Penina V. Adelman, was written for this volume. Her "A Ritual of Loss" was published in her *Miriam's Well: Rituals for Jewish Women Around the Year* (New York: Biblio, 1986), 84–90. Reprinted by permission of Biblio Press.

AGUILAR *The Spirit of Judaism* by Grace Aguilar (1842; Philadelphia: Jewish Publication Society of America, 1864), 13–19, 23–26, 30, 118–19, 122–24.

AMIR Anda Amir, "Eve" and "Lot's Wife," trans. Sue Ann Wasserman, in Wasserman's "Women's Voices: The Present through the Past" (rabbinic thesis, Hebrew Union College–Jewish Institute of Religion, 1987). Used with permission of Sue Ann Wasserman.

BECKMAN "A Letter of Counsel to N. Henry Beckman before Sailing For America, by His Mother, 1880," by Yette Beckman. American Jewish Archives, Cincinnati.

BENJAMIN "God and Abuse: A Survivor's Story," by Sophia Benjamin (pseud.), was written for this volume.

BERKELEY "A Convert's Road to Prayer," by Gail Berkeley, first appeared in *Response: A Contemporary Jewish Review* 13 (Fall–Winter 1982): 1–2. © Gail Berkeley. Reprinted with permission of the author.

BREITMAN "For Sheila," by Barbara E. Breitman. Used with permission of the author.

BRONER "Body Memories" and "Sitting *Shiva* for a Lost Love" (1986), by E. M. Broner. Used with permission of the author.

COHEN "The Influence of the Jewish Religion in the Home" (1893), by Mary M. Cohen, appeared in *Papers of the Jewish Women's Congress* (Philadelphia: Jewish Publication Society of America, 1894), 115–21.

DANIEL "We Learned from the Grandparents: Memories of a Cochin Jewish Woman," by Ruby Daniel, with Barbara Johnson, was prepared for this volume in 1990. It is excerpted from a forthcoming work by Johnson (with Daniel) on Cochin Jewry.

EILBERG "The Gifts of First Fruits," by Amy Eilberg, a sermon delivered 3 September 1988. Used with permission of the author.

EISENSTEIN "The Spiritual Power of Music," by Judith Kaplan Eisenstein, was written expressly for this volume.

ELWELL "Rosh Hashana Sermon, 24 September 1987," by Sue Levi Elwell. Used with permission of the author.

ERDOS "A Personal Reflection," by Karen Erdos, with Dianne Ashton, was written for this volume in 1990.

FALK "Sabbath," "Dialogues," and *"Kiddush,"* by Marcia Falk, © 1990, 1992, and 1992 by Marcia Lee Falk. Used with permission of the author. "Sabbath" first appeared under the title "Saturday Morning" in *A State Street Reader* (State Street Press, 1990). *"Kiddush"* excerpted from *The Book of Blessings: A Feminist-Jewish Reconstruction of Prayer* by Marcia Falk (San Francisco: Harper San Francisco, 1992). Used with permission.

FELD Merle Feld's "Healing after a Miscarriage" first appeared in *Response: A Contemporary Jewish Review* 14 (Spring 1985): 4. © Merle Feld. Reprinted with permission of the author. Her "Meditation on Menstruation" and "We All Stood Together" (first published in the Reconstructionist Siddur, *Kol Haneshamah,* 1989) used with permission of Merle Feld.

FRANK "Yom Kippur Sermon (1890)," by Ray Frank, in *Ray Frank Litman: A Memoir,* by Simon Litman (New York: American Jewish Historical Society, 1957), 9–11, 15, 16, 22–23. Reprinted by permission of the American Jewish Historical Society. Frank's "Prayer" (1893) and "Woman in the Synagogue" (1893) appeared in *Papers of the Jewish Women's Congress* (Philadelphia: Jewish Publication Society of America, 1894), 8, 52–65.

GELLER "Encountering the Divine Presence," by Laura Geller, an address delivered in 1986 and published in *Central Conference of American Rabbis Yearbook, 1987*. Reprinted with permission of the Central Conference of American Rabbis.

GEMSON "All Alone among the Vikings," by Constance Gemson, was first published in the October 1983 issue of *Jewish Currents* and is reprinted with permission. Gemson's "Lot's Wife" is used with permission of Constance Gemson.

GLÜCKEL Excerpts from *The Memoirs of Glückel of Hameln,* trans. Marvin Lowenthal (New York: Schocken, 1977). Used with permission of Rosamond Fischer.

GRATZ Letters to Maria Fenno Hoffman (10 July 1809) and Miriam Moses Cohen (12 September 1853), by Rebecca Gratz, American Jewish Archives, Cincinnati. "Hebrew Sunday School Report," 25 April 1858, in *Occident and American Jewish Advocate* 16 (1858): 164–65.

GREENBERG "Resisting Yom Hashoah 1985" and "The *Mikvah,*" by Blu Greenberg. Used with permission of the author.

GROSSMAN "On *Tefillin,*" by Susan Grossman. © 1986 by Susan Grossman. Used with permission of the author.

HART "Address to a Graduating Student of the Hebrew Sunday School," by Louisa B. Hart, from "A Memoir of Louisa B. Hart with Extracts from Her Diary and Letters," *Jewish Record,* no. 189 (Philadelphia). Courtesy, Jonathan Sarna.

HELLERSTEIN "Tishe b'Av on 48th Street," by Kathryn Hellerstein. Used with permission of the author.

HENELE "Private Letters from the Ghetto of Prague," by Henele, daughter of Abraham Ha-Levi Heller, to her sister Bona and to Simon Wolf Auerbach, in *A Treasury of Jewish Letters: Letters from the Famous and the Humble,* ed. Franz Kobler (Philadelphia: Jewish Publication Society of America, 1953). Reprinted with permission of the Jewish Publication Society of America.

HOLLANDER "A Rosh Hodesh Ceremony," by Vicki Hollander. © February 1990, by Vicki Hollander. Used with permission of the author.

HYNEMAN "The Destruction of Jerusalem," by Rebekah Hyneman, appeared in *Occident* 10 (1853): 16. Her "Ruth's Song" appeared in *Israelite* 1, no. 28 (1855): 222.

KOHUT "Welcoming Address," by Rebecca Kohut, in *Proceedings of the First Convention of the National Council of Jewish Women* (Philadelphia: Jewish Publication Society of America, 1896), 19–23.

KOLMAR "The Woman Poet," "The Jewish Woman," and "We Jews," by Gertrud Kolmar, in *Dark Soliloquy: The Selected Poems of Gertrud Kolmar*, translated and with introduction by Henry A. Smith (New York: Seabury, 1975). Reprinted by permission of Harper Collins.

KUSSY *The Women's League Handbook and Guide*, by Sarah Kussy (New York: National Women's League of the United Synagogue of America, 1947), 11–13, 20, 87, 94–95. Her "Judaism and Its Ceremonies" appeared in *American Jewess* 4 (November 1896): 78–81.

LAZARUS, E. "In the Jewish Synagogue at Newport" and "The New Year, Rosh-Hashanah, 5643 (1882)" appeared in *Emma Lazarus: Selections from Her Poetry and Prose*, ed. Morris U. Schappes (New York, 1967), 33–41, 48, 52. Reprinted with permission of Morris Schappes. Lazarus's "An Epistle to the Hebrews" (New York: Federation of American Zionists, Philip Cowen, 1900) was originally published as a sixteen-part essay in the *American Hebrew* (3 November 1882–23 February 1883).

LAZARUS, J. "Judaism, Old and New" (1894), by Josephine Lazarus, in *The Spirit of Judaism* (New York: Dodd, Mead, 1895), 85–100.

LEVITT AND WASSERMAN "*Mikvah* Ceremony for Laura," by Laura Levitt and Sue Ann Wasserman, November 1989. Used with permission of the authors.

LICHTENSTEIN "Believing Is *Seeing*," by Tehilla Lichtenstein, *Jewish Science Interpreter* 26, no. 5 (April 1955): 3–11, and "God in the Silence," *Jewish Science Interpreter* 21, no. 10 (1947): 8–12. Used with permission of the Society of Jewish Science.

LOUIS "The Influence of Women in Bringing Religious Conviction to Bear upon Daily Life," by Minnie D. Louis, *American Hebrew* (28 June 1895), 183–86.

MENKEN "Drifts That Bar My Door," by Adah Isaacs Menken, from *Infelicia* (1869), appears in *The American Jewish Woman: A Documentary History*, ed. Jacob Rader Marcus (New York: Ktav; and Cincinnati: American Jewish Archives, 1981), 279–82. Reprinted with permission of Jacob Rader Marcus.

MILGROM "Sermon, Yom Kippur, 5749," by Shira Milgrom. Used with permission of the author.

MIRIAM "A Song to Jacob Who Removed the Stone from the Mouth of the Wall," by Rivka Miriam, translated by Sue Ann Wasserman in her "Women's Voices through the Past and Present" (rabbinic thesis, Hebrew Union College–Jewish Institute of Religion, New York, 1987) under the advisership of Dr. Stanley Nash. Used with permission of Sue Ann Wasserman.

MOISE "Hymn," "Piety," and "Man's Dignity," by Penina Moise, in *Hymnal of Penina Moise* (1856). American Jewish Archives, Cincinnati.

MOLODOWSKY "Prayers" and "Songs of Women" (from *Kheshvndike Nekht* [Vilna, 1927]), by Kadya Molodowsky, trans. Kathryn Hellerstein. These translations will appear in *Selected Poems of Kadya Molodowsky*, ed. and trans. Kathryn Hellerstein (Philadelphia: Jewish Publication Society, forthcoming). Used with permission of Kathryn Hellerstein.

MONTAGU "For Reform Synagogue, Berlin" (1928), by Lily H. Montagu, in *Lily Montagu: Sermons, Addresses, Letters and Prayers*, ed. Ellen M. Umansky (Lewiston, N.Y.: Edwin Mellen, 1985), 327–35.

MONTEFIORE Excerpts from the diary of Judith Lady Montefiore, appeared in Lucien Wolf, "Lady Montefiore's Honeymoon," in *Essays in Jewish History*, ed. Cecil Roth (London: Jewish Historical Society of England, 1934), 241–58; her "Private Journal of a Visit to Egypt and Palestine" is dated 1836.

MORDECAI Selected excerpts from the Emma Mordecai Diary, no. 2155. Southern Historical Collection, Library of the University of North Carolina at Chapel Hill.

MORPURGO "Lament no more," "Ah! Vale of woe," and "Woe! my knowledge is weak," by Rahel Luzzatto Morpurgo, trans. Nina Davis Salaman, appearing in the Arthur Davis Memorial Lecture (London: George Allen & Unwin, 1923).

NATHAN "To My Son," by Grace Nathan, in *The American Jewish Woman: A Documentary History,* ed. Jacob Rader Marcus (New York: Ktav; and Cincinnati: American Jewish Archives, 1981), 73–74. Printed with permission of Jacob Rader Marcus.

NEUDA "Morning Prayer" and "Prayer after Safe Delivery," by Fanny Neuda, appeared in her *Hours of Devotion,* trans. M. Mayer, 5th ed. (New York: Hebrew Publishing Co., 1866), 8–9, 81.

OREN "Eve," by Miriam Oren, translated by Sue Ann Wasserman in her "Women's Voices through the Past and Present" (rabbinic thesis, Hebrew Union College–Jewish Institute, New York, 1987). Used with permission of Sue Ann Wasserman.

PAPPENHEIM "The Jewish Woman in Religious Life," by Bertha Pappenheim, was read at the Women's Congress in Munich, 1912. Reprinted from the *Jewish Review* (January 1913) by the Jewish League for Woman Suffrage (London). Pappenheim's *Prayers* was translated by Stephanie Forchheimer (New York: A. Stein, 1946).

PLASKOW "The Coming of Lilith," by Judith Plaskow, has appeared in a number of Plaskow's essays, including "The Jewish Feminist-Conflict in Identities," in *The Jewish Woman: New Perspectives,* ed. Elizabeth Koltun (New York: Schocken, 1976), and "The Coming of Lilith: Toward a Feminist Theology," in *Womanspirit Rising: A Feminist Reader in Religion,* ed. Carol P. Christ and Judith Plaskow (New York: Harper & Row, 1979). © Judith Plaskow. Used with permission of the author.

RACHEL "A Yiddish Letter of a Mother to her Son from Jerusalem to Cairo," in *A Treasury of Jewish Letters: Letters from the Famous and the Humble,* ed. Franz Kobler (Philadelphia: Jewish Publication Society of America, 1953), 2:364–67. Reprinted with permission of the Jewish Publication Society of America.

RICHMAN "Report of the National Committee on Religious School Work," by Julia Richman, appeared in *Proceedings of the First Convention of the National Council of Jewish Women* (Philadelphia: Jewish Publication Society of America, 1896), 200–208.

ROTH "To Her Son" (1854), by Lena Roth, American Jewish Archives, Cincinnati.

SALAMAN, N. "The Power of the Spirit" and "Of Prayer," by Nina Davis Salaman, in her *Voices of the River* (Cambridge: Bowes & Bowes, 1910), 35, 36.

SALAMAN, R. "The Angel and the Child," by Rosa Emma Salaman, appeared in *Occident* 13 (1855): 36–38.

SAREL "Private Letter from the Ghetto of Prague," by Sarel, daughter of Moses, to her husband, Loeb Sarel Gutmans, in *A Treasury of Jewish Letters: Letters from the Famous and the Humble,* ed. Franz Kobler (Philadelphia: Jewish Publication Society of America, 1953). Reprinted with permission of the Jewish Publication Society of America.

SENESH Hannah Senesh's diary entries (1 October 1938, 27 October 1938, 12 November 1938, 20 November 1938, 11 December 1938, and 6 February 1939) from *Hannah Senesh: Her Life and Diary,* by Hannah Senesh.

© 1971 Nigel Marsh. Reprinted by permission of Schocken Books, published by Pantheon Books, a division of Random House Inc.

SHOHET   "Prayer Composed for Dedication of Temple Israel Museum," by Grace Cohen Shohet (Mrs. Harmon Shohet), 3 November 1953. Grace Shohet Collection, American Jewish Archives, Cincinnati.

SHUR   "My Dance Work as a Reflection Of a Jewish Woman's Spirituality," by Fanchon Shur, was commissioned by the rabbinic organization of women at Hebrew Union College, 1984, for a journal that was never published. The article was revised in 1989 for this volume. For booking dance performances and workshops, contact: Growth in Motion, 4019 Red Bud Ave., Cincinnati, Ohio 45229.

SIMON   *Records and Reflections,* by Rachel Simon, (1894).

SOCIETY ESRATH NASHIM   Minutes of the Society Esrath Nashim, Philadelphia, June 1891. Philadelphia Jewish Archives at the Balch Institute for Ethnic Studies.

SOLOMON   "Presidential Address," by Hannah Greenbaum Solomon, in *Proceedings of the First Convention of the National Council of Jewish Women* (Philadelphia: Jewish Publication Society of America, 1896), 400–404.

SPIEGEL   "Growing Up Jewish," by Marcia Cohn Spiegel, was written for this volume in 1989.

SULLAM   Sara Copia Sullam to Baldassar Bonifaccio, Venice, 1621, in *A Treasury of Jewish Letters: Letters from the Famous and the Humble,* ed. Franz Kobler (Philadelphia: Jewish Publication Society of America, 1953). Reprinted with permission of the Jewish Publication Society of America.

SZOLD   Henrietta Szold to Alice Seligsberg (12 December 1909), to Mrs. Julius Rosenwald (17 January 1915), to Haym Peretz (16 September 1916), and to Adele Szold Setzer and Bertha Szold Levin (27 August 1938) in *Henrietta Szold: Her Life and Letters,* by Marvin Lowenthal (New York: Viking, 1942), copyright renewed © 1970 by Harold C. Emer and Harry L. Shapiro, executors of the estate of Marvin Lowenthal. Reprinted by permission of Viking Penguin a division of Penguin USA.

TEMPLE ISRAEL SISTERHOOD   Minute Book of Temple Israel Sisterhood, 1891, New York City. American Jewish Archives on the campus of Hebrew Union College–Jewish Institute of Religion, Cincinnati.

TEUBAL   "Simchat Hochmah: A Crone Ritual," by Savina J. Teubal. Used with permission of the author. The introduction to the ritual was written for this volume. Videotapes of "Simhat Hochmah" are available from Sounds Write Productions, Inc., P.O. Box 608078, San Diego, Calif. 92160–8078. Cassettes, CDs, song books, and sheet music of Debbie Friedman's compositions for this service are also available.

TUSSMAN   "Leaves," "Last Apple," "Mild, My Wild," and "I Say," by Malka Heifetz Tussman, translated from the Yiddish by Marcia Falk. © 1992 by Marcia Lee Falk. Excerpted from *With Teeth in the Earth: Selected Poems of Malka Heifetz Tussman translated by Marcia Falk* (Detroit: Wayne State University Press, forthcoming). Used by permission.

UKELES   "Mikva Dreams—A Performance," by Mierle Laderman Ukeles, appeared in *Heresies: The Great Goddess 5* (Spring 1978). Reprinted courtesy of the author/artist and Ronald Feldman Fine Arts, Inc., New York City.

ULINOVER   "The Old Prayer Book" (from *Der Bobes Oytser* [Lodz, 1922]) and "With the *Taytsh-Khumesh,*" by Miriam Ulinover, trans. Kathryn Hellerstein. Used with permission of Kathryn Hellerstein.

UMANSKY   A portion of "Piety, Persuasion, and Friendship: A History of Jewish Women's Spirituality" has been adapted from Ellen M. Umansky's "Spiritual Expressions: Jewish Women's Religious Lives in the Twentieth

Century United States" in *Jewish Women in Historical Perspective,* ed. Judith Baskin (Detroit: Wayne State University Press, 1991). Umansky's "Reclaiming the Convenant: A Jewish Feminist's Search for Meaning" appeared in *A Time to Weep, a Time to Sing: Faith Journeys of Women Scholars of Religion,* ed. Mary Jo Meadow and Carole A. Rayburn (Winston Press, 1985). "Re-Visioning Sarah" first appeared in Umansky's "Creating a Jewish Feminist Theology: Possibilities and Problems," in *Anima* Ten/2, reprinted in *Weaving the Visions: New Patterns in Feminist Spirituality,* ed. Judith Plaskow and Carol P. Christ (New York: Harper & Row, 1989).

WEINBERG   "Campus Pilgrimage to Reverse the Nuclear Arms Race," by Sheila Pelz Weinberg, an address delivered at peace rally in Philadelphia, spring 1983. Used with permission of the author.

WEISBERG   "The Study of Torah as a Religious Act," by Dvora Weisberg, was written for this volume in 1989.

WEISSLER   "Four *Tkhines,*" translated by Chava Weissler. Selected for this volume by Chava Weissler. Weissler's description of the *tkhines,* in the introductory material to this section, is revised (by Weissler) and reprinted from "Images of the Matriarchs in Yiddish Supplicatory Prayers," *Bulletin of the Center for the Study of World Religions* (Harvard University) 14, no. 1 (1988). Reprinted with permission of the *Bulletin.*

YEMENITE WOMEN   "I Shall Begin to Sing" and "In the Name of God I Shall Begin," in Mishael Maswari Caspi, ed. and trans., *Daughters of Yemen* (Berkeley and Los Angeles: University of California Press, 1985). Reprinted with permission of University of California Press. © 1985 the Regents of the University of California.

ZELDA   "I Am a Dead Bird," "Yom Kippur Eve," "Sun-Startled Pines," "A Heavy Silence," and "Moon Is Teaching Bible," by Zelda, translated from the Hebrew by Marcia Falk. © 1992 by Marcia Lee Falk. Used with permission of the translator.

ZYGMUNTOWICZ   "Survival and Memory," by Itka Frajman Zygmuntowicz, with Sara Horowitz. © Itka Zygmuntowicz and Sara Horowitz. Used with their permission.

Bonifaccio, Baldassar, 5, 34

The Book of Blessings: A Feminist-Jewish Reconstruction of Prayer (Falk), 199

Breitman, Barbara E., 205, 210n2, 285–86

Broner, E. M., 202, 210n2, 274–75

Brotherhood week, 163

"Campus Pilgrimage to Reverse the Nuclear Arms Race" (Weinberg), 196–97, 228–29

Cantors, 21–22, 30n65, 191

Care for Women, 113

Carlbach, Schlomo, 204

Challah, 2–3, 210–11n5

Cheder, 112

Chicago World's Fair (1893), 17, 108–9, 123n2, 129–38

Childbirth, 25n7, 68, 284. *See also* Miscarriages

Children: death of, 23, 66, 200, 221–22, 247–57, 309; as first fruits, 282–85; prayers for, 62, 82; as sinless, 66; as women's responsibility, 3. *See also* Education

Choirs, 10–11

Christian-Jewish relations: and barriers between women, 145; between 1890 and 1960, 13–14, 129–30; and differences in religion, 148; as field of study, 232; and Hebrew Sunday School, 63, 85; and hymns, 65; and Jewish Women's Congress (1893), 129–30; in nineteenth century, 6–8, 61, 62, 63, 68, 69, 79–80, 81, 85, 102–3; and Protestant missionizing, 6, 7–8; and religious apathy, 139; and "Sunday Movement," 68; and tribalism, 102–3; and unity of God, 79–80, 81; and Zionism, 165–66

Christian Science, 13–14

Cochin Jews, 202–3, 298–304

Cohen, Eleanor H., 28n46

Cohen, Mary M., 109–10, 136–38

Cohen, Miriam Moses, 63, 84

Cohn, Belle, 128

Cohn, Marta, 171–76

"The Coming of Lilith" (Plaskow), 193, 214–16

Compton, Alwyne, 98–99

Confirmation, 22, 143, 231

"Congregational Address" (Ackerman), 185–86

Conservative Judaism, 21, 22, 24, 29n54, 30n65, 111, 116, 118

Conversions, 131, 195, 210–11n5, 223–26, 325n1

"A Convert's Road to Prayer" (Berkeley), 195, 223–26

Covenant: and crone ceremony, 258–59, 261, 263, 264; reclaiming the, 197–98, 230–34

Creative Jewish Women's Alliance, 295

Crone ceremony, 200–201, 257–65

Cult of True Womanhood, 9–10

Dance, 198, 235–39, 274–75

Daniel, Ruby, 202–3, 298–304

Death: angel of, 66, 248; of children, 23, 66, 200, 221–22, 247–57, 309; and crone ceremony, 261; and guilt, 327; and life cycle, 258; and mourners, 63; and mysticism, 301–4; as physical separation, 289; welcoming of, 67. *See also* Grief/mourning

Deborah (the prophet), 26n18, 55, 69, 131, 259

"The Destruction of Jerusalem" (Hyneman), 64, 86

"Dialogues" (Falk), 198–99, 240–41

Dietary laws, 2, 11, 78n1, 116, 137, 150–51, 161, 230, 233, 308

Domesticity, myth of, 26n24

Domestic religion, 123

"Drifts That Bar My Door" (Menken), 67, 91–93

Dry Tears (Tec), 20

The Duties of the Heart (Bahya Ibn Pakuda), 59

Dvar Torah, 22

Eddy, Mary Baker, 13–14

Education: between 1890 and 1960, 13; God's role in, 143; and immigrants, 6–7, 117; and National Committee on Religious School Work, 142–44; and National Women's League, 161, 162; in nineteenth century, 6–7, 62, 82–83, 142–44; pre-1800, 5–6, 34, 35; and rabbis, 142; and sabbath, 116. *See also* Hebrew Sunday School

Educational organizations, 6–7, 15–16, 111, 112, 142–44

Eilberg, Amy, 30n69, 204–5, 282–85

Eisenstein, Judith Kaplan, 22, 206, 290–92

Elders: learning from, 202–3, 299–301. *See also* Crone ceremony

Elul, 209, 318–20

Elwell, Sue Levi, 201–2, 210n2, 269–73

Emancipation, 5–6, 11–12, 26n11, 26n14

"Encountering the Divine Presence" (Geller), 199, 242–47

"An Epistle to the Hebrews" (Emma Lazarus), 70, 102–3

Epstein, Sarah, 291